The Next Mormons

THE NEXT MORMONS

*How Millennials Are Changing
the LDS Church*

Jana Riess

OXFORD
UNIVERSITY PRESS

UNIVERSITY PRESS

Oxford University Press is a department of the University of Oxford. It furthers
the University's objective of excellence in research, scholarship, and education
by publishing worldwide. Oxford is a registered trademark of Oxford University
Press in the UK and certain other countries.

Published in the United States of America by Oxford University Press
198 Madison Avenue, New York, NY 10016, United States of America.

Library of Congress Cataloging-in-Publication Data
Names: Riess, Jana, author.
Title: The next Mormons : how Millennials are changing the LDS church / Jana Riess.
Description: New York : Oxford University Press, [2019] |
Includes bibliographical references and index.
Identifiers: LCCN 2018037059 | ISBN 9780190885205 (hardcover : alk. paper) |
ISBN 9780190885229 (epub)
Subjects: LCSH: Church of Jesus Christ of Latter-day Saints—History—21st century. |
Mormon Church—History—21st century. | Generation Y—Religious life. |
Generation Y—Attitudes. | Church of Jesus Christ of Latter-day Saints—Public opinion. |
Mormon Church—Public opinion.
Classification: LCC BX8611.R54 2019 | DDC 289.3/7309051—dc23
LC record available at https://lccn.loc.gov/2018037059

9 8 7 6 5 4 3 2 1

Printed by Sheridan Books, Inc., United States of America

For A. B.

CONTENTS

The Next Mormons

Introduction

The Changing Face of Mormonism in America

This book tells two very different and apparently contradictory stories about young adult Mormons in America. Both of them happen to be true.

The first is embodied by Jack, a twenty-six-year-old graduate student at a midwestern university.[1] His Mormon faith became important to him around age twelve or thirteen, when he began studying the scriptures for himself. In part this was sparked by a problem at home: Jack's father had begun distancing himself from the Church of Jesus Christ of Latter-day Saints (LDS Church), so Jack had to decide what role the church was going to play in his own life. He decided that its message—what Mormons refer to as "the restored gospel of Jesus Christ"—was essential to his own eternal happiness. He attended Brigham Young University (BYU) because he valued "being among people who for the most part shared my standards," and then after one semester at BYU he took a leave of absence to serve a two-year mission in South America. Jack loved his mission and the sense of purpose it provided. "It was just a wonderful opportunity to deepen my knowledge of the gospel and attempt to apply it to myself, and live in a way where I could feel God's influence in my life regularly," he reflects now. At age twenty-three, not long after returning from his mission, Jack got married in a Mormon temple, fulfilling one of his religion's highest goals: to be married not just for this life, but for all eternity. He and his wife started having children almost immediately—they already have one son and a baby on the way—and they plan to raise those children as faithful Latter-day Saints. While Jack and his wife are avid believers, they're not as strict as some older Mormons they know, including his mom. If they watch a movie that features a few light swear words, they just shrug it off. More significantly, Jack says he does not see the LDS prophet and apostles as infallible, which older Mormons might be more prone to do. "I don't think the church will ever derail completely and go in a direction that's contrary to God's will, but that said, I think there is room for error," he explains. "We shouldn't expect perfection from ourselves, from our leaders, or from the church as a whole." But when asked where he falls on a scale of one to ten—where a ten means he will always stay a Latter-day Saint and a one means he will someday leave the church—Jack doesn't hesitate a moment to declare himself a ten. He is all in, a fully committed Mormon.

The second story is illustrated by Emily, who, like Jack, grew up in a large LDS family.[2] An eighth-generation Mormon, Emily had orthodox parents who took her to church each week, got her involved in LDS youth activities, and forbade her to drink caffeinated soda.[3] In her family a significant focus was placed on being, or at least acting, happy; Emily's mother had a sign in her house that said, "If you're unhappy, you're ungrateful." Although Emily sometimes struggled with anxiety and depression, her parents "didn't think it was a real thing," so she did not get treatment.

When Emily went to a state university in Utah, it never crossed her mind to stop going to church; church was what she had always done, and she enjoyed it. She had particular goals for her life, and being an active Mormon was a major part of that. "I just expected to go to school, meet my husband, get married, and then be a stay-at-home mom." But that did not happen. When she turned thirty she was distressed to still be single in a religion that heavily emphasizes marriage and children.[4] Now thirty-four, she endured a recent breakup and says that in the aftermath her "shelf broke," using a term that is common among Mormons who begin to question their faith. Emily felt emotionally vulnerable, and her doubts about Mormonism, which she had long suppressed, began taking center stage. She had previously tried to cure her mental health problems by praying and attending the temple, but that had never worked. She also felt unmoored when, in November 2015, the LDS Church instituted a new policy that, among other things, prohibited any children who were in the custody of same-sex couples from being baptized or blessed. Emily simply did not understand it. She continued trying to go to church, but the religion's teachings about gay people bothered her.

Emily eventually stopped attending church and wearing her temple garments, the special underclothing that adult Mormons wear after going through the temple the first time. She still puts them on for family functions, worried someone might notice if she does not have telltale "garment lines" under her clothing. She's not sure she can call herself Mormon anymore, which grieves her. And she knows it will sadden her parents when she can muster the courage to tell them, especially her mother. "One of the accomplishments for stay-at-home moms is to be able to say 'all of my children are still in the church, and have married in the temple,' and I hate taking that accomplishment away." But Emily can't deny that she feels profound relief now, because going to church had begun to cause her pain. She has gotten therapy, which has helped with her depression, and says she feels more at peace and closer to God than she did when she was a "TBM"—a True Believing Mormon.

> I know that in my former TBM ways, and in the eyes of my family, not going to church is a sin. I don't pay tithing anymore. All the things I don't do anymore, like I don't read my scriptures, those were [considered] such horrible things to not do. But all the time I *was* doing all those things, I never felt this much love, not like I do now.

Emily says she is a three on the one-to-ten scale of her predicted future church activity—she doesn't think she's coming back, but she doesn't rule it out.

Jack and Emily represent two very different trajectories for the Millennial generation of Latter-day Saints. This book uses survey data, historical research, and in-depth interviews to explore those forking paths. What can we learn from Mormon and former Mormon young adults about the spiritual, intellectual, and emotional experiences that successfully imprint—or fail to imprint—an enduring Mormon identity?

RETHINKING MORMON EXCEPTIONALISM

LDS teens are "tops in living faith," ran a proud headline in the church-owned *Deseret News* in 2005, highlighting data from the National Study of Youth and Religion (NSYR), a major study of the religious beliefs and behaviors of American teenagers. Lead researcher Christian Smith and others found that compared with other religiously identified teens, Mormon youth were more likely to hold religious beliefs similar to their parents', share their faith with others, pray regularly, and discuss religion in their families.[5] They were also markedly less likely to have sexual intercourse and engage in risky behaviors. This groundbreaking study generated other books that presented positive findings about Mormons alongside discouraging news about many other teens, who had embraced a watered-down and vague "moralistic therapeutic deism" in the place of traditional doctrine, and were indifferent to rigorous spiritual practices that required time and sacrifice. Mormon kids, said NSYR researcher Kenda Creasey Dean in a chapter of her book called "Mormon Envy," were the "'spiritual athletes' of their generation," often rolling out of bed before dawn to attend weekday seminary classes (religious instruction for high schoolers) and using their adolescence to prepare for a full-time mission.[6]

The admiration of these researchers was palpable, and I'm not questioning that it's well deserved. As a Mormon myself, of course I am gratified to hear that my church is producing young people who place a high value on service and are devoted to their faith. I have seen it first-hand and in my own research, which focuses not on adolescents but on young adults. There's abundant evidence that young Mormons are often profoundly religious, and that many make great sacrifices to practice their faith, often contributing up to two years of unpaid labor as volunteer missionaries, and paying 10 percent of their income as tithing.

There's another side to this, though, which is that the number of young adults who are leaving Mormonism appears to be rising sharply. Some minority groups such as singles and LGBT members appear to be more vulnerable to leaving Mormonism than those who are married and straight. How is the church's well-known emphasis on the "traditional" family, which was such a successful calling card in the second half of the twentieth century, being received in the twenty-first, when social constructions of family are changing rapidly in American culture, and women's roles have been redefined?[7]

I also address how different generations of Mormons feel about religious behavior, political issues, and institutional authority. There is evidence that Millennials who remain in the church are less exacting about some (not all) of its religious practices, especially church attendance and dietary restrictions, even if they consider themselves orthodox or what Mormons call "active." There are also indications that those who disaffiliate may do so for reasons that are as political as they are theological. It's not that these young adults have abandoned belief in God, but that the church's conservatism on social issues has become an obstacle to their continued participation. Although it seems paradoxical, Emily's story is as true as Jack's tale of steadfast religiosity. Those young adults who remain in the LDS Church are in many ways as devout as ever, but defections are also increasing.

Over the past decade, both the Pew Research Center and the General Social Survey (GSS) have noted a quietly rising tide of disaffiliation from the LDS Church in the United States. Pew discovered that in 2007, 70 percent of respondents who had been in the LDS Church in childhood still self-identified as Mormons as adults, but in 2014 that figure had dipped to 64 percent. Among Millennials, the rate of retention was slightly lower still, at 62 percent.[8] (Note that this does not gauge how often they attend or how active they consider themselves to be, only that they claim the label

"Mormon" or "LDS" when asked their religion.) The GSS shows more dramatic losses among Mormons and confirms that much of this change is being driven by Generation Xers and Millennials. Drawing on four decades of longitudinal data from the GSS, social scientist Darren Sherkat has reported that Mormons have "high rates of loyalty in generations born prior to 1971," but the declining retention rate "ranks Mormons among the least loyal groups in the youngest generations."[9] As shown in Table 0.1, which includes GSS data through 2016, Mormonism used to keep about three-quarters of its adherents. Among young adults it is now retaining less than half.

There are reasons to be cautious about this finding, because as you can see from the sample sizes I've included here (the "n" refers to each group's sample size), the GSS does not include a large number of Mormons for each generation.[10] That's particularly true of Millennials, those born in the 1980s and 1990s. That does not mean the GSS is unreliable for understanding Mormonism's basic trajectory of losses, however. If we combine the Millennials and GenXers together in the GSS, we get a larger sample of over two hundred people and thus a lower margin of error. The combined retention rate of those two generations is 57 percent, which is significantly

Table 0.1. GENERAL SOCIAL SURVEY (GSS) DATA ON RELIGIOUS RETENTION, 1973–2016

GSS Cohort	Born before 1943 (Silent)	Born 1944–1954 (Older Boomers)	Born 1955–1964 (Younger Boomers)	Born 1965–1980 (GenX)	Born since 1981 (Millennial)
Mormon retention	75% (n = 192)	72% (n = 130)	72% (n = 152)	62.5% (n = 152)	46% (n = 52)
Baptist retention	72%	69%	71%	69%	63%
Catholic and Orthodox retention	84%	73%	73%	71%	64.5%
Jewish retention	88%	82%	80%	74%	89%
"Liberal Protestant" retention	55%	50%	55%	56%	53%
"Sectarian Protestant" retention	55%	61%	63%	63%	58%

lower than the roughly three-quarters of Mormons from older generations who remained in the fold, but higher than the 46 percent the GSS records for the small number of Millennials it includes.

Clearly, there is evidence that in the United States, more young adults are leaving Mormonism than they did in the past. We should keep in mind that this is due in part to the environment of widespread religious disaffiliation that is occurring in America; it is not unique to the LDS Church. In recent years, according to the Public Religion Research Institute, the rate of young adults self-identifying as "Nones," or people with no religious affiliation, has climbed to 39 percent, the highest proportion in recent US history.[11] Almost every organized religion is experiencing losses in this new climate.

It's important that when we talk about Mormonism in America we remember the *in America* aspect—a wider context that is too often neglected. From the 1950s to the 1980s, many proud Mormons talked about the "miracle growth" their church was experiencing. And indeed, Mormon growth often hovered between 4 and 8 percent per year in those decades, outstripping general population growth several times over. What the "miracle growth" stories often failed to mention was that many other religions also thrived in America during these same decades. The immediate postwar environment was strong for mainline Protestants and Catholics, and the 1970s and 1980s were particularly hospitable for evangelicals. Most of those religions are shrinking in the twenty-first century.[12] Mormonism too has not been immune, even if its problems with disaffiliation are more recent. It's tempting to fixate on things the LDS Church is or is not doing as the primary explanation for those membership losses, arguing that the church is alienating young people with its antigay rhetoric, its treatment of women, and its superannuated leadership. While this book presents statistical evidence that some of those reasons do factor into why more Millennials are leaving the LDS Church, a major explanation for disaffiliation is the changing religious landscape in America. Mormonism is not an island.

In fact, compared to some other religions, Mormonism is not doing too badly. Mormonism's US growth rate of .75 percent in 2017—kept in positive territory by still-higher-than-average fertility among Mormons—is actually somewhat enviable when compared to, for example, the once-thriving Southern Baptists, who have bled out more than a million members in the last ten years.[13] Mormonism is not yet declining in membership, but it has entered a period of decelerated growth.[14] In terms of congregational expansion, the LDS Church in the United States added only sixty-five new congregations in 2016, for an increase of half a percentage point.[15] In 2017, the church created 184 new wards and branches in the United States, but 184 units also closed, resulting in no net gain at all.[16]

Church activity and fervor also appear to be waning among some younger members. In a leaked video of a 2008 meeting of the top leaders of the LDS Church, internal research was presented indicating that only 30 percent of young single adult Mormons in North America could be considered active participants.[17] (This would include both those who no longer self-identify as Mormon but are still on the official rolls and those who continue to call themselves Mormon but do not attend meetings.) That fewer than a third of single Millennial Mormons attend church regularly is a startling revelation for a religious movement whose most visible exponents are young adults who give a year and a half to two years of their lives to serve unpaid missions—a remarkable sacrifice of time, money, and energy.

Based on the findings of both Pew and the GSS, we can say with confidence that Mormon retention is declining from one generation to the next, and that the LDS Church is losing a greater share of young adults than it has in the past. We appear to be looking at a current retention rate of 50 to 60 percent. Given other research on disaffiliation among the youngest Millennials and Generation Z, this may drop further as younger people age into the data pool ("cohort replacement"). Mormonism is exceptional in many ways, but it is not able to wholly resist the larger forces at work in American religion.

THE NEXT MORMONS SURVEY

To dig deeper into these trends, political scientist Benjamin Knoll and I created the Next Mormons Survey (NMS), a major national study of 1,156 Mormons and 540 former Mormons. We wanted to understand who Mormons are, what they believe, and what generational differences may pertain among them. What can we say about the attitudes and beliefs of Mormons who stay versus those who leave? How do those two groups compare—and how do four generations of Latter-day Saints respond to questions about faith, practice, and social views? (A full explanation of the survey's methodology can be found in the data appendix at the back of the book.)

We sought answers to many questions. For example, are Millennials more likely than older generations to value LGBT inclusion and believe that same-sex marriage is socially acceptable (chapter 7)? Are they less likely than older Mormons to privilege institutional authority and obedience (chapter 10)? And are they postponing marriage and childbearing, despite the clear profamily message that is a cornerstone of the Church of Jesus Christ of Latter-day Saints (chapter 4)? Some of the answers to these questions were what we expected, but many surprised us.

The NMS used slightly different generational parameters than the General Social Survey data that was presented in Table 0.1 (see Table 0.2). The year-to-year cutoffs that researchers select for each generation may seem arbitrary: Why is someone born in 1998 still regarded as a Millennial when her younger sibling, born just two years later, is branded as being from Generation Z? The NMS largely followed Pew's methodology for distinguishing each generation, so that we would be able to meaningfully compare our data with research that Pew has already done on Mormons in America, and on Millennials.[18] Other surveys may have slightly different generational boundaries, but the basic contours are the same. We speak of generations or cohorts because each group is united by certain shared experiences and, often, by shared values—though an individual born at the tail end of GenX in 1979 may have more in common with the Millennials, while one born on the vanguard of GenX in the mid-1960s may feel more comfortable with the values of the Baby Boomers. While members of each generation share some common traits and views, there is also great variation.

In most of the NMS results explained in this report, we have combined the Baby Boomer and Silent generations into a single "Boomer/Silent" cohort, since there were not enough members of the Silent Generation for that cohort's results to be statistically reliable when considered alone. Occasionally I'll make reference to the Silent Generation's responses in comparison to the other three generations under consideration, but the small sample size of Silent members means that those results should be interpreted with caution.

While there is excellent reason to be confident that the NMS data is comprehensive and reliable, the study does have three limitations. First, this survey only focuses on the United States. All of the data in this book is about Mormons and former Mormons in America. There are significant and often interesting differences that social science research is only beginning to tease out about Mormons in other nations, but those will not be addressed here.[19] Second, while this is a large enough sample that we

Table 0.2. GENERATIONS AND AGE AT TIME OF SURVEY

Generation	Year Born	Age at Time of Survey
Greatest Generation	1927 or before (not surveyed)	89 or older (not surveyed)
Silent Generation	1928–1944	72–88
Baby Boomer Generation	1945–1964	52–71
Generation X	1965–1979	37–51
Millennial Generation	1980–1998	18–36

can draw meaningful conclusions about Mormon beliefs and attitudes, we must always be aware that when we slice the data into smaller subsets—only Millennial Mormon women, for example, or only African American Mormons—the margin of error rises accordingly. Therefore, we are always going to be more confident about findings that emerge from the entire sample or from large subsamples of several hundred people, such as each generation of current Mormons. Finally, the NMS is a snapshot in time, and is not longitudinal. To supplement it I draw frequently on longitudinal data from other studies, like exit polls showing Mormon voting patterns since 1992, to point to change over time and possible generational effects. But many of the questions in the NMS have never been asked before, so we have no previous benchmarks to compare findings about, for example, temple garment habits (chapter 3) or views on authority (chapter 10). In those cases I can point to current generational *differences*, which are sometimes profound, but not necessarily draw conclusions about generational *change*.

As we'll see, many young adult Mormons are intensely loyal to the church. But they also struggle with whether they will be able to live all the commandments of a strict Mormon lifestyle; resolve doctrinal questions about various controversies in Mormon belief or history; and—a persistent theme—reconcile the tensions they feel between exclusivist claims and their generation's generally inclusive, tolerant, and open-minded worldview. The high standards of personal morality and clear emphasis on the heterosexual nuclear family that served Mormon interests so well in the national religious retrenchment of the postwar period may be the very elements that prove to be stumbling blocks for the next generation.

PART ONE

Foundations

CHAPTER 1

The Continuity of Religious Belief

When Daniel, now twenty-eight, was eight years old, he and his twin brother were baptized and confirmed as members of the LDS Church.[1] At the time, getting baptized was just another item on the checklist for a Mormon boy; it wasn't a decision Daniel thought much about. Nor did he wonder seriously about whether to be ordained to the priesthood at age twelve—it was the "normal order of things" as he followed in the footsteps of his father and older brothers. He didn't question the religion taught to him, nor did he claim it fully and personally as his own. He also had a secret known only to his twin brother: he had discovered pornography online. Though he felt terribly guilty about it, looking at porn gradually became a focus of his early adolescence, as did hiding that secret. "I played the Mormon card very well," he says. "I knew exactly what I was supposed to do, what to appear as, what to say. I was a smart kid and I knew all the expected answers."

His feelings about Mormonism changed during his sophomore year of high school, when he met a girl who simply exuded happiness. He found himself wanting to spend as much time with Jenna as possible to learn the secret of her joy. "I came around to realizing it was because of the gospel, because of the church. That was enough to compel me to do some of my own searching." He began to pray seriously and to read the scriptures for himself, "to search and dig and change." LDS President Gordon B. Hinckley had challenged members to read the Book of Mormon in its entirety by the end of that calendar year, so Daniel did that and prayed to know whether it was true:

> I can honestly say that God was with me. He confirmed to me that the gospel was true, and Christ was real. I truly felt him and his love. I had that testimony for myself for the

first time, and it totally changed my perspective. It changed how I felt and lived, and I became a new person. I gave up the pornography; I was able to release that. I became known as the happiest person in my school, and it was natural. It was real.

Daniel became a convert to his own religion. He decided to serve a mission to share what he had discovered, hoping the LDS gospel would change other people's lives as it had his. If the tale ended here, it would be the kind of success story you might find in the *Ensign*, the monthly LDS magazine. But Daniel's narrative is more complex than that. His life in his twenties has been a fascinating mix of religious zeal and doubt, as well as the regular life upheavals that many people experience in emerging adulthood: moves to new places, romantic relationships that end in bewildering ways, and struggles to establish a career. Daniel's story has been complicated by the fact that six of his eight siblings have now left the church—including his beloved twin. All these defections left him wondering about his own religious beliefs. "I had to go through every part of the gospel one by one: What makes us different from other churches? Why should it matter that I'm Mormon? What does it mean to have the priesthood? What is Christ in my life?" This questioning occurred when he had recently moved to the East Coast for a new job and knew almost no one. Nobody there cared whether he stayed in the church, or sought to "keep [him] accountable" to its standards.

Daniel emerged from the cloud of doubt and remains active in the church. He has multiple callings (assignments or responsibilities in his local congregation) and also volunteers as a temple ordinance worker. He continues to have what Mormons call "a strong testimony" of religious belief, in part because he has had too many beautiful and powerful experiences to discount. "I have seen miracles; I have performed miracles. I have seen things and been part of things that I can't deny," he says. He expresses humble wonder that his faith was strengthened by his dark night of the soul, especially because he loves and trusts his siblings who have left the church and believes they did so for good reasons. Daniel's story illuminates several themes we'll be exploring in this chapter, including the strength of religious belief among Mormon Millennials (despite some uncertainty compared to their elders) and what factors may help to sustain that faith.

BELIEF IN GOD AND CHRISTIAN TEACHINGS

Daniel's story, like all religious conversion narratives, is a product of a particular place and time. The advantage of using both interviews and social science data is that we have a chance to see where individual stories like his reflect broader patterns. Mormon doctrine may seem to be a static thing, but its emphases have shifted measurably over time. Certain themes have been downplayed since World War II (apocalypticism, persecution, the Gathering of Zion), while others have gained prominence, especially the nuclear family as the unit of exaltation and Jesus Christ as the Savior of the world. Looking at General Conference, a twice-annual event where Mormon leaders address the faithful, highlights these changes over time. For example, the topic of family only began appearing among the top ten General Conference themes in the postwar period, when family, marriage, and parenthood all made the list.[2] The trend has only accelerated since then; there were three thousand references to family in the first half of the 2010s, versus just over five hundred citations in the entire decade of the 1930s.[3] Jesus Christ became the most referenced conference theme only after 1950, having not ranked in the top ten for any period until just before World War II.[4] Today's Mormons grew up in a church that was more overtly Christ centered than at previous times in LDS history; it also had grown comfortable using the traditional nuclear family as its calling card to the world. In that context I was particularly interested to see how the themes of Jesus Christ and the family would emerge in contemporary Mormons' religious beliefs.

The NMS asked respondents to choose their top three favorite aspects of being Mormon from a list of nine options.[5] The most popular items were the same for all generations: the peace that faith provides, the doctrine of eternal families, and the church's emphasis on the Savior. In other words, Mormons' preferences on this question reflect almost perfectly the church's own emphases in the postwar era. Mormons are absorbing the key theological messages that the LDS Church has sought to impart, and the youngest Mormons are no different.

Almost all self-identified Mormons say they believe in God, which is similar to the findings of other studies about Mormons.[6] However, the NMS presented respondents with a six-point scale of belief rather than a simple binary yes-or-no question. The choices encompassed a broad spectrum, from a doubt-free certainty about God to an equally rock-solid atheism (which almost no self-identifying Mormons of any generation chose).[7] It was in these nuanced, middling expressions of belief that generational differences became more apparent (Figure 1.1).

In the oldest generations, 85 percent chose the first option ("I know God really exists and have no doubts about it"), while only 9 percent selected the second ("While I have doubts, I feel that I do believe in God"). GenXers, by contrast, showed a bit less certainty, with only 76 percent choosing the first statement. Millennials were less certain still, with 70.5 percent saying they had no doubts and 20 percent believing despite their doubts. In all, then, while more than 90 percent of each generation believes in God, this belief

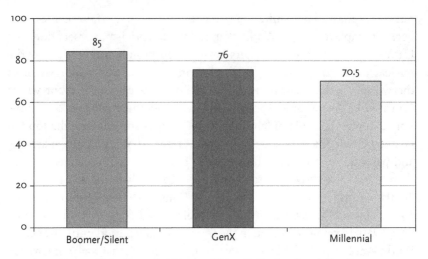

Figure 1.1. Mormons Who Know God Exists and "Have No Doubts about It," by Generation.

may be softer around the edges for Millennials. Doubters are still in the minority among current Latter-day Saints—a topic we will explore later in the chapter—but the percentage who aren't sure that God exists has doubled from the oldest generation to the youngest.

These findings track with what the Pew Research Center has discovered about generational difference and religious belief in the US population at large. For example, Pew's 2014 Religious Landscape Study highlights a twenty-one-point difference between the Silent Generation members who say they believe in God with "absolute certainty" (71 percent) and the younger Millennials who do (50 percent).[8] Although every generation of Mormons has a higher baseline than the general population in their belief in God, the erosion of certainty is similar. In the NMS, even within the Millennial cohort itself there is a decline. Three-quarters of older Millennial Mormons (ages twenty-seven to thirty-six) are certain God exists, compared to only two-thirds of the younger ones (ages eighteen to twenty-six).

This same generational pattern also emerged in a series of "testimony" questions that we asked Mormons about traditional Christian beliefs. In this series, we used a five-point scale (see wording in Table 1.2). If we reduce their answers to a binary agreement or disagreement, Millennials resemble their elders in being staunch believers. If, however, we look at their responses on the five-point scale used in the original question, it appears that Millennials are neither as certain nor as rigid in their beliefs as older Mormons are (Table 1.1).

What we see here is a notable drop in certainty on every theological measure, with an average decline of eighteen points. Just to reiterate, this

Table 1.1. MORMONS' CERTAINTY ABOUT TRADITIONAL CHRISTIAN TEACHINGS, BY GENERATION

	Boomer/ Silents Who Are "Confident and Know This Is True"	GenXers Who Are "Confident and Know This Is True"	Millennials Who Are "Confident and Know This Is True"	Delta (Ordered from Greatest to Least Difference)
Jesus Christ was literally resurrected and rose from the dead.	83%	70%	57%	−26
Jesus Christ is the Savior of the world and died to reconcile humanity to God.	84%	74%	65%	−19
God is real.	86%	76%	68%	−18
There is life after death.	80%	70%	62%	−18
God has a plan for my life and I will be happier if I follow that plan.	74%	68%	60%	−14
God created Adam and Eve sometime in the last 10,000 years and humans did not evolve from other life forms.	61%	53%	47%	−14
Average				−18

does not mean that Millennial Mormons are unbelievers. For example, on the question about Christ's literal resurrection, which showed a twenty-six-point drop in certainty between generations, more than nine in ten Millennials do affirm this belief to varying degrees; they're just less sure about it than older Mormons (Table 1.2). Notably, the growth in the middle category ("I believe this might be true, but I have my doubts") has grown exponentially.

How much of this difference is the result of generational change and how much is due to a life cycle effect is hard to tell from this snapshot. If it's the latter,

Table 1.2. BELIEF AND DOUBT THAT "JESUS CHRIST WAS LITERALLY
RESURRECTED FROM THE DEAD," BY GENERATION

	Boomer/Silent	GenX	Millennial
I am confident and know this is true.	83%	70%	57%
I believe and have faith that this is probably true.	14%	18%	22%
I believe this might be true, but I have my doubts.	1%	8%	14%
I believe this is probably NOT true.	1%	4%	4%
I am confident and know this is NOT true.	1%	1%	4%

Millennials may grow into greater theological certainty with time. It's also possible that there has been some self-selective winnowing here, in which the older respondents who remain in the current Mormon sample are the ones who had the most certain faith to begin with.[9] Yet the trend is nonetheless striking.

BELIEF IN MORMON TEACHINGS

As with belief in God, Millennials exhibit a strong overall trust in LDS teachings, affirming doctrines like Joseph Smith's prophetic role, the historical accuracy of the Book of Mormon, and the LDS Church's authority in matters of salvation. Again, however, when we parse that more carefully, we begin to spot generational differences. For starters, Millennials are less likely than their elders to embrace an all-or-nothing theology. Among the Boomer/Silent generation, 56 percent believe "wholeheartedly in all of the teachings of the LDS Church," while both GenXers (46 percent) and Millennials (47 percent) are more reserved. Overall, then, fewer than half of Millennials and GenXers say they believe in the whole package of LDS truth claims without any reservations.

On particular points of LDS doctrine, we also see a fading certainty among Millennials. On these questions, there is on average a twelve-point drop from the oldest generation to the youngest in the percentage choosing the most certain option on a five-point scale ranging from "I am confident and know this is true" to "I am confident and know this is *not* true" (see Table 1.3).

Other than the downward generational trajectory, there are three things worth noting. First, *every* generation of Mormons shows a drop in confidence on these specific questions about LDS belief compared to more general beliefs in God and Jesus. Second, the largest drops occur between the Boomer/Silents and GenXers, not between GenXers and Millennials.[10] We will see this many times throughout the book: GenXers' views and behaviors are often closer to Millennials' than they are to Boomer/Silents',

Table 1.3. MORMONS' CERTAINTY ABOUT SPECIFIC LDS TEACHINGS, BY GENERATION

	Boomer/ Silents Who Are "Confident and Know This Is True"	GenXers Who Are "Confident and Know This Is True"	Millennials Who Are "Confident and Know This Is True"	Delta (Ordered from Greatest to Least Difference)
God's priesthood authority is reserved only for men, not women.	57%	46%	41%	−16
Joseph Smith was a prophet of God.	67%	54%	51%	−16
The LDS First Presidency members and apostles are God's prophets on the earth today.	67%	55%	53%	−14
God is an exalted person of flesh and bone.	68%	55%	55%	−13
The Book of Mormon is a literal, historical account.	62%	53%	50%	−12
The LDS Church is the only true faith leading to exaltation.	56%	49%	48%	−8
LDS sealing ordinances are ultimately the only way for families to be eternal.	56%	49%	49%	−7
The priesthood and temple ban on members of African descent was inspired of God and was God's will for the Church until 1978.	44%	30%	37%	−7
Average				*−12*

and this finding is not just true of the NMS, but other studies as well.[11] So when we investigate the tremendous changes that are happening in the LDS Church with Millennials, it's important to remember that many of these shifts began before Millennials came of age. Mormon GenXers first tested the boundaries of belief, paving the way for their younger siblings to later do the same.

Third, the areas that see the greatest decline in certainty all have to do with questions of prophetic and priestly authority. Barely half of Millennials say they know without a doubt that Joseph Smith is a prophet and that today's LDS leaders are apostles and prophets, while only four in ten are sure the priesthood is reserved only for men and not for women. As we will see in chapter 10, authority issues are far-reaching with the Millennial generation as a whole, since their trust in institutions is often lower than their elders'.[12] The NMS data shows that LDS Millennials are not hostile to the church's institutional authority, but they are less keenly wedded to it than older Mormons are.

Overall, the NMS findings confirm that Mormons are strong believers in core Christian doctrines, if more qualified believers in specific LDS doctrines. Generationally, Millennials show less absolutism than their elders, but they are still remarkably devout compared with their non-LDS Millennial peers. These findings about Mormons' piety are very much in line with what the National Study of Youth and Religion learned about Mormon youth in 2002 and 2003; LDS teens at that time (who are today's Millennials) professed exceptionally high belief in a personal God and strong convictions about traditional Christian doctrines such as the existence of life after death, angels, and miracles.[13] The study found that while teenagers have a reputation for being rebellious and thinking independently, most of those surveyed were actually "exceedingly conventional" in their religious beliefs and practices, accepting whatever they were raised to think was true.[14]

Among current Mormons, such conventional orthodoxy is still the rule, even for the rising generation. Take Jack, twenty-six, whose story opened this book. He says that if it weren't for the Book of Mormon, he would not be a member of the LDS Church, and that serving a mission was one of the best experiences of his life. Having recently become a father, he hopes to pass on this legacy of faith to his children, raising them "to focus on Jesus Christ." He theorizes that there may be a growing polarization within his Millennial generation of Mormons. Some, like him, "are staying very strong" in the church, while many others—like at least one and possibly two of his four siblings—have disengaged from it. Despite his own vibrant faith, he can see why many people from his generation report feeling judged by fellow Mormons, and he worries that the church's culture is too exclusivist. "Just the other morning in my scripture study in Mark, there's a verse about how culture and tradition would get in the way of people living the gospel," he explains. "I think sometimes if the Savior were to come today to our wards, who would he be spending his time with? I think he would spend some time with faithful believers, but he would also reach out to those who feel judged, without condoning any type of sin or unrighteousness."

RELATIONSHIP WITH GOD

Jack's ruminations on what Jesus might think of modern-day Mormonism point to his generation's desire for a relevant faith that can remain both solid and flexible. But propositional belief is only one aspect of that kind of enduring faith. I would posit that the successful transmission of a religious identity is based on a combination of three indispensable elements: orthodox belief, an accepted code of behavior, and a fuzzier category I would describe as transformative religious experience. This third category is paramount if rising generations are to fully inhabit the faith of their parents. In other words, the "secret sauce" of religion as a core identity has to include not just the shoulds and shouldn'ts of belief and behavior, but also a palpable sense that a devotee has personally encountered the divine. This is an area in which Mormonism seems to excel.

Millennial Mormons, like all Mormons, report feeling close to God. Eighty-two percent of LDS Millennials say they feel God's presence at least once a week, almost identical to the rate of GenXers and the combined Boomer/Silent generations (83 percent in both cases). More than three-quarters of Mormon Millennials report feeling a deep sense of peace and well-being at least weekly, which is likewise virtually unchanged from older generations of Mormons; most feel guided by God when they pray or are in the midst of their daily activities. Only one-half of 1 percent of LDS Millennials report they "never" feel God's presence and love, a remarkably low number. While of course we have seen that more Mormon young adults are leaving the religion than in the past (and are not therefore canvassed in this "current Mormon" sample of respondents), it is also true that those who stay feel spiritually connected.

It is fascinating that despite the aforementioned softening of Mormon Millennials' certainty in their beliefs (and, as we'll see in chapter 8, far more pronounced dips in their adherence to some expected religious behaviors), in experiencing the transcendent they are every bit as confident as their elders. Mormon Millennials who remain in the faith regularly feel God's presence, a factor that came up often in interviews. Many cited Mormonism's unusual ability to help them experience God's presence in their lives—what Mormons and many other Christians call "the Spirit," "the Holy Spirit," or "the Holy Ghost." In particular, adult converts spoke of the deepened relationship with God they feel the LDS Church made possible for them. Such is the case with Robin, an attorney who says Mormonism's focus on spirituality was a tremendous draw.[15] "There was this power there," says Robin, who converted when she was twenty-two, just after the September 11 terrorist attacks. She had been reading about Mormonism and corresponding with a missionary, but in the immediate aftermath of 9/11 she needed spiritual guidance. The terrorists' actions shocked her deeply, "and it struck me that if there could be organized darkness in the world—not referring to Muslims, but just to acts of violence that required planning and quite a lot of organization—that there would need to be an equal, opposite organized good in the world. Or at least, I was open to that idea." So on the Sunday after 9/11, she visited the LDS chapel that was a few blocks from her house, and was "overwhelmed by this feeling" of being spiritually connected. "What was most attractive to me at first was just sort of the feeling of inspiration and revelation and the presence of the Holy Spirit," she says, citing "that sense of power and truth that was clear and available." Robin joined the LDS Church despite the objections of her nonreligious parents, whom she describes as "traditional hippies with a bent of Buddhism." She married a Latter-day Saint and they are raising their two children to be Mormon.

Another convert, Brittany, also joined in her early twenties, and also did so because she felt the power of the transcendent in the Mormon community.[16] "The Mormon Church was the first church where I felt God," says the former Catholic, who also tried Unitarianism and the liberal United Church of Christ (UCC) denomination before being baptized into the LDS Church. In Mormonism, Brittany "saw that no matter who I was and where I was, God loved me." Her social values actually aligned most closely with the UCC, especially since her parents were gay and she advocated for LGBT equality, but it was through Mormonism that she most felt the power of God. Now thirty, Brittany still holds to her Mormon identity, but says her testimony has been shaken by the church's actions toward LGBT people like her parents—and, possibly, like herself. When asked about her own sexual orientation, she responds that it is a "really tough question" and that she "would have to say bisexual," but she's not sure. Largely because of this, her Mormon identity is in flux: she is a passionate believer in many tenets of Mormon theology and has felt God's presence most strongly in the LDS Church, but she's not certain she can stay active in it.

Interviewees found different facets of the Mormon faith appealing. Some are unique to Mormonism, like the Book of Mormon. Annabel, twenty-nine, was raised in the LDS Church in Utah, and says the Book of Mormon and other LDS scriptures have been conduits of spirituality for her.[17] "I believe that we can feel the numinous through any number of sources, but I always tend to feel it the most strongly and the most regularly when I'm in the Mormon faith, when I'm around those things like reading the scriptures or having spiritual discussions," she says. Other churches "are beautiful and they give me a sense of peace, but I don't always feel the numinous there."

Annabel and other interviewees also circled back periodically to LDS ideas about the afterlife. In particular, she resonates with the uniquely Mormon teaching that all people will be sorted into different kingdoms for eternity, based on what will make them happy. "I feel like being who I am here, being my absolute true self, will essentially take me to my heaven, whatever kingdom that is." Annabel's words highlight an element of personalization that applies even to eternity; Mormonism does not hold with a one-size-fits-all afterlife, which may be especially attractive to a generation that has been raised to expect customization to their individual tastes.[18] But her statement also goes a step further; whereas the LDS Church has taught that people "will be assigned to an eternal dwelling place in a specific kingdom" based on their faith and obedience, Annabel's understanding of heaven honors her own desires and sense of being true to herself.[19]

The Mormon afterlife also features the timeless and captivating notion that people who have been sealed in the temple can be reunited with their loved ones in eternity as a "forever family." A thirty-two-year-old interviewee, Rachel, cites the Mormon doctrine of eternal families as especially formative for her belief system.[20] When she was five years old, her brother died of cancer, a profound loss that was only made bearable by the knowledge that they would be reunited after death.

> I remember feeling that it was totally natural that of course I would get to see him again in heaven. I think that belief mitigated, somewhat, the pain of him dying. I do remember, though, that it was also a horribly sad experience. . . . It definitely made me more thoughtful about my faith and the kind of claims that the gospel makes.

Young adult Mormons like Rachel show themselves to be very interested in spiritual experiences that tie them to the transcendent and the eternal. In the data, they cite regular experiences of God's presence and a sense of delight at the universe; in interviews, they often reflected deeply on how their faith is animated by various elements of Mormon theology and practice. From this it's clear that the third element of a successful faith—the "secret sauce" of transformative religious experience—is alive and well among Millennial Mormons.

FACTORS ASSOCIATED WITH GREATER BELIEF

What contributes, overall, to Mormons' strong rates of belief and sense of God's presence? Which factors correlate with increased orthodoxy, both in the population at large and within the LDS community itself? Many Mormon parents, teachers, and bishops have told me how concerned they are about the rate at which young adults they know seem to be either losing interest in church activity or wholly disengaging. Given that concern, are there things that might make Mormonism a more "sticky" faith? This is the memorable term some evangelicals have employed to describe their efforts to create long-term disciples, and it's an apt one for Mormonism as well. Research at Fuller Theological Seminary on evangelical young adults confirms that the most important factors in "sticky" religion continue to be the classic ones: being raised in homes where parents practiced their faith openly and with warmth, and where children were enmeshed in intergenerational networks that also supported the family's religion.[21] This conclusion about parental influence is hardly new, and is backed by longitudinal data spanning several generations. While there is no perfect formula for raising children who remain devout in adulthood—especially given the unprecedentedly rapid disaffiliation of the Millennial generation as a whole—the best chances for successful transmission of a religious identity from one generation to the next remain within the family.[22]

Another factor that contributes to higher rates of religious orthodoxy may be a surprise—a college education. Sociologists once predicted that education would eventually prove a death knell for belief—that once people were exposed to secular knowledge and strategies for critical thinking, they would jettison their faith.[23] For the most part, this has not occurred in America; if anything, a college education appears to provide a modest boost toward greater belief and religious activity.[24] In the NMS, 21 percent of current Mormons had a high school education or less; 45 percent had done some college or an associate's degree; 22 percent had a four-year college degree; and the remaining 12 percent had a postgraduate degree. Those who received only a high school education were less orthodox on nearly every testimony question. For example, nearly two-thirds of Mormons with a college degree are confident that "the LDS First Presidency members and apostles are God's prophets on the earth today," but under half of those with a high school education agree (63 vs. 48 percent).[25] An even wider gap separates those groups on the question of whether Jesus Christ was literally resurrected from the dead. Seventy-four percent of Mormons with a college diploma say they know this is true, compared to just 57 percent of those who did not attend college. Overall, the most religiously believing Mormons were those who had obtained a college degree, and the least orthodox were those with only a high school education. On questions of religious *transcendence*, though, those with a high school education edged out those with a bachelor's degree by an average of five points, showing the highest scores on measures like being guided by God through their prayers, experiencing deep spiritual peace and well-being, and feeling God's presence and love. Overall, we can say that a college education is positively correlated with greater confidence in almost all Mormon doctrines, but not necessarily with stronger feelings of closeness to God.

In addition to factors like family socialization and a college education that appear to spur greater religiosity across many faith traditions, let me also suggest two additional influences that may be unique to Mormonism: seminary attendance and geography.

The Mormon youth experience has come to include a pivotal component that is not present in most other religions and may help with later retention: seminary for high school students. For Mormon teens in Utah and other places with sizable LDS populations, seminary is a "release time" educational experience that occurs during the regular school day as a noncredit class. Release-time students typically walk from their high school to a nearby building for an hour of daily religious instruction covering scriptures, church history, and doctrinal foundations. For high schoolers growing up outside of LDS-heavy areas, seminary generally occurs at a church member's home in the early morning before the regular school day. The curriculum is the same everywhere.[26] High school students are not required by the church to enroll in seminary, though it is strongly encouraged—particularly if students want to eventually become missionaries or attend a church-owned university. Many Mormon families require their teenagers to attend seminary if they want certain privileges. For Nicole, twenty-six, "there was the expectation that we would go if we wanted to continue to drive the car." She attended seminary even though rising at the crack of dawn was often challenging because she was an athlete who sometimes had away games until after midnight on weeknights.[27]

Considering its importance in the Mormon youth experience today, it's surprising how recent a development seminary is in LDS history; it was not made a standardized program of the LDS Church until "Correlation," an umbrella term used to describe the sweeping corporatization of Mormonism in the 1960s and 1970s. The church for the first time instituted global programs on a massive scale, with unified curricula, training materials, and missionary tools. Many of the foundational programs that are considered essential to inculcating a Mormon identity today, including seminary, date from this period. According to historian Rebecca de Schweinetz, the number of students enrolled in seminary increased by 40 percent between 1965 and 1971.[28] This growth is reflected in our data, which shows the seminary experience to be conspicuously more common among younger Mormons. We asked respondents to describe their seminary attendance in high school—whether they had attended regularly all four years, semiregularly, infrequently, or not at all. Only 15 percent of Mormon Millennials reported not attending seminary at all or attending infrequently, compared to 33 percent of Boomer/Silents. GenXers were, as usual, in the middle but closer to the Millennials (21 percent). Put another way, one in three Boomer/Silents did not attend seminary, but that shrinks to one in five GenXers and roughly one in seven Millennials. This reflects the expansion of the seminary program over time.

In the NMS data, seminary attendance is positively correlated with a number of outcomes Mormon leaders would consider desirable: people who attend seminary regularly are more likely to later serve a mission, for example, and to get married in the temple. When they reach adulthood, they report higher levels of church activity and stronger levels of belief than Mormons who did not attend seminary. This led to another question: Is this the case only because the LDS youth who attended seminary were also more likely to have had parents who were orthodox and committed enough to make their kids go to seminary? Is the "seminary effect" really just a factor of growing up in orthodox homes and being surrounded by LDS peers? While some prior research done in the 1980s did not show seminary to have an effect independent of family socialization and peer groups, the NMS did.[29] In fact, the difference is noteworthy, as Figure 1.2 suggests with its list of many different youth activities. People who remain in the church were marginally more likely to have been involved in ward potlucks, road shows, and church camps than those who have since defected. But for seminary, the difference was nearly two to one. Six in ten Mormon Millennials participated in seminary when they were in high school, compared to just a third of former Mormon respondents of the same generation.

This difference remains intact when we factor in how often these people attended church when they were growing up. If we exclude adult converts and those who grew up Mormon but rarely or never attended church, those who enrolled in seminary all four years were still 33 percent more likely to be self-identifying Mormons today.[30] Among high school students who are already Sunday worshipers, seminary appears to provide something extra that helps to cement a Mormon identity. However, it is not clear from the research whether that is a result of the content taught in the curriculum, the friendships that form with other students, or—for those who did early

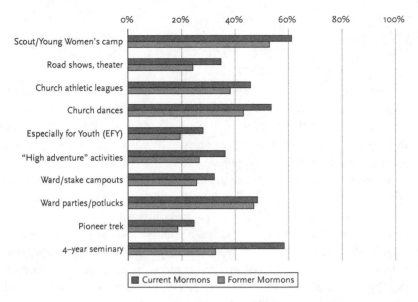

Figure 1.2. LDS Seminary Attendance as a Predictor of Future Retention.

morning seminary—the habit of sacrifice that is instilled by getting up so early to seek religious knowledge.

Marie, now twenty-four, credits seminary not just with giving her a solid grounding in the scriptures during her adolescence, but also with keeping her in the church now, as an adult. "I feel like my experience in seminary—the teachers I had there and in the Young Women program—were so important and foundational to me that I am still a member of the church today because of what I went through as a youth," she says. In our in-person interview, Marie gestures to the other side of the room at a line in the carpet and asks me to consider that line a threshold. Her experience during seminary, she says, pushed her "back really far this way," toward where we were sitting, far away from that line across the room. "But as I've grown intellectually and spiritually, I've gone closer to that threshold. And if I hadn't been anchored in that way from seminary and Young Women, I would have passed through." She says the difference wasn't just the knowledge she gained in seminary, though she enjoyed diving deeply into the scriptures and learning about church history. It was more that seminary fills "your life with goodness, and it's hard to forget that." She loved her teacher, who was charismatic and funny and kind; she also thinks that preparing devotions for her fellow students and writing spiritual thoughts in a journal helped with her faith formation. In all, seminary for Marie was a deeply positive experience, and from the data we see that it has a noticeable effect for many on retention in the church.

One other factor that influences Mormons' belief and practice is geography, specifically whether Mormons live in Utah or somewhere else in the United States. In a nutshell, Utah Mormons are often, but not always, more theologically orthodox (Table 1.4).[31]

Some differences can be explained by convert status; nearly half of all Mormons outside of Utah are converts to the church (47 percent) versus just one in five Utah Mormons (19 percent). And despite the old adage about the zeal of converts, they are consistently *not* as religiously orthodox as those born and raised in the faith.[32]

Although Utah Mormons are generally more orthodox, in a few areas of what we might call "private" or "family" religiosity, the reverse is true. For example, 81 percent of Mormon parents outside Utah say they read the scriptures and pray with their families regularly, while only 72 percent of Utah Mormon parents do. This was surprising but may reflect the fact that in Utah, multiple support systems are in place for inculcating a Mormon identity in children. When a majority of a child's neighbors, teachers, and community leaders are LDS, there is perhaps not so much pressure on parents to be their children's sole conduit to the Mormon faith. This conclusion is supported by the fact that 37 percent of non-Utah Mormons chose

Table 1.4. RELIGIOUS BELIEFS AMONG MORMONS IN UTAH VERSUS MORMONS ELSEWHERE IN THE UNITED STATES

	Utah Mormons (All Generations)	Non-Utah Mormons (All Generations)
Agrees with the statement "I believe wholeheartedly in all of the teachings of the LDS Church"	56%	46%
Attended seminary all four years	67%	57%
Describes self as currently "very active" in the LDS Church (as opposed to somewhat, not very, or not at all active)	62%	52%
Holds a current temple recommend	63%	47%
Cites knowledge that "families can be together forever" as one of the top three favorite parts of being Mormon	64%	40%
Agrees that "religious organizations are a great force for good"	84%	66%
Views "moral or religious decline" as one of the top three issues facing the nation	42%	30%

"the strong community I enjoy at church" as one of their favorite aspects of being Mormon, but only 15 percent of Utah Mormons did. It would seem that many Utah Saints are experiencing Mormon community almost by osmosis, so it is not something they remark upon as being special.

Mormonism is unusual among American religions because its strong geographical concentration in Utah creates an enclave in which a minority religion can achieve majority status. Only a few other minority faith traditions can boast a similar concentration of coreligionists within a single area, and those tend to be particular cities rather than entire states— Brooklyn for Orthodox Jews, Dearborn for Muslims. The percentage of Utah that is Mormon has been declining in recent years, from a high of 75 percent in 2000 to about 63 percent in 2017. One study has even claimed it is as low as 51 percent.[33] Despite this decline, the religion's majority status there continues to make it possible for the state's Mormons to feel enveloped by a culture that supports their religious choices. For some of my interviewees who grew up in Utah, that was a comforting experience, while for others it felt confining—and sometimes it was both at once. Colby, twenty, moved to Utah partway through high school, transferring from a Michigan school where he'd been the only Mormon to one that was dominated by Mormons.[34] In Utah he fell in with "a very active LDS friend group," he explains, with peers who "were doing everything they were supposed to, often because they *wanted* to—all the activities, the campouts, the youth conferences—and I just didn't feel like I fit completely into that mold." He felt social pressure to be more involved in the church than he had been previously and "to do a lot of things since all my friends were doing them. I didn't even think about getting my patriarchal blessing until all my friends were getting theirs. I got mine not because I was ready, but because my friends were all doing that and they would talk about it."[35] In Colby's experience of Utah, full activity in the church was not just about religion but also defined Colby's social life, which is a vital part of adolescence. He became more active in the church partly out of a desire to fit in with his peers. Because of pro-Mormon peer pressure, he signed up to serve a mission when he turned eighteen, even though he says he was not mentally or spiritually ready. The decision to go on a mission was, he reflects now, similar to other "significant church milestones in my life. . . . [I]t was something I felt was expected of me, something that all my friends were doing." He wound up returning early because of feelings of depression and anxiety.

Other interviewees made the reverse pilgrimage, growing up in Utah or southern Idaho and then moving to the "mission field" (what Mormons have traditionally called every place that is *not* Utah or southern Idaho) as adults. Brooke, a thirty-six-year-old mother of five, didn't interact with many non-Mormons until after she was married and she and her husband moved east for their continued education.[36] "I finally found myself in the minority, religion-wise." Her class "had almost any religion or nonreligion you could think of," including Muslims, Jews, Sikhs, and Seventh-day Adventists. "We had every-thing, and it was fantastic." While she sees this as having been a positive and eye-opening experience, she also acknowledges that she's not quite as orthodox now as she was before this exposure. "I guess that I have a more doubting com-ponent now," she admits. "I think that component comes from being more aware of the skeptical world around me and the criticisms of the Church."

Living in Utah and other Mormon-dominated areas, then, may provide a sort of protective barrier in the form of a shared community—what Peter Berger half a century ago called a "sacred canopy"—that instructs people in what it means to be Mormon and utilizes social leverage to maintain certain accepted standards of behavior and belief. Being surrounded so completely by other Mormons creates an environment in which LDS beliefs may be regarded as both normal and normative.

THE DOUBTERS WHO REMAIN

Like Brooke, Catherine is a mom in her midthirties whose Mormon faith began shifting when she moved to the Northeast with her husband about ten years ago.[37] She made friends with several other young mothers who were not Mormon. "That was the kicker," she remembers. "I had a friend who was evangelical and believed firmly that she was right, and another friend who was an Orthodox Jew and didn't eat bacon. It sounds naïve for me to say, but it was the first time I saw how other people had as strong a tes-timony as we did." During this period, Catherine began delving into LDS history for the first time, reading books and listening to podcasts about topics she hadn't considered before. She realized she had doubts about the Mormon temple ceremony, the history of polygamy, and the exclusive truth claims of the LDS Church. She is still active in the church—in fact, she has a calling in the Primary presidency—but she no longer believes. She doesn't have "much belief or faith in" core tenets like Joseph Smith and the Book of Mormon, "but I also see so much good in the way I was raised, and I would like to be a spiritual person. I think it's healthy for us to try and connect with some sort of spirituality. So I'm choosing Mormonism to practice that spirituality, but I do not consider myself to be a True Believing Mormon."

Catherine is unusual. In this chapter we've seen that the vast majority of self-identified Mormons in the United States report a strong level of belief in the teachings of the LDS Church.[38] Only about 17 percent of respondents who still identify as Mormons express even a moderate degree of doubt in the teachings of the LDS Church.[39] Not surprisingly, those who say they are most active in the church report having few if any doubts, and those who are inactive have the most—just over half of people who still consider themselves Mormon but are inactive in the church say that at least some of its teachings are hard for them to believe. So while about one in six self-identified Mormons in the United States claims a degree of doubt, only about one in ten active members who attend church weekly and about one in twenty of those with current temple recommends express doubt in some, most, or all of the church's teachings. This means that people like Catherine, who is not a believer but holds a current temple recommend, are thin on the ground.

What are the shared characteristics, if any, of those who doubt the church's teachings but still identify as LDS? Given the higher percentage of young adult Mormons who have left the church, it seems logical to assume that a higher percentage of Millennial doubters are still in the pews, but that's not actually the case. The level of doubting among Mormons is stubbornly identical from one generation to the next: 17 percent across all age groups. Nor do we see any major differences by race or gender. Factors that do make a difference are education— as we saw earlier, those lacking a college degree are less orthodox—and marital status. Mormons who are divorced or separated are more than twice as likely to be doubters as those who are married (28 vs. 12 percent). When it comes to politics, Independents are more likely to identify as doubters than either Republicans or Democrats (31 vs. 13 and 20 percent, respectively).

The factor that makes the most difference, though, is not about age or political affiliation or marital status. It has to do with the people around you. Table 1.5 displays the frequency of doubting among people with

Table 1.5. PREVALENCE OF DOUBTING AND MORMON SOCIAL NETWORKS

	% Doubter
None or few immediate family left the church	11%
Some or more immediate family left the church	22%
No immediate family are/were LDS	30%
None or few childhood/youth friends left the church	10.5%
Some or more childhood/youth friends left the church	21%
No childhood/youth friends are/were LDS	23.5%
None of closest friends are LDS	44%
Some of closest friends are LDS	18%
All closest friends are LDS	4%
No LDS in extended family	35%
Some/most extended family LDS	16%
All extended family LDS	7%

varying levels of Mormons in their family and friendship circles. In each case, the fewer Mormon family members and friends people have, the more likely they are to be doubters. This is most often the case for those who have zero close friends or extended family members who are Mormon (44 and 35 percent). Doubting also rises as the number of loved ones who have left the church increases, as we saw with Daniel's experience. Doubting is least common among those whose closest friends are all Mormon (4 percent) and whose extended family are all Mormon (7 percent).[40]

These findings underscore the importance of social networks in the spectrum of belief and doubt. Relationships matter. When LDS leader Henry B. Eyring used the phrase "infected with doubt" in 2013, he faced heavy criticism. But his metaphor was appropriate at least in one way: doubting is statistically more likely to be associated with the Mormon composition of people's social networks than it is with their demographic characteristics.[41] Those who have friends and family who are Mormon and stay Mormon tend to be believers, while those with friends and family who are not Mormon or stop identifying as Mormon are more likely to be doubters.

What's important to remember is that these categories of "doubter" and "believer" are dynamic: individuals may move from one category to the other multiple times during their faith journey, whether they remain engaged with institutional Mormonism or not. For some, a period of doubt is a way station before leaving the church, as we'll see in chapter 11. But sometimes, as was the case with Daniel, doubt can become a catalyst for a deeper and even more committed Mormon faith. This was also true of Rachel, whose belief in eternal families was cemented in her youth after the death of her brother. She had sometimes felt overwhelmed by serious doubts, especially on her mission to France. At that time she was plagued by "what if" questions, "feeling like I was making this all up, that everyone is making this all up. Also I was wrestling with the absence of great spiritual manifestations when I really wanted to have them." Rachel came to see believing as a choice: "Coming through on the other side of those questions and challenges I was realizing that my faith was an exercise in commitment and holding on to the bits of the spiritual experiences that did come my way, and not giving up on those." For this reason and others, her mission was a transformative experience, intensifying her loyalty to the Mormon faith and her desire to serve others. As we will see in the next chapter, Rachel is part of a generation that has made such missionary service a rite of passage for both men and women.

CHAPTER 2

Called to Serve

The Missionary Experience

When Lee, now thirty-eight, was in college, she loved a passage in the Book of Mormon about the sons of Mosiah being overcome with joy at the thought of all the people who had been converted to the gospel because of their missionary efforts.[1] In the story, these sons had given up their own privilege in Nephite society to preach to their enemies, the Lamanite people, risking their lives on a gamble: that God's message was for everyone, and that if they ventured forth to share that message they would be blessed. Lee was on fire because of that passage. "I couldn't bear the thought that there might be someone out there that I was supposed to reach. And if I didn't go, I wouldn't reach them," Lee explains. "That was horrifying to me."

So when she was twenty-one—the age when women were permitted to serve missions at that time—she was called to serve in Uruguay.[2] She was thrilled to teach the gospel in Spanish, becoming enmeshed with members' and investigators' lives as she served people all day, every day.[3] And she was not overly concerned at first when she got word that her father, who was just fifty years old and in perfect health, had fallen off his bicycle back home. Cheerful letters from her mother, which arrived in Uruguay several weeks after they were written, assured her that her father had been released from the hospital and would soon be fine. She also received a letter directly from her dad, which was comforting. Yet that day the mission president called Lee to inform her that her father had died of internal bleeding. The letter Lee had just received had been written before his condition suddenly worsened.

Lee was in shock, and collapsed against a wall in an outpouring of grief. Her memories of that day are surreal: the baby-faced mission elders who had no idea what to say, the kind Seventh-day Adventist landlady who tried to help, the round-the-clock mission companion for whom she wanted to be strong. And piercing through the shock was the question: Should she go home? Her mother, she knew, could likely use her support there, especially as Lee was the oldest child. However, her father's last words as he was wheeled into emergency surgery had been to the effect of "if something should happen, tell the kids that I love them, and to keep on doing what they're doing, because they're doing such good things." And there was the plain fact that Lee felt *called* to serve her mission. While a part of her wanted to return home to her family's embrace, "I also knew that I'd been sent there, and I truly believe that it was by God. He knew what he was doing. And if I went home, even just for the funeral, they wouldn't have sent me back to Uruguay. So I stayed." Lee heard the news on a Monday. On Thursday, she went back to work as a missionary.

Lee's story encapsulates many of the themes we will encounter in this chapter: the personal sacrifice that is required of LDS missionaries, and the deep faith that sees them through tough times; the positive feelings most missionaries have about their experience; the sense that a mission demarcates a bright line between childhood and adulthood in Mormon culture; the growing presence of women in the mission force; and the great statistical likelihood that returned missionaries who served the full tenure of their assigned time will remain as lifelong members of the LDS Church. Now the Young Women president in her ward, Lee is preparing the next generation of female missionaries, and is solidly grounded in her own faith.

A CULTURE OF RESPONSIBILITY

Lee's dedication did not develop in a vacuum, but is part of an ingrained culture of responsibility in the LDS world. Although Mormon families are getting smaller, they are still statistically larger than average, which can lead to children taking on greater responsibilities at home, especially if they have younger siblings. Mormons' commitment to raising children who work hard is clear in their responses to certain questions in the NMS. Adapting a question used by Pew, we asked respondents to look at twelve traits in children and choose up to three that they considered most important to instill, selecting from a list that included qualities like creativity, good manners, empathy, curiosity, and helping others.[4] Among the current Mormon respondents, the top traits were responsibility, hard work, and religious faith. It is significant that responsibility and hard work edged out religious faith even in this steadfast pool of believers.

From an early age Mormons are given jobs to help the ward (congregation) run effectively. Beginning at age three, children give mini-talks in Primary, a dress rehearsal for when they are teenagers and will be expected to give regular talks to the entire congregation in sacrament meeting. Boys are ordained to the Aaronic priesthood at the age of twelve, which gives them responsibilities both sacred (administering the sacrament, or communion bread and water) and quotidian (taking out the trash at the end of church meetings). Many Mormon boys have traditionally been heavily involved in the Scouting program, working to obtain the rank of Eagle Scout and its accompanying Court of Honor. In some LDS families, completion of the Eagle Scout program has been a prerequisite before parents will give a son permission to drive, something that was mentioned by several male interviewees.[5]

Girls have fewer formal religious responsibilities than boys, but they experience a litany of cultural and spiritual hoops to jump through as part of the Personal Progress program from ages twelve to eighteen, in which they set and achieve individual goals that are related to the eight "values" of the Young Women organization. Some tasks are simple and can be accomplished in an hour or two, like reading certain scriptures or preparing a meal for their family. Others are more involved and require at least ten hours of work.

For Mormon teens, the work is also generally fun. The church has a robust program for youth that blends activities like scavenger hunts, camping, and games with learning the gospel. However, several older Mormon interviewees told me that while the wider culture has in recent decades downplayed religious responsibility in favor of entertainment, the LDS youth experience has gone in the opposite direction, becoming more overtly religious and less lively over time. This starts with Primary, which until 1980 was a weekday after-school activity that was more about doing crafts and singing songs than imbibing doctrine; it is now a Sabbath-day meeting in which children in their Sunday best might earn a star for memorizing each Article of Faith. This more concentrated focus on religious instruction extends to youth activities, and in particular Young Women Camp (formerly called "Girls' Camp"), which several women mentioned as something that has changed significantly since their own childhoods—and not necessarily for the better. Sarah, a thirty-eight-year-old mother of six in Utah, remembers that when she went to camp as a teenager, the experience was remarkably fun, and every day there would be water sports like tubing on the river.[6] Camp was primarily intended for bonding with peers and having a great time, not cramming in an extra helping of religiosity. "There was an obligatory sobbing testimony meeting on the last night, but other than that they kind of just let us run free," she remembers. Now an adult camp leader, she would like to recreate that experience for her daughters and their friends, but says the focus has changed. Male priesthood leaders from the bishopric and stake presidency come up to camp in the evenings to deliver a spiritual thought and oversee the proceedings. Great emphasis is placed on "modest" clothing—not just eschewing two-piece bathing suits, as was the case when Sarah was younger, but even in some camps forbidding girls to wear shorts at all despite temperatures that climb into the triple digits. And throughout, there is a greater emphasis on religious devotion, with "testimony hikes" and other spiritually focused activities replacing the freer, more boisterous experiences she remembers. "I feel that they're trying to create such an intense spiritual experience for the girls, where when I went it was more like a Scout camp," Sarah says.

If the focus of Mormon youth programs has tended more toward devotion than diversion in recent decades, the results have been mixed. In terms of belief, we found in the last chapter that Mormon Millennials are definitely internalizing the basic messages the church's curriculum has tried to communicate. But we will see later that Millennials are less rigid than their elders in observing some Mormon standards of behavior. I wonder how much of this is inevitable—a result of their coming of age in an era in which coffee, R-rated content, and Sunday brunch have become cultural norms—and how much might relate to the church's own internal changes. The shift from Mormonism as an entire social world that encircled nearly every aspect of members' lives to a denomination that focuses primarily on doctrine might be a double-edged sword.

THE MISSION EXPERIENCE

Mormonism's culture of responsibility extends to the mission experience itself, in which young people are asked to give up eighteen months to two years of their lives to volunteer wherever the church elects to send them. What's more, they are often expected to help pay for it. Young missionaries from North America pay an average of $400 a month wherever they are serving, but that cost is standardized around the world so that those called to the most and least expensive areas will bear roughly the same financial burden.[7] For example, the monthly costs for serving in London, England, are among the highest anywhere, with actual expenses reaching several thousand dollars a month. Other high-rent missions are found in Western Europe, Hawaii, and parts of Oceania, while low-cost areas include places in Central and South America. Even these less expensive missions, however, are heavily subsidized by the church, with actual costs exceeding the missionary's contribution by a factor of three or four.[8] For a two-year mission, then, the cost paid by the missionary's family would start around $10,000, not including extra spending money. (The church officially discourages parents from sending more, though some do.[9]) To save for this, very young Mormon children—especially boys—are sometimes given a special piggy bank that has three slots: for tithing, mission, and spending.[10] Some LDS kids are therefore saving their pennies toward their future missions more than a decade before they ever send in their applications to serve. "When you would get an allowance as a five- or six-year-old, you have some to spend, some to tithe, and some to put in your mission account," says Taylor, now thirty-seven, who served a mission in Taiwan—an experience he paid for himself with savings from various summer jobs.[11]

While they are in the field, Mormon missionaries' time is not their own. In 2017, the church unveiled a new, more flexible schedule for missionaries, but even under the revised version the demands are intense: They rise at 6:30, do a half hour of exercise, take one hour for personal scripture study and a half hour for planning the day, eat breakfast, and shower. At 10:00 AM they are expected to head out to preach the gospel and stay at it through 9 PM, with short meal breaks. Then they can return to their apartments, write in their journals, and pray before lights out at 10:30 PM.[12] Missionaries have one personal day off a week for writing home, doing laundry, shopping for groceries, and attending to other needs. They communicate regularly with their supervisors, who are also fellow missionaries, to report their progress with investigators (their term for potential converts)—specifically, who has been baptized or is willing to set a date for a baptism, who has attended sacrament meeting, and who is just starting to learn about the church.

Today's missionaries are aided by a sophisticated preparation system that begins at an MTC, or Missionary Training Center. The largest one, located in Provo, Utah, was renovated and expanded in 2017 so that it can accommodate several thousand new recruits at any one time, but there are more than a dozen other MTCs throughout the world.[13] At all of the centers trainees say a brief goodbye to their families before immersing themselves in learning foreign languages, studying the gospel, and preparing physically for the rigors of their coming experience. (Missionaries need to be able to walk and bike for many miles per day, so the MTC schedule includes daily exercise.) At the Provo MTC, those who will be serving English-speaking missions may only stay a few weeks, since language acquisition is not required. Those who are learning foreign languages will remain there for something closer to two or two and a half months. While at the MTC, missionaries must adhere to the same "mission rules" that will regulate their days while they're in the field. In particular, they are required to be within sight of their assigned companion at all times, study the scriptures and the teachings of the church every day, and attend regular conferences with the other missionaries serving in their zone.

Such highly regimented schedules are a far cry from what some missions were like before Correlation. For example, when sociologist Armand Mauss served his mission in rural New England in 1947, there was no standard curriculum from which missionaries were supposed to teach, and no centralized missionary department in Salt Lake City to prescribe what missionary life was supposed to be like. This resulted in great local variation, and in Mauss's case, a reprise of the "without purse or script" model used by Jesus's own disciples in the first century. In other words, they had no fixed place to stay for seven months of the year, traveling homeless from one village to the next and carrying a small valise with only underclothing, socks, shirts, and pamphlets about the church. (He also carried an umbrella, which served the dual purpose of warding off both "the sudden summer rains of New England" and "suspicious dogs.") The missionaries depended on local people for food and lodging, sometimes sleeping in barns and washing in streams.[14] This impromptu model was not the norm even at the time, but the fact that the church was willing to experiment with it demonstrates the differences between then and now. In the late 1950s, under the leadership of modernizing prophet David O. McKay, the First Presidency brought the mission program under its direct supervision, so that the whole effort was coordinated from a single office and overseen on a top-down basis. The church began to run its missionary program according to contemporary business practices, with the now-iconic dark suit and tie becoming standard for all male missionaries.[15] McKay also favored calling mission presidents who were younger than the avuncular retirees who had previously held those posts; during his tenure, successful middle-aged businessmen became the norm.[16]

For well over half a century, this hierarchical structure has defined the missionary experience, with little deviation from the patterns and expectations set in Salt Lake City. And for the most part, the program has been phenomenally effective. In 1960, there were just over 9,000 LDS missionaries serving around the world; by 1995 there were more than 48,000, almost six times as many.[17] Since the 1990s there have been two major changes in the missionary force, both based on new policies instituted by the church. In 2002, Elder M. Russell Ballard announced the church would be "raising the bar" concerning which applicants would be accepted to serve a mission. Speaking to an audience of Aaronic priesthood holders, Ballard said that "the day of the 'repent and go' missionary is over." Specifically, he was refuting the idea that young men who had been immoral at eighteen would be able to repent of those sins and serve a mission at nineteen.[18] Repentance was always available, Elder Ballard told them; however, even if forgiven by the Lord such young men "may or may not qualify to serve" a mission.[19] The decision to raise the bar came hand in hand with a new curriculum for missionaries called *Preach My Gospel*, which emphasized teaching by the Spirit rather than rote memorization, as had been the case previously. To accommodate that new curriculum, the church needed missionaries who were mature enough in the gospel to be able to go off script.[20] The loftier standards had an immediate impact on the size of the LDS missionary force. In 2002, just prior to the standards being elevated, there were 61,638 LDS missionaries, but two years later there were 51,067, representing a drop of more than 10,000 missionaries.

These numbers stayed deflated throughout the decade but received a huge boost in 2012 when the church instituted a second change: it lowered the minimum age for men and women to eighteen and nineteen, respectively. Almost immediately, missionary applications shot up in what has since been labeled "the surge"—the period from 2013 to 2015 when the force included both the college-age missionaries who had expected to serve during this time and a crop of fresh high school graduates who were suddenly faced with the exciting prospect of going on a mission sooner than they had planned. In 2013 and 2014, missionary numbers hovered in the mid-80,000s before settling down; in early 2018, there were just under 67,000 missionaries in service.[21] Since this number no longer reflects the double rate that attended during the surge, it shows that lowering the age requirement spurred tremendous enthusiasm among LDS young adults. Given falling LDS birth rates, it's uncertain whether the swelled numbers of the missionary force will be fully sustainable in the years to come. However, it is clear that thousands more are serving missions now compared to before the age change—and for most of them, the mission is proving a positive experience.

THE "BEST TWO YEARS"?: MILLENNIALS AS MISSIONARIES

The NMS data on missionary service is generally quite heartening (Figure 2.1). More than half of Mormon Millennials have served a full-time mission (55 percent), which is clearly the highest proportion of any generation; among GenXers, 40 percent served, and in the Boomer/Silent generation, it was 28 percent. As Armand Mauss has noted, missionary service was actually rather rare in the first half of the twentieth century, and even by the early 1990s as many as two-thirds of LDS young men did not take part.[22] The data we see in the NMS reflects an ever-increasing push to normalize missionary service as an expected path of behavior for active Mormons.

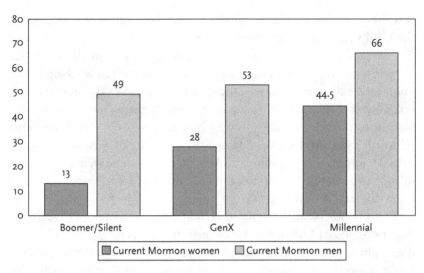

Figure 2.1. LDS Missionary Service by Generation and Gender. *Includes those who returned early.

Millennials have the closest gender parity in missionary service: 44.5 percent of Millennial women who remain in the church have served a mission, a significant leap from the 13 percent and 28 percent of prior generations. Before the age change, about one in six young missionaries was female; today it is closer to one in three.[23] Not to be outdone, however, Millennial men have the highest rates of missionary service of any generation of either men or women. Clearly, missionary service has been increasing for both genders with each successive generation, with the highest spikes occurring among women. With the wave of women serving missions, the LDS Church has also created a new supervisory role called the "Sister Training Leader," choosing some female missionaries to train others and participate in previously all-male mission leadership councils. In a denomination that has provided few managerial opportunities to women (see chapter 5), such changes may have far-reaching and positive future effects in normalizing female leadership.[24]

Most Mormons who served a mission regard it as a positive experience that helped them in many areas of their lives (Figure 2.2). We asked returned missionaries (RMs) to evaluate whether their missions had helped them strengthen their faith, prepare for a career, prepare for marriage and a family, gain converts for the LDS Church, and teach them to appreciate diversity. On nearly every measure, nine out of ten RMs who are still Mormon said the mission was "very helpful" or "somewhat helpful" in these areas. The only area to generate slightly less enthusiasm was "gaining converts for the LDS Church": about 85 percent of RMs considered their mission to be "very" or "somewhat" helpful in that. Interestingly, there was

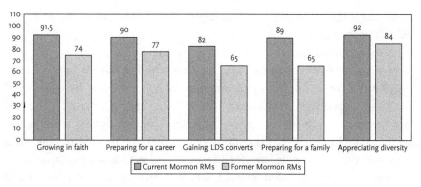

110
100
90
80
70
60
50
40
30
20
10
0

91.5   74   90   77   82   65   89   65   92   84

Growing in faith   Preparing for a career   Gaining LDS converts   Preparing for a family   Appreciating diversity

☐ Current Mormon RMs   ☐ Former Mormon RMs

Figure 2.2. Returned Missionaries Who Viewed the Mission as "Very" or "Somewhat" Positive. *Includes those who returned early.

very little generational difference in any of these categories; almost all RMs who still self-identify as Mormons had a positive mission experience, at least in hindsight.

Even in the smaller pool of returned missionaries who are now former Mormons, most view the mission as a positive experience. For this group, the numbers are not in the 90 percent range, but they are still clear majorities in all five areas. Three-quarters say the mission helped them develop religious faith and be successful in a career, while more than eight in ten report that the mission taught them to appreciate diversity. Because the sample size of RMs who are now former Mormons is small, the margin of error is in the low double digits; however, the overall trend seems clear that even missionaries who subsequently left the church believe their missions were beneficial.

This was the experience of Rob, thirty-eight, who is no longer Mormon but considered his mission helpful in four of the five areas specified (with the exception of gaining converts). In particular, he says it was instrumental in preparing him for the career he now has in sales of high-end scientific equipment.[25] "When I applied for this job, they asked, 'How do you deal with rejection?' I was like, 'I served a mission in Germany for two years. I can deal with rejection just fine.'" The mission, he says, schooled him on following through with things he didn't necessarily want to do, which is an important value in any career; even jobs you love can be "filled with things that aren't super-fun, like writing a dissertation, or doing experiments where it seems like you're just banging your head against a wall. A mission is very much about self-motivation, and my sales job is like that too." Rob also credits his mission with teaching him how to be more loving in relationships, which has helped his marriage. "There were some experiences working with companions in particular when I had to learn to step back and see things from someone else's point of view, and that I wasn't always right.

Sometimes the moral high ground lecture isn't what actually helps you to solve a problem."

Gloria, thirty-one, who is still active in the church, looks to her mission in South Korea as foundational in teaching her how to love others.[26] A culture of perfectionism in her mission led her to want to be working all the time. Gloria was "very serious about the rules," feeling that if she and her companion kept every rule to the letter, their missionary work would be blessed. "I noticed that the message was that 100 percent obedience is how you can show your love for the Lord and get blessings. I would try my heart out for that, but it would create friction with my companions and others," she explains. A turning point came when she was assigned a companion who was struggling, which hampered her ability to go out to preach. Because missionaries have to stay with their companions around the clock, that meant that Gloria too was grounded. Stuck in the apartment, she experienced "a lot of guilt" that she wasn't working, and she blew up when the companion broke a cardinal rule and called a family member at home in the United States. (Missionaries are only permitted two phone calls a year, on Christmas and Mother's Day.) Gloria's companion was angry right back. "Sister," she said, "it is not about the rules. It's about the people." Gloria was struck by that comment. She realized she did not truly love her companion, and was in fact often irritated by her. If Gloria didn't love her companion, she wondered, how was she going to love all the people she was supposed to teach about the gospel?

Gloria then experienced a gradual "letting go," in which she relaxed her stranglehold on rules and focused instead on learning to love. It was not easy—in fact, the word that Gloria used three times in describing the experience was that the mission "broke" her identity in a painful but ultimately constructive way. She had always viewed herself as a good person, but the stress of the mission made her acknowledge a shadow side of herself she had not known existed. Still active in the church, she views the mission as "one of the most transformative catalysts in my life, but not in that 'this was the best two years' narrative kind of way. It was the hardest two years, and therefore it transformed me because it was so difficult."

Among NMS respondents who have served a mission, the area of greatest agreement was that it taught them to appreciate diversity. This was particularly true of Millennials, who were about six points more likely than older RMs to say their mission was "very valuable" in this particular way. While that is a modest difference, it's an interesting one given that Millennials as a generation have been shown to prize values such as diversity and inclusion. Younger Millennials (eighteen to twenty-six) were even more likely than older Millennials (twenty-seven to thirty-six) to single out appreciating diversity as a "very" valuable skill they learned on their mission.

Examples of this came up frequently in interviews. Nicole, twenty-six, says her mission in the Pacific Northwest showed her many different kinds of lives and families.[27] Having grown up in an affluent area where a majority of teens went on to college, she realized on her mission that college was not possible for everyone. "I learned to change my question from 'Where are you going to go to school?' to 'What are your plans for after high school?'" Likewise, Jamie, thirty-three, credits her mission with opening her eyes to how privileged she was. Born into a white, middle-class Mormon family in Utah, her mission in the urban South put her in close personal contact with people whose lives had been very different:

> I was working with mostly illegal immigrants who had walked from Central America and Mexico and had so little. They didn't speak English very well. Some couldn't read or write, and I saw that I had so much more access to resources than they did, based in part on my race and where I was from. So in that way it opened my eyes, which was a good thing.[28]

Yet it was also Jamie's openness to diversity that led to doubts about her faith. "I remember talking with a lady who was a Bahá'í at one point," she explains. "And I remember walking away thinking that her belief system, and who she was, was actually very beautiful, and I could not find fault with it even though I was supposed to."

Oddly, an encounter with a Bahá'í woman while serving a mission was also the beginning of questions for Lisa, now thirty-two, who in a separate interview told a similar story of coming face to face with religious pluralism while on an LDS mission:

> We knocked on a door and a woman immediately started telling me about the Bahá'í Faith. I was interested, sort of recreationally. But standing there in her foyer, that feeling of the Spirit came on so strong. I think my companion felt it too. And when we walked out the door and down the sidewalk, I turned to my companion and said, "Did you feel that?" And she said, "Yeah, but I don't want to talk about it." So I told her that even though we didn't understand it, if we felt it was God, then we needed to listen to it.[29]

Lisa felt the Spirit as forcefully while listening to this woman explain her faith as she often had when defending her own religion to other people who, she had always believed, needed the life-altering message she offered them. The experience was confusing to say the least. What if this other religion was also true? What if the same litmus test Lisa had applied to the Book of Mormon—telling investigators they would recognize its truth when they experienced good feelings about it—also applied to sacred texts from other religions? "To me, it was and is a giant question," she reflects.

Encountering religious diversity can be both a boon and a challenge to a person's own beliefs.

While Millennial RMs were more likely than older Mormons to say their missions had been "very valuable" in exposing them to diversity, they were less likely to convey that their mission helped them to grow in their own faith. Two-thirds of Millennial RMs who are still in the LDS Church felt this way, compared to four out of five RMs from the Boomer/Silent cohort. Still, this is a majority of Millennials.[30] This finding about the value of missions for faith development confirms existing research on the lasting effect of short-term missions on personal religiosity.[31]

For all that most missionaries look back on their experience with appreciation, many also say they would never, ever want to do it again. It was simply too difficult. Several people I spoke to—all of whom reported having mostly positive experiences—said they have occasionally experienced postmission nightmares in which they are called once again to serve. According to Rob, whose mission to Germany was discussed earlier, this nightmare recurred for years after his return. "In the dream I would already be married with kids, but I would still accept the mission call," he says. In his humorous and touching memoir *Way Below the Angels*, BYU professor Craig Harline observes, "Whether someone had the bad dream or not wasn't so much a matter of where they'd been on a mission, or of how much faith they'd had, but of how well they managed to fit into mission-culture-as-currently-constituted." The natural salespeople rarely had the dream, but it plagued "the born introverts and born introspectives and born sensitives who engaged in all sorts of personality-bending and will-breaking and metaphorical Chinese footbinding *trying* to fit in."[32]

EARLY-RETURN MISSIONARIES

The statistics I have just discussed are based on all returned missionaries in the sample, including those who came home early. Not surprisingly, though, the ones who returned earlier than expected had less glowing things to say about their experiences than those who stayed the entire time. Overall, early returnees were more likely to choose the "somewhat valuable" option than those who stayed for the duration. We did not ask respondents who returned early to indicate whether they had done so because of physical health, mental health, behavioral problems, loss of testimony, or some other reason, so we have limited information about why they did not serve the entire time. What we can say, though, is that early returns are becoming noticeably more common.

No respondents in either the Boomer or Silent generations returned home early; 5.5 percent of GenX missionaries did; that number climbs to 17 percent for the Millennials.[33] One theory is that perhaps the lowered age of service means that the mission is often the first time an individual has lived away from home for an extended period, or held what amounts to a (more than) full-time job, and that this immaturity has led to higher rates of early return. It certainly sounds plausible. However, when we break the Millennial generation in half into older and younger members, we don't see that expected upsurge in the younger group. In fact, the number actually decreases slightly to 16 percent of younger Millennial missionaries who returned early, versus 19 percent of older Millennials. While we need to be cautious because we are dealing with a subset of the subset of the data, it is interesting that the trend toward early mission returns seems to have been well underway before the 2012 age change.

Earlier I mentioned the LDS Church's decision in 2002 to "raise the bar" for missionary service, elevating its standards so that only the most spiritually prepared and morally circumspect young people would be accepted. Now that we can review empirical data about the increase in early returns among Millennials, this policy makes sense in hindsight. In fact, it is possible that it was exactly this escalation in early returns that precipitated the new standards in the first place; the oldest Millennials, born in the early 1980s, would have been serving missions in the late 1990s and early 2000s, shortly before the policy was implemented. If nearly one in five was returning early from the field, it is not surprising that the church would have done whatever it could to ensure that future missionaries would be better prepared.

It used to be that early returnees felt stigmatized by what they saw as a failure. In a 2003 article on the subject, Mormon writer and scholar Levi Peterson (who nearly left his own mission in 1955 but was dissuaded by the prospect of disappointing his mother) said, "If anything, an aborted mission seems worse than none at all. Young Latter-day Saints have been taught to view their mission as a test of their devotion to the Lord; now they feel they have failed that test."[34] Blogger Russell Arben Fox thought seriously about returning home early from his mission in the late 1980s, but his mother had indicated that no son of hers who did so would still be acknowledged as a son, so that was that. He stayed.[35] The unspoken motto of the church in those days, he writes, was "Come home honorably or come home in a coffin."

Today, there appears to be greater social acceptance of missionaries who return home early for health or other reasons; some of the old stigma is gone. There are online support groups for early RMs (and for their parents, for whom the experience can be a profound loss), professional counseling through the church, and new videos and training materials that prospective missionaries are asked to watch even before they send in their application, so they can realistically gauge their readiness.

In part this evolution may reflect society's greater acceptance of mental health conditions, some of which manifest for the first time in the college years—exactly the period when Mormon missionaries are serving and are often under unprecedented stress. One small study found that the top reason for returning early was indeed mental health (36 percent), closely followed by physical health (34 percent). Far less common were being sent home because of a previously unresolved transgression (12 percent) or disobeying mission rules (11 percent).[36]

The NMS finds that a completed mission correlates well with staying Mormon for the long term, even among people who were not very active in the LDS Church growing up. Among respondents who had less-than-weekly church attendance in childhood, only 19 percent who completed a full-term mission are no longer Mormon. In other words, eight in ten people who had been less active as kids were still Mormon in adulthood if they had served a full-term mission.[37] Retention is even stronger among those who were weekly attenders during childhood. Only 9 percent of those who were active growing up and served a full-term mission are no longer Mormon today, compared to 29 percent who served a partial mission and nearly half, 45 percent, who didn't serve at all. Put another way, the LDS Church is losing almost half of previously active youth if they didn't serve a mission and nearly a third of those who started a mission but returned early, but only one in ten of those who served the full term.

One such early return was Zachary, now twenty-one, who says he was "about as worthy as you can get" when he put in his mission papers immediately after he turned eighteen.[38] Zachary's family had been inactive in the church while he was in high school, so there were a couple of years in his adolescence in which he, like them, stayed home from sacrament meeting and other activities. However, he independently decided to reactivate when he was seventeen. He'd continued attending seminary because it was a class in his regular school day, and in that class he was challenged to gain a testimony of the Book of Mormon. He went home, read about sixty pages, and asked God if it was true:

> And at that moment, I received an answer. I could feel that this was right, and that it was true. So I wrote down my testimony of the Book of Mormon, and decided that I wanted to go on a mission and be a really upstanding Mormon person. I wanted to make God proud.

The following year, Zachary was called on a mission to Chile and spent a happy six weeks learning Spanish at the Chilean MTC. He greatly enjoyed the mission and the feeling that he "knew that this was what God wanted for me to do." Then he began getting sick. Riddled with intestinal problems, he lost an alarming sixty pounds in three and a half months. He received skillful medical attention, but nothing seemed to help; his condition continued to deteriorate. "It was eventually decided that I should go home," he reports. Zachary's use of the passive voice here ("it was . . . decided," not "I decided") and the fact that he remembers the exact date he was made to return both hint at the pain he associates with leaving early. When he came home, he was "devastated" at this upending of his expectations. His physical problems were successfully diagnosed as stemming from a hereditary bowel disorder, but his emotional travail was just beginning. His girlfriend dumped him and he swiftly became depressed. "I was so crushed by this loss of what I had my life planned out to be," he says. To counter that disappointment, he doubled down on his religion by attending the temple weekly, praying hard, and throwing himself into his calling in a young single adult ward. He was "the most devout" he had ever been—which, he explains, was saying something.

Yet his faith fell apart. In our interview a year and a half after his early return, Zachary was still trying to make sense of it, seemingly mystified at the way his once-solid LDS testimony had evaporated. His loss of faith started, oddly enough, when he became friends with some FLDS young men who had grown up as polygamists.[39] Though they were no longer practicing polygamy, they did challenge his view of Mormon history, introducing him to the fact that Joseph Smith had been married to several dozen women. "I kind of knew that, but hadn't really *known* that," he admits. "I was like, 'What else don't I know about the history of the church?'" It turned out there was a great deal, and as he kept reading and listening to podcasts, several things weren't adding up. Desperate to have God confirm his previous beliefs, he prayed every night for confirmation, only to receive . . . nothing. Finally he went to the temple again in hopes of a dramatic answer to prayer. Sitting in the Celestial Room, Zachary poured out his heart to God: "I've researched and read and prayed and done everything I can think of to do, and you've been silent," he pled. "I think I should leave the church. God, is that what I'm supposed to do?" He finally experienced his long-awaited epiphany. "I felt, as clearly as I had felt when I got a testimony of the Book of Mormon, that I was supposed to leave the church." And so he did.

Zachary's most intense period of Mormon life, from ages seventeen to nineteen, was bookended by two dramatic spiritual experiences: one that sealed his testimony in the Book of Mormon and another that cemented his feeling that he should quit. But in the middle of that period was his brief but powerful tenure of missionary service, an experience that began in optimism and ended in anguish. One wonders if Zachary's Mormon life might have turned out differently if his mission had been completed. Statistically, we have seen that there's a correlation between serving a full-term mission and remaining a member of the LDS Church. We have also seen that for the growing numbers of people who serve, a mission is largely a positive experience, helping individuals engage faith more deeply, prepare for adult life, and appreciate diversity. While the mission experience has changed significantly over the last decades, it remains—like the temple endowment ritual we turn to in the next chapter—a vital rite of passage in the transition from Mormon adolescence to adulthood.

CHAPTER 3

Rites of Passage and the LDS Temple

When Chrissy was twenty-three, she was ready to marry her fiancé in an LDS temple, capping a lifetime of Mormon faithfulness.[1] As a child in Primary, she had sung songs about someday going to the temple; now that dream was coming true. Whereas regular Sunday services are open to the public at thousands of LDS chapel meetinghouses around the world, temples are rare—there are just over 150 around the globe—and closed to everyone but the most committed Latter-day Saints. Inside, Chrissy would first receive temple ordinances for herself and then return the next day to marry her BYU sweetheart, being sealed to him for, as Mormons say, "time and all eternity." This ritual of sealing is a foundation of Mormonism, and Chrissy was excited to fortify the bonds of love she and her fiancé shared.

She was also curious about what would happen. Growing up, she and her eight siblings had been aware of their parents' regular trips to the temple, returning again and again to conduct the same rituals for the deceased that they performed once in a lifetime for themselves in their own endowment ceremonies. Her parents had spoken to her in general terms about the temple, and Chrissy had even gone inside its hallowed walls a few times to perform baptisms for the dead with other youth, but youth are not permitted in most areas beyond the baptistery. This would be the first time that Chrissy had an all-access pass in the form of an adult "temple recommend," a card she carries in her wallet that testifies to her worthiness as established in private interviews with her ward and stake leaders. In those qualifying interviews, she affirmed that she believed in the church's main doctrines, supported its leadership, paid her tithing, kept the Word of Wisdom (the Mormon dietary law), and was honest and chaste. In the final catch-all interview question, she declared herself "worthy to enter the Lord's house and participate in temple ordinances."

After passing the interviews, Chrissy became eligible to participate in the ordinances of the initiatory ("washing and anointing"), where women would symbolically wash and bless her body in preparation for the longer "endowment ceremony," a dramatic re-enactment of the biblical creation, fall, and redemption of the world. During this ceremony Chrissy would, with other temple patrons, make eternally binding covenants and put on special ritual clothing. This would be the first time Chrissy knew the details of the endowment, because faithful Mormons refrain from discussing the specific symbols and actions they learn in the temple (and so will this chapter, though it will explore how participants like Chrissy *felt* about those rituals).

Chrissy loved her day at the temple, surrounded by family and supportive friends. Anytime a new step came along, she looked to her mother for guidance, "and it never felt awkward, because she would just show me or help me to do what I was supposed to do." Even though none of the rituals she encountered in the temple were "familiar or even expected," she felt safe there. It *felt* familiar even though it wasn't—"like I was coming home," she explains.

BOTH POSITIVE AND NEGATIVE EXPERIENCES

Mormon leaders and parents want all young adults to have positive, loving temple experiences like Chrissy's. And while there are vivid stories of people who did not—a few of which will be discussed in this chapter— the NMS data shows that most Mormons who have been to the temple do have a good first experience. Six in ten current Mormon respondents reported that they had been to the temple for the initiatory followed by the endowment ceremony, which are the two essential rites of initiation for the LDS temple. People who grow up Mormon tend to participate for the first time in early adulthood, since these two rituals are required before serving a mission or getting married in the temple. But Mormon adults with a recommend can go at any time, so those who join the LDS Church later in life, for example, may be initiated in the temple at any age.

More than 90 percent of Mormon respondents who had been through the temple said they felt "very" or "somewhat" positive about their first experience. There is only a tiny difference generationally, with younger Mormons being three to five points more likely to have had a positive experience than older ones. In interviews, many people echoed the basic substance of these findings. One of the most eager Millennial temple attendees was Chelsea, a twenty-five-year-old convert from Manhattan who, before becoming a Mormon, had often seen the LDS temple near Lincoln Center and been curious about the people who went in and out.[2] In fact, she first expressed interest in learning more about the religion by flagging down a group of well-dressed young people as they exited the building. They turned out to be missionaries who were "flabbergasted" that a New Yorker was actually approaching *them* to inquire about the church. When Chelsea received her temple endowment several years later, she was thrilled:

> Pretty much all of my friends and my Young Women leaders were there, and they were all supporting me. It was like a glimpse of heaven in that way. It was powerful. And because I had been spiritually exploring before, and had been to Catholic services, some of the "high church" nature of it, with standing up and sitting down, and repetition and hand movements you do, that was not shocking to me.

Chelsea and other interviewees spoke about the peace of the Celestial Room, where all temple-goers wind up after the endowment ceremony, having passed through a veil that symbolizes the separation between mortal life and eternity. The Celestial Room is a place of plush carpets and soft whispers, where individuals dressed in white can sit as long as they like to pray or contemplate their experience. Brittany, age thirty, who is also a convert, explains her love for the temple in terms of an iconic moment from popular culture:

> Do you remember the scene from *Titanic* where after Rose dies, everyone from the ship, and Jack, are there waiting for her? In the Celestial Room, that was my experience. Everyone I knew was there. . . . This is what heaven is going to be like: I'm going to walk in and be welcomed by everyone who knows and loves me, and it's going to be wonderful.[3]

Not everyone, however, has a positive first experience. Colby, twenty, recounts that he "didn't really know what to think about the whole thing. It was pretty confusing, as well as weird, especially when the temple clothing became involved." No one had explained that in addition to his all-white suit, he would have to put on several other pieces of clothing in a prescribed way throughout the endowment ceremony to symbolize elements of the creation story. Despite that confusion, he hastens to add, "it was an overall good experience."[4]

It's possible there is a disconnect between what Millennials say about loving their first time in the temple and what some of them actually felt at the time. Although Colby uses adjectives like "confusing" and "weird" to describe his initial reaction, he still summarizes the experience as "very positive." In Mormonism there are two strong impulses concerning the temple: the first is not to talk about it much at all, and the second is that on the rare occasions it is discussed it should be depicted in vague and sunny terms. Given these patterns, it is difficult to admit to not understanding—or worse, understanding but not enjoying—your first temple experience in a culture that speaks about it in such guarded and eulogistic ways.

That struggle may be exacerbated by the presence of loved ones who come to cheer new initiates on. The communal support that Chelsea and Brittany both cherished about their experience can feel like intense social pressure when your family and friends all appear to be enjoying the temple and you feel you must pretend to adore it for their sake. Karianne, twenty-five, cried during most of the temple portion of our interview as she remembered her first experience, which occurred shortly before her wedding several years before:[5]

> I cannot remember—I might get teary, I'm sorry—but I cannot remember a worse night
> of my life. My mother came and my husband's family came, and suddenly it was me in
> the spotlight. I was the only one who hadn't been through the temple ceremony be-
> fore. . . . I was in an unfamiliar place, in unfamiliar clothing, and I was hearing words
> and performing rites that made me feel robotic and small. Nothing like all of the warm,
> welcoming, God-loving feelings that people had told me would happen.

It was difficult for Karianne to explain what was so devastating. Part of it was the clothing, which no one had prepared her for, but it was also that she had been promised that in the temple she would receive a special, sacred name, and that this name would be so unique "that it required getting revelation because it was part of who you are." So it was a huge disappointment to her that the temple worker who gave her the name merely "picked it from a [pre-prepared] list."[6] Karianne "was a little heartbroken about that. It didn't feel personal anymore. And suddenly I didn't feel like I was getting something from God. I wasn't *given* something from God." The evening was an uncomfortable blur, but she managed to hold herself together until she was alone with her fiancé in the parking lot. Then she broke down and had a full-on panic attack, sobbing that she hated the temple and never wanted to return—which was a problem, because she and her fiancé were scheduled to be sealed in marriage there the following week. Together they agreed that they would return for their wedding, but that she would never have to go to the temple again after that if she did not want to.

They got through the wedding and settled in happily together as husband and wife. At church on the first few Sundays after their marriage, though, it felt to Karianne like the topic of the temple kept cropping up. "The people giving the lessons would just glow as they talked about their wonderful feelings and the beautiful things they experienced, and I just felt broken, like my temple-ometer was not functioning," Karianne remembers. "I felt so alone." She tried to confide her anguish to a friend but was rebuffed and told, condescendingly, that she obviously needed to try harder. Gradually, Karianne pulled away from the church—a decision that was not *only* about the temple, but began with her despair about it.

Unlike Karianne, most former Mormons do not cite a negative experience at the temple as one of their top reasons for leaving the church; it tied for eighteenth among thirty possible reasons for cutting religious ties (see chapter 11). However, that doesn't mean those individuals had positive experiences. Just under half of our sample of former Mormons had gone to the temple for their own endowment. Of those, only 11 percent characterized it as a "very positive" experience, which is a sharp contrast to the 59 percent of current Mormons who chose "very positive."[7] About four in ten former Mormons had a negative experience, which is a fivefold increase from the percentage of current Mormons who did (8 percent). Overall, then, the temple emerges as a complex site of contention for many former Mormons: few left the church because of it, but it's unlikely that they miss it.

CURRENT MORMON MILLENNIALS AND TEMPLE RECOMMEND STATUS

We've seen so far that many current Mormons report very positive first experiences of the temple. But in Mormonism, this initial foray is supposed to be followed by regular temple attendance throughout a member's life; an unwritten but oft-cited rule of thumb is that endowed members who live near a temple should try to attend once a month.[8] Members are encouraged to keep their temple recommend card current, which requires being interviewed by their local church leaders every two years. Whenever they return to the temple, they engage in the same rituals for the deceased that they have done for themselves, serving as proxies as ancestors are baptized, washed, endowed, and, in the case of men, ordained posthumously to the priesthood. Those rituals prepare the deceased to be sealed to spouses, parents, and children, just as Mormons can be in this life. Church members believe that merely having these rituals performed on behalf of a deceased person does not force a conversion beyond the grave; it merely opens a door of opportunity should that soul wish to take it. The first step, however, requires temple recommend–holding Mormons who are willing to serve as proxy recipients and attend the temple again and again.

This is where the NMS data becomes less encouraging of the idea that Millennial Mormons—and GenXers as well—are truly enthusiastic about the temple (Table 3.1).

Table 3.1. ENDOWED MORMONS WHO HAVE RETURNED TO THE TEMPLE,
BY GENERATION

	Boomer/Silent	GenX	Millennial
Percent who received own endowment and have returned to perform endowments for the deceased	87%	59%	56%

Those numbers are startling. Whereas almost nine in ten Boomer/Silent respondents had returned to the temple on behalf of the deceased, just over half of Millennials had, and six in ten GenXers. For the Boomer/Silent respondents, temple attendance appears to be more of a priority. It seems that a number of Mormons under age fifty-two have attended the temple once for their own ordinances, possibly (like Karianne) to get married, but have not returned.

Others have returned, but only sporadically. Marie, twenty-four, got married in the temple last year and has gone back once since then. That's not because she had a negative experience. She seems a bit sheepish as she tries to explain why she's stayed away, especially considering there's a temple right in her Utah town. "It's something that I want to do, but I just have not created the time for it, unfortunately. But I'll probably go this week." She thinks Millennials are busier with careers and school than any generation before them, so time is definitely a factor. She ventures to say that the temple might also feel a bit remote to her faith. "I think that especially people who've grown up in the church value the temple and we think it's an important step to get through, but it doesn't really hold a lot of water for religion and spirituality in our everyday lives."

Since the NMS data is episodic and not longitudinal, it's difficult to say whether Millennials' and GenXers' temple attendance will pick up as they age. Perhaps regular temple attendance is an aspect of religious observance that becomes more attractive to people as they edge closer to mortality.[9] Since the temple is very much about meeting the needs of individuals who have passed on, it's possible that those needs are felt more acutely by people who are winding down their own lives. And on a practical note, Mormons who are retired and whose children are raised likely have more time for temple rituals than GenXers and Millennials, as Marie suggested.

A related area of concern for church leaders is how few Millennials hold a current temple recommend. In fact, they are the only generation of Mormons for whom fewer than half (47 percent) are fully qualified to enter

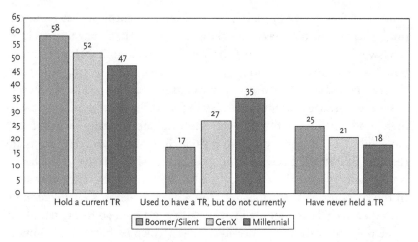

Figure 3.1. Temple Recommend Status among Mormons, by Generation.

the temple. It's not just because they're young, either, given that four out of five (83 percent) say they've held a temple recommend at some point in their lives. That's actually higher than GenX (79 percent) or the Boomer/Silent group (75 percent). But Millennials are more likely to have allowed that temple credential to lapse (Figure 3.1).

A final note about generational differences regarding the temple comes from the survey question about respondents' favorite part of being Mormon. As we discovered in chapter 1, all generations listed the same top three aspects of the religion (though in a slightly different order), making it clear that the church's postwar emphases on eternal families, the Savior Jesus Christ, and the importance of faith have hit home. However, after the remarkable similarity in attitudes toward those top three, there were modest but interesting generational differences in how each cohort ranked the remaining six items, including temple worship. Both Millennials and GenXers ordered temple worship dead last out of nine possible favorite aspects of being Mormon. For Boomer/Silents, the temple was sixth, which is hardly a ringing endorsement, but still more positive than younger Mormons' assessment. What are we to make of this? Something about the temple is not "clicking" with Millennials and GenXers, and both data and interviews suggest that concerns center around exclusion and women's roles.

EXCLUSION, GENDER, AND TEMPLE ANXIETY

Troy, thirty-seven, holds a current recommend but has not been to an endowment session in several years.[10] He keeps his recommend current so he can attend family weddings, but he feels some resentment that he would not be able to see his loved ones get married if he didn't pay tithing, keep the law of chastity, and observe the Word of Wisdom. It feels coercive to him. "I used to totally support the idea that people had to be worthy to go to the temple, and that some people just wouldn't be able to go into the temple to see the marriage of a family member or friend," he says. "But I am increasingly more uncomfortable with that idea. It's unnecessarily exclusionary." He points out that in many nations outside the United States, Mormons are required by law to hold civil wedding ceremonies because the LDS Church is not universally recognized as having the authority to contract marriages. In those countries, the bride and groom get married in a civil ceremony with their friends and family in attendance, and then go to the temple at some point afterward for a private sealing (which is theologically important but not legally binding). Troy thinks this should be the practice everywhere, so no one is excluded from attending weddings. "Even if I marry a Mormon, I likely won't get married in the temple initially," he says. "I don't want to perpetuate the exclusion."

Troy's comments illuminate a tension that came up several times in my interviews with Millennials, who often view the temple simultaneously as a place of inclusion and exclusion. On the side of inclusion is the daunting enterprise of sealing the entire human family to one another and to God; no human is to be left behind. Jason, thirty-one, had a rough initial experience with the temple but came to treasure it for precisely this reason— that the gospel includes every single person, even the dead.[11] "I think the reason I love the temple so much is just the view of God's love that I feel like temple ordinances give me," he explains. "We go there to try to bless *everybody*. We don't want anybody to be left out." Jason put this into practice when he participated in temple rituals on behalf of a great-uncle who had been taught the Mormon gospel many times but never joined the church. In doing his great-uncle's sealing, Jason was struck by the fundamental equality and justice in Mormon ideals about salvation. Even though his great-uncle had rejected Mormonism in life, "still there was this chance for him to receive the ordinances so that he was treated exactly the same as people who were born of two parents who were married in the temple."

Such universalism also appeals to Chrissy, whose story opened this chapter. "There's no other Christian religion that claims to have an answer to this question of what happens to people who didn't know Christ when they were alive," she tells me. "That is the backbone of my testimony of the temple. How unfair it would be that all those people would have no way to find their path to Christ." Millennials as a generation care a great deal about values such as inclusion, justice, and equality, so it is not surprising that many would lift up this universalistic aspect of LDS theology as particularly attractive.

But as Troy's frustration about temple recommends suggests, the temple can also be a place of deep exclusion. Like Troy, Miranda, thirty-five, is troubled that nonmembers can't attend Mormon weddings.[12] As a girl, she had dreamed of "a regular church wedding with my friends, flower girls, and a sleeveless dress." Temple weddings seem a throwback to an earlier era before religious pluralism was common; if all of your extended family and close friends were LDS, a temple wedding was a celebration everyone could attend, with no feelings of loss or grief at anyone being excluded. Miranda went ahead with her wedding in the temple, rather than following her own inclination to get married in a separate ceremony and then be sealed in the temple after the year-long waiting period that is obligatory in the United States. She did so because she felt intense family and community pressure to be sealed from day one. "I knew that people would think there was something wrong if we didn't get married in the temple," she explains. "That we were unworthy, or we weren't committed Mormons, or that I was pregnant." Miranda was alluding to the reality that when a Mormon wedding happens outside the temple, there is sometimes speculation that the couple did not keep the law of chastity, or were barred entrance for some other infraction. She worried that few people would understand that hers was a legitimate choice to wait until she felt ready to go to the temple, not an indication of unworthiness. She was concerned that her family might be embarrassed or frustrated by her decision, so she caved to their wishes.[13]

Unfortunately, Miranda had a disastrous response to the temple, which made her feel "violated" because she felt "coerced in being there." A large part of her distress was caused by the second reason some young adult Mormons have complicated relationships with the temple, which is how women are treated in the endowment ceremony. Miranda gets very specific about ritual language she finds troubling:

> I felt I was being asked to promise things I didn't believe in, like the part about obeying one's husband.[14] Really, any language in which women's relationship to God is being mediated through the spouse. I was not pleased with the language . . . where the woman is supposed to tell her husband her sacred name and he is not asked to reciprocate.

Miranda's issues with the temple have not prevented her from staying active in the LDS Church; she has a calling in the Relief Society and plans to raise her two young children as believing, involved Mormons. But it took ten years of sporadically attending the temple for her to have even one positive experience there—a breakthrough that was made possible, she says, because her feelings about gender have "mellowed" over the last decade.

The issue of gender inequality came up with surprising frequency in my conversations, as women (and it was almost always women) commented on how uncomfortable they felt with the same elements Miranda disliked: promising to hearken to their husbands while their husbands, in turn, promised to hearken directly to God; hearing they would be queens and priestesses unto their husbands while those husbands would be kings and priests directly to God; having to veil their faces during prayer; seeing Eve portrayed as subordinate to Adam; and having to reveal their sacred names to their husbands without receiving their husbands' sacred names in return. Even Chrissy, whose marvelously positive first temple experience we heard about earlier, began questioning elements of the temple about six years ago, when several female friends were leaving the church over women's issues. Around that time she stumbled upon a blog post that changed her perspective on the temple.

> This article . . . said that we are told as Young Women that we have this direct connection to Heavenly Father, that he wants the best for us individually. And then she [the author] said that in the temple, however, everything is mediated through the man—that there's no real direct connection to God for women. I read that and thought it was interesting, and then I started really paying attention to what is said in the temple, and how Eve is communicated to or not. . . . This blog post got me thinking about the temple endowment in a different way, and now I can't *not* see that.

Some women said the temple's emphasis on women serving men who in turn serve God just doesn't jibe with the marriages they have (or, in the case of several single interviewees, hope to have). Nor is it consistent with their own previously unmediated, direct, loving relationships with God—relationships they were taught to cultivate in Mormon classes, camps, and programs. The language of the temple, mostly unchanged in this respect since the endowment was settled in the nineteenth century, feels like a relic from another age. It was interesting that in interviews, several women mentioned that their husbands had volunteered their own temple names to their wives, so that both spouses would be on equal footing. (Some wives, in turn, demanded it; as Roe, thirty-two, told her brand-new husband, "This is *not* going to fly. Out with it!"[15]) The disclosure of a person's sacred name technically violates an explicit promise made in the temple, so it is key to consider how these otherwise orthodox young adult Mormons might weigh competing ideals: they want to maintain the secrecy that is associated with certain aspects of the temple, but when that secrecy threatens the bond that many want to experience in their marriages, some choose marital equality over the temple's code of silence.[16] There is no way to quantify that, or to compare the experience generationally to see if this is a new development, since the NMS did not include a survey question about the reciprocity of temple names.

There is one element of the temple experience that female interviewees found especially positive: being washed and blessed by other women. The initiatory is the only remaining place in Mormon life where women still give priesthood blessings as they did both in and out of the temple in the nineteenth and early twentieth centuries.[17] Women continue to bless and symbolically wash other women in the temple, and men do the same for other men. Sarah, thirty-eight, says, "When women put their hands on my head to bless me, I was like, 'That's it.'"[18] Roe agrees and adds that while she has stopped going to the temple for endowments, she still enjoys the initiatory and "seeing my fellow sisters use their priesthood to officiate." For Brittany, the convert with the *Titanic*-like experience of seeing her loved ones together in the Celestial Room, the initiatory took some getting used to, but she gradually began to look forward to it. "A woman was serving another woman in pronouncing her clean and ready to enter the temple. We are really here on earth to cleanse each other's souls."

A number of female interviewees, then, developed favorable associations with the initiatory, which they see as a rite of female empowerment that is only available in the temple. And because Mormons can often choose which temple rituals they want to perform (only endowments, only the initiatory, only sealings, or some combination), it is possible for some of these women to carefully negotiate a path where they can still attend the temple and contribute to saving the deceased, but avoid the endowment ceremony with elements they consider hurtful. Contrasted with the endowment, the initiatory feels like a sacred space in which women's authority is celebrated.

Given this pattern in the interviews, I was curious to see how women felt about the temple compared to men. Would the preference women showed for the initiatory in our conversations be replicated on the larger canvas of the data? The short answer is not really. Women in the survey liked both the endowment *and* the initiatory. In Figure 3.2, we see they report nearly identical "very positive" responses to both rituals (62 and 63 percent, respectively). In terms of gender, actually, what is particularly notable about the data is not that two-thirds of women viewed both rituals so positively, but that men were not as enthusiastic, especially toward the initiatory. We'll see in the next chapter that it's par for the course for Mormon women to be more religiously observant than men, so the fact that women come out ahead is not unusual. However, the gap that exists in initiatory responses (63 percent for women, 46 percent for men) is significant.

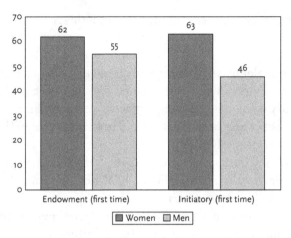

Figure 3.2. Current Mormons Who Had a "Very Positive" First Temple Experience, by Gender.

THE RISE OF TEMPLE PREPARATION

In the survey and also in interviews, both current and former Mormons were asked how they felt about their own temple preparation (Table 3.2). Because the temple is not openly discussed in Mormonism, I wanted to know whether people felt ready for this rite of passage or, as Colby put it, they "pretty much went in blind." It turns out that it depends not only on individual factors like how open people's parents or bishops were to forthright conversations but also on their year of birth. Older Mormons were more likely to say they did not receive any helpful information about the temple before their first time.

There are several interesting insights to glean from this data. First, Boomer/Silent Mormons were two and a half times more likely than GenXers and more than four times more likely than Millennials to say they did not receive any useful information about the temple before their first time. A scant 6 percent of Millennials reported not receiving valuable information from family members, local leaders, or church curriculum. In contrast, 26 percent of Boomer/Silent respondents said they were wholly unprepared, with some of their write-in comments including words like "confusing" and "didn't understand." Many of these older respondents would have gone through the temple before the 1970s, which is when LDS leaders began taking official measures to better prepare people. ("It has come to our attention that many of those planning to go to the temple for the first time are not properly oriented as to what to expect there," the First Presidency wrote to local leaders in 1971, attaching a pamphlet called "So You Are Going to the Temple."[19])

Table 3.2. TEMPLE PREPARATION BY GENERATION

When preparing for the first experience with the temple endowment ceremony, I received the most useful information about what to expect from:

	Boomer/Silent	GenX	Millennial
A church-sponsored temple preparation class	17%	32%	35%
One of the church leaders who interviewed me for a temple recommend	17%	15%	22%
Family and friends	37%	39%	32%
Books	2%	4%	< 1%
The internet	< 1%	< 1%	3%
I did not receive any useful information	26%	10%	6%

If only one in twenty Millennial Mormons chose the "no preparation" option, where are they getting their information? Not from books, alas; fewer than 1 percent say they cracked a book before receiving their endowment. And it's not the internet, either, which is the second main takeaway: despite copious hand-wringing on the part of LDS leaders and parents about the dangers of the internet, there is no evidence to suggest that members of this digital-savvy generation are going online to uncover temple rites. As Elaine, thirty-five, put it, "I know I could just Google the temple ceremony, but I don't want to do that. I don't want to find out about it from an anti-Mormon website. I want to find out about it from a parent, or a trusted friend."[20] In interviews, only a couple of Millennials admitted to having looked up the temple ceremony beforehand, and one of those said she regretted it. In addition to being forbidden, such online forays may not even be very helpful. That's because some of what people find surprising about the temple is not what is said but what is worn, what is done, what is performed. It is an all-encompassing and physical ritual of a kind not experienced in regular Mormon Sunday chapel services, and as such, merely reading a text can only take a neophyte so far.

This brings us to our final point, which is that the institutional church appears to be getting better at preparing people for the temple. Some local leaders such as bishops and stake presidents may be more explicit than they used to be about what to expect. Taylor, thirty-seven, was jealous of his future wife's temple prep class, since his own, taken years before, had been lackluster. The stake president who taught his wife's class "went through the whole endowment. He told them what covenants they would be making.

He only did not talk about the few very specific things you're told not to talk about. Everything else was fair game."[21]

Temple preparation classes are a relatively recent phenomenon in LDS history, only becoming an official program in 1978. Given that history, it's understandable that fewer than one in five Boomer/Silents named a temple class as their most significant preparation. Such classes weren't even available yet when the oldest people in our survey would have been in their late teens and early twenties. The rate of people who say that temple prep classes were their most helpful source of information doubled from the oldest generation (17 percent) to the youngest (35 percent), which is a laudable success for the church.

However, there is a perception even among the luckier younger generation that these classes are hit-or-miss. Sometimes, the classes are truly open, like with Taylor's wife's experience. More often they are vague and focused on the scriptural reasons that temples exist, not on what actually happens there. Jamie, thirty-three, took a temple prep class and doesn't remember a single thing about it.[22] Daniel, twenty-eight, thought the focus was misleading because "all it did was talk about symbolism. Yes, there's a lot of symbolism in there, but that's not really what you need to be prepared for. I was so thrown off guard by the clothing and the ceremony of it, the ritual of it, that I was worried that I'd gotten myself into a cult!"[23]

Several interviewees mentioned how much more useful the class would be if it showed prospective temple-goers the ritual clothing used in the endowment. As Janelle, thirty-six, pointed out, it's common at Mormon funeral visitations for bodies to be laid out in full temple regalia, so there's already a precedent for letting these items be seen outside the temple. "It feels a little bit like a double standard, that we don't talk about this and hush it up, but we don't keep non-Mormons from attending Mormon funerals where people can be dressed in their temple clothing," Janelle says.[24] In 2014, the LDS Church released a video on sacred temple clothing that briefly showed the various items spread out on a table, which was a helpful and positive step forward; this video can be used by individuals or classes that are preparing for the temple.[25] Sometimes an informal tutorial on ritual clothing happens outside the official confines of a class; for example, Chelsea, the New York convert who loved her first experience at the temple, felt particularly well prepared because she had a Young Women leader who took her aside to discreetly explain the ritual attire.

> We were talking, and she just said, "I'll show you the clothes." She took out her temple bag and just laid all the clothes out for me, like her grandmother's apron. And she showed me the robe and the garments. This woman was very politically and socially conservative, but in this she was free. She said, "You can't expect people to do things if

they don't know what to expect." So it wasn't at all a shock for me when I had to put the clothes on for the first time in the temple.

Mikey, also twenty-five, had something like this experience with the ritual clothing—but he only understood what it was when he got his endowment. In high school, he had a seminary teacher who was also a temple worker and knew the ceremony very well. For reasons that were not clear to him at the time, she kept emphasizing obscure aspects of the Old Testament as she had the class decorate a gingerbread man with frosting: first they would read a scripture about ancient priestly clothing, and then they would add that clothing item to the cookie. "At the time I wondered why we were spending so much time on it. So when I saw the temple clothing I was like, 'Wow! So that's why she did it. This must be so weird for other people who didn't have that teacher.' "[26] Mikey says this teacher's tactful preparation made all the difference when he actually entered the temple.

Some Millennials who feel passionate about their love for the temple are equally passionate about improving the way the church prepares people for it. For example, Jacob, thirty-five, reordered the material in his fiancée's temple prep booklet so it would be more logically arranged according to the order of what actually happens in the temple.[27] Much of that material is already present in the standard-issue booklet, he says, but it's buried. So he created a differently ordered temple prep kit for his fiancée to use, and his bishop and stake president both expressed interest in making this more logical curriculum available to others. Given what we see from the data—that the older generations that were the most likely to say they had no useful information before entering the temple were also the generations who had less frequent "very positive" temple initiations—such attention to how the temple is taught seems likely to enhance Mormons' experiences with it. Continuing to improve the temple preparation class may be even more important for LDS men than it is for women. In the NMS data, a third of men said the class was their most important source of temple information, compared to just over a quarter of women, whose most important resource was family and friends. Improving temple preparation may be a key to improving outcomes for men, including the majority who did not have a very positive first experience with the initiatory.

GARMENTS

When Mormons go through the temple for the first time, they receive "garments," which are sacred underclothes that symbolize the holy priesthood. These garments have sometimes been the subject of ridicule from outsiders who accuse Mormons of wearing "holy underwear," which is a gross oversimplification of how Mormons see them. So it's little wonder that Mormons have been cautious about discussing them. In the same 2014 video that discussed temple clothing, the church also depicted LDS temple garments in a matter-of-fact way, with surprising transparency.[28]

Historically, some Mormons believed their garments had almost magical properties of physical protection, but many today consider the protection to be less physical than spiritual.[29] Mormons are instructed in the temple to regard the garments as sacred, but how this relates to day-to-day life can vary; often specific instruction is not given in the temple itself but is passed down within families from one generation to the next.[30] One family never allows garments to touch the floor as a way of respecting their sacred character; in another they are piled up with the rest of the whites at the base of the washing machine. In one family women put on their regular bras and underwear first and then layer the garments on top; in another this is seen as heresy because garments are meant to be worn as a second skin, closest to the heart. There are also differences about when people think it is permissible to remove their garments: Is it all right not to wear them while exercising? What about when you're going to the doctor and don't want your underclothes to be a source of undue curiosity?

The point is that apart from two standard things—the mandate that garments are to be worn henceforth after going through the temple, and the temple recommend interview question that asks if they are being worn "both night and day as instructed in the endowment"—in practice there is a surprising amount of variation around garments. To learn more, the NMS presented a number of different scenarios to current Mormons who had been to the temple, asking when they believed it was permissible to remove their garments.

With only a couple of exceptions, Millennials appear to have adopted a more relaxed understanding about when it is acceptable to remove temple garments, as shown in Table 3.3. Consider the question about exercising or hiking. Just over a quarter of Boomer/Silents think it's acceptable to remove their garments for that purpose, compared to nearly half of Millennials. In other cases, the generational change likewise shows doubling, but the overall approval numbers are lower. Only about 10 percent of Boomer/Silents feel a break in garment usage is all right if a person is in a play, the weather is especially hot, or a job requires manual labor, but the number is twice that among Millennials. Of particular interest are two scenarios in which support has actually quadrupled. Only one in twenty older Mormons approve of shedding garments during vacations or women's menstruation, but among Millennials it's one in five. So while those exceptions still only

Table 3.3. TEMPLE GARMENT EXCEPTIONS BY GENERATION

Thinking about LDS temple garments, whether you currently wear them or did at one point in the past, when do/did you consider it acceptable to remove them? (CHECK ALL THAT APPLY)

	Boomer/Silent	GenX	Millennial
When going to the doctor's office	35%	33%	45%
When exercising or hiking	26%	37%	46%
When having sexual relations	75%	58%	51%
When doing yard work	11%	23%	27%
When the weather is very hot and/or humid	8%	16%	21%
When on vacation	5%	18%	20%
When ill or when there is a medical reason	42%	37%	38%
When working in a job, such as construction or the military, that requires manual labor	8%	13%	23%
When in a play or some other kind of performance	11%	13%	22%
If you lose your testimony of the truthfulness of the LDS Church	26%	27%	25%
When attending special events, such as weddings or formal dances	4%	12%	14%
When garments fit poorly or are uncomfortable for your body type	6%	9%	14%
When women are menstruating or having menopausal hot flashes	5%	12%	19%
When women are pregnant or nursing	3%	11%	17%
When sleeping	10%	16%	22%
When you don't feel like wearing them	6%	9%	12%

have minority status even among Millennials, they are four times more accepted than they are among Boomer/Silents.[31]

Looking at the data according to gender, women are more conservative about garment use than men, making fewer allowances for situations in which a person might wish to take them off. Many of these differences are within a few percentage points, but some are seven, eight, or nine points. Women take an especially dim view of removing garments while on vacation, for example; only one in ten women feel this is acceptable, versus one in five men. There are only two areas where women are more lenient than men by any significant margin, and these are during sexual intercourse or when a person is ill and has a medical reason not to wear them.

Garment practices for women were another area where the interviews were illuminating. Women were sometimes vocal about their frustrations with garments, in a way that men were not. Most male interviewees seemed easygoing about garments and reported no problems. As Taylor, thirty-seven, put it, the transition to wearing garments is "probably easier for men than women" because many men already wear an undershirt and boxers, so replacing those with their garment equivalents is not much of a shift. (It's also possible that male interviewees were reticent to discuss problems with garments because of the inherent awkwardness of talking to an interviewer of the other gender about very private issues like underwear—an awkwardness that is, of course, replicated every time an LDS woman has to be interviewed for a temple recommend by a male church leader.)

Female interviewees had a lot to say about garments. Chelsea, twenty-five, loved them from the outset and says they were "like in the *Sisterhood of the Traveling Pants* where the jeans just fit everyone perfectly." But at the beginning of this book we also met Emily, thirty-four, who is leaving the church and has mostly stopped wearing garments, though she still puts them on for family gatherings.[32] Not wearing them most of the time was "a very easy change to make" because she found garments hot and uncomfortable, and since she is tall, they never fit quite right. When she someday finds the courage to tell her parents that she has stopped going to church, Emily plans to stop wearing garments entirely, even around her family. She says that will be "freedom."

Other women negotiate their practice of wearing garments *while* they are still in the church, including a few who hold temple recommends. Miranda, who felt coerced by her family to have her wedding in the temple, wrote to the LDS Distribution Center several years ago with detailed complaints about changes she wanted to the fit and fabric of women's garments. She didn't like the lace used to trim them, thought the "sizing charts did not correspond to reality," and reported that the waistband on the bottoms was ridiculously high, almost up to her breasts. She felt listened to and validated, she says. "They responded to my complaints and actually sent me samples of ones they wanted me to try out. I think the church is trying to be more responsive." She believes that women's garments now are much better cut than they were when she first started wearing them in her twenties, though the church still has not bent to the number one item on her wish list: a tank-top version so women can wear sleeveless outfits. "I don't think they were willing to go that far," she laughs.[33]

Still, Miranda has stopped wearing garments at night. Since she holds a current temple recommend, I asked how she responds in the recommend interview to the question about wearing garments "night and day":

> I just say yes. I don't explain. . . . I think the question of how I wear my underwear is no one's business but my own. I really don't think a bishop should ask about it. It's inappropriate. . . . I'm willing to wear garments during the day, but my bedroom is my own.

Miranda does, however, feel a fair amount of guilt about this and says that if the guilt becomes too much, she "may think about if it is time to give sleeping in them another try." She may be pleased to learn that in 2018, months after our interview, the LDS Church released a new version of the women's garment with breathable stretch cotton fabric, an improved fit, and lower-riding waistbands for the bottoms—in short, many of the changes Miranda and other women had requested.[34]

Catherine, whom we met in chapter 1 and who remains active in the church though she no longer believes, has also reached a point where she holds a temple recommend but has stopped wearing garments.[35] This decision was a very long time in coming, because she thinks there is great value in making promises in the temple and she wants to be a person of her word. She believes covenants should be respected. On the other hand, she says, "I no longer believe in what they [the garments] represent." They remind her of things she did not enjoy about the temple, particularly regarding gender. So she gave them up:

> Almost a year ago, not quite, I just had this feeling like I am done doing things that make me feel sick. I don't think God wants me to feel frustrated or angry because I'm putting on garments. . . .
> I will not miss a wedding of a close family member. So I will go in and just say whatever I need to say. . . . I know that can seem dishonest, but I didn't make this system. If it comes to me seeing my daughter's wedding or my son's wedding, I will put on my garments and I would be there.

The experiences of Emily, Miranda, and Catherine point to different paths of negotiation. Emily's story is in some ways the most straightforward: she has mostly stopped wearing garments and she is leaving the church. This is a standard narrative that has been told and retold many times, in which shedding garments is often viewed as an overall "system failure," a sign of an individual's deteriorating relationship with the church.[36] But this is not the only narrative for Millennials, if it ever was for previous generations. (And how would we know, if no one who stayed in the church talked about being anything less than fully compliant about garments?) We will see evidence in chapter 8 that Millennials are less rigid about a number of religious practices, from the Word of Wisdom to church attendance. Yet they are still Mormon, and many still hold temple recommends. Miranda and Catherine may be in the minority in terms of staying LDS but not wearing their garments, but they may also be the proverbial canaries in the coal mine, portending trouble for the future—particularly over gender, which we turn to in the next two chapters.

PART TWO

Changing Definitions of Family and Culture

CHAPTER 4

Single Mormons in a Married Church

When Naomi was a teenager, she and the other young women in her ward were assigned to make lists of the qualities they were looking for in a future husband, and to work on acquiring the qualities a future husband might want in a wife.[1] Many lessons on Sundays and weeknights involved preparing for the marriages the girls would one day have. No alternatives to marriage were presented. Singleness was not mentioned as a desirable life choice, either in the curriculum or by way of example. Most of her Young Women leaders were themselves married, though Naomi remembers a few "older" single women in their late twenties and early thirties whom she regarded with something like pity. She was confident she "would never be like that." She knew this because she had a plan: she would graduate from college, serve a mission, get married, and have babies, in that order. "That was the narrative, that all those things would happen in a row."

Only they didn't. She didn't meet her eternal companion and have a chubby Mormon baby within a year of a temple wedding. Apart from the college degree, none of her original plans came to pass. Perhaps the hardest part was that the narrative *did* seem to work out for others:

> You also watch people around you where it does happen exactly like that. Your friend, your roommate, meets someone one day and gets married. And you think, "Wait. I've been doing exactly what that person is doing, and why is the outcome so different?" Not that I see life as a vending machine, where you put certain things in and can expect certain things to come out. But it's easy to fall into the trap of questioning yourself when you can see the narrative working out for people all around you.

Now thirty-eight and still single, Naomi has had to re-evaluate what the absence of a ring on her finger means—not only for her family life, but also for her faith. Mormons have the highest rate of marriage of any Christian group in the United States, which can make it lonely and painful to be in the unmarried minority. Naomi, like most other Mormon singles I spoke to, has built a rich and fulfilling life for herself. She earned a PhD, started a social media affinity group for working LDS women, and is the editor of an anthology of personal essays from single Mormons. Every single contributor, she says, told her the essay was the hardest thing they had ever written. Many Mormon singles feel judged or shamed, or express frustration that the church seems to be worshiping the nuclear family instead of Christ. For some—including Naomi herself, now—the grief has been strong enough that they're no longer active in the faith. She's not ready to say she is done with Mormonism, but she has stopped going to the temple and seems wary of being hurt again by the church's barrage of promarriage rhetoric. She's still open to marriage, but has widened the dating pool to include non-Mormons.

Naomi's story encapsulates well the journey of many single adult Mormons, in that the "plan of happiness" they imbibed when they were younger included a partner who never materialized for them in adulthood. Because marriage and children are so central to the Mormon concepts of happiness in this life and exaltation in the next, living without them can be acutely painful. Like Naomi, some singles wind up leaving the church; as we will see later in this chapter, they do so at higher rates than their married peers. For its part, the LDS Church has tried different approaches to meet the needs of single members, including "singles wards," or congregations where unmarried members can worship together outside the multigenerational wards that constitute the usual Mormon experience. There are pros and cons to singles wards, however, and no easy solutions to the low activity rate among older singles.

MARRIAGE IN THE UNITED STATES

The story of single adults in the LDS Church takes place against a backdrop of major shifts in the American family, which are essential to understanding the fuller picture of Mormonism today. The last half century has seen a number of significant social transformations, including to the institution of marriage. These changes can be summed up in three broad trends.

First, marriage is less common overall, and it is not because divorce is up. Divorce rates have actually fallen since their peak in the late 1970s and early 1980s, especially among college-educated Americans, who have somewhat higher rates of marital stability than those with a high school education or less.[2] Rather, it is because fewer people are tying the knot in the first place. To see how this shift plays out generationally, let's take a snapshot of some of the oldest and youngest Americans side by side, comparing their marital situations at roughly the same ages fifty years apart (Table 4.1). Among the Silent Generation, two-thirds were married in 1960, when they were in their late teens to early thirties.[3] For example, current LDS First Presidency member Dallin H. Oaks (born in 1932) got married at nineteen. As marriage in early adulthood was the norm in the 1950s, his experiences were typical of the time. Compare that to the Millennial generation. When they reached that age range in 2013, only 26 percent were married (Table 4.1).[4] This means that within the span of about half a century, America went from having two-thirds of its young adults married to just over a quarter, a drop of nearly forty points nationally. This is a large-scale social reversal.

This does not mean that only a quarter of the Millennial generation will *ever* marry. Some people are marrying later in life, which is a second broad trend. The median age at marriage in 1960 was 22.8 for American men and 20.3 for women.[5] Admittedly, that era was a bit unusual in that the median ages at marriage actually decreased from the higher ages that had pertained in the late nineteenth and early twentieth centuries, especially for men. Still, there's no question that the median age has now not only reverted to historical norms but also exceeded them: by 2016, the median age of marriage had increased by roughly seven years for both genders to 29.5 for men and 27.4 for women.[6] Many Millennials and GenXers who marry are not doing so until their thirties, meaning that, as some researchers have put it, marriage has moved from being a "cornerstone" foundation to a "capstone" aspiration.[7] Marriage is something many young adults view as desirable after other goals, like education, have been achieved. In many ways the findings of social science bolster the idea that delaying marriage can be a wise idea,

Table 4.1. A SNAPSHOT OF MARRIAGE IN THE UNITED STATES, 1960 VERSUS TODAY

	1960	Today
Median age at marriage for women	20.3	27.4
Median age at marriage for men	22.8	29.5
Percentage of adults married by age 32	65%	26%
Marriage among college-educated Americans	76%	63%
Marriage among those with a high school diploma or less	72%	45%

as getting married very young and being financially unstable are both risk factors for divorce.[8]

This brings us to our third point, which is that the national phenomenon of delayed marriage has not affected all groups equally. Marriage has seen its most significant declines among populations that are socioeconomically more at risk: minorities, those with less than a college education, and those earning lower incomes (all of which often correlate together). In 1960, only four percentage points separated marriage rates between the college-educated (76 percent) and those with a high school diploma or less (72 percent). By 2013, according to Pew researchers, "the gap had ballooned to 18 percentage points (63% versus 45%)," with the sharpest marital declines occurring among minority groups and the poor.[9] Marriage has become something for the "haves" in America, and not so much for the "have nots." And that's unfortunate, because as many researchers have pointed out, marriage is itself associated with greater economic mobility, better health, and increased self-reported happiness. Marriage is declining most sharply among the very groups who could most benefit from it.

MARRIAGE AMONG MORMONS

What do these three trends look like for Mormons? Are Latter-day Saints starting to skip out on the institution of marriage? Are younger Mormons as likely to delay marriage as their non-Mormon Millennial peers?

The NMS finds that Mormons are by and large holding steady in their marital status, despite the rapid pace of change in American society more generally. Mormons still rank highest among all Christian groups in the overall rate of members who are married, and second highest among all religious groups.[10] In Pew's 2014 Religious Landscape Study (RLS), 66 percent of US Mormons were married, a finding that was repeated almost exactly in the NMS two years later, with 65 percent. (The rates of marriage are noticeably lower among former Mormons, which I will discuss later in this chapter.) That compares to about 48 percent of all US adults who are currently married. Mormons, then, are about a third more likely to be married than members of the general population, which is statistically very significant.

However, it's worth noting that the percentage of Mormons who are married has decreased since Pew's 2007 RLS, from 71 percent in 2007 to the mid-60s now, as Table 4.2 demonstrates (with a slightly higher rate reported by the Public Religion Research Institute [PRRI]). More Mormons have never married: this category climbed from 12 percent in 2007 to 19 percent in the Pew survey seven years later. This seven-point rise in

Table 4.2. MORMONS WHO ARE MARRIED, SINGLE, WIDOWED, DIVORCED, OR COHABITING

	2007 Pew RLS	2011 Pew, Mormons in America	2014 Pew RLS	2016, PRRI American Values Atlas	2016, The Next Mormons
Married (including remarriage)	71%	67%	66%	68%	65%
Cohabiting with a partner	3%	2%	3%	3%	5%
Divorced/separated	9%	9%	7%	8%	8%
Widowed	5%	6%	5%	5%	3%
Never married	12%	16%	19%	16%	18%

singleness is within the margin of error for these studies but could represent a change worth watching given the strong national trends toward singleness in US society.

The second issue, whether Mormons are delaying marriage, has been a topic of speculation. Journalist Naomi Schafer Riley expressed concern that the 2006 General Social Survey pegged Mormons as getting married at age 22.6, whereas in the 1990s it had been 21.6. "This age may not seem high yet, but if the Mormon population follows the trend of the rest of the American population (albeit at a slower pace), the church could be in real trouble."[11] The NMS results suggest it's not quite time to sound the alarms, since the median age for Mormons to marry is holding steady at 22. In other words, Mormons who do get married waste no time in doing so. They are bucking the larger national trend of delayed marriage.

It's true that Boomer/Silent Mormons were more likely than the Millennials to have married while still in their teens—a quarter of the Boomer/Silents were married by age nineteen, compared to just 13 percent of Millennials—but Millennial Mormons find their sweet spot immediately afterward, when they are in their early twenties. However, we should remember that this is not the final say about Mormons resisting the national trend toward delayed marriage, because Millennials and even some GenXers are not finished yet. What we can say is that delays are not occurring *among those who have gotten married so far.* It remains to be seen what will happen with the rising numbers of Mormons who have never married (18 percent, in the NMS) and those who are cohabiting (5 percent, and nearly twice that among Mormon Millennials).[12]

Overall, then, it would seem that the larger US trend toward delaying marriage has not yet occurred in the active LDS community, though there is an evident decrease in marriage among Mormon teenagers. There is also, as we've noted, a rise in the number of Mormons who have not married at all. The fact that little is changing in regard to LDS marital practices underscores the final point about which groups in America are most likely to be unmarried. The majority of Mormons in the United States inhabit a privileged demographic space where marriage is concerned because they are primarily white, middle class, and educated. That puts them in the most favorable demographic categories of people who tend to get married and stay married.

Then too, since World War II the LDS Church has created its distinctive religious identity in the crowded American religious landscape by emphasizing marriage and the nuclear family. Marriage is hammered home as not just a cultural goal but a deeply religious mandate for Latter-day Saints. In the postwar period, Mormonism's familial ideals coincided perfectly with certain trends in American society that favored earlier marriage and larger families. As the church navigates the twenty-first century, however, it must do so knowing that the society that supported Mormonism's emphases on marriage and "traditional" gender roles in the 1950s has turned in another direction, either expanding marriage to include same-sex couples (see chapter 7) or questioning its value altogether. The church must find a way to speak to the growing percentage of never-married Mormons, who often feel great strain in a church that has taught them that marriage is fundamental not only to their happiness in this life but also to celestial exaltation in the world to come.

SINGLE WOMEN, SINGLE MEN

Within that rising percentage in which nearly one-fifth of the NMS sample has never married, there is a slight gender imbalance. It was not, however, the imbalance I was expecting. Throughout the oral history interviews and also in some nonrandomly collected data, it seemed that single LDS women might outnumber their male counterparts by a significant margin. As I conducted this research, many people volunteered observations about how few single men there are in Mormon wards compared to the number of women. However, the NMS numbers tell a different story (Table 4.3). The ranks of never-married Mormons include 20 percent of men and 17 percent of women, which is within the margin of error but still an interesting finding, especially when we consider that it is confirmed by two other large-scale studies.

Taken together, these three national samples all show a higher percentage of never-married men than women. This upends a common narrative within Mormonism that there are more single women than men, but

Table 4.3. MORMON MARITAL STATUS BY GENDER IN THREE NATIONAL STUDIES

	Pew, 2014*		PRRI, 2016**		NMS, 2016	
	Men	Women	Men	Women	Men	Women
Married or remarried	66%	65%	69%	67%	66%	64%
Cohabiting/living with a partner	3%	4%	3%	3%	7%	4%
Divorced or separated	6%	9%	6%	9%	5%	8%
Widowed	1%	8%	3%	6%	2%	4%
Never married	24%	14%	18%	15%	20%	17%

* I'm grateful to Alexis Straka for performing this analysis of the 2014 Pew data.
** Email to author from Joanna Piacenza, editor and communications manager for PRRI, and Daniel Cox, research director for PRRI, September 18, 2017.

it reflects a broader national tendency in which men slightly outnumber women among the ranks of the never-married in America.[13] This remains true nationally if we limit consideration to active Mormons who report attending church each week—but it is not true for active members in Mormon-dominated areas. In Utah, never-married women who were active in the church outnumbered their male counterparts by more than two to one, a sharp divergence from the national situation.[14] This likely accounts for the prominence of the idea that there are more single Mormon women than men. One of my interviewees, a divorced New Yorker named Mala, told me she thought she should move to Salt Lake City to increase her chances of remarriage, but she had resisted because of "zero desire to live in a Mormon majority culture."[15] Mala can rest easy about remaining right where she is, as her chances of finding a temple-worthy partner may actually be worse in Utah.

It's clear that both single women and men face challenges in the LDS Church. Some of those challenges are the same, like feeling lonely or misunderstood. Some, however, are uniquely associated with gender. Jessica, a twenty-seven-year-old graduate student in North Carolina, says that single women can experience a crisis of identity in the church because of its constant emphasis on motherhood. She notes there's no shortage of rhetoric about how wonderful and important women are, but church leaders also continue stating that the only divinely appointed job women have is to bear and nurture children.[16] That, she says, can be confusing:

> My biggest issue is that I think I'm foreordained to not only be a mother but to do a lot of other things. As a single woman, I don't know what my role is, or what other ways in which I'm important to the gospel or the building of the community. . . . With most of

the single women, it feels like the church is saying that we're just biding our time until we get married, and that's when our "real" lives will begin.

Jessica has remained active in the church, and her feelings of isolation have lessened in a singles ward with a robust cohort of other graduate students. But for Jamie, thirty-three, the identity crisis has become acute. Starting in her late twenties, she began to be "increasingly depressed" because of the disconnect between her life as a single woman and what the LDS Church always taught was her destiny: marriage and children. "I was facing a life of not ever having love or companionship or sex or children," she says, so she started professional therapy and read a great deal about human psychology and intimacy. This experience showed her that she could not stay in the LDS Church and also hold on to her sense of self-worth. Slowly, quietly, she left the fold. "I just knew that I couldn't stay. I did not agree with the expectation that if I was single, I had missed the boat." Now, she is in a happier place emotionally and plans to start dating again—non-Mormons exclusively this time. "I find even a lot of the post-Mormon men that I've associated with, that patriarchal mindset is still very much a part of who they are, and I am looking for a more egalitarian relationship," she says.

Several single Mormon women I interviewed mentioned their search for an egalitarian relationship. They emphasized that women no longer need men financially the way they did two or more generations ago. As women become more educated and self-sufficient, they do not depend on men as breadwinners, which means they may be less willing to settle for a partner who does not treat them as equals. As Naomi, whose story began this chapter, put it, marriage needs to enhance the terrific life she already has, not limit it.

In the NMS, we asked Mormon and former Mormon respondents whether they preferred egalitarian or traditional marriage, with "egalitarian" meaning both partners have jobs and share responsibility for chores and raising children, and "traditional" meaning the man is the breadwinner and the woman is primarily responsible for raising children. While a majority of Mormons prefer a traditional marriage, it's more popular among men (65 percent) than among women (58 percent). Generationally, there is change afoot: nearly half (48 percent) of Millennial women want the egalitarian marriage, and we see movement toward the nontraditional even within that generation of women: for younger Millennial women (eighteen to twenty-six), egalitarian marriage carries the majority at 54 percent. But six in ten younger Millennial men prefer the traditional arrangement, creating a gap between what young Mormon women want from their prospective marriage partners and what those men appear willing to offer.[17]

Single Mormon men express many of the same frustrations as single women, especially a sense of failure once they reach what one interviewee referred to as a "sell-by date" with no marriage prospects. But several men I spoke to were also sensitive to the fact that the structure of patriarchy puts the ball in their court. Says Troy, a thirty-seven-year-old economic researcher:

> Part of it is that in Mormon culture, it's men's responsibility to initiate. I've had priesthood leaders call me to task for not dating enough. But women are not considered at fault for not getting married, because they're not *supposed* to initiate. A lot of the single Mormon women I know are suffering from depression. They're in a position where they want to achieve something, and the culture is telling them they have no power to achieve that, so it's very debilitating in terms of self-actualization.[18]

That's not to say that single Mormon men are in a terrific position either. Whereas single women are pitied in Mormon culture, Troy says, single men are condemned, and "I don't feel like either one of those is a good position." I asked Troy if he was aware of a disturbing quotation, often (wrongly) attributed to Brigham Young, that any single man over the age of twenty-five is a "menace to society."[19] He was well aware of the comment and its ramifications. Single men, he says, rarely receive invitations to social events that involve families; some people "don't want you to be around kids because they think you're a pedophile or something," while married women "can't be friends with you because that would be inappropriate." This means that overall, "if you are an older single man in a family ward, you are likely pretty isolated."

Other men confirm the strain of being single and male in the LDS community. Brandon, now forty-one and married, was single until age thirty-seven, so he spent nearly two decades in singles wards. Although in his early twenties he enjoyed the vibrant social scene of the singles ward, the relentless push to get married became a turnoff as he matured. He once sat in an Elders Quorum meeting in which the president taught that "if you're not getting married or dating, you're sinning and you need to go see the bishop about it and change your life"—which was ironic, since this occurred in a singles ward and the teacher was himself single. "I wanted to raise my hand and say, 'OK, then, dude, what's wrong with *you*?'"[20]

Like many singles, Brandon had assumed as a very young man that marriage would occur naturally when he got home from his mission, and he remembers feeling judgmental toward a cousin who didn't marry until he was two years off his mission. That seemed incredibly old to Brandon. Years later, he found himself in the same situation, and when his late twenties became his early thirties and beyond, he found that the church's message of "incompleteness" without marriage "made me feel like I was sinning." He also felt displaced by the church's ever-evolving policies about singles wards:

> I was 31 or 32 when the church had that hard and strict policy that once you're 31 you're out of the singles ward and have to go to a family ward. I talked with a friend who said, "It was the first time of my life that I ever got kicked out of something." And that's how I felt. I loved that singles ward, where I was the Gospel Doctrine teacher, and literally the next week the bishop came to me and said I couldn't come to that ward anymore. So right around that age, a lot of people just stopped going to church.

Today, the church is experimenting with a variety of options, including "midsingles" wards that pick up where the young single adult (YSA) wards leave off. The goal is that no one in their early thirties will find themselves like Brandon, *Logan's Run* style, suddenly evicted from the community they've loved just because they've had a birthday. As of 2017 the church had thirty-six of these wards in the United States and two in Canada; of these thirty-eight units, two-thirds had been organized within the previous eight years.[21] Yet even these communities for singles in their thirties and early forties aren't always a refuge from the pain of being unmarried in a church that so relentlessly pushes marriage. A bishop of a singles ward that meets the needs of thirty-one- to forty-five-year-olds echoes interviewees' comments.[22] Yes, he says, there is "depression among the sisters" who reach their thirties and find themselves still single. Even though "so many of these women are leading remarkably wonderful and productive lives, blessing corporations and campuses," unmarried women cry in his office periodically, and his heart goes out to them. "I think it's hard to escape a certain level of insecurity that comes from this voice in the back of the head asking, 'What's wrong with me? Why have I not been chosen?'" However, the bishop cautions that there is another side to this story:

> A lot of men, a lot more than maybe we as a Mormon community would guess, feel that same thing. For those that feel it's easy for a man to get married, they are doing a real disservice to good men who are finding this difficult too. And I think we should be less quick to judge. The experience has made *me* less quick to judge. There have been a lot of tears shed by men asking, "Why have I not been chosen?" too.

The loneliness and bewilderment often felt by older Mormon singles, he says, is gender neutral. As a result his ward has actively sought to be a gentle, healing place for these Latter-day Saints. They don't have lessons on marriage, having been instructed by their stake president "not to pound that drum." They don't pile on the guilt by asking singles why they aren't dating more. Instead, they offer community and solidarity, creating a safe space for singles to worship. "There's something special that the Lord is trying to tell them, not to give up on the church, not to give up on all the things they can enjoy," says the bishop.

SINGLES, BELIEF, AND PRACTICE

The bishop's comment for singles "not to give up on the church" reflects a certain reality: many singles do give up. Statistically, single people are more likely to leave Mormonism or become inactive than married people. Whereas two-thirds of married adult members report having attended church in the last month (64 percent), fewer than half of unmarried Mormons have attended (48 percent), though the numbers are a bit stronger among those singles who are currently members of a dedicated singles ward. The fact that singles' attendance is higher in singles wards *might* mean that singles wards are more effective in engaging singles, but it also could mean that those particular singles were already motivated to be active in the church. No one is forced to go to a singles ward—and in some, individuals actually have to submit an application and meet a worthiness standard just for the privilege of being there. So there is a sense in which singles wards are a self-selecting clientele.

The NMS results deviated from previous studies of Mormons in showing a clear decline in attendance among single members versus married ones. A 2004 study noted with surprise that "contrary to other churches, the highest rate of adult attendance in the LDS Church is by the never-married."[23] While the NMS data contradicts that, it actually offers a rosier picture than the one discussed by members of the LDS Quorum of the Twelve in a private 2008 meeting, at which the church's own research division indicated that the rate of church activity for single North American eighteen- to thirty-year-olds was around 30 percent, half what it was for married members of the same age.[24]

Just as inactivity is higher among singles, so is disaffiliation. Whereas we saw that 18 percent of the current Mormon sample has never married, among former Mormons it is a quarter (25 percent). Just under half of former Mormons are currently married (46 percent), including those who are remarried after a divorce or bereavement, versus 65 percent of Mormons who are now married.[25] This represents nearly a twenty-point drop in marital rates between current and former Mormons. In addition to the greater percentage of never-married individuals, we see a higher percentage of former Mormons who are divorced (14 percent) or cohabiting (13 percent).

Even among those singles who continue to identify as Mormon, some devotional habits are less common than they are among married Mormons, which is also the case nationally.[26] Daily scripture reading, for example, is claimed by 42 percent of married Mormons but only 31 percent of singles, an eleven-point drop. Daily prayer is about the same between both groups: seven in ten for both married and single Mormons. Married Mormons are sixteen points more likely to believe "wholeheartedly in all" LDS teachings (54 percent, compared to single Mormons at 38 percent) and twenty points more likely to have seen General Conference in the last six months. Some of this is due to age effects; single Mormons are generally younger than married ones, and as we've seen across most of the findings of this book, younger Mormons are in some ways (not all) less exacting than their elders. That would explain much of the drop in General Conference viewing, which has a clear generational plunge from the oldest Mormons to the youngest (chapter 10). Age doesn't explain all these differences in religiosity, however. As we'll see in chapter 8, Millennial Mormons are actually *more* devout on some measures of religious practice, including daily scripture reading. So for single Mormons to lag married ones on this particular measure does not represent an age effect, but something else.

More pronounced drops in religiosity occur among single Mormon men than among women. Consider the example above about viewing General Conference. Single Mormon women were less likely to have seen General Conference in the last six months compared to married Mormon women— 45 percent of single women versus 61 percent of married women. Among men, however, the discrepancy between married and single men was even wider. About 57 percent of married men had seen General Conference, but only 33 percent of single men had, a gap of twenty-four points. Most single men appear to give General Conference a pass. Across the NMS data, single men's measurable religious behavior was the lowest of any marital category for men or women.[27]

SEX AND THE SINGLE MORMON

Among the various benchmarks of religious belief and behavior that LDS leaders are concerned about, none looms so large as sexual activity. The church has consistently taught that sex is reserved for marriage, full stop. Getting married in the temple is predicated on both partners either being virgins or having undertaken a repentance process under a bishop's supervision to qualify them for temple worthiness. Mormons take what they call the "law of chastity" very seriously, and teach not only that unauthorized sexual intercourse violates that law but also nonmarital oral sex, anal sex, and even masturbation. All are possible grounds for church discipline, such as having a temple recommend temporarily taken away or being denied access to the sacrament (the Lord's Supper).

Prior research on Mormons' sexual behavior finds that most Mormons don't just "talk the talk," saying one thing but then doing another. In the National Study of Youth and Religion, for example, about three-quarters of Mormon teens said they believed in waiting until marriage, and about three-quarters of Mormon teens actually *were* apparently waiting.[28] A separate study conducted by BYU found that the more religious LDS teenagers were, the less likely they were to engage in sex. Nationwide, eighteen-year-old girls were three and a half times more likely to have had sex than eighteen-year-old Mormon girls (65 vs. 19 percent), and US boys were more than five times more likely to have had sex than Mormon boys (59 vs. 11 percent).[29] Clearly, LDS teens are taking the chastity message seriously.

But there is potentially a great difference between an eighteen-year-old single and a thirty-eight-year-old single, at least in terms of the expectation of virginity. Are unmarried Mormon adults in their twenties and thirties having sex? Are they able to resist the mandate of their biology and the influence of the general culture, which positions thirty-something virginity as a mockable trait worthy of a Judd Apatow comedy?

The answer is complicated. The good news, in the eyes of church leaders, is surely this: single Mormons who are still affiliated with the church are not much more likely to have experienced sexual intercourse, oral sex, anal sex, or what prior generations called "heavy petting" than now-married church members did prior to tying the knot. For example, 26 percent of married Mormons had intercourse before they got married, and 28 percent of never-married Mormons have. In fact, among all ten sexual experiences we asked about, the only one where single Mormons have a statistically significant advantage over now-married ones is in the percentage who masturbated alone before marriage: nearly a third of never-married Mormons say they have done this, compared to a quarter of Mormons who are now married (Table 4.4).[30]

Considering that the never-married population canvassed in the NMS includes singles of all ages, it is impressive that these respondents have held fast to the sexual expectations of their religion. The vast majority of single Mormons who are still in the church are not having sex.

That is only half the story, however. One thing the NMS allows us to do that previous studies have not is to compare current and former Mormons in their ideas, attitudes, and behaviors. On questions of premarital sexual behavior, we see a startling pattern: former Mormons are about twice as likely to have engaged in forbidden practices like sexual intercourse outside

Table 4.4. PREMARITAL SEXUAL EXPERIENCE AMONG CURRENT MORMONS, BY MARITAL STATUS

	Currently Married to First Spouse ($n = 639$)	Never Married ($n = 211$)
Fondling breasts or genitals over clothing	34%	33%
Fondling breasts or genitals without clothing	30%	29%
Masturbation alone	25%	31%
Oral sex	25%	27%
Anal sex	8%	10%
Sexual intercourse	26%	28%

of marriage (Figure 4.1). Two-thirds had sex before marriage, for example, compared to just under a third of the sample that still identifies as LDS.

Overall, we see a much higher percentage of premarital or nonmarital sexual experience in the former Mormon sample—approximately twice as much. These findings complicate the victorious narrative about Mormons' remarkable rates of abstinence from premarital sex, and should prompt us to ask: Are Mormons' astonishing rates of resistance to premarital sex artificially inflated in surveys because those who did have sex have left the church?

More research is needed on this score, particularly to determine whether there is any kind of causal relationship.[31] Are some single Mormons having sex and then—perhaps because they want to continue being sexually active or they cannot handle the shame of having broken the law of chastity—leaving the fold entirely? Or had they already left Mormonism before they engaged in these sexual behaviors? These remain questions for future researchers.

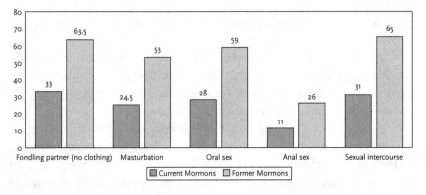

Figure 4.1. Premarital Sexual Activity among Current and Former Mormons.

In this discussion of singles' religious beliefs and behaviors, it goes without saying that the LDS Church has proven itself willing to institute whatever programs leaders believe will best contribute to singles' spiritual flourishing—and help them marry and start families of their own. Throughout this chapter, I have referred to the phenomenon of singles wards, which the LDS Church began creating in the late twentieth century as vehicles for young adults to exercise leadership responsibility and to meet fellow members who might be viable candidates for marriage. The idea of wards that specifically catered to students began taking hold after World War II at church-owned Brigham Young University and spread outward from there; by the end of the twentieth century they were becoming common outside of Utah in urban and some suburban areas. Over the years, singles wards have changed to fit the needs of unmarried members, with church leaders experimenting with various age cutoffs and, in 2011, dissolving "student" wards in favor of singles wards for all unmarried members, whether they were students or not.[32] Not all of these changes have been popular. These wards are beloved and they are hated, sometimes by the very same individuals, so it is worthwhile to weigh their potential pros and cons.

There are several advantages to having single members worship by themselves, the first of which is obvious: singles wards aim to promote marriage by gathering all local Mormon singles in one place for regular interaction. We don't have statistics on how many marriages actually result from singles wards, but there is anecdotal evidence that such congregations are at least modestly successful in introducing people to one another and that this does sometimes end in the much-desired temple wedding. What's more, meeting a spouse at church makes it extremely likely that you will share the same faith. Mormons are second only to Hindus in marrying within the fold, which in turn significantly increases the likelihood that any children born to that family will also elect to stay in the religion.[33] Marriages in which both partners are committed to the same faith tradition have a greater chance of retaining children in that tradition than ones in which the partners are members of different religions or one is not affiliated at all.[34] So singles wards, from the perspective of LDS leaders, aren't just enabling single members to meet and marry, but are boosting the health of the entire religion. That's because married people are more likely to stay Mormon than singles, and any children they raise together religiously will also have a strong foundation for retention.

But while marriage is one of the church's stated goals in creating sin-gles wards, it's not a theme that came up often in personal interviews. Rather, people who have been involved in singles wards cite the many opportunities to be with friends their own age as the chief attraction. As several interviewees mentioned, a singles ward can offer an instant com-munity for Mormons who are moving to a new area. Jason, thirty-one, opens his apartment to fellow singles each Sunday evening for dinner and a movie, and likes the fact that there are always people in the ward he can take with him on road trips or hiking excursions. He says he's "formed a lot of friendships" in the ward that have been important for his life and faith.[35]

Emily, whom we met at the beginning of the book, says the singles ward she began attending at age twenty-three introduced her to fabulous women she considered to be not only friends but also role models.[36] Coming off a bad breakup of a relationship she had expected to culminate at the altar, Emily had no "plan B" for how to live life as a single person. Not one woman in her life had paved the way to show that a Mormon woman could be happy to be single and working: no aunts, older cousins, or Young Women leaders had forged that path. It was in the singles ward that she found the direction she needed. "That was actually really helpful, to see lots of single women who were older than me and doing such awesome things with their lives," she says now, a decade later. "They were my first real role models of what being single would be like." Friendship, not potential romantic relationships, is sometimes the real payoff of singles wards.

Finally, one of the most important functions of singles wards is to groom young adults for religious leadership. In singles wards, almost every calling except the bishop and his two counselors is filled by single members, many of whom are in their twenties. They are the Relief Society presidents, the Elders Quorum presidents, the Gospel Doctrine teachers. In this they are training in the gospel in the most hands-on and effective way possible; their own commitment is strengthened because they are teaching and leading others.

Having single people as leaders is rare outside of singles wards. In con-ventional or "family" wards, single adults are too often passed over for leadership opportunities. Clayton Christensen, an author and professor at Harvard Business School, is a Mormon who has held many leadership positions in the LDS Church, especially in the New England area. Speaking in 2015 to an audience of single adults in New York, Christensen shared the results of an informal study he did when he was assigned to be an "area authority" (the next level up from a stake president in the LDS hi-erarchy at that time).[37] He was concerned about the abysmal activity rates for singles in his area: only 17 percent of the single women on the church rolls attended church regularly or even occasionally, versus 68 percent of the married women. Among single men, attendance was even lower: just 8 percent. When he dug deeper, he discovered one district of the church in Upstate New York that did not have that problem. In that district's six branches, married and single members attended at roughly equal rates. What was the difference, he wondered? The answer was callings. Those small branches were "so desperate for anybody who could walk" that single men and women were given heavy responsibilities—and they responded with faithful dedication. Christensen believes that every conventional ward needs to take a hard look at the membership of its "ward council," which consists of leaders from all the various auxiliaries like the Relief Society, the Young Men, and the Primary. If there are no single members serving in important callings that require their presence at ward council, those wards have missed an opportunity to not only diversify the ranks of leadership but also extend to single members the knowledge that they are valuable contributors.

As we've seen, there remain compelling reasons for the existence of singles wards. Not only do they foster relationships—even, for some, marriages—among Mormons who are in similar stages of life, but they also cultivate leadership, which is essential in a church that lives and dies by the effectiveness of its grassroots organization. Not all Mormons agree about singles wards, however—especially when they sometimes seem like a better idea in theory than they do in execution.

THE CASE AGAINST SINGLES WARDS

"I'm not sure it's a good idea to separate singles at all," writes Nicole Hardy in her memoir, *Confessions of a Latter-day Virgin.* "Because we're absent from regular congregations, we singles—and our concerns—aren't often considered."[38] Several of my interviewees agreed, saying the practice of shunting single adults into separate wards reinforces the notion that singleness is a problem to be solved. When single members are ghettoized, they can be either invisible to the married majority or viewed paternalistically. Janelle, thirty-six, proposes a lower age cutoff for singles wards—around age twenty-five—and says that after that, singles should be integrated into conventional wards and given leadership opportunities there, as Clayton Christensen has suggested.[39] "Over time, changing that would create understanding that would break down some of the stereotypes and judgments" about single adults, Janelle says. Singles could still have social activities together, such as their own weekly Family Home Evening meetings, but their Sunday worship experience would occur in conventional wards with people of all ages. Several interviewees who are currently in singles wards particularly mentioned how much they miss being around children at church.

And many unmarried Mormons I interviewed brought up the idea that single adults are *treated* like children at church, or at least like teenagers. Says Tinesha, a twenty-three-year-old student:

> They've had married couples from BYU come and talk to us about marriage, and these people were all the same age as us and had been married for like a year and a half. I think the church acts like once you get married, then you'll be treated as adults. I went to a dance once where the chaperones were only eighteen or nineteen, a couple years younger than I was, but they were married so they could be chaperones.[40]

It gets worse. One of the recent activities her ward conducted was throwing flour balloons (like water balloons but filled with flour). Tinesha felt this was something she wouldn't have even enjoyed when she was eight; why should she participate at twenty-three? Other social activities single Mormons mentioned included going on scavenger hunts, building forts, drawing pictures in chocolate pudding, and carving pumpkins. As Chelsea, twenty-five, put it, "At BYU, I felt so infantilized. After one evening stake conference, they literally had Capri Suns and fruit snacks. Why are they giving us juice boxes when we're twenty-something years old?"[41]

It's a valid question. In the aforementioned video of a 2008 meeting of major LDS leaders, the Brethren's discussions about YSAs revealed that they are deeply concerned about the low levels of church activity among singles, but they don't all seem to register the "adult" part of the phrase "single adults." The language used in that meeting indicates that some view single adults as still under the direct supervision of parents. More than halfway through the meeting, Elder Boyd K. Packer complained, "The one word that's been missing in all of this is family. It hasn't been said once." (It had.) "The original jurisdiction until they're married is in the parental home, in the family." Elder Packer's comments suggest a possible disconnect between the demographic reality of most LDS singles being mature and financially independent and the view that some leaders may harbor, that they are embracing a perpetual adolescence.

Some singles also complained about the "meat market" mentality that often pertained in singles wards, fostering unhealthy competition for dates and a relentless round of gossip. Char, forty-two, says her fifteen years in singles wards made her appreciate something she'd never noticed before about Jane Austen novels: that there was a social "season" for only one part of each calendar year. In Mormon singles wards, by contrast, "there was one long exhausting season."[42] Brandon thinks this social preoccupation of many singles wards detracts from the religious emphasis that should be present on Sundays. "Church can be distinct and focused on the Savior," he says. "It doesn't need to meet all the social needs."

As it moves forward, the LDS Church faces a potential minefield, since some members love singles wards and may even stop attending church altogether if they are reassigned to a conventional ward, and others passionately wish singles wards did not exist. This conversation about singles at church takes place against the backdrop of the church's growing emphases on marriage and the family, with some singles feeling left out of a "plan of happiness" that is predicated on temple marriage. "I feel like the family has become an idol to the church, and we worship it," says Chelsea. The church's expectations of the nuclear family are also inextricably tied to its understanding of the sacred role of women, which is the topic we turn to next.

CHAPTER 5

Millennial Women and Shifting Gender Expectations

At the start of her sophomore year at BYU, Elysse went to the neuroscience department to officially declare her major.[1] She arrived at the appointment ten minutes early, armed with her résumé and a list of impressive academic achievements from high school, when she had been a National Merit Scholar and a straight-A student. She handed her documents across the desk to the man, who did not even look at them, but instead eyed her with disdain, taking in the pink dress she was wearing, the styled blond hair. Throughout the awkward interview, she posed several of the questions she had prepared in advance, and he replied in vague terms before handing the documents back to her—still unread.

"It's a lot of math and science," he said dismissively. "If you're bad at that, you probably shouldn't be here." Elysse was stunned. She had completed three medical internships and won a state gold medal and a national bronze medal for her medical work. Who was he to say she was bad at math and science? She started to protest, but he cut her off. "Look, a lot of students who thought they were academically inclined in high school get here and realize they're really social butterflies, and they don't do as well as they expected," he said.

The experience stung, particularly because at no time did this would-be adviser ask Elysse about her experience or research interests. He did not regard her as a serious candidate, and it was because of her gender. He viewed her as a "social butterfly," someone who had come to the university mostly to date and meet a husband. "If it were 1970, I'd expect this kind of treatment," Elysse says. But this happened in 2008. She never did major in neuroscience at BYU, but the story has a happy ending: now twenty-six, she's getting a doctorate in neuroscience at Harvard University, where her talents are appreciated and she works around a hundred hours a week. Nobody today would ever accuse her of not being serious about science.

Elysse's experience of sexism in Mormon culture is dramatic, but it differs from other women's more in degree than in kind. Dedicated to a particular version of family values in which women are seen as primarily responsible for bearing and nurturing children, Mormonism is sometimes at odds with recent shifts that have taken place in American culture, a divide that is more keenly felt in the younger generation.

NINE POINTS MORE RELIGIOUS

Many studies have pointed out that, in the United States, women tend to be more religious than men, particularly in conservative faith traditions.[2] The NMS was no different. On average, Mormon women are about nine points more religiously orthodox than men, as seen in Table 5.1. Given a scale of belief, women came out ahead on nearly every measure in selecting the most certain, confident response.[3] Many men chose the second possible response ("I believe and have faith that this is probably true"), so it's not like Mormon men are unbelievers. However, they do not profess the same degree of theological certainty as women, on average. Women's certainty flags only with questions of exclusion: the four testimony questions that ranked last for both women and men all have to do with Mormons having exclusive access to eternal families and exaltation, or with priesthood restrictions on women or African Americans.

Women's more pronounced religiosity was evident in other parts of the survey as well. For example, in the question about favorite parts of being Mormon, women were more likely than men to identify specific theological tenets such as the church's emphasis on the Savior, the comfort of having a prophet, and the knowledge that families can be together forever (Table 5.2). These ranked highly for men as well, though not as highly as for women. Where men surpassed women was in pragmatic assessments of what Mormonism might add to their lives here on Earth, like keeping them free from addiction, presenting them with opportunities to serve others, and embedding them in a strong community that focuses on children and youth. The only overtly religious area in which men even slightly outstripped women was in the temple, which as we saw in chapter 3 can sometimes be a problematic experience for women. However, the temple results are so close that it is difficult to draw conclusions from that slight gender difference.

In terms of religious behavior, LDS women are a bit more likely than LDS men to pray and read their scriptures daily, watch General Conference,

Table 5.1. MORMON TESTIMONY STATEMENTS, BY GENDER

	Men Who Are "Confident and Know This Is True"	Women Who Are "Confident and Know This Is True"	Delta (Ordered from Greatest to Least Difference)
Jesus Christ was literally resurrected and rose from the dead.	61	76	+15
God is real.	69	83	+14
There is life after death.	63	76	+13
God has a plan for my life and I will be happier if I follow that plan.	60	73	+13
God created Adam and Eve sometime in the last 10,000 years and humans did not evolve from other life forms.	47	59	+12
Jesus Christ is the Savior of the world and died to reconcile humanity to God.	68	79	+11
The LDS First Presidency members and apostles are God's prophets on the earth today.	53	62	+9
The Book of Mormon is a literal, historical account.	50	59	+9
Joseph Smith was a prophet of God.	52	61	+9
God is an exalted person of flesh and bone.	55	62	+7
God's priesthood authority is reserved only for men, not women.	44	51	+7
The LDS Church is the only true faith leading to exaltation.	48	53	+5
LDS temple sealings are ultimately the only way for families to be eternal.	50	53	+3
The priesthood and temple ban on members of African descent was inspired of God and was God's will for the Church until 1978.	37	36	−1
Average	54	63	+9

Table 5.2. FAVORITE PARTS OF BEING MORMON, BY GENDER

	All	Men	Women
Emphasis on the Savior	47	42	51
The knowledge that families can be together forever	47	42	51
The peace my faith provides in hard times	42	36	48
The strong community I enjoy at church	31	36	27
The comfort of having a prophet on the earth today	26	22	28
The opportunities the Church provides me to serve other people	21	25	18
The focus on children and youth	20	22	19
Temple worship	18	19	18
The good health and freedom from addiction that comes with keeping the Word of Wisdom	17	22	13

steer clear of R-rated movies, see sacrament meeting as "uplifting and interesting," and hold a current temple recommend. Mormon women are also nine points more likely to strongly agree that being Mormon is an essential part of their core identity, and more likely to feel proud if a fellow Mormon were elected president of the United States.

In multiple measures of belief and belonging, then, women appear to be more orthodox than men.[4] This trope is reinforced in Mormon leaders' statements about women, which evince a consistent emphasis on women being inherently spiritual and selfless. So it is a live question whether Mormon women are more orthodox because they are "naturally" religious or because they have been socialized all their lives by leaders' assertions that women are more loving, kind, and in tune with the Lord.[5] Regardless of the genesis of women's religiosity, its existence is frequently remarked upon in Mormon culture. "My wife is extremely proactive and she is a saint," says Ammon, twenty-five.[6] She has instituted a tradition where every evening, no matter what kind of day they have had or how they are feeling, she and Ammon open a scripture app and take turns reading aloud for at least twenty minutes. His wife has also been instrumental in upping the ante on their family tithing habits. He credits her initiative with keeping him on the straight and narrow. "She's one of the good ones, you know? She keeps me strong. I feel like I don't do nearly as much to push her as she pushes me."

SEPARATE SPHERES

Segregation by sex begins early in Mormonism, starting in a limited way at age eight, which is also the age of accountability and baptism. That's when boys and girls who have been together in Primary since age three begin to attend single-sex evening activities like Cub Scouts for young boys (weekly) and "Activity Days" for girls (biweekly or less often). At twelve, gender segregation becomes more pronounced, as girls begin attending the Young Women program on Sundays and one evening a week, and boys are ordained to the Aaronic priesthood (and generally continue in Scouting on weeknights and occasional weekends). Throughout adolescence, boys advance through the ranks of the Aaronic priesthood, with growing responsibilities as they go. Even a twelve-year-old deacon, the entry-level position of the Aaronic priesthood, can pass the sacrament on Sunday, gather fast offerings, and help with the upkeep of the building. At age sixteen, a young man can become a priest, the highest level in the Aaronic priesthood, where he is authorized to baptize new members, bless and administer the sacrament, and teach the gospel.[7]

In the LDS Church's instructions about the duties of the Aaronic priesthood, there are three paragraphs addressed to girls. The blessings of the priesthood, the instructions state, are available to everyone—male and female, rich and poor. Everyone is entitled to its saving ordinances. Girls are not missing out on anything by not exercising the priesthood or having important responsibilities themselves; it is enough merely to be on the receiving end of priesthood ordinances. This is quite different from the message that boys receive about priesthood in these same instructions: that it is the exercising of it that helps a young man grow in faith. The article itself indicates that actions such as giving priesthood blessings, caring for the sacrament, and contributing to the temporal health of ward members will bring boys closer to God. Girls, however, are expected to deepen their relationship with God in a more passive way that is unspecified. This subordinate role is reinforced by the remarks of a boy quoted in the instructions, explaining how teen girls can further the cause of the priesthood: "I think two of the biggest things they do are to dress modestly and be kind to everyone. The modest dress helps me keep my thoughts in check, and I can actually look at them while talking!"[8] Girls, according to this message, should strive to be kind and to dress conservatively so they do not tempt boys to have sexual thoughts. The subtext of these remarks is that girls *do* have a responsibility in church—namely, to be supportive and not attract attention to themselves.

Adolescence, then, is a time when gender expectations begin to be clearly defined in Mormonism. This can be painful at times, especially for girls who don't submit easily to being groomed for marriage and motherhood. In interviews, I asked what respondents thought about the different roles Mormon boys and girls played while they were in high school. Most men said it was simply not on their radar at that time (and some were surprised enough by the question that I suspect it is not much on their minds even now). But many women had clearly thought a good deal about the question, and not just in hindsight. At one point in high school, Miranda, thirty-five, discovered the huge budget disparity that existed between the amount spent on boys' Scouting activities and the much smaller amount allocated to the Young Women. "It was like, 'Here's a dollar figure attached to how much less I am valued than the Young Men in the ward,'" she says.[9] Throughout adolescence she was a square peg in the round hole of meekness and motherhood. "Everywhere but church, the message was focused on achievement and careers." The focus at church rankled her since she was academically oriented (she would go on to become an attorney). As a stay-at-home parent now, though, she has a somewhat different perspective. The church is the only environment she is part of where focusing solely on family and home is seen as a valid life choice by those around her, and she appreciates that. Right now she is still struggling with very mixed feelings about women's roles in Mormonism.

Many Mormons will take exception to this portrayal of the "separate spheres" in the LDS Church. Women and men are equal, they say, but they have different and clearly defined roles; men have priesthood and women have motherhood.[10] This focus on the strictly gendered division of duties in the church became a hallmark of Mormonism after World War II, so it is the religious and cultural expectation most living Mormons have always known. Men have gone out to work, and women have stayed home with the children; men run the church, and women do not. A content analysis of Mormon periodicals finds that women's roles as a topic of special consideration became paramount in the 1960s and 1970s, when the LDS Church was publicly resisting the social changes wrought by second-wave feminism.[11] Over the course of several turbulent years in the late 1970s and early 1980s, it worked to defeat the Equal Rights Amendment (ERA) and excommunicated ERA activist Sonia Johnson.[12] In subsequent decades, Mormon leaders' statements about issues like working mothers have softened, though the church has continued to define itself by what it calls the "traditional" family. The church resisted a push for women's ordination in the early 2010s, culminating in the widely publicized 2014 excommunication of feminist activist Kate Kelly. It did, however, allow for minor incremental changes in women's roles, such as permitting a woman to pray in General Conference for the first time, allowing a female leader to sit in on three of the previously all-male meetings at the highest levels of church governance, and—in 2017—expanding parental leave and reversing a policy that forbade female church employees from wearing pants to work.[13] In 2018, the church tempered its "separate spheres" ideology by discontinuing the gender-segregated home and visiting teaching programs in favor of a joint emphasis on "ministering" that can involve men and women, boys and girls.[14] It also introduced changes to the Young Women Camp program that aim to give teenage girls more leadership experience.[15]

In some ways, recent changes that give Mormon women more authority are a reversion to an earlier norm. Although women have never been ordained to the priesthood in Mormonism, they historically did some of the things that are today exclusively priesthood activities. Until the twentieth century, women regularly gave blessings for healing laying hands on sick women, men, and children.[16] They also controlled their own separate and autonomous organization, the Relief Society, until the 1970s, running its finances, magazine, curriculum, and charitable efforts without male supervision. Today, the Relief Society is an auxiliary organization of the church and is entirely under the direction of the all-male priesthood, and with the exception of one initiatory ritual in the temple (see chapter 3), women are no longer authorized to give priesthood blessings.

Yet theologically, Mormonism has something to offer that most Christian religions don't: a belief in a Heavenly Mother who works together with Heavenly Father for "the salvation of the human family."[17] Heavenly Mother has not been given much attention by LDS leaders, but in recent years some have begun mentioning "heavenly parents" as a divine couple, and the church issued a brief Gospel Topics essay about her in 2015. Mormons are not permitted to pray to her, but the church recognizes her existence. Penny, twenty-four, says this belief in Heavenly Mother is one of the things that helps her stay in the LDS Church.[18] "Even though we never talk about it, and it's a hidden doctrine, I appreciate that we acknowledge the possibility of a Heavenly Mother," she says. "I think Mormonism has some more feminist possibility than some other faiths, even if it's very unrealized."

Then there is the reality, noted by LDS scholars Richard and Claudia Bushman and others, that Mormonism feels to insiders more egalitarian in practice than it appears to outsiders in theory.[19] Mormon women can preach and pray in sacrament meetings, for example, and give input to male leaders when asked. It's the "when asked" part that is a sticking point. Women might speak in sacrament meeting, but men are in charge of every aspect of the service; women might teach a mixed-gender Gospel Doctrine class, but they are otherwise only given oversight of children and other women, never men. They cannot be Sunday School presidents, ward clerks, or stake executive secretaries. And while they are called to leadership positions within the Relief Society, most major decisions—even whom a Relief Society president may call as her counselors—are ultimately made by the ward bishop.

At the core of Mormonism's gendered division of labor is the question of leadership and the priesthood. Most contemporary Latter-day Saints support the church's position that the priesthood should be reserved only for men, a fact that has been confirmed by several previous studies of Mormons' attitudes toward women's ordination. These studies have also found that women themselves, somewhat counterintuitively, are more opposed to women's ordination than men are.[20]

The NMS confirmed both of these findings, but differed in two key areas. First, there are significant generational differences in how older Mormons view women and priesthood compared to younger ones.[21] We asked respondents their level of agreement with the statement "The fact that women do not hold the priesthood sometimes bothers me," a question that was first asked by David Campbell, John Green, and Quin Monson in a 2012 survey.[22] A majority of Millennial Mormons are indeed sometimes "bothered" by the fact that women do not hold the priesthood, which is a significant reversal of the views of older Mormons (Table 5.3). Overall, more than twice as many Millennials (59 percent) are bothered by women's exclusion from the priesthood as Boomer/Silents (24 percent). It's particularly interesting to note the high percentage of Boomers and Silents who "strongly" disagree about women and priesthood: 61 percent. This is not a tepid opposition.

Although this question raises the fraught issue of women's ordination, it is worded in such a way that believers are not called to go against the LDS prophet or apostles if they are troubled by women's lack of priesthood. There's no advocacy here or agitation for change, but merely an inquiry about feelings. So this question doesn't necessarily measure whether Mormons actively want things to change. Still, these results are interesting, especially insofar as they reveal major generational differences between Millennial Mormons and older ones.[23]

Another question, differently worded, may shed additional light. When we remove the word "priesthood" and pose a more general question about

Table 5.3. MORMONS WHO AGREE THAT "THE FACT THAT WOMEN DO NOT HOLD THE PRIESTHOOD SOMETIMES BOTHERS ME," BY GENERATION

	Boomer/Silent	GenX	Millennial
"Strongly" or "somewhat" agree	24	48	59
"Strongly" or "somewhat" disagree	77	52	41

how Mormons feel about women's influence in the church, Boomer/Silent Mormons soften a bit (Table 5.4). Respondents were asked whether they agreed or disagreed with the notion that "women do not have enough say in the LDS Church." This is a broader statement about the visibility of female leadership, not the specific flashpoint issue of priesthood ordination. Women can have "say" without priesthood, and in fact some could argue that they had more "say" in the church in earlier decades when women controlled the Relief Society's budget, expenditures, and activities. In fact, many Boomer/Silent Mormons would personally remember a time when that was the case.

As we can see by comparing Tables 5.3 and 5.4, the numbers rise only slightly for Millennials and GenXers when we take priesthood ordination off the agenda. The difference is greater for older Mormons: an eight-point rise for the Boomer/Silent generations. This may suggest that the word "priesthood" itself is a trigger for older Mormons in a way that is not true of younger ones. Among Boomers and Silents, the idea of women's leadership is still unpopular, but it has gone from just a quarter who said they were sometimes bothered that women don't have the priesthood to nearly a third who believe that women don't have enough "say."

These findings indicate that a generational shift in attitudes about women's religious leadership may be underway. But what can we learn from also surveying *former* Mormons? Not surprisingly, former Mormons are significantly more supportive of women's ordination than current Mormons are. Overall, three-quarters of them are troubled that the priesthood is reserved only for men in the church; moreover, of that 74 percent who say they are troubled, the vast majority are "very troubled." Only 8 percent of former Mormons say they are confident and know for certain that "God's priesthood authority is reserved for men, not women."

One trend in the research on current Mormons—that men were more likely to be supportive of women's leadership than women were—does not hold true among former Mormons. Former Mormon women seem particularly exercised about women's roles. For example, just over a third of former Mormon men said they were "very troubled" that women do not hold the

Table 5.4. MORMONS WHO AGREE THAT "WOMEN DO NOT HAVE ENOUGH SAY IN THE LDS CHURCH," BY GENERATION

	Boomer/Silent	GenX	Millennial
"Strongly" or "somewhat" agree	32	52	61
"Strongly" or "somewhat" disagree	68	48	39

priesthood, compared to 57 percent of former Mormon women. Women's issues turn out to be a significant reason that women choose to leave the LDS Church, as we will see in chapter 11.

Why does women's religious leadership matter? The "Gender and Religious Representation" survey by Benjamin Knoll and Cammie Jo Bolin, which used a religiously diverse sample of Americans, demonstrates that women who attend congregations in which women make up at least half of the religious leadership have higher levels of religious belief, identity, and "efficacy" (confidence that their opinions matter in their congregations) than other women.[24] This effect is not limited to how women feel and behave religiously, but extends to other areas of their lives. For example, the presence of women as religious leaders in female respondents' childhoods contributed to better educational and socioeconomic outcomes for those women as adults, even after controlling for other factors. The positive results were particularly marked for women with more liberal theological and political views—the very ones who may be, in Mormonism at least, more likely to simply leave the church than to continue to chafe at restrictions they feel within it.

GENDER: AN ETERNAL CHARACTERISTIC

The church's evolving tug of war over women's roles is encapsulated by "The Family: A Proclamation to the World," a 1995 First Presidency statement that upholds a gendered division of labor as divinely ordained. Although the Proclamation is not included as scripture in the LDS canon, it is often quoted in General Conference and has been framed and displayed in thousands of Mormon homes. "By divine design, fathers are to preside over their families in love and righteousness and are responsible to provide the necessities of life and protection for their families," it reads. "Mothers are primarily responsible for the nurture of their children. In these sacred responsibilities, fathers and mothers are obligated to help one another as equal partners." Herein lies a tension, because in Mormonism to "preside" means to have charge over. In the home, then, the task of presiding is given to the husband "by divine design," which would seem to be a clear approval of patriarchy. However, the Proclamation also insists that husbands and wives are "equal partners," which makes the old-fashioned idea of a man presiding significantly more complicated. If a disagreement arises, does the husband have the right to overrule his wife? Do they take turns deciding? How are terms like "equality" and "partnership" to coexist next to ones like "preside"? These are the kinds of questions that define Mormonism's ongoing negotiation of women's roles.

In addition to supporting a gendered division of labor, the Proclamation on the Family makes a significant theological claim about gender in Mormonism. "Gender is an essential characteristic of individual premortal, mortal, and eternal identity and purpose," it reads. Gender, in the Mormon view, is not a social construct or something that is absorbed in childhood; it carries through each stage of premortal, mortal, and postmortal life. Gender is forever.

One ardent supporter of this part of the Proclamation is Annabel, twenty-nine. "My spirit is female," she says. "That's eternal. . . . I will always be a woman."[25] Like many LDS women, she is deeply religious, prays every day, and thinks the Bible and the Book of Mormon are the word of God. She feels called to be a mother and begins to cry during our interview because she worries that despite her "very strong maternal instincts" she may never have a child of her own, for a couple of reasons.

The first is that Annabel was born as Christopher, and is transgender. When she was eight or nine, she knew that something was different about her, but she didn't have fancy words like "transgender" to describe what she was feeling. Nor did she have any examples of transgender individuals who might guide her through it. All she knew was that she wanted, more than anything, to be a girl. But she mentioned none of this gender dysphoria to her straight-laced Mormon family until she was twenty-four, when she sat shaking on her parents' couch and worked up the courage to tell them the truth. "They didn't really know how to respond, or what questions to ask. They were just lost, I guess." That was five years ago, and while her parents have made some concessions—eventually allowing her to wear dresses at their house, for example—they still will not call her Annabel.

Some rapprochement has occurred recently because of the second major issue in Annabel's life: she is dying. Two years ago, she was diagnosed with glioblastoma multiforme (GBM), an aggressive form of brain cancer, and she's defied the odds by surviving even this long. In our interview, I asked Annabel if she was glad, knowing that her life will be short, that she decided to live her final years authentically, as the woman she knew herself to be.

> I am grateful for all the choices I've made—the transition, all the things. I have some regrets, but . . . I'm a person who likes to live in the now. Maybe that's a side effect of not having a future to live in, but for me it's always been the now. And right now, I am happy.

One bright spot in Annabel's life has been the church, even though her Mormon family has mostly kept their distance (when I interviewed her, Annabel said she thought her youngest brother was leaving for a mission that week, but she had not been invited to say goodbye). The ward has become like a surrogate family. When she first arrived, she introduced herself to the bishop as a trans woman and he said, "Great!," immediately followed by, "I don't know what transgender is." So he called in the Relief Society president, who was also a professional therapist, while Annabel was sitting there in his office. "So she comes in and says, 'What's up?' And I go, 'I'm transgender.' And she goes, 'Wonderful! Do you want to be a visiting teacher?' And I've had a great experience with the entire ward ever since."

Annabel's story, while unusual, points toward a complex reality of Mormonism and gender in the twenty-first century. The binary division of "male" and "female" is being challenged in an era when some people, especially younger people, are coming to understand gender, like sexual orientation, as a broad spectrum more than an either-or proposition. Transgender people remain a tiny minority in the American population, around one-half of 1 percent.[26] This means that in every thousand people, only five or six will identify as transgender. That's true of the NMS as well; only eight individuals in our full sample of 1,696 respondents said they were "transgender" or "other." (Incidentally, all eight identified as former Mormons. Annabel, who as an interviewee was not part of the survey sample, is exceptional in her determination to stay active in the LDS Church.) It remains to be seen how the church will navigate a landscape in which the gender binary of male and female may not be clear-cut for everyone. Given how important gender roles and gender segregation are in Mormonism, anything that crosses those boundaries—the literal meaning of "trans"—leads to terra incognita.

As of this writing, the LDS Handbook states that transgender individuals should not have sex reassignment surgery, which will result in certain restrictions on temple recommends or priesthood ordination.[27] However, there is no Handbook guidance about persons who are transgender but have *not* had surgery to change their sexual organs or physical appearance. Annabel is in this category. She has never had surgery, but she takes daily hormones, including an estrogen pill and a testosterone blocker. She looks, sounds, and dresses like a woman. Also in this category is Grayson, a twenty-three-year-old Mormon who transitioned to male while in adolescence.[28] Unlike Annabel's family, Grayson's parents have been tremendously supportive throughout. His mom in particular "has always been in my corner," even serving as the president of the Mama Dragons, an advocacy organization for parents of LGBT youth. Despite the unconditional love of his family, it has been a tough road for Grayson at times. The church did not permit him to serve a mission when he came of age, and he has never held a temple recommend. "I have been temple recommend worthy this whole time, but I don't fit in the gender boxes, so I can't go," he says. Still, he has found his local wards to be mostly supportive, and when he transitioned, his bishop was compassionate. "Because there's very little guidance about transgender issues in the Handbook, it just comes down to how empathetic your particular bishop happens to be," Grayson says, citing the common Mormon phrase "bishop roulette" to describe how much depends on the chance assignment of local leaders. "If you get lucky, as I did, you can kind of skate by on 'ain't no rule.'"

Given how crucial gender roles are to Mormonism's self-definition—and the attention transgender issues have received in the wider culture—it is unlikely that policies about transgender Mormons will remain this vague. Mormon theology is deeply invested in the Proclamation's notion that gender is an eternal characteristic, and Mormon culture often manifests strict gender binaries in ways that are unwritten yet important. Even dress standards that blur those boundaries and are considered appropriate outside Mormon culture, such as women wearing pants to church or men sporting a "man bun," are criticized within some pockets of Mormondom.[29] Transgender individuals who question the sex assignment they received at birth—or, worse in the eyes of the LDS Church, challenge the notion that gender expression should be limited to the binary categories of male and female—raise new questions about gender roles and sex segregation in Mormonism.

NEW HORIZONS FOR MORMON WOMEN

As the LDS Church continues to navigate the evolving gender roles of the twenty-first century, it does so amidst a changing landscape of opportunities for women. Three significant shifts in particular have altered young Mormon women's lives, potentially expanding their opportunities in the world.

The first of these is family size. Where fertility is concerned, Mormon couples have consistently and handily beaten the national average for decades, averaging nearly four children apiece.[30] In our survey of current Mormons, that held true almost exactly: the current Mormons in our sample reported that they grew up in families of 4.02 children, on average. Large families were a staple of Mormon life into the twenty-first century, with Armand Mauss noting in 1994 that "Mormon family size has remained close to twice the national average."[31]

Yet this appears to be changing, as the NMS data shows a smaller family size among younger Mormons. In Table 5.5, for example, the option of "1–2 children" accounted for just over one in five Boomer/Silent respondents as they described the families they grew up in, versus one in three Millennials. Large families of five or more children went from 39 percent of the

Table 5.5. NUMBER OF CHILDREN IN MORMONS' FAMILIES OF ORIGIN, BY GENERATION

Number of Children in Your Family Growing Up	Boomer/Silent	GenX	Millennial
1–2 children	22%	30%	32%
3–4 children	40%	33%	38%
5–6 children	24%	25%	18%
7 or more children	15%	13%	12%

Boomer/Silent respondents to 30 percent among today's Millennials when they were growing up.

This trend becomes even more apparent when we look at fertility in the respondents' own families that they have created as adults. For this purpose, we will focus on comparing the Boomer/Silent generation with GenX, since most of the Millennials in our survey are still within their childbearing years. (The Millennials' data is presented in Table 5.6, but it should be taken with a grain of salt because it will surely change as they age.) The GenXers in our sample, ages thirty-seven to fifty-one at the time of the survey, are nearing the end of their childbearing years, and therefore offer a more valid basis of comparison with the Boomer/Silent cohort.

As expected, LDS families appear to be getting smaller. Between the oldest Mormons and the GenXers, the categories that showed an increase were "no children" and "1–2 children." Every one of the large-family categories shows a decline, and the decline is especially precipitous in the "super-sized" clans of five or more children. While nearly a quarter of Boomer/Silents had five or more, only about 12 percent of GenXers can say the same—meaning that the rate of super-sized families was cut in half between just two generations. Looked at another way, a majority of current Mormon GenXers have zero, one, or two children.

What does this mean for Millennials? Overall, we have seen that Millennial Mormons are a sort of hybrid: they are in some ways like older Mormons but also like their non-Mormon peers. So Millennials' families will likely be smaller than their Mormon grandparents' and parents' families, but larger than their non-Mormon friends'. As one social scientist put it upon seeing preliminary data, for younger Mormons' families, "four is the new six, and two is the new four."

What do smaller families mean for Mormon women? Many studies have shown that having fewer children correlates with additional years of completed education for women, which leads to the second point: many Mormon women are taking advantage of higher education. Education in

Table 5.6. NUMBER OF CHILDREN IN MORMONS' OWN FAMILIES, BY GENERATION

The Number of Children You Have Had	Boomer/Silent	GenX	(Millennial)*
0 children	11%	18%	(49%)
1–2 children	29%	40%	(37%)
3–4 children	36%	30%	(12%)
5–6 children	16%	9%	(2%)
7 or more children	8%	3%	(.2%)

* In this table, Millennials' fertility information is presented in parentheses because it should be viewed as a current snapshot that is going to change as more Millennials (ages eighteen to thirty-six at the time of the survey) have children.

Mormonism has long been put forward as a positive good, with church leaders encouraging young people to get all the education they can and emphasizing an LDS scripture that "the glory of God is intelligence."[32] Mormons believe that education is not merely a stepping stone to a better career in this life but also a valuable refining fire for the soul, since any knowledge gained here on Earth can be taken into the world to come. However, church leaders have not always given the same advice about education to men and women. They have instructed men to magnify their skills so they can become successful at work and provide for a family. For women, by contrast, education is portrayed as a means to become better mothers who are able to teach and guide their children, and as a practical stopgap measure should a husband's death or disability ever force a woman into the workplace.[33]

Mormon women are now surpassing men in certain kinds of educational achievement. Two-thirds of the women in the NMS's current Mormon sample have completed at least some college (65 percent), compared to just over half of men (54 percent). This reflects the larger national trend that women are outstripping men in college attendance and college degrees, which reverses the trajectory of older generations.[34] For Boomer/Silent Mormons, for whom college graduation in general was a relatively rare phenomenon, one in five men earned a college degree (21 percent) but only 14 percent of women did. Among GenX men, just over a quarter had a four-year college degree (27 percent) and more than a third of GenX women did (35 percent). So from the Boomer/Silent age group to GenX, men only increased their college degree attainment by six points (21 to 27 percent), while women's jumped by more than twenty points (14 to 35 percent).[35] This reflects a remarkable change in just one to two generations.

For postgraduate education (master's degrees, doctorates, or professional education such as law or medical degrees), Mormon men still lead women: 13 percent of men have earned such degrees, compared to just under 7 percent of women. The male advantage in postgraduate education is particularly pronounced in Utah, where nearly three times as many men as women earn advanced degrees (20 percent of men vs. 7 percent of women). For Mormons outside Utah, 10 percent of women obtain such degrees, while the rate for men dips slightly, to 16 percent. So while substantially more Utah Mormon men earned a postgraduate degree compared to Utah Mormon women, outside of Utah that gap shrinks considerably. On another note, women in Utah are ten points more likely to have completed "some college" but not have earned a college degree than LDS women elsewhere in the country.[36]

When it comes to education and gender, culture and geographic location, not just religion, influence a person's trajectory. Mormon women as a whole are more likely than women of the general population to have completed some college, though they are a little less likely to have finished their college degree. This reflects the fact that a portion of Mormon women continue to marry young, have children early, and drop out of school, sometimes forever. This trend is clearly more pronounced in Utah, however, where early marriage and higher fertility remain cultural touchstones. Outside of Utah, Mormon women are more likely to finish college and even to pursue postgraduate education, while men are a bit less likely to do so. What we can take from this is that in Utah, there is still a strong cultural imperative for men to succeed in their careers, which means getting a good education; this has been less of a mandate for Utah women.

Education matters, not just to women's own socioeconomic opportunities and personal fulfillment, but to their future religious adherence as well. Although some religious leaders have through the years expressed suspicion that higher education would lead to skepticism about organized religion, there's evidence that Christians with a college education are more likely to stay religiously active, as we saw in chapter 1.[37] The NMS confirmed that Mormons with college degrees are 15 percent less likely to leave the church, but also discovered something else: this is not always the case for women. Having a college degree decreases women's likelihood of disaffiliating, yes, but women who follow college with certain kinds of postgraduate education like an MA or a PhD are actually *more* likely to leave. Women's retention does not appear to be adversely affected when they receive professional degrees in law, medicine, or business; the correlation between postgraduate education and leaving the church exists solely for women with academic degrees. Among men, additional education correlates with greater retention no matter what kind of advanced degree is

Table 5.7. CURRENT MORMONS WHO HAD A MOTHER WHO WORKED OUTSIDE THE HOME, BY GENERATION

"Growing Up, Did Your Mother Work outside the Home, and If So, Was It Full Time or Part Time?"	Boomer/ Silent	GenX	Millennial
Yes, full time	33%	46%	54%
Yes, part time	24%	25%	21%
No	43%	29%	25%

pursued. If further research bears this out (and we should keep in mind that the number of Mormon women with advanced degrees is small enough to encourage caution about generalizing these results), it is worth asking why some very highly educated women are more likely to leave the fold.

Fertility and education aren't the only matters reflecting significant transformation. Mormon women's lives are changing in the arena of employment—as are women's nationally. For example, in 1950, only 34 percent of US women participated in the workforce; in 1998 it was 60 percent.[38] In the NMS, this trajectory is clear: Millennials were more likely than members of any other generation of Mormons to have grown up with mothers who worked outside the home (Table 5.7). Three-quarters of LDS Millennials were raised by working moms, with more than half of those mothers working full time. Among the Boomer/Silent generations, full-time working mothers were considerably more rare.

In the former Mormon sample, the picture looks a bit different (Table 5.8). Only 67 percent of Millennial former Mormons had mothers who worked outside the home, compared to 75 percent of those who remain self-identified as Mormons. In fact, Millennials and GenXers in the former Mormon sample were more likely to have had a stay-at-home mother than those same generations in the current Mormon sample, while among Boomers and Silents the percentage was almost exactly the same.

This does not necessarily mean there is a causal factor at work here. There is no evidence that merely having a stay-at-home mother makes a person more inclined to leave the church later. As we will see in chapter 11, a constellation of factors contribute to retention and disaffiliation, and in this case we would say that working mothers are also often mothers with at least some college education, and as we've just discussed, college-educated mothers are more likely to stay in the church (and presumably to raise their children to do the same). Nevertheless, the fact that younger people who have left Mormonism are more likely to have had stay-at-home mothers is an interesting correlation. Certainly the hardline rhetoric of former LDS leaders like Ezra Taft Benson, who linked working mothers to all kinds of

Table 5.8. FORMER MORMONS WHO HAD A MOTHER WHO WORKED OUTSIDE THE HOME, BY GENERATION

"Growing Up, Did Your Mother Work outside the Home, and If So, Was It Full Time or Part Time?"	Boomer/ Silent	GenX	Millennial
Yes, full time	36%	49%	46%
Yes, part time	21%	15%	21%
No	44%	36%	33%

disastrous outcomes for their children, does not bear up under scrutiny. As Benson told the sisters of the church in 1981, when the oldest of our survey's Millennials were in diapers, many active LDS families were "experiencing difficulties with their children because mother is not where she ought to be—in the home."[39] Several decades later, we can see that many children of working Mormon mothers appear to have turned out just fine.

We have explored how smaller families, rising access to higher education, and growing full-time employment mean that Mormonism is undergoing a transformation in women's roles, at least outside the governance of the church itself. While Mormonism's all-male priesthood structure is unlikely to change, women's roles are expanding in measurable ways outside of it. Mormon women today more closely resemble non-Mormon women in their family size, education, and employment choices than they did a generation ago. Mormons are still a "peculiar people," but LDS women's lives are less markedly circumscribed outside of church. Those trends, coupled with new social questions about the nature of gender itself, may be a harbinger of the soul-searching that is ahead for Mormon women, as they strive to be faithful to their religion and their heritage while also navigating a twenty-first-century world. At the same time, the church itself must determine whether its insistence on traditional gender roles remains an attractive asset that sets the religion apart in a positive way or has become a liability in the minds of younger members.[40]

CHAPTER 6

Minority Mormons and Racial Attitudes

Chelsea, twenty-five, was with fellow BYU students in the temple when she had an awkward experience.[1] She had just changed out of her wet baptismal jumpsuit into dry clothes, and was waiting for elders of the church to place their hands on her head and pronounce words of blessing for the deceased women for whom Chelsea served as proxy. Something, however, was not proceeding according to the script. The man assigned to perform the blessing was fascinated by Chelsea's hair. Though she normally wore it straightened, it had reverted back to its naturally curly state after getting wet in the baptismal font. Perhaps the man had never touched an African American woman's hair before, because he exclaimed, "Oh my gosh! Feel her hair! It's so fluffy and fuzzy." He then motioned for another man who was officially witnessing the ordinance to check it out: "Brother, you've got to feel her hair!" The second brother merely "smiled awkwardly" and ignored the invitation, so the first went ahead with the blessings. Even as he was saying the sacred words, Chelsea said, "he was still feeling and rubbing his fingers through my hair. It was so uncomfortable."

It was not Chelsea's first uneasy experience at BYU. The native New Yorker counts herself "very, very lucky and blessed to never have experienced overt racism" while living in Utah, though she says "there were definitely microaggressions."[2] Fellow students asked whether she had enrolled at BYU to play sports, for example, but she is not athletic. They presumed she would like rap music, whereas she prefers Shania Twain and Celine Dion. They inquired whether she knew this or that African American student on campus, "like we all know each other." And people assumed she liked fried chicken and watermelon just because she was black. (She does happen to like fried chicken and watermelon but, as she rightly asks, "really, who *doesn't*?")

Students' conjectures were not generally made with harmful intentions, and in fact one student who believed Chelsea would like rap music purposely blasted rap in their shared dorm space because she was hoping Chelsea would be attracted to it and become her friend.[3] Still, each incident carried a sting, and it was hard to know how to respond. "I was so determined not to cause waves about it that I was complacent about whatever was said to me. In a homogeneous white state like Utah, if you are out of that box you are seen as representative of the entire demographic you came from—for me, that all black people were haughty or rude or whatever." So during that awkward moment in the temple when a white man felt free to plunge his hands into her hair—and invite another man to do so without Chelsea's permission—she said nothing even though she felt "deeply uncomfortable." She didn't have the confidence then that she has now, she says, so she tried to laugh and go along. "I tried to blend in and not stand out, as much as I could." She regrets that now.

Chelsea is no longer an active Mormon, but her disaffection was catalyzed not by racism so much as by the LDS Church's actions toward LGBT members, which we'll learn more about in the next chapter. (The church's LGBT policy was leaked on November 5, 2015; on November 6, Chelsea stopped wearing her temple garments.) Race, however, did not make her time as an active Mormon very easy. One time at BYU, she was having a conversation with her stake president about dating when he remarked, "I imagine it's a little difficult for you because of your situation." He didn't say, "Dating is harder for you because you are black," but they both knew he was talking about race. Being African American *did* limit her dating options within the church, because racial prejudice still exists. "You still have a lot of Mormons thinking they can't marry outside their race," she explains.

Chelsea's story fits into a long and complex story about Mormonism and race, particularly about African Americans. Until 1978, the church forbade priesthood ordination to men of African descent and temple entrance to black men and women, prohibiting them from participating in sacred rituals such as endowments and eternal marriage. Even though that policy was rescinded more than forty years ago, its legacy is unsettling for some Mormons who wonder what to do with it theologically—was it a human mistake, or a policy inspired by God for reasons people don't understand? Mormons' views on race are complex, as this chapter will show, and the experiences and views of Mormons of color defy easy characterization.

Mormons are not a racially diverse people in the United States, with nearly nine out of ten respondents self-identifying as white. Overall, the racial breakdown in the NMS was similar to previous research that has surveyed Latter-day Saints in America. Table 6.1 presents a sampling of various studies on Mormonism's racial profile over recent years, showing continuity over time.

There was some variation by age group. Whereas 93 percent of Mormonism's Boomer/Silent generation is white, only 81 percent of LDS Millennials are. Although Millennials are the most racially diverse of all Mormons, with two in ten being nonwhite, they are not as racially diverse as non-Mormons of their generation; among Millennials in the US population generally, more than four in ten are nonwhite.[4] Mormonism's Millennial generation is not diversifying at a rate that matches the rapidly changing general population, which is expected to be majority nonwhite by 2042.[5] While the nation changes, Mormonism has remained much the same racially.

Table 6.1. MORMONISM'S RACIAL COMPOSITION

	Faith Matters Survey, 2006[a]	American Religious Identification Survey (ARIS), 2007–2008[b]	Pew, 2007 Religious Landscape Study (RLS)[c]	Pew, 2011 Mormons in America Study[d]	Pew, 2014 RLS[e]	The Next Mormons, 2016
White	86%	91%	86%	88%	85%	87%
Black		3%	3%	1%	1%	4%
Hispanic/Latino[f]		3%	7%	7%	8%	4%
Asian					1%	2%
Native American						1%
Other	14%	3%	5%	4%	5%	1%

[a] See Robert D. Putnam and David E. Campbell, *American Grace: How Religion Divides and Unites Us* (New York: Simon & Schuster, 2010), 293.
[b] Rick Phillips and Ryan T. Cragun, "Mormons in the United States, 1990–2008: Socio-demographic Trends and Regional Differences," American Religious Identification Survey 2008, http://commons.trincoll.edu/aris/files/2011/12/Mormons2008.pdf.
[c] Pew Forum, "A Portrait of Mormons in America," Pew Research Center, http://www.pewforum.org/2009/07/24/a-portrait-of-mormons-in-the-us/#3.
[d] Pew Forum, "Mormons in America: Certain in Their Beliefs, Uncertain of Their Place in Society," January 12, 2012, 76, http://www.pewforum.org/2012/01/12/mormons-in-america-executive-summary/.
[e] Pew Forum, "Mormons," 2014 Religious Landscape Study, http://www.pewforum.org/religious-landscape-study/religious-tradition/mormon/.
[f] The NMS used the category "Hispanic/Latino," which included fifty current Mormon respondents. This language conflates ethnicity (Hispanic) with race (Latino) but was chosen because of its compatibility with previous surveys. In the book I have referred to this group by the less problematic word "Latinx," which is a gender-neutral term that includes multiple identities.

This can be lonely for nonwhite Mormons. Rebecca, thirty-seven, grew up in Mauritius to parents of Indian descent, and came to Utah for college when she was twenty-one.[6] She had long been attracted to the LDS religion, but her father, a staunch Catholic, had never allowed her or her brother to be baptized as Mormons when they were living at home. So coming to Utah offered not only the prospect of a solid education but also the possibility that she might fulfill her dream of joining the church, which she did. It was a culture shock, however. In a Sunday School lesson when she was a new convert, for example, she was surprised when an older man raised his hand and said, "You know, regarding the Negroes. . . ."

> I remember looking around the room and thinking, "Wow, he just used the word 'Negro' and no one is saying anything." Back home we don't identify people by color, but by nationality. To hear people define others or themselves by colors was just shocking to me, and I felt it was wrong. How was that even OK?

Rebecca frequently endured stereotypes that white Americans made about Mauritius, knowing nothing about her country. For an international cultural activity at church, Rebecca wore Indian clothing, made some treats from her culture, and brought artifacts to show. But some of the questions were bizarre, she says, like where people in her country obtained their food. "They were thinking I live on an island that's primitive. They probably think I row in a boat to go find food, or something. And I was like, 'No, this is like Hawaii. It's a major place, very cosmopolitan.' I found that misunderstanding a lot in Utah."

More disturbingly, Rebecca also heard some church members repeat a lingering folk belief that the reason some people were born outside the United States in non-LDS families was because they were not righteous in the premortal life. "Sometimes they wouldn't say it openly, but use nice lingo, but that was what they were saying: 'You were born on that small island because in the spirit world you were not valiant. People who were valiant were born into white, strong LDS families in the United States.'" Rebecca held to her understanding that the gospel was distinct from any cultural attitudes that Utah Mormons may have held, and did not take such remarks to heart. She loves the LDS Church and its community, but seeks to counter racial stereotypes. For example, when she started dating, some friends warned her that "the boys who marry colored girls in Utah" did so because "they cannot marry a white girl" due to some flaw or defect the boys had, like not serving a mission. Rebecca was shocked. "The idea that superrighteous RMs [returned missionaries] wouldn't even look at a colored girl" was abhorrent to her. Now married and still living in Utah, Rebecca teaches her children about their inherent worth despite any contrary messages they might be receiving from the culture, and models for them the mantra that has carried her thus far: the culture is not the gospel.

Lillian, an Asian American thirty-eight-year-old from the Midwest, had a similar experience with the BYU dating scene.[7] "There was an unspoken understanding that white people married white people, which meant that white people also dated only white people," she says. (However, the idea does not always remain unspoken; the church's current curriculum for marriage preparation still contains a 1976 quote from a former church president advising marriage partners to be "of the same racial background generally."[8]) Lillian says she experienced some racism in the church growing up—not so much at the ward level where everyone knew her family, but in the stake where her family was considered exotic or, as she puts it, "other." The racism she felt in her midwestern stake wasn't that different from racism she experienced elsewhere in American culture, but it actually hurt more "because I expected better. If this was 'the true church,' then we were expected to be better." The fact that it was *not* much better was "hard to come to terms with as a kid." She's also had some uncomfortable experiences with racial stereotyping as an adult. When her boyfriend took her to meet people in his home ward, a friend of his parents' could not get it through her head that Lillian had been born and raised in America:

> One of the first things she asked me as I sat on her couch was, "What language do they speak in your country?" To which I replied, "Well, we speak English in America." This was followed up by, "Well, yes, but you know, what do they manufacture in your country?" And then, "What are the major exports of your country?" . . . From that moment, I knew what topics I could broach with this sister, and whether I could leave my parents alone with her if I was not there to act as a buffer.

Not everyone I talked to had experienced racism in LDS circles. Alex, twenty-three, says being a racial minority has been more of a problem with non-Mormons than it has been within the church.[9] Growing up in North Carolina, there weren't that many Mormons to begin with—just ten in his large high school—and he was the only African American, garnering him the nickname "Blackie the Mormon." His peers didn't quite know what to do with someone who was both Mormon and black. With people at church, though, he felt accepted. After seminary each morning, he would go to other members' houses for breakfast and they would drive him to school. "I had really good relationships with my peers in the church, and their parents. I would see the kids in school, and we weren't necessarily buddy-buddy, but we were definitely amiable when we saw each other. I always felt safe among my peers at church." Alex never felt ostracism in the church because of his race, though he has had difficulties as a member of another minority group: he is not strictly heterosexual. That, as we will see in the next chapter, has been a more challenging circumstance for Alex personally.

Race made it more difficult for Char, forty-two, to date and be part of the social scene when she was an undergraduate student at BYU.[10] Because she looked Asian, male students would walk up to her on campus and start speaking whatever language they had mastered on their missions: "Japanese, Chinese, Thai—I do *not* look Thai—Korean, Cambodian. Just assuming." When they asked where she was from, she would say Seattle. When they continued pressing and asked where her parents had come from, she would answer "Upstate New York and Texas." What they actually wanted to know, of course, was her ancestry, which she would finally reveal—she was born in Korea, then adopted into a huge American family that later converted to Mormonism.[11] She made a point of emphasizing to them that Mormon theology made national differences obsolete: "I was sealed to my family, which makes *that* my ancestry." What she experienced at BYU was friendly curiosity, but often with an edge: categorizing her by race and background mattered more than it should have to her fellow students. "It was never a negative racism, but it doesn't have to be negative to still be racism."

Among the people I spoke to, the worst experience I heard came from Tinesha, a student at BYU.[12] For her, racism in the church has usually been experienced as a series of microaggressions—except for one unforgettable experience when she was a child growing up in the state of Washington. She had a Primary teacher who refused to call her by her name, referring to her instead as "it" because Tinesha's parents were in an interracial marriage. The family petitioned officials in Salt Lake City for permission to attend a different ward.

Tinesha is only twenty-three years old, so she is talking about an appalling experience that happened in the twenty-first century. While the church as an institution has made serious efforts to counter racism, the ghosts of past attitudes have not been fully exorcised, and the racial composition of the membership is not staying in step with the racial diversification occurring in American society.[13]

MORMONS OF COLOR IN PROFILE

To date, little research has been done on the characteristics of nonwhite Mormons. Because Mormons as a whole constitute such a small percentage of the population (between 1.5 and 2 percent), and nonwhite Mormons appear to be about a tenth of that, it's likely that less than two-tenths of 1 percent of Americans are Mormons of color. As some of the stories above would suggest, that can make it a lonely road. In the NMS's sampling of current

Mormons, there were 146 nonwhites, including 50 African American and 50 Latinx respondents, as well as a smattering of Asian Americans, Native Americans, and people who selected the category "other." In general in this chapter, the responses of nonwhite Mormons are placed together in a single group to reduce the margin of error, giving us more confidence in any conclusions. However, there will be times where I break out African American or Latinx respondents' data specifically. Readers should be aware when this happens that the margin of error is high.

In many of their religious beliefs, Mormons of color are similar to white American Mormons, and sometimes more devout. Ninety-two percent say they are either very active or somewhat active in the LDS Church, compared to 85 percent of whites; they report equal rates of weekly prayer and slightly higher rates of daily scripture study. Nonwhite Mormons are more likely to have served a mission for the LDS Church: nearly six in ten have done so, while only four in ten white Mormons have. This is especially impressive considering that more than half of nonwhite Mormons (54.5 percent) are converts and presumably were not brought up with the goal of serving a Mormon mission. By comparison, just over a third of white Mormons report being converts (36.5 percent). Nonwhite Mormons report feeling God's presence and spiritual well-being at levels similar to white Mormons, though they are slightly less likely to "know" without a doubt that God is real. About half "believe wholeheartedly in all of the teachings of the LDS Church," which is almost exactly the same as whites. Mormons of color are a bit more likely to say the scriptures should be taken literally (46 percent, compared to 38 percent of whites). These NMS findings confirm other studies that suggest some minority groups, particularly African Americans, tend to be more religious than white Americans, with high religious attendance and belief.[14]

On other theological questions, nonwhite Mormons express lower levels of religiosity. Whereas six in ten white Mormons say they know the LDS First Presidency members and apostles are God's prophets on the earth today, only four in ten nonwhites do. Mormons of color are slightly less confident of life after death, the resurrection of Jesus, and the teaching that God is an exalted person of flesh and bone than white Mormons are. Nonwhite Mormons show a significant drop in confidence on the question of whether Joseph Smith was a prophet. While 58.5 percent of whites "know" without a doubt that this is true, only 44 percent of nonwhites do. Significantly, the drop is steepest among blacks, only a quarter of whom are sure that Smith was a prophet.[15]

There are demographic differences beyond religious belief and behavior. More than half of nonwhite Mormons grew up with a mother who worked full time outside the home (55.5 percent), compared to 43 percent of whites. About a third have never married (33 percent, vs. just 16 percent of white Mormons). It is possible that this reflects the fact that interracial marriage was for many years discouraged by the church, and it's hard for nonwhites to marry other Mormons within their race because the number of possible same-race partners is so small. Another demographic difference is that nonwhite Mormons are considerably less likely to live in Utah; only about 8 percent do, compared to nearly a third of white US Mormons. (Incidentally, not a single one of the NMS's fifty African American Mormon respondents lived in Utah; this is perhaps not surprising given that only 1 percent of Utah's population is black.[16])

It's in politics where we see the greatest divergence. Nonwhite Mormons are significantly to the left of white Mormons. Sixty-eight percent voted for or supported Barack Obama in 2012, versus 31 percent of white Latter-day Saints; two-thirds also backed Hillary Clinton in 2016. Consistent with those election patterns, a majority of nonwhite Mormons say they vote Democratic or lean toward the Democratic Party (58 percent). As we'll see in chapter 9, Mormons as a whole in the United States are politically conservative, so this is a major departure. But it's very much in line with the political habits of other Americans of color, who tend to vote Democratic. Race, then, appears to be a more central determinant of party identification than does Mormon affiliation. Race also plays a role in how different groups view the United States. Whereas seven in ten white Mormons believe that the United States is the greatest country in the world, this view is shared by only half of nonwhite Mormons.

Nonwhite Mormons are more progressive on a variety of social issues, such as the moral acceptability of drinking alcohol, gambling, getting an abortion, or having an extramarital affair. They are not, however, any more supportive of homosexuality or same-sex marriage than white Mormons. Only 28 percent of the survey's African American LDS respondents believe that same-sex marriage should be legal in all fifty states. This divide—that a majority of African Americans would oppose same-sex marriage, despite high support for other progressive social positions—has also been observed among African American Protestants.[17]

Finally, the NMS confirmed earlier research about education and race. A nonrepresentative study in the 1980s had suggested African American Mormons were better educated and more affluent than African Americans generally, which the NMS corroborated.[18] For example, 46 percent of black respondents in the NMS have a four-year college degree, which is more than double the educational achievement of African Americans nationally (21 percent) and also higher than that of white Mormons (33 percent).[19] Again, we have to be guarded given the small number of respondents, but the findings are suggestive. Theologically, African American Mormons (and other Mormons of color) are more similar to the white majority than they are different, but there are demographic, educational, and especially political dissimilarities.

BLACKS AND THE PRIESTHOOD/TEMPLE BAN

Hovering in the background of any discussion of Mormonism and race is the lingering specter of Mormonism's priesthood/temple ban, in place until 1978. (Calling it "the priesthood ban" without reference to blacks' simultaneous exclusion from the temple erases women from the story, so this book uses the term "priesthood/temple.") While the history of the ban is complex, it appears to have been codified as policy during the presidency of Brigham Young, since during Joseph Smith's era at least one African American man, Elijah Abel, was ordained to the priesthood in 1836. (He was also ordained as a Seventy and served a mission.[20]) There is evidence of other black men who held the priesthood in the 1830s and 1840s, including Q. Walker Lewis and Joseph T. Ball. In 1852, however, Young declared black men ineligible because "the people that are commonly called negroes are the children of old Cain" and "cannot bear rule in the priesthood" because of Cain's curse.[21] Young also permitted race-based slavery in Utah Territory.

Although Joseph Smith was not the primary author of the priesthood/ temple ban, he held many of the racial views that were prominent among whites in the early nineteenth century. The Book of Mormon taught that dark skin was a punishment, for example, and Smith did not apparently question the popular interpretation of Genesis that the "curse of Cain" was tied to perpetual servitude.[22] According to historian Max Perry Mueller, the difference was that Joseph Smith taught that it was possible for righteous individuals to overcome that curse, believing "race is not destiny." The Book of Mormon, for example, spoke of dark-skinned Lamanites who, upon joining with their former enemies, the Nephites, actually became light-skinned and appeared "white like unto the Nephites."[23] LDS leaders who followed Smith, however, did not adhere to his idea that race itself was mutable or impermanent, emphasizing instead that a racial hierarchy was ordained of God and only God could change it.[24]

The ban became an enduring set piece of LDS identity formation. Well into the twentieth century, LDS leaders pronounced additional reasons for it, like the notion that those with black skin had been less valiant in their premortal lives (a variation of the folk belief that Rebecca heard as the reason she was born in Mauritius). During the civil rights movement in the 1960s, Mormons' racial ban garnered negative media attention. Several college athletic teams refused to play games at BYU, and BYU athletes' appearances at other universities incited protests and accusations that the LDS Church was a racist institution.[25] For many Mormons, the experience of seeing their church at odds with the ideals of the civil rights movement was painful, and they can still describe where they were and what they were doing on June 8, 1978, when LDS President Spencer W. Kimball announced that all the blessings of the priesthood and the temple would be available henceforth to every worthy Mormon, regardless of race.[26]

The 1978 revelation did not fully resolve Mormonism's racial tensions, of course. The religion professes a core belief that God the Father is a personage of flesh and bone, rather than an ethereal being without "body, parts, or passions" as other traditions might teach.[27] Mormonism's commitment to this embodied God raises the logical question of race: in a religion that insists God has skin, what color is that skin? This is an area where Mormonism has room for theological—and artistic—growth. To date, the LDS Church's official artistic depictions of God the Father have shown him only as a white man, floating in the air next to his son Jesus, who is also white.[28] Jesus and God differ only in the color of their hair and beards: brown for the Savior and a Santa Claus white for God. Having only one kind of official artistic depiction of God the Father sends a visual signal that God is to be understood as having white skin, even if this is not a signal that LDS leaders have crafted intentionally or have articulated in living memory. Perhaps the absence of diverse renderings of God helps to explain why, when nonwhite Mormons often have religious zeal that equals or exceeds that of white Mormons, their agreement with the particular statement that "God is a being of flesh and bone" was nearly ten points lower than white Mormons'. Given the history of the church's portrayals of God the Father, saying yes to God as flesh and bone may also mean saying yes to God as a white man.[29]

The church's continuing visual emphasis on God as white is not the only racial issue that lingers in the era after the priesthood/temple ban. As Rebecca's story suggests, folk notions about "a lack of valiance" in the premortal life did not disappear after 1978. Lillian explains that when she was growing up, such explanations were all too common:

> I heard over and over again growing up that black people were unrighteous in the war in heaven so they carried the curse of Cain on earth, that they had been fence sitters. I remember even hearing some young woman at girls' camp or something say that maybe other races had been fence sitters and so they were not white either. I also heard from my parents and their educated friends that that was a load of crap, and so I knew that it was untrue, but that meant I never felt entirely safe with fellow Mormons until I knew if they were "progressive" and didn't hold with those kinds of old-school, false ideas about race.

Growing up, Lillian was never sure that other Mormons would be "safe" for her to be around, and her parents sometimes had to counter toxic messages. To determine how common such messages might be, the NMS asked respondents a series of questions about folk beliefs that were no longer official doctrine but may have been taught in church anyway, including whether the priesthood/temple ban occurred because people of African descent were less valiant in the premortal life. Overall, fewer than a quarter of Mormons said they had ever heard that taught in a church meeting or lesson, though the numbers were a bit higher among African American Mormons (30 percent). The encouraging news about these figures is that they are low, suggesting that this particularly upsetting folk belief may finally be passing out of existence. That does not make the experience easier, however, for Mormons like Lillian who have encountered such ugliness.

In 2012, racism in the LDS Church was in the news once again because a BYU religion professor was quoted in the *Washington Post* as claiming the priesthood/temple ban had been in place until 1978 because blacks were not spiritually ready to receive the priesthood before that time. He compared the situation to a child asking for car keys before being mature enough to use them.[30] The ensuing controversy was not pretty, especially since this occurred when a Mormon, Mitt Romney, was running for president of the United States and the LDS Church was in the public eye more than usual. That same month, the church issued an official statement condemning all forms of racism.[31] The next year, in 2013, it followed up with a Gospel Topics essay that denounced any prior justifications that had been advanced throughout Mormon history by various LDS apostles and prophets: "that black skin is a sign of divine disfavor or curse, or that it reflects unrighteous actions in a premortal life; that mixed-race marriages are a sin; or that blacks or people of any other race or ethnicity are inferior in any way to anyone else."[32] In Mormonism, such a clear and specific disavowal of earlier prophetic teachings is astonishingly rare, so the church was clearly making an effort to reject white supremacism. The Gospel Topics essay was also unusual in that it suggested the ban itself was the result of LDS leaders' cultural conditioning in the racial hierarchies of the nineteenth century. The essay carefully places the ban within the context of American society before and after the Civil War, and it never states that the ban was God's will.

This is interesting in light of the NMS data, because if the church is now distancing itself from its earlier teaching that the priesthood/temple ban was God's will, a majority of Mormons have not yet gotten the memo. The NMS asked whether respondents felt that the ban on members of African descent was "inspired of God and was God's will for the Church until 1978."

Respondents were given a five-point scale of possible responses, with the upshot being that nearly two-thirds of Latter-day Saints say they either know (37 percent) or believe (25.5 percent) that the ban was God's will. Another 17 percent think it *might* be true, and 22 percent say they know or believe it is false. Overall, then, a majority of Mormons still support the idea that the priesthood/temple ban was inspired by God.

On the other hand, Mormons' faith in this particular LDS teaching was significantly lower than the credence they attached to every other testimony statement in that particular series of questions (see chapter 1). The fact that only 37 percent of current Mormons said they knew it was true is downright lukewarm compared to their certainty on other testimony statements, like the number who know confidently that "God is real" (76 percent) or "Jesus Christ is the Savior of the world and died to reconcile humanity to its sins" (74 percent). Compared to that, a far lower number of Mormons are *certain* that the priesthood/temple ban was inspired.

We can also see how Mormons differed on this testimony question by gender, generation, and race. Table 6.2 shows very little difference by gender: men and women are nearly in lockstep on this question. This in itself is interesting, since as we saw in the last chapter, women come out ahead of men on testimony questions by an average of nine points. A rate of only 36 percent certainty among current Mormon women is palpably

Table 6.2. MORMONS' VIEWS ON THE PRIESTHOOD/TEMPLE BAN BY RACE, GENDER, AND GENERATION

"The priesthood and temple ban on members of African descent was inspired of God and was God's will for the church until 1978."

	I Am Confident and Know This Is True.	I Believe and Have Faith This Is Probably True.	I Believe This Might Be True, but I Have My Doubts.	I Believe This Is Probably *Not* True.	I Am Confident and Know This Is *Not* True.
Men	37%	27%	18%	7%	11%
Women	36%	24%	16%	13%	11%
Boomer/Silent	44%	22%	14%	10%	10%
GenX	30%	29%	20%	11%	11%
Millennial	37%	25%	16%	11%	11%
White	37%	24%	18%	11%	10%
Nonwhite	32%	38%	12%	6%	12%

unenthusiastic by comparison with their other responses on questions of belief. In terms of generation, we see a difference between the confidence of Boomer/Silents, 44 percent of whom view the ban as God's will, when compared to Millennials (37 percent) and especially GenXers (30 percent). It seems the idea that the ban was God's will is marginally less popular with younger Mormons, especially GenXers.

There is a slight difference in certainty when we break the data out by race, but it's more modest than I was expecting. Whereas 37 percent of white Mormons say they know the ban was God's will, just under a third (32 percent) of nonwhite Mormons view it this way. When we add together those who know with confidence that the ban was God's will with those who believe it was, *more nonwhite Mormons than white ones actually support the ban:* 70 percent of nonwhites, compared to 61 percent of whites. That also remains true when we consider only African American respondents in a group by themselves: 67 percent of African Americans know or believe the priesthood/temple ban was God's will, which is six points higher than the rate for whites.

What accounts for this counterintuitive finding? Again, we have to remember that the margin of error is high when we consider only African Americans' responses. But there is also a growing body of research that explores the views of individuals in minority populations who, paradoxically, are sometimes strong supporters of systems that justify the status quo, even if they personally are harmed by that status quo.[33] System justification theory suggests that individuals do not always act in their own self-interest if forfeiting that interest might help bolster a system or institution they care about and benefit from—in this case, the LDS Church and its belief in prophetic authority. System justification theory acknowledges that groups that appear to be oppressed have their own opinions on the matter—whether, for our purposes, that is black Mormons who have found ways to justify the priesthood/temple ban that used to be in place or Mormon women who are often the strongest defenders of gender-based priesthood restrictions.

Just because many nonwhite Mormons view the priesthood/temple ban as having been inspired by God does not mean they have warm feelings about it. About four in five say they are at least a little troubled by the ban, while only one in five are not at all troubled. (Among whites, by contrast, about one in three were not at all troubled.) One African American who is definitely bothered by it is Chelsea, whose story opened this chapter. She also is in the minority in that she is confident that the priesthood/temple ban was not God's will. "I refuse to believe that God would withhold spiritually necessary blessings because of race," she says. She places the blame for the ban on Brigham Young, whom she calls "a product of his time." Throughout our interview, Chelsea circles back several times to the temple, which she loves. She notes that Mormons believe that temple ordinances such as endowment and sealing are necessary to receive the highest levels of celestial glory in the afterlife, so she cannot accept that God would prohibit some people from receiving those ordinances and entering the celestial kingdom just because of skin color, thereby perpetuating an eternal racism.

Paul, a forty-four-year-old convert from Haiti, also views Brigham Young as responsible for the priesthood/temple ban. "Joseph Smith was a pioneer like John Brown or Harriet Tubman," he asserts.[34] An avid history buff, Paul wishes the LDS Church would more actively emphasize the stories of early African American Mormons, who traveled with the LDS pioneers and contributed to the building of Zion. The history of the priesthood/temple ban was a real problem for Paul to overcome before he would agree to be baptized with his mother and sister in 1993. "We were investigating [the church] for two months, and by that I mean I was doing some research and always bringing up racism and race in our lessons. I was like, 'The church didn't give minorities the priesthood until 1978, and I don't like that. Why are there references to being black as flint as a negative thing? Why are the Lamanites dark and the fair-skinned people good?' " During that same period, Paul's sister competed in a beauty pageant and was the runner-up. He was convinced she should have won ("my sister is ten times more beautiful, and smarter than everyone"), and that she lost because of the judges' racism, plain and simple. He was terribly angry about it, but then had a spiritual experience where he felt like the Holy Ghost commanded him to let it go. "I heard the Spirit say, 'Stop using racism for all your answers. It's keeping you from all the blessings.' Something came over me." He was baptized with his family shortly thereafter.

How Mormons of color grapple with the legacy of the priesthood/temple ban clearly varies greatly from one individual to another, with some, like Chelsea, rejecting the possibility that it could have been God's will and others, like Paul, making an uneasy peace with it. (In our interview he implies that the ban was more Brigham Young's idea than God's, but never comes out and declares it.) As seen in the data, a majority of Mormons, including those of color, believe that the priesthood/temple ban was God's will, even though this may not be the church's most recent teaching on the subject. Perhaps it will take some time before the viewpoint expressed in the Gospel Topics essay trickles down to more members in the pews. African American convert Janan Graham-Russell has observed that while the purpose of the document was to "repudiate the racism and racist folklore that had been used to explain the restriction in the past, ... the attitudes of white members, who make up the majority of the Church in the U.S., have not necessarily changed."[35]

In addition to assessing Mormons' ideas about the priesthood/temple ban, the NMS asked respondents about their racial views, particularly about racial discrimination. For example, in one question people were asked to choose which of two statements best represented their views: "Blacks who can't get ahead in this country are mostly responsible for their own condition" or "Racial discrimination is the main reason why many black people can't get ahead these days." Because this is a long-standing Pew question, we can compare the NMS data with broader US trends. Among Americans generally, 49 percent say that blacks who can't get ahead in this country are mostly responsible for their own condition, and 41 percent say racial discrimination is the main reason many black people can't get ahead.[36] Yet there are deep differences in how Americans answer this question. Over the years, the political divide Pew has measured has widened to a chasm: two-thirds of Democrats (64 percent) now say black people are the victims of racism, while only 14 percent of Republicans agree.

The Mormon data is somewhere in between, as seen in Table 6.3. About two-thirds of Mormons overall think blacks are responsible for their own

Table 6.3. MORMONS' VIEWS ON SYSTEMIC RACISM, BY RACE, GENDER, AND GENERATION

	"Blacks Who Can't Get Ahead in This Country Are Mostly Responsible for Their Own Condition."	"Racial Discrimination Is the Main Reason Why Many Black People Can't Get Ahead These Days."
All Mormons	64%	36%
White	66.5%	33.5%
Nonwhite	46% (and 38% when just considering African Americans)	54% (and 62% when just considering African Americans)
Men	66%	34%
Women	62%	38%
Boomer/Silent	71.5%	28.5%
GenX	66%	33%
Millennial	55%	45%
Democrats (and leaners)	44%	56%
Republicans (and leaners)	75%	25%

condition, with 36 percent pointing to systemic discrimination. LDS Republicans are slightly more likely than US Republicans to cite discrimination (25 vs. 14 percent), but the national patterns basically hold true among Mormons: Democrats, nonwhites, and younger people point to racism more than Republicans, whites, and older people do.

In addition to the political divide, there is also a racial one. A slim majority of nonwhite Mormons agree that discrimination is the more likely cause if African Americans can't get ahead (54 percent). Those numbers are even higher among blacks themselves, 62 percent of whom point to racial discrimination, which is slightly higher than among blacks nationally.[37] Put more simply, two-thirds of white Mormons say blacks are responsible for their own condition if they are behind economically, and two-thirds of black Mormons indicate instead that it's the result of racism.

Age-wise, while seven in ten Boomer/Silent Mormons believe blacks are responsible for their own condition, among Millennials it's closer to half. This is in line with the national trajectory, though Mormon Millennials are still less likely to see systemic racism than Millennials nationally—45 percent did in the Mormon sample, versus 54 percent among eighteen- to twenty-nine-year-olds throughout the United States.[38] Tinesha, the twenty-three-year-old student who once had a Primary teacher refer to her as "it," has encountered this attitude first-hand as a teaching assistant for an introductory sociology course. "Even among people my age, I don't think that many believe that systemic discrimination is a thing," she says. "They think it ended with the civil rights movement." As an African American, she has experienced racism first-hand and asserts, "I absolutely believe that it's real." It is hurtful for her when fellow Mormons discount her experiences and her interpretations of them. For example, one time her father and siblings stopped at an ATM so he could take out some cash. He had just gotten off work and was wearing a suit, but someone actually called the police because they thought he looked suspicious. Tinesha says if she were to describe this experience (or one of many others) to people at church, "Mormons are like, 'That's not racist! We're not racist.' . . . If I shared that story people would say, 'That's just one person doing one thing. The rest of the world is not like that. That's not racism.'"

The NMS also asked LDS respondents whether they felt, overall, that the nation's growing racial diversity is a positive trend for the future. In a word: no. Overall, only about four in ten Mormons view racial diversification positively. One surprise about this is that the large differences we saw earlier in the question on systemic racism, such as between political parties or generations, really don't pertain here. The "roughly four in ten" rule holds true for both Republicans and Democrats, for both men and women, and for all three generations (with Millennials and women slightly more likely to view racial diversity favorably). Another surprise is that it even holds true for nonwhite Mormons, who are actually a bit *less* likely to view proliferating diversity optimistically: only 36 percent of nonwhite Mormons feel positive about the nation's growing diversity, compared to 42 percent of whites. When we break that down a bit further, we see that optimism dips significantly among African American Mormons, to just 22 percent. This means that among black Mormons, four in five do not view growing racial diversity favorably. Although this is surprising, there is a national precedent for this unexpected finding that blacks are more doubtful about racial diversity than whites. In a similar question, Pew asked respondents whether they felt that "having an increasing number of people of many different races, ethnic groups and nationalities makes the United States a better place to live." Overall, 57 percent of Americans agreed with this statement, but only 50 percent of African Americans did.[39]

Despite Mormons' general rejection of racial diversity as a positive trend, they do not demonstrate any unusual tendencies toward racism or discrimination in national surveys. When surveyed about the desirability of racial segregation or the superiority of one race over another, Mormons' responses have been in line with other Americans' for more than half a century—even before the priesthood/temple ban was removed.[40] Long-term data from the General Social Survey suggests that white Mormons are no more likely to object to a child bringing home a friend of another race for dinner, or to oppose interracial marriage, than white non-Mormons are. In some cases, white Mormons are more supportive of progressive views than other whites.[41] In general, individuals' views on race seem most shaped by education, age, and proximity to other races, and less by religion.[42]

One area where Mormon views are considerably more positive than other predominately white groups is immigration, and in this religion does seem to play a role. In recent years, the LDS Church has taken public stands that can be viewed as proimmigration, from urging the federal government to allow young Deferred Action for Childhood Arrivals (DACA) designees to remain in the United States legally to forcefully stating, after then-candidate Donald Trump called for a ban on all Muslims entering the country, that the LDS Church supported religious freedom for everyone.[43] Nearly six in ten Mormon respondents in the NMS felt that "immigrants today strengthen our country because of their hard work and talents," while only four in ten indicated that "immigrants today are a burden on our country because they take our jobs, housing, and health care."[44] This breakdown among Mormons is similar to views in the United States as a whole (in which 65 percent of people surveyed by Pew in 2017 said that immigrants strengthen our country), and considerably more favorable than the spread among US Republicans, who generally have negative views about immigration.[45] Mormons, then, veer away from the views of other white and politically conservative Americans when it comes to immigration.[46] This suggests that many Mormons listen when their church makes political statements and might even depart from otherwise conservative attitudes if LDS leaders ask them to.

Previous research indicates that there may also be a "missionary effect" at work here, meaning that Mormons' views on immigration may be more positive than other conservative Americans' because many Mormons have been immersed in missionary service abroad. The NMS confirmed that too: returned missionaries demonstrate a higher regard for the contributions of immigrants than Mormons who did not serve a mission, 64 percent to 58 percent. The appreciation for immigrants is highest of all among those missionaries who had to learn a foreign language for their mission (68 percent).[47]

GLOBAL RELIGION OR AMERICAN CHURCH?

Mormons' positive views on immigration seem at odds with their simultaneous concern that increasing racial diversity does not bode well for the future: recall that six in ten Mormons think the nation's growing racial diversity is a problem. Given that most immigrants to the United States are nonwhite, immigration naturally leads to greater racial diversity, so Mormons' views present an interesting paradox.[48] Mormons are positive about immigration in the abstract, but less sanguine about its results.

In some ways this ambivalence about diversity is present in the structure of the church itself. On the one hand, the LDS Church prides itself on being a global religion. Its scriptures have been translated into 188 languages, and its temples dot six of seven continents.[49] On the other hand, its top leadership has been predominately white and American. Until 2018, all fifteen members of the First Presidency and Quorum of the Twelve were white men, and only one (Dieter F. Uchtdorf, who is German) was from outside the United States. In 2018, the Quorum of the Twelve diversified by appointing an Asian American and a Brazilian to be apostles, signaling a welcome shift away from the traditional focus on white men from Utah.[50] In the upper echelons of LDS leadership, there has long been a certain dynastic quality in which many (not all) apostles have been descendants of the original Mormon pioneers or at least long-time fixtures in the Utah church. This has presented a colonial face to the world in which new converts are welcome, but the leadership has been distinctly American. In 2018, with the appointment of those two apostles and a number of additional international leaders in the Quorums of the Seventy, the ratio of general authorities who were born outside the United States increased to nearly 40 percent.[51]

It is unclear what effect greater diversity at the upper echelons may have on specific decisions made by the church, but several studies have shown that having greater racial and ethnic diversity in management contributes to better leadership in general. Diverse juries, for example, have been found to make fewer factual errors in their deliberations, while businesses with racially diverse management see higher financial returns and are more likely to develop innovative products.[52] Incorporating diverse points of view sharpens a group's thinking and increases its ability to respond creatively to change.[53] Moreover, greater racial diversity in church leadership could go a long way toward helping nonwhite Mormons feel more represented in the LDS community. Several major studies have testified to the importance of seeing and hearing leaders who have had experiences similar to one's own. Rebecca, the thirty-seven-year-old convert from Mauritius, thinks many white Mormons in the United States, particularly Utah, live in a bubble of their own making. "I think in our mind, we think that if we don't talk about it [racism], it will never come back." But racism is already present, often unacknowledged because the privilege of white majority status is that whites can close their eyes to the lived experiences of minorities.

On the other hand, several people I spoke to had positive experiences of American culture and minimal trials due to racial or ethnic differences. Mikey, twenty-five, moved to Southern California from Taiwan when he was nine years old.[54] Although "it was a huge culture shock to a kid from an Asian background," and he was startled by how little respect the other students in Primary seemed to have for their teachers, he gradually adapted. "I realized that in the relationship between the teacher and students, and even the bishop-student relationship, the power difference is a lot closer in the United States," he says. "Eventually I even got comfortable telling my teachers about things that were going on in my life, as opposed to telling my parents. My teachers became my friends." Mikey's experience suggests that on the local level at least, the church outside the United States may sometimes be run in accordance with local customs, as well as American ones; he was a bit scandalized when he came to America and experienced a less formal approach than he was used to in Taiwan.[55] Yet culturally, Americanism is often exported right along with Mormonism when US missionaries go abroad to spread the gospel. Some expectations are implemented the world over: men will dress in Western suits, drums are unacceptable instruments for a sacrament meeting, and chapel buildings should come equipped with basketball courts. It may be that some of these colonialist assumptions are now being challenged at least a little, as with recent temple designs that incorporate subtle elements of the host country rather than simply replicating standard-issue Mormon architectural styles from the United States.[56]

Where leadership is concerned, however, change is slow. In the meantime, Mormons of color look to the few examples they have encountered of leaders who look like them. Lillian, as an Asian American, has wonderful memories of Chieko Okazaki, one of the most recognizable nonwhite world leaders the LDS Church has had; Okazaki served in the general Relief Society presidency in the 1990s. "She didn't speak with the painful Utah 'Primary teacher' voice, she had had a career, she had experienced racism and sexism and other-ism and she had overcome so many things that women loved her because we could feel her love and truth," Lillian says.[57] Lillian mostly enjoys watching General Conference, when top Mormon leaders address the faithful twice a year (see chapter 10), but she also finds it hard work. "Although I appreciate the fundamental truths I hear in General Conference, sometimes they are harder to hear because I have to sift through layers of Utah culture to get to the spirit of the message," she says. "And this can be exhausting." Having only "white Utah-based leadership talking to us and explaining different principles of the gospel" means that nonwhite Mormons sometimes "have to put on special ears to hear the gospel through the noise."

In the last few decades, Mormonism has experienced its fastest growth abroad. Yet it remains an American-led church overseas and a predominately white one at home, despite very recent nods to racial diversity. Many US Mormons, particularly ones who benefit from white privilege, often resist recognizing how much the LDS Church is tied to white American culture. Mormons are, according to Roe, thirty-two, "very insular."[58] Roe, who is white herself, says too many Latter-day Saints are in their own world much of the time. "I've seen racism and sexism in the church," she says. "All of this comes from being a homogeneous little group. We say that everybody needs the truth that we have, but we don't really want to accept them when they do come if they don't look and talk and smell and act like us." As we'll see in the next chapter, race is not the only area where Mormonism has found itself struggling to keep pace with changes in society; LGBT inclusivity is another.

CHAPTER 7

Rainbow Fault Lines

LGBT Inclusion

When he was thirteen years old, Ellis, now twenty-four, confessed to his bishop that he thought he might be gay.[1] Ellis was appalled at the thought. Growing up as the tenth of eleven children in a traditional Mormon family, he had imbibed the belief that homosexuality was an abomination, something to be ashamed of and overcome. In fact, he wondered whether he could ever be forgiven. In a Primary class he had once asked his teacher what the church meant by the "infinite atonement" of Christ. Did that mean even Satan could be forgiven? The teacher said no, that of course Satan could not be forgiven. Some horrors were simply out of bounds. This caused him to wonder: "What is too bad to be forgiven? How far is too far? If I'm like this for the rest of my life, what does that mean?"

Feeling guilty, he confessed his anxiety to the bishop, whose reaction was to pack Ellis off to an LDS therapist for counseling in Houston, a couple of hours away. "My bishop's comment was that this therapist would fix me, which was welcome news to me. I think the bishop saw that it would become more of an issue when I was older, and he wanted to pass the baton to the therapist about my sexuality," Ellis remembers.

He begged the bishop not to tell his parents why he was being sent for counseling, and the bishop honored this wish. So his mother did not know as she drove him to his sessions every Tuesday that he was seeing a therapist because the bishop thought it would be the best way to cure him of thinking he was gay. For his part, Ellis was relieved at the hope that a professional might be able to help him. He had been disgusted when he first said "the G word" aloud to himself in the sixth grade. He knew he was different in noticeable ways from his brothers and his guy friends, and like most people going through puberty, his main desire was to fit in. He wanted to try to change.

At the first appointment, the LDS therapist closed the door to the office and told Ellis they could speak privately. "Your bishop told me that your parents don't know why you're here, because you don't want them to," he said. Then came the statement that shocked Ellis. "The bishop asked me to make you not gay anymore. But that's not how this works. That's impossible. You don't need fixing." Ellis recalls:

> And his very next comment was, "Let's talk about penises." And I was like, "Is this a trap?" But it wasn't a trap. He just kind of normalized stuff that I was feeling terrible about. That was a very liberating feeling to have him tell me that everybody my age checked out other people's bodies in the locker room. He said, "There are things you can fix about yourself, and this isn't one of them. Let's focus on the things you can change, like self-esteem and how to fit in in a heterosexual society." Then he encouraged me to get out of Texas.

Ellis did indeed get out of Texas. He graduated early from high school, served an LDS mission in Italy, and is now a full-time student in New York. He remains very close with his family and says he's proud of them for the "huge concessions and compromises" they have made with his coming out. To pay for school, he's interning at a private equity firm and works two other jobs. He still prays every day and attends Institute regularly, even though he doesn't go to church on Sundays. He misses some aspects of going to the temple, which he used to visit frequently, and feels a little wistful whenever he's down near Lincoln Center and sees the Manhattan temple. But he also feels free and whole. His "new openness and big-P, rainbow-font Pride" is not a "detour or a disconnect" from his Mormon upbringing, he explains, but another piece of the same journey. And he still remembers that LDS therapist with gratitude and fondness. "When I'm processing things or decompressing, I remember what he said," Ellis says. "Because it was such a positive experience, I'm glad that he was part of my life formation."

EVOLVING VIEWS ON HOMOSEXUALITY

Ellis would be the first to tell you that his life as a gay Mormon has been easier than the journey other LGBT Latter-day Saints have had, especially those of older generations. For most young Mormons who are gay, acceptance is more likely than it was even in the recent past. "My younger Mormon friends know people who are coming out as teenagers," he reports. "I was 21. And my older Mormon friends didn't come out until they were like 29." Their decision to make their sexual identity public has been aided by a more widespread acceptance of homosexuality—not only in American culture more generally but also within the Mormon subculture. Mormon views on homosexuality have undergone a rapid change just within the last decade. For example, the NMS asked whether respondents believed "homosexuality should be accepted by society" or "homosexuality should be discouraged by society." The Pew Research Center asked this question in 2007 and 2014, so we have some data to which we can compare these answers. Overall, Mormons' acceptance of homosexuality grew from 24 percent in 2007 to 36 percent in 2014 and 48 percent in the 2016 NMS (Figure 7.1). So while acceptance doesn't command majority support, that support has doubled in less than a decade.[2] This movement is driven in large part by Millennials, more than half of whom say homosexuality should be accepted. And among younger Millennials like Ellis (those in the eighteen to twenty-six age bracket), six in ten believe it should. By contrast, only 38 percent of the combined Boomer/Silent generation feels homosexuality should be accepted by society—a view that is reinforced by many statements from LDS Church leaders, who are themselves of the Silent Generation or even older.

Over the past couple of decades, the church has softened its stance toward homosexuality in several ways. Most significantly, it has moved away from the teaching that homosexual orientation is itself a sin. In 1969, then-apostle Spencer W. Kimball published *The Miracle of Forgiveness*, which shaped LDS attitudes toward sexuality in the years to come, especially after he became the president of the church in 1973. At that time, the church's

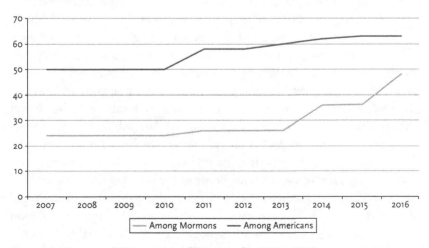

Figure 7.1. Mormon and US Acceptance of Homosexuality, 2007 to 2016.

position was that while homosexual orientation constituted a grievous sin, only homosexual acts warranted excommunication.[3] In *Miracle*, which addressed a host of various sexual sins, Kimball singled out homosexuality for particularly damning censure, calling it "an ugly sin, repugnant to those who find no temptation in it, as well as to many past offenders who are seeking a way out of its clutches."[4] Kimball's rhetoric established the pattern for future LDS discourse in four key ways: by referring to homosexuality as "unnatural," by rejecting any attempts to normalize it under the law, by insisting that the church's own stance would never change, and by omitting women from the discussion. (The possibility of lesbianism does not appear to have been on the author's radar.[5]) LDS leaders' subsequent discussions of homosexuality through the end of the twentieth century reflect all four of these ideas. Under Kimball's presidency, the church's position became more entrenched, replacing "homosexual acts" with "homosexuality" as grounds for excommunication in 1976. As historian D. Michael Quinn has argued, "This seemed to make Mormons vulnerable to church punishment for their homosexual orientation, even if they had not engaged in homosexual activities."[6] The church has since returned to the earlier policy, with the most recent Handbook of Instruction stating unequivocally, "Homosexual behavior violates the commandments of God, is contrary to the purposes of human sexuality, and deprives people of the blessings that can be found in family life and in the saving ordinances of the gospel. Those who persist in such behavior or who influence others to do so are subject to church discipline." Yet homosexual orientation—which the Handbook refers to merely as "same-gender attraction"—is no longer an excommunicable offense. Bishops are instructed to "support and encourage" gay members who "resolve to live the law of chastity and to control unrighteous thoughts," offer them church callings, and approve them for temple recommends if they are worthy in every other way.[7] Therefore, gay Latter-day Saints might conceivably remain members of the church as long as they are not sexually active. However, in lived experience, the standards are not always the same. For example, a heterosexual Mormon couple could hold hands in sacrament meeting and even kiss in public without anyone questioning their worthiness to hold a temple recommend or a calling at church, but the same is not necessarily true of gay couples. Any public displays of affection are considered suspect at church-owned Brigham Young University, for example, where the Honor Code stipulates that "homosexual behavior includes not only sexual relations between members of the same sex, but all forms of physical intimacy that give expression to homosexual feelings." Administration officials have sometimes interpreted this vague prohibition on "all forms" of physical contact as including hugs, handshakes, and even prolonged eye contact.[8]

Two other major changes have occurred since the Kimball era. First, in the late 1980s, LDS general authorities ceased recommending that homosexuals "cure" themselves by marrying someone of the opposite sex. This represents a departure from Kimball's rhetoric, which had advised that a gay man "force himself" to enter into heterosexual marriage so that he could engage in a holy and natural life.[9] However, some bishops and stake presidents were still abiding by the church's older policy. Since those pronouncements urging gay members to marry someone of the opposite sex had never been officially or publicly refuted, some local leaders continued to advise mixed-orientation marriages. As we saw in chapter 6 on race, in Mormonism, earlier statements from apostles and prophets can stay "on the books" and even in the teaching curriculum long after they have disappeared from the pulpit in General Conference.

A second, and related, change is that in the early twenty-first century the church began distancing itself from conversion therapy efforts that promised to "cure" individuals of their same-sex attraction. Such efforts had ranged from the violent (electric shock treatments used on some gay BYU students in the 1960s[10]) to the emotionally abusive, as when gay teen Alex Cooper was signed away to a "residential treatment center" in Utah and forced to endure taunts, punishments, and isolation by fellow Mormons who had been enlisted to make her repent of being gay.[11] Cooper's nightmarish experiences occurred in the early 2010s, but by that time conversion therapy was slowly becoming the exception in Mormonism, not the norm. Also in the 2010s, the LDS Church scaled back its involvement with the organization Evergreen, a "reparative therapy" group that featured LDS general authorities on its board of trustees and as speakers at many of its conferences.[12] The Mormon turn away from conversion therapy happened slowly—years, in fact, after the US Surgeon General reported there was "no valid evidence that sexual orientation can be changed"—but it appears to now be endorsed from the top.[13] The church's official website for gay members answers the question "If I'm faithful enough, will my attractions go away?" by stating that "many people pray for years and do all they can to be obedient in an effort to reduce same-sex attraction, yet find they are still attracted to the same sex." What's more, "a change in attraction should not be expected or demanded as an outcome by parents or leaders."[14]

STANDING FAST ON SAME-SEX MARRIAGE

Yet even as the LDS Church moderated its stance in these areas, it held the line on same-sex marriage. Throughout the 1990s and into the early twenty-first century, the church engaged in costly political battles on this issue.

In 1998 in Hawaii, Mormons contributed a majority of the $1.5 million raised by opponents of same-sex marriage, while that same year in Alaska, according to Harvard Law School professor Michael J. Klarman, "The Mormon Church in Utah contributed $500,000 to the pro-amendment campaign—the vast majority of that side's funding. By contrast, amendment opponents were able to raise only about $100,000."[15] In 2000, Mormons were also instrumental, along with Catholics and evangelicals, in passing traditional marriage measures in California (Proposition 22) and Nebraska.[16]

But Mormons' most notable politicking against same-sex marriage came in California in 2008, after the California Supreme Court struck down Proposition 22 as violating the state constitution. That measure's successor, Proposition 8, left nothing to chance, moving to amend the state's constitution and define marriage as being only between a man and a woman. Although the LDS Church did not directly donate tithing money to support Proposition 8, it did apply pressure on Mormons to give generously. A First Presidency letter, read from the pulpit of all LDS congregations in California, instructed members to "do all you can to support the proposed constitutional amendment by donating of your means and time to assure that marriage in California is legally defined as being between a man and a woman. Our best efforts are required to preserve the sacred institution of marriage."[17] Church members responded to the call, contributing stunning amounts of money and volunteer hours to the cause. Of the $40 million raised to support Proposition 8, an estimated 50 to 70 percent of the initiative's funding came from Mormon donors, who made up only about 2 percent of the state's population. Meanwhile, "in many areas, Mormons also constituted the majority of the on-the-ground grassroots political operation," which included staffing phone banks and canvassing from door to door.[18]

Mormons and other supporters of Proposition 8 were successful in their efforts to defeat same-sex marriage in California, at least for a time; the measure passed with a slight 52 percent majority. However, it was a pyrrhic victory for the LDS Church, as the public relations fallout proved a headache once the outsized extent of Mormons' campaigning and fundraising became known. In the days that followed the election, more than a thousand demonstrators gathered outside the Los Angeles temple to protest Mormon involvement, and media coverage across the nation was very critical of the church.[19] In New York City, several thousand people took to the streets outside Manhattan's LDS temple. "Would Jesus spend tax-free dollars to support hate and injustice?" one slogan read.[20]

That negative response to Mormons' Proposition 8 activism may help to explain why, even though the church's core doctrine of marriage between one man and one woman did not change, some leaders' ways of talking about it did. One case study for exploring this development can be seen in 2010, when President Boyd K. Packer, then one of the most senior members of the Quorum of the Twelve Apostles, gave a talk in General Conference called "Cleansing the Inner Vessel." The homily was primarily about the dangers of pornography, but he also clarified that sex was intended "only and solely between a man and woman, husband and wife," and that the church sought to protect society from "Satan's many substitutes or counterfeits for marriage." He railed against "those today who not only tolerate but advocate voting to change laws that would legalize immorality." Laws to permit same-sex marriage were doomed to fail because they would "alter the designs of God's laws and nature. A law against nature would be impossible to enforce. Do you think a vote to repeal the law of gravity would do any good?" Packer rejected the idea that homosexuality was an inborn trait. God would never design some people with "inborn tendencies toward the impure and unnatural," he taught. "Not so! Why would our Heavenly Father do that to anyone?"

Though four decades had passed, Packer's language came straight from the Kimball playbook. In fact, even the structure of the argument aligns with *The Miracle of Forgiveness*: "Many have been misinformed that they are powerless in the matter, not responsible for the tendency, and that 'God made them that way,'" Kimball wrote in 1969. "This is as untrue as any other of the diabolical lies Satan has concocted. It is blasphemy. Man is made in the image of God. Does the pervert think God to be 'that way'?"[21] But in the very different climate of 2010, the Kimball-Packer harangue sparked an outcry, not only from national media outlets, but also from within the church itself—enough so that when the talk was posted online days later, the language had been slightly altered. Gone was the "why would our Heavenly Father do that to anyone?" line, effectively removing the theological claim that God would never create anyone to be homosexual. The edited version of the talk also removed a statement that equated the 1995 Proclamation on the Family with Holy Scripture, calling it instead "a guide that members of the Church would do well to read and follow."[22] What did not change, ironically, was President Packer's insistence in the talk that "we cannot change; we will not change the moral standard." Meanwhile, that standard was indeed changing all around him.

SEXUAL DIVERSITY WITHIN MORMONISM

In one important sense, President Packer's talk was preaching to the choir—and it is a heterosexual choir. The NMS data shows that 95 percent of current Latter-day Saints identify as heterosexual.[23] This number is similar to the general national population, for which reliable estimates of those who self-identify as gay, lesbian, bisexual, or transgender have ranged from 3 to 6 percent. (This is *not* the same as the higher percentage of Americans who say they have ever experienced same-sex attraction.) While several reputable studies exist, the most helpful is likely Gallup, which has included sexual orientation as one of its Daily Tracking questions every day for years. From 2012 to 2016, its ongoing canvas of more than 1.6 million American adults revealed a population that was 3.5 percent LGBT in 2012 and had slowly ticked up to 4.1 percent by 2016.[24] As an additional data point, the National Health Interview Survey by the Centers for Disease Control and Prevention (CDC) found in 2013 that the self-identified LGBT population was 3.4 percent.[25] In both studies, younger Americans were significantly more likely to self-identify as nonheterosexual than respondents of older generations, to the tune of around 7 percent for Millennials.[26]

One factor to consider here is that the self-reported rates of homosexuality are considerably higher in the *former* Mormon sample of the NMS: 6 percent identify themselves as gay or lesbian, as opposed to just over 1 percent across all generations in the current Mormon population (see Table 7.1). An additional 5.5 percent of former Mormons consider themselves bisexual and just under 1 percent "other," meaning that overall, 12.5 percent of former Mormons self-identify as not strictly heterosexual, compared to just 5 percent of current Mormons. The fact that the proportion of nonheterosexual people among former Mormons is two and a half times what it is among current Mormons strongly suggests that

Table 7.1. SEXUAL ORIENTATION OF MORMONS AND FORMER MORMONS

	All Current Mormons (Ages 18–88)	Only Current Millennial Mormons (Ages 18–36)	All Former Mormons (Ages 18–88)	Only Former Millennial Mormons* (Ages 18–36)
Heterosexual/straight	95%	90%	87%	83%
Homosexual/gay/lesbian	1%	2%	6%	5.5%
Bisexual	3%	7%	5.5%	9%
Other/Don't know/Prefer not to answer	< 1%	< 1%	< 1%	2%

* The sample size of Millennial former Mormons is only 150 respondents, so the margin of error is higher than it is when we break out different generations in the current Mormon sample.

LGBT members may be more likely to leave the church than heterosexual Mormons, a finding we will discuss further in chapter 11.

The NMS findings about LGBT Mormons are consistent with a 2014 Public Religion Research Institute (PRRI) report on homosexuality and religion in America. In nearly every religious group surveyed, the percentage of gays and lesbians who adhered to a particular faith was lower than that religion's market share in the general population. For instance, 8 percent of the nation was at that time affiliated with black Protestantism, but only 5 percent of the LGBT population was; 19 percent of Americans identified as white evangelical Protestants, but only 8 percent of LGBT Americans did. In Mormonism, the gap was especially profound. Mormonism claimed 2 percent of the national population (rounding up) but less than half a percent of the LGBT population, which rounded down to zero in the report. It was the only religion listed that claimed 0 percent of the nation's LGBT community.[27]

Age is a factor here. Millennials are the most sexually diverse cohort of US Mormons. Whereas 97 percent of members of the Boomer/Silent generation report being heterosexual, that figure drops to 90 percent among Mormon Millennials. Two percent of Millennials report being homosexual, 7 percent bisexual, and less than 1 percent "other." (For this question, the write-in explanations included nonsexual and asexual. Note that this option was not about being transgender, which was assessed in the gender identity question and is discussed in chapter 5.) So while the active Mormon population remains strongly heterosexual, on par with the self-reported figures in the general population, there is a seven-point drop in heterosexual identity among young adult Mormons compared to their grandparents' and great-grandparents' generations.[28] This trend mirrors on a smaller scale the generational findings in the National Health Interview Survey, in which younger Americans were more than twice as likely as adults over age sixty-five to self-identify as homosexual, and five times more likely to identify as bisexual.[29]

What these statistics cannot tell us is anything useful about sexual fluidity, or the idea that sexual orientation is a more complex spectrum than the gay/straight binary that has long defined the tenor of conversation within the LDS Church. This subtlety is particularly important to recognize when talking about Millennials, who as a generation have coalesced around less binary labels such as "bisexual" or "queer." A 2017 study by GLAAD found, for instance, that just 84 percent of Millennials consider themselves to be strictly heterosexual (similar to the 83 percent in our population of former Mormon Millennials), and that the categories showing the most growth from earlier generations are bisexual, asexual, pansexual, and unsure/questioning.[30] In fact, the more traditional categories of gay and lesbian had not kept pace in "market share" among Millennials compared to their elders; the "strictly gay/lesbian" option held steady at 3 percent while more fluid classifications expanded.

One interesting and surprising finding of the GLAAD study was that Millennials were the generation least likely to say they personally know someone who is gay, while Baby Boomers were the most likely, which is exactly what we also found in the NMS—contrary to our expectations.[31] At first glance, these statistics seem to fly in the face of other studies that show a clear correlation between having personal exposure to LGBT persons and being more sympathetic toward those persons; how can Millennials have the highest rates of sympathy but the lowest rates of personal contact? One thing to keep in mind is simply that older individuals have more years of life experience and are acquainted with more people overall, so it makes sense that they also know more gay people. Yet there is more going on here. The answer, GLAAD says, is not that Millennials really don't know gay people but that they have a more nuanced understanding of sexual diversity than their predecessors. Only the "gay and lesbian" subcategory has older Americans edging out Millennials in terms of personal contact. While older Americans said they had more personal contact with "gays and lesbians," for every other group—bisexuals, queers, pansexuals, asexuals, and others— Millennials rank first. The upshot of all this, then, is that Millennials "appear more likely to identify in terminology that falls outside those previously traditional binaries," says GLAAD.

LIVING BEYOND THE BINARY

In conducting interviews for this book, it proved difficult to find LGBT Millennial Latter-day Saints who remain fully active in the church. One who is trying to make it work is Alex, the twenty-three-year-old African American teacher we met in the last chapter.[32] However, he gently rejects the term "gay," because "homosexual to me implies a permanency and a singularity that I may not subscribe to. By singularity I mean that the term homosexual means I'm only attracted to men, that I'll only ever be attracted to men. But I have hopes that one day I will be able to be attracted to a woman, that I will have a family." He says he has occasionally experienced a mild attraction to women, but that it "pales in comparison" to how physically and emotionally drawn he is to men. He does know some gay men who are married to women, and he is optimistic that those marriages will turn out happily. "The wives knew going in what was going on with their husbands," he explains. "The majority of these relationships are working out."

Alex admires gay men who have been able to marry women and have children—becoming a father, he says, is one of his most cherished dreams. He believes in eternal families and wants to be sealed in the temple, cementing forever the sense of connection he's had to the Mormon faith for more than a decade. Alex was twelve when he decided to be baptized in the LDS Church that his mother belonged to but did not attend. Ever since, the church has functioned like a surrogate family for him—what he calls "a safe haven." With divorced parents and a mother he describes as sometimes being verbally abusive, Alex considered Mormonism a life-line. "Going to church just brought such positivity and optimism to my life when things could get pretty dark otherwise," he says. Interestingly, both of Alex's parents are themselves gay, which was somewhat confusing during his childhood, especially as he was trying to sort through his own sexuality. His relationship with his mom reached a crisis point when he was in the middle of high school, so he went out of state to live with his dad. His father was not a believer, but was supportive of Alex's determination to stay active in the LDS Church, getting up at 5:15 AM to drive his son to seminary. As a result, Alex remained fully engaged with the church and graduated from seminary.

But during his senior year he became sexually active with men, a fact he felt terribly guilty about. What followed was a years-long roller coaster of sexual activity, tearful confession to the bishop, and lapsed church attendance, always followed by repentance and renewed church involvement. He finds this cycle exhausting and embarrassing. During college he "was having sex, including sexual hookups with anonymous men. I got tired of having the same conversation with the bishop, and going through the same repentance process with the bishop and thinking I had gotten over it, and then falling again. I had been battling with porn and masturbation since I was nine years old, even before I joined the church." There have been some bright spots. Alex briefly dated a wonderful girl he met at a Family Home Evening held by his university's singles ward. She encouraged him to get more involved in church since he had such a strong testimony of the gospel. They only dated for a few months but remain good friends. She's one of two members of the ward who know about his struggles, and it's a relief to be able to tell someone. In our interview it also seemed a relief to him to talk about what he has been through; he told me he agreed to be part of the book because he hopes his story can help other young Mormons who are attracted to members of the same sex (again, he would not use the word "gay" to describe himself). Because those people might not have had "the resources or the caring, compassionate leaders that I've had," he worries "that they might get discouraged and leave the church. They might think that this life isn't suitable for them, and they might commit suicide.[33] I just want to help however I can."

Alex's story points to the politicization of debates about human sexuality, in which even language can be a minefield.[34] Many Millennials resist the typology that one must be either gay or straight, male or female. While it may be true that Alex is avoiding the term "gay" simply because his deep Mormon religiosity has caused him to fear that label when applied to himself, it's also entirely possible that he speaks for a generation of people who are challenging *all* tidy sexual labels. In my conversations, I did not find any Mormons or former Mormons who volunteered the language of queering or intersectionality, but their descriptions of their experiences and feelings certainly upend binary ways of thinking. Consider the case of Falencia, who is a Haitian American former Mormon. While she was a young student at BYU, she quickly became engaged to a man, but she was also deeply attracted to a female friend and gradually came to realize she preferred that friend's company to her fiancé's. She felt the engagement was more "playing at a relationship, just going through the motions because it was just another step towards the Celestial Kingdom."[35] She chose the woman, dropping out of BYU so they could finish their educations together in an eastern city. "It turned out that she was more what I was looking for than he was," Falencia explains simply. They have been married for seven years, and neither is active in the LDS Church.

LGBT MORMON RELIGIOSITY

Falencia is one of many LGBT Mormons who reach a point where they can no longer reconcile church activity with their own values and self-understanding. For most of them, this is a gradual decision. Lauren is one such person.[36] Now thirty-one, she tried for years to deny, or at least hide, the feelings she had for women. In adolescence she internalized the message that a large part of her future involved marrying a man and having children, so even though she had known since around age thirteen that she was not attracted to boys, she tried to fit into the heterosexual mold. As a student at BYU she dated men—at the very least "to keep up appearances," she says—including one guy she took on a date to Salt Lake City so she could hear Mandy Moore in concert. Standing just a few feet away from Moore in the small, crowded club, Lauren realized that if the singer just said the word, she would gladly ditch her male date and run away with her. Lauren made the mistake of being honest with her date about this attraction to Moore. A few days later he sat her down and sternly called attention to their differences. "You're OK with gay marriage," he said. "I'm not OK with gay marriage. What are we going to tell our children?" Lauren was taken aback. "I was like, 'We've only been dating a month. We don't have hypothetical children!' We broke up a month later."

Being at BYU represented a gradual awakening of her sense of self. A part of her expected other people to automatically know she was a lesbian; after all, she had a *Brokeback Mountain* poster on her wall and all the DVDs of *The L Word*; how could her roommates not see it? Yet it was empowering for her to tell people. Lauren was at BYU when the university's Honor Code policy became slightly less draconian. When she arrived, merely admitting you were gay, even if you were celibate, was possible grounds for expulsion:

> And there were plenty of gay witch hunts. Somehow, people would suspect a person of being gay, so all of their friends would be called into the Honor Code office. We would always save their academic career by saying they were just friends. And 99 percent of the time, even though those people were gay, they weren't doing anything about it. We knew we had signed an Honor Code. We were just trying to get through school unscathed.

In 2007, the Honor Code changed so that merely confessing to a gay identity was not enough to force a student out of school, so Lauren began telling a few people. She remembers one powerful meeting of the BYU Democrats group where a friend got up and said, "You know what? I'm gay." Even though she already knew that student's secret, hearing it declared aloud was empowering—someone at BYU was out and proud. "It proved there were more of us than I had ever thought," she says. "So many people came out." After that night, Lauren came out to more people, including her roommates. They seemed to take it in stride. One of the roommates, a Utah Mormon who had never met an openly gay person before, sort of adopted Lauren as her token LGBT resource, the person she would go to whenever she had a question about homosexuality. Lauren didn't mind at all. "I loved it, that I could be that example for her, and show that we weren't crazy and we weren't all sleeping around with each other."

But not long after graduation, Lauren drifted away from the church. She tried the local singles ward but didn't care for it; nor did she feel at home in her parents' family ward, which felt narrow and judgmental. She began going to church about every other week, then once a month, then only once every other month. After coming out to her parents in her late twenties, she also told them she was done with church. It wasn't that all of her experiences had been bad. In fact, for a while she had an incredibly understanding bishop who had a gay son himself. "Lauren, I don't care that you're gay," he told her. "But come to church." Thrilled that she had "won bishop roulette," Lauren soon learned she could just as easily lose at that game—when the bishop's wife passed away, he was released from his calling.[37] "I'm sure the new guy is nice enough, but it was much easier to go to church when I had a bishop who understood me," she explains. She's not opposed to the idea of returning to church someday, but says the institution's party line would have to change in some major ways for that to happen. "I would like to think the church would someday change its tune on gay marriage, but if nothing else, I would really like them to at least re-word how the Handbook is written. I understand how it feels to be that homosexual kid who sees in the Handbook that being gay is as serious a transgression as rape and murder. And then they figure, what's the point?"

Grouping all nonheterosexual respondents together in the NMS allows us to offer some general observations about LGBT members and former members.[38] In terms of testimony, they are less religiously orthodox than heterosexual respondents by almost every measure; not only is their confidence in specifically Mormon teachings lower, but also their belief in more generically Christian tenets (God is real, there is an afterlife, Jesus Christ was literally resurrected from the dead). Most interesting are the responses of nonheterosexual Mormons and former Mormons on the questions about what they find "very troubling," "a little troubling," or "not at all troubling" about the LDS Church. It is not surprising that far more, proportionally, cite LGBT issues as being very troubling. What is more surprising is how many other issues showed a similarly pronounced divide. LGBT former Mormons were deeply concerned about the church's lack of financial transparency; emphasis on conformity and obedience; strong culture of political conservatism; and excommunications of feminists, intellectuals, and activists. On closer examination, these issues all touch upon the church's behavior toward LGBT persons. It's hard to not be concerned about how the church spends its money when you know how much Mormons have contributed to defeat same-sex marriage, just as it's difficult to be sanguine about the church's emphasis on conformity when you may have known since childhood that a fundamental part of your core identity did not, in fact, conform. Theologically, believing in prophets whose teachings have undermined your very existence is challenging in a way that most heterosexual Mormons will never have to experience. In other words, for LGBT Mormons, leaving the church is never "just" about LGBT issues per se. It's that those issues strike at the very heart of Mormon ideas of authority.

"THE POLICY" AND SAME-SEX MARRIAGE

LGBT Mormons themselves are not the only members who struggle with the way the church has addressed LGBT people. Troy, a heterosexual Mormon in California, had just boarded an airplane in November 2015 when his sister texted him an article that claimed the LDS Church was going to prohibit baptisms and baby blessings for any children born to church members who were in a same-sex marriage.[39] "I read it and thought at first that it could not be real," he remembers. "When I landed later I found out that it was real, that it was really happening, and I was so disappointed. It was a pretty difficult week. It makes no sense to me and feels antithetical to the teachings of the church." Troy says that now, at age thirty-seven, he is more sensitive to LGBT issues than he was in his twenties, when he "took the standard church position that this was something they had to deal with. We all have trials and difficulties in life, and this was their trial." Through in-depth conversations with friends, he gradually began to perceive an unfair double standard at the heart of the church's policies toward gay members: there is no path to citizenship for them. "A heterosexual person might be single now, but potentially they have the hope of getting married in the future," he explains. "Under current church philosophy, that isn't true for an LGBT person. An eighteen-year-old LGBT person who wants to stay in the church must stay single and be alone for their entire life. This is fundamentally a different condition than the single, never married person—there is no hope of a better future."

The more Troy has thought about it, the more he believes the church's position is untenable, especially now that Mormon leaders have backed away from the idea that being gay is a choice and not an inborn trait. "If being gay is not a choice, which the church concedes, why would God want one of his children to suffer and be alone forever through no fault of their own? That isn't a God that I know or recognize," he concludes. For his part, Troy has chosen to remain very active in the church despite his growing misgivings that its LGBT policy is "fundamentally wrong." He believes the policy is unnecessarily punitive, and he says he's surprised by the negative reactions it has engendered even among his more conservative Mormon friends. "Even some of them have posted things on Facebook that would indicate that they don't agree with the policy either."

According to the NMS data, however, a robust majority of currently identified Mormons do support the LGBT exclusion policy, but that support is not universal. Overall, 71 percent of current Mormons either "strongly" or "somewhat" agreed with the first part of the policy (labeling same-sex Mormon couples as apostates), with only 29 percent saying they disagreed. Yet the nuances of this acquiescence are worth exploring. When compared with people born before 1965, Millennial Mormons showed a drop of eighteen points in the number who "strongly" agreed that same-sex marriage should trigger a disciplinary council and possible excommunication. Members of Generation X felt similarly. Support for the second half of the policy, which prevents children of same-sex couples from being

Table 7.2. CURRENT MORMONS' SUPPORT FOR BOTH PARTS OF LDS LGBT
POLICY, BY GENERATION

	All Current Mormons	Boomer/Silent	GenX	Millennial
Part 1: Labeling members involved in same-sex marriages as apostates who are automatically subject to a disciplinary council				
Strongly agree	47%	58%	45%	40%
Somewhat agree	24%	14%	25%	30%
Somewhat disagree	11%	12%	10%	12%
Strongly disagree	18%	15%	19%	18%
Part 2: Barring children of same-sex couples from being baptized or blessed				
Strongly agree	36%	44%	34%	32%
Somewhat agree	25%	19%	28%	28%
Somewhat disagree	15%	16%	13%	16%
Strongly disagree	24%	21%	25%	24%

baptized, was less enthusiastic in all age groups (Table 7.2). There was an eleven-point drop among the entire active Mormon sample in the percentage of people who chose "strongly agree" (from 47 to 36 percent) and a corresponding ten-point rise in the percentage who either strongly or somewhat disagreed (from 29 to 39 percent).

One surprise in the data about children's baptism was a nine-point gender divide (Table 7.3). Two-thirds of men (66 percent) agreed with the policy, but only 57 percent of Mormon women did. In fact, 28 percent of current Mormon women "strongly" disagreed with the policy about children—a ten-point jump from the men who strongly disagreed—while another 14 percent of women "somewhat" disagreed. That means that overall, more than four in ten LDS women disagree with the church's policy that children of same-sex couples should be denied baptism (42 percent).

Former Mormons are even more strongly opposed. If most active Mormons at least halfheartedly agree with the LGBT policy, the opposite can be said of former or inactive Mormons: most of them hate it. Seventy-seven percent disagree with barring same-sex couples' children from blessings and baptisms. Moreover, the respondents who said they "strongly" disagree far outweighed the more tepid "somewhat" disagreement. Most former Mormons are not just opposed to this policy, but passionately so. Overall, just under two-thirds of former Mormons "strongly" disagree with the second half of the LGBT policy (63 percent), with only 14 percent "somewhat" disagreeing. What differs in comparison to the data on current Mormons is that there's little generational change among former Mormons. Just seven points separate the Boomer/Silents (59 percent)

Table 7.3. CURRENT AND FORMER MORMONS' SUPPORT FOR THE LDS CHURCH'S POLICY BARRING CHILDREN OF SAME-SEX COUPLES FROM BEING BAPTIZED OR BLESSED, BY GENDER

	Current Mormon Men	Current Mormon Women	Former Mormon Men	Former Mormon Women
Strongly agree	37%	35%	13%	4%
Somewhat agree	29%	22%	18%	9%
Somewhat disagree	15.5%	14%	16%	11%
Strongly disagree	18%	28%	53%	75%

from GenXers (66 percent), with Millennials falling in between (64 percent). Overall, we see closer alignment among the various generations of former Latter-day Saints in how they feel about the church's LGBT policies than we do among currently identified Mormons, where the generation gap between older adults and younger ones is more pronounced.

Clearly, there is a generational difference in current Mormons' social views about LGBT issues. For example, 40 percent of younger Millennials in the NMS feel that same-sex marriage should be legal in all fifty states, while only 20 percent of Boomer/Silent respondents agree.[40] This is consistent with other findings about Mormons' evolving views about same-sex marriage. In PRRI's 2016 American Values Atlas, Millennial Mormons showed even more support for same-sex marriage, with 47 percent favoring it compared to 28 percent of the Boomer/Silent cohort. Though the numbers are higher overall in the PRRI sample, both surveys showed an approximately twenty-point generation gap between the oldest and youngest adult Mormons.

The PRRI survey also found that among all Mormons, opinions about same-sex marriage had reached a tipping point between 2015 and 2016.[41] In 2015, two-thirds of Mormons (66 percent) opposed same-sex marriage, and in 2016 barely half did (55 percent).[42] This eleven-point erosion of opposition, and corresponding eleven-point spike in support (from 26 to 37 percent), occurred during the exact period in which the church's official position against same-sex marriage was made abundantly clear through its November 2015 policy changes. Even as the church stiffened its posture, the rank and file softened theirs, contributing to a growing disconnect between the leadership and the membership.

So although a majority of Mormons still disagree with same-sex marriage, and the church's official position is clearly opposed, the tide of LDS opinion may well be turning—particularly because the generation after the Millennials, Generation Z, will never have lived in a world where same-sex marriage is unthinkable. As PRRI CEO Robert P. Jones has put it, "Young adults are generally uncomfortable with politicized religion, and for them, same-sex marriage is not a moral battleground but simply a feature of everyday life."[43]

It will be quite some time before those younger and more progressive Mormons have any institutional authority in the church, if in fact they elect to stay. In the meantime, tensions over LGBT issues have reached a new level of intensity. As we will see later in the book, LGBT issues were Millennial former Mormons' third most common reason for leaving the church. As one Millennial expressed it to me, this is the civil rights issue of their generation.

PART THREE

Passages of Faith and Doubt

CHAPTER 8

Navigating Religious Practice for a New Generation

Elaine, now thirty-five, was about fifteen when she went off the rails.[1] The oldest of three daughters in a devout Mormon family, she had always done the usual things: attending Primary and Young Women, making crafts at Girls' Camp, and starting seminary her freshman year of high school. But during her sophomore year, something shifted. "I decided that I didn't think the Church was true," she explains. Along with that loss of testimony came a number of behavioral differences, like experimenting sexually with boys: "I was doing everything but having vaginal intercourse." She loved how the boys made her feel, so she jumped in and out of numerous relationships, mostly hiding it from her parents. She flat-out refused to go to seminary anymore because she had butted heads with the teacher, but her parents insisted she continue going to church on Sundays. Elaine felt at the time like there was no point to attending church because "I was not good enough to be there. . . . I thought it was just me making evil choices, and that I wasn't worthy to even be there. So why bother?" She was horrible to her family during this time, she says, and failed some of her classes.

Her parents sent her to an LDS musical theater camp the summer before her senior year of high school, betting on their belief that music, if nothing else, might get through to their daughter. She loved to sing and dance. Sure enough, Elaine had a religious awakening and "felt the Spirit for the first time in who knows how long." When her parents arrived at the end of camp, they were overjoyed to find their daughter's heart so softened. She recommitted herself to the LDS Church during her senior year of high school, re-enrolling in seminary, "making better choices" in her dating life, and becoming "more invested on Sundays."

Now that she is older, Elaine says a lot of her behavior in high school makes more sense to her, especially since she was diagnosed with bipolar disorder in her early thirties. One of the classic symptoms of the manic phase of bipolar disorder is hypersexuality, which she wishes she had known at the time, when she ruthlessly blamed herself for her behavior. Elaine continues to be active in the church, and she's grateful for a number of things about Mormonism that helped her survive the dark years before she got treatment, like committed parents, an understanding bishop, music that fed her soul, and—much to my surprise—the Word of Wisdom.

> I think it has probably saved my life from addiction. I have such an addictive person-
> ality, and with my mental illness history, there are so many times that I have looked at
> someone drinking a glass of wine and thought, "Holy moly, if I didn't have the Word of
> Wisdom that would be me, and it would be a huge problem. I would not be able to stop."

Elaine's experience illuminates the push-pull relationship of behavior and belief in Mormonism. Adherence to expected behaviors, like sexual absti-nence before marriage and keeping the religion's strict dietary code, is in-tricately related to belief. In Elaine's case, a loss of her testimony (belief) led to sexual experimentation (a behavior), which led to a sense that she was unworthy in God's eyes (a belief) and therefore should not even attend church (a behavior). Belief and behavior tend to reinforce one another, which is something the Mormon religion has understood very well: it has consistently emphasized high behavioral standards, as well as doctrinal in-struction, and Mormon youth have outpaced their non-Mormon peers on many behavioral measures. Some of these behaviors continue to be just as strongly adopted by Millennials in the NMS as by older generations, while on others they are departing from the ideal. Most Millennial Mormons consider themselves "active" in the LDS Church—but the way they define "active" may look different than it does for older generations.

HOLDING THE LINE ON SPIRITUALITY

"I do believe God answers prayers," says Rachel, thirty-two, "but I also be-lieve prayer is an exercise in refining our own desires, shedding selfishness and trying to get to a mindset where I might be able to hear the message that God has for me."[2] She's not alone in praying regularly. In my interviews with Millennial Latter-day Saints, most said they prayed daily or at least weekly. Most also felt that God answered their prayers, with some qualifications, like "I don't think he answers them in ways that make sense to us right away" (Brittany, thirty) or "It's hard to see a pattern to why certain people seem to have their prayers answered and others don't" (Taylor, thirty-seven).[3] In other words, young adult Mormons pray frequently, but they are not expecting magical answers or immediate gratification from God. "Sometimes we pray for things that maybe we shouldn't pray for," says Lauren, thirty-one. "It's not like in Primary where you're told you can pray and get whatever you want."[4]

The NMS data showed that when it comes to prayer, Millennial Mormons are less religious than older Mormons but considerably more religious than non-Mormons of their generation. There is a double-digit drop between the Boomer/Silent Mormons who pray in private every day (76.5 percent) and the Millennial Mormons who do (65 percent), but these numbers are still very high when compared to younger Millennials in the general population (39 percent).[5] Millennial Mormons, then, are considerably more likely than their non-Mormon peers to pray daily. Also, one in five Millennial Mormons pray at least once a week, though not every day; this means that overall, 84 percent of Mormon Millennials pray at least weekly, which is not a large decline from the Boomer/Silent Mormons who say the same (88.5 percent). Clearly, prayer is alive and well among Mormons, even younger ones.

In Mormonism, prayer and scripture study often go hand in hand; church members are taught to do both daily. However, the NMS showed that across all generations, daily scripture study was not quite as common as daily prayer.[6] Only 38 percent of all Mormons read the scriptures every day, and there's little variation by generation: 40 percent of Boomer/Silents and Millennials both say they do this, compared to 34.5 percent of GenXers. (GenXers, it might be pointed out, are the generation most likely to have children at home, and a common thread in interviews was that when children came along, daily scripture habits were harder to maintain.) Another 30 percent of Millennials say they read the scriptures at least once a week, which means that combined, seven in ten Millennials read the scriptures daily or weekly—which slightly edges out the older generations (Table 8.1).[7]

Table 8.1. PRAYER AND SCRIPTURE STUDY AMONG MORMONS, BY GENERATION

	Boomer/Silent	GenX	Millennial
How often do you pray in private?			
Daily	76.5%	64%	65%
At least once a week	12%	20%	19%
How often do you read the scriptures outside of religious services?			
Daily	40%	34.5%	40%
At least once a week	26.5%	33%	30%

Millennials also have the highest rates of literal belief in the scriptures of any generation: 45 percent agree that the "scriptures are the word of God and are to be taken word for word," almost a ten-point jump over the Boomer/Silent group.[8] This is an interesting and somewhat surprising development, given the clear downward generational trend on this same question in research by Pew and Gallup. In those studies, the oldest respondents profess the most literal belief in the scriptures, and Millennials the least.[9] In Mormonism that seems to be reversed, as the youngest survey respondents were actually the most likely to choose the "word for word" option. It could be argued, however, that the idea of scriptures being taken word for word is not a classically Mormon theological position, since the eighth Article of Faith stipulates that the Bible is only the Word of God "as far as it is translated correctly." Perhaps Baby Boomers and members of the Silent Generation are articulating a more conventional LDS notion about the scriptures, whereas Millennials have been influenced by what they have seen in their lifetimes in the wider culture: the rise and pervasive influence of evangelical Protestantism in the public square. In that context, a belief that scriptures are to be taken "word for word" may reflect the way evangelicalism has often determined the language and terms for discussing religion. Another possible explanation is that in Millennials' lifetimes, the LDS Church curriculum has emphasized cherry-picking certain passages to illustrate particular doctrinal issues, rather than exploring the whole of scripture.[10] The majority of church leaders over the last half century have modeled a literal understanding of scripture, even for books like Jonah or Job that are widely regarded by Jews and other Christians as allegory or poetry.[11]

In any case, one thing is clear: Mormon Millennials have a high view of the scriptures, and try to read them with some regularity. "I would like my children to become familiar with the Bible and the Book of Mormon as massively important texts to humanity," says Elysse, twenty-six.[12] She does not yet have children but wants them to learn the scriptures when she does. A number of people I interviewed referred to their belief that the Bible and the Book of Mormon helped them to become better people. Grayson, twenty-three, reflected, "I do think there's a lot of inspired things in the Bible, and even if it's not a factually accurate historical document, it can teach us how to be good people."[13]

SHARING THE FAITH WITH OTHERS

In addition to these devotional habits of prayer and scripture study, Millennial Mormons also excel in religious practices that involve sharing the faith with others, both inside and outside the LDS Church. For an example of the former, we need look no further than home and visiting teaching, which until 2018 were long-standing programs for adult church members. In Mormonism, a "home teacher" was a priesthood holder who was assigned to another family in the ward. Ideally, the home teacher visited the family once a month to check up on them, and was on call if they ever needed help with anything (moving furniture was a common request). In turn, the male priesthood holder in that family, if there was one, would be assigned to do the same for someone else's family. Visiting teaching worked in much the same way, but specifically for the women in the ward: a sister was assigned to check in on one or more other women each month. The idea behind home and visiting teaching was to strengthen families, develop strong friendships within the ward community, and identify any practical needs people might have. For example, if a visiting teacher learned that a family was low on food, she would bring it to the attention of the Relief Society president and bishop, who might arrange to bring groceries for that family. Since 2018, such family-to-family relationships have been facilitated through a combined program called "ministering," but at the time of the NMS in 2016, home and visiting teaching were still in full swing.

Given the intergenerational nature of home and visiting teaching, you might expect that older Mormons would report being more diligent about keeping that commitment—it could conceivably be hard for younger people, for example, to be in a supervisory role over older ones. Yet in the data we see that Millennial men edge out their elders as having been the most faithful home teachers of any generation, with 56 percent saying they went at least once a month (Table 8.2). Millennial women said they did their visiting teaching at almost exactly the same rate as Boomer/Silent women.

Perhaps the practice of home and visiting teaching resonated with Millennials because, as many have noted about this generation, they place a strong value on interpersonal relationships. Research from the Barna Group about Protestant young adults suggests that Millennials' most positive experiences and feelings about church are focused on relationships and opportunities to serve.[14] Some Protestants who are concerned about retaining Millennials have written about the need for churches to become more relational and authentic, moving "away from the church-as-business

Table 8.2. MONTHLY HOME AND VISITING TEACHING, BY GENERATION

	Boomer/Silent	GenX	Millennial
Men (home teaching)	52%	49%	56%
Women (visiting teaching)	45%	40%	46%

model and into the church-as-relational-community model."[15] Through home and visiting teaching, Mormons may have had an advantage in engaging this generation, because the "church-as-relational-community model" is what those programs were all about. It remains to be seen whether the less formal program of "ministering" will also hold appeal for Millennial Mormons, but with its emphasis on fostering relationships and everyday fellowship outside of church, it seems poised to do so.

Another relational practice at which Millennial Mormons excel is sharing their faith. When asked "How often do you share your views on God or religion with others?," Millennials outshine the Boomer/Silents by nearly twenty points (Table 8.3).

In a religion that stresses the motto "every member a missionary," Millennials are following the church's emphasis on being public ambassadors for the faith. Sixty-four percent say that they share their views on God or religion with others at least once a week, compared with just over half of GenXers (56 percent) and only 45 percent of the Boomer/Silent group. What's more, 28 percent of Mormon Millennials say that they make such a public witness of their religious beliefs *every day*—nearly twice as much daily missionary work as any other generation. In part, there may be an age effect here: Millennials are the closest in age to the time they would have served an LDS mission, and we've already seen that they are the generation most likely to have served a mission. So for them, sharing their faith may simply feel more natural because doing so all day, every day was a recent experience. Another cause might be the sensibility that in this generation, every topic is on the table for discussion: whereas previous generations of Americans were taught that religion was one of the two topics not to be broached in polite company (the other being politics), Millennials have grown up with the notion that nothing is taboo.[16] Also, the NMS question did not specify exactly what "sharing your faith" might entail, so it's possible that social media comes into play here; Millennials might consider reposting an inspirational meme to count, for example.

Table 8.3. SHARING VIEWS ON GOD OR RELIGION WITH OTHERS, BY GENERATION

	Boomer/Silent	GenX	Millennial
Daily or once a week	45%	56%	64%
Once or twice a month	28%	26.5%	17%
Seldom or never	27%	17%	19%

Overall, the above findings will likely hearten the leaders of the church. What, if anything, connects these practices at which Millennials excel? One keyword to keep in mind is "relationality." Research has shown this generation to have an extraordinary affinity for one-on-one relationships outside of an institutional setting.[17] Activities such as sharing their faith and teaching fellow Mormons in their homes are built upon personal relationships more than upon doctrine or ideology. While Baby Boomers adopted the mantra "Think globally, but act locally," Millennials may be the cohort to carry it out.

CHURCH ATTENDANCE AND SABBATH KEEPING

There are other areas of religious behavior in which Millennial Mormons seem to be deviating more markedly from their elders. One of the most important is church attendance, about which the NMS garnered conflicting information. When asked a general question about how often they attend church, most Mormons respond confidently, with about three-quarters saying they attend at least weekly.[18] That includes Millennials, who lead the pack in saying they attend at least once a week, at 79 percent. But when asked specifically whether they had attended church meetings on any Sunday within the last *month*, fewer than half of Millennials say yes, the lowest of any generation (Table 8.4). What we see here is a sizable gap between the way Mormon Millennials view their church attendance in the abstract and the way things appear when we drill down more precisely to ascertain recent behavior. More than thirty points separate Millennials' ideal from their apparent reality, compared to just half a point in difference among the Boomer/Silent respondents.[19]

This second question was added because there is a desirability bias in almost every survey that deals with church attendance. People tend to overestimate their pleasing behaviors on surveys, so it's helpful to be as concrete

Table 8.4. CHURCH ATTENDANCE IN THEORY AND PRACTICE, BY GENERATION

	Boomer/Silent	GenX	Millennial
Reports attending religious services at least weekly	69.5%	72%	79%
Reports attending Sunday church meetings within the last 30 days	69%	57%	47%

as possible about actual recent activities.[20] Having to think about whether they really did attend church in the last month is different than merely asking how people might categorize themselves in general. This second question allowed respondents some leeway because it only asked about the last month, not the last week, so built in to the question is the expectation that even the most regular attenders will miss occasionally because of illness or travel.[21] I was expecting that there would be some discrepancy between these two questions, but it was surprising to see such a wide divergence among Millennials—coupled with a near-zero divergence among the oldest respondents. With the Boomer/Silent Mormons, what you see is what you get.

When we cross-tabulate these findings not only by generation but also by whether respondents identified themselves as "very active" in the church, an interesting trend emerges. Whereas only one in ten of the oldest generations who described themselves as "very active" reported never attending church in the last thirty days, 43 percent of "very active" Millennials had not been to church. In other words, four times as many Millennials consider themselves "very active" even though they have not recently attended church (Table 8.5).

In Mormonism, there is a strong cultural imperative to attend church regularly, and the temple recommend interview process contains a question that includes attendance at "sacrament and other meetings." Perhaps the way older Mormons conceive of the designation "very active" has been predicated upon regular church attendance, and that norm is changing. Several interviewees told me about their parents' very strict rules about Sunday church attendance, and acknowledged that their own were not as exacting. "We had full attendance of church when I was a kid—like if we were on vacation in Hawaii or California, we would pack Sunday clothes, take the day off, and find a ward house," says Thomas, thirty-six.[22] "The focus was: What are the rules, and how can we obey them even better? That was our family culture, and I think it was very common in that whole generation."

Just because Millennials are skipping church does not necessarily mean they dislike sacrament meeting. The NMS asked a battery of questions about

Table 8.5. "VERY ACTIVE" MORMONS WHO HAVE NOT ATTENDED CHURCH IN THE LAST 30 DAYS, BY GENERATION

	Boomer/Silent	GenX	Millennial
Have not attended Sunday church meetings within the last 30 days	10%	29%	43%

people's experiences of Sunday worship, including whether they felt primarily "spiritually fed and inspired" by going to church or "tired or burned out." Millennials were only a little less likely than Boomer/Silents to choose the first option (86 percent of Boomers feel spiritually fed, compared to 76 percent of Millennials). Overall, then, just a quarter of Millennial Mormons seem to find church uninspiring. And when respondents were asked to choose up to three ways sacrament meeting might be improved (e.g., planning more music, allowing different instruments, having occasional guest speakers from the community, sending children under age eight to their own class), the only item that garnered any real traction was limiting sacrament meetings to forty-five minutes. That proved a popular idea. However, every generation liked this possibility, not just Millennials.

Therefore, it's unclear why Millennial Mormons' church attendance is markedly lower than older generations'. For Rion, thirty-five, it's not necessary to attend church to be an orthodox Mormon.[23] "I consider myself a TBM [True Believing Mormon] in my own way," he says, despite attending just once or twice a month. He believes the most important role of religion is to teach people to lead moral lives, but he doesn't think it requires several hours of church a week to do that. When asked whether he considers himself an active Mormon, Rion is thoughtful:

> Church attendance has claimed the monopoly on the term "activity," and I don't think that's wise. I consider myself very active in my faith, in my conduct, in my religion. "Religion" is a strange word to put your finger on. But yeah, I consider myself more active in my own way than most church-attending people. Sitting in a pew does not have a monopoly on the definition of activity.

Rion's deliberations might help explain the seemingly contradictory NMS data: a super-majority of Millennials declare themselves to be faithful attenders of church, but most have not attended in the last month even though they don't seem to feel that church is boring or otherwise lacking. Rion has simply decoupled the term "active Mormon" from the practice of going to church.

WORD OF WISDOM ADHERENCE

Thomas, whose family was so devout they would still go to church when they were on vacation in faraway places, decided as a young teenager that he wanted to make a break from Mormonism, and the most decisive way he could think to accomplish that was by violating the Word of Wisdom. At thirteen, he was taking shots of hard liquor, and by the end of high school, he was regularly smoking pot and failing his classes. Thomas had grown up in an unusual kind of Mormon family; in fact, if Mormonism had royalty, his family would be among its nobility. The great-nephew of one apostle and the grandson of another, he carried the burden of high expectations, as communicated by his by-the-book father. Thomas responded by rebelling in a way that was sure to garner negative attention. "So in terms of Word of Wisdom, and chastity, there was a sense of defiance in it. And also a sense of relief. I felt like crossing those boundaries left me on the other side of the Rubicon. And I needed to be on the other side of the line—it gave me some psychological distance from the toxic environment I'd grown up in."

Thomas understood intuitively that the Word of Wisdom was a boundary marker, a line that could not be crossed without burning the bridges that connected him to his family and his church. For Mormons, experimenting with alcohol or drugs is not considered a normal, if regrettable, part of adolescence. It's a more serious form of self-definition, a signal that one is choosing to be less than fully LDS. Given that parameter, I was not surprised to see that a majority of the former Mormons in the NMS drink coffee and alcohol, at rates that aren't terribly different from the general population.[24] That made sense with the usual narrative: violating the Word of Wisdom is often a sign that someone is out of the church, or on the way there. What I did not expect was how many currently identified Mormons were also disregarding parts of the Word of Wisdom but still saying they are active in the church.[25]

The most straightforward way we can examine patterns of Word of Wisdom adherence is by analyzing how many members are "squeaky clean" observers. In other words, how many Mormons reported that they have consumed nonherbal tea, alcohol, coffee, tobacco, marijuana, psychedelics, or other illegal substances (including heroin and cocaine) in the last six months? The NMS reveals that 45 percent of self-identified Mormons in the United States have not consumed any of these substances.[26] Another 22 percent said they have consumed only one of them, and 15 percent said they have consumed two. The rest (about 17 percent) said they have consumed three or more. It seems that fewer than half of American Mormons faithfully observe a literal prevailing interpretation of the Word of Wisdom.

When examining only Mormons who describe themselves as "very active" (regardless of frequency of church attendance), 60.5 percent of survey respondents reported that they avoided each of the substances prohibited by the Word of Wisdom. This decreases to 30 percent of those who say that they're "somewhat active" and 16 percent who say they're "not very active" or "not at all" active. Slightly more than half (53 percent) who claim they attend church every week report avoiding each of the substances listed previously, compared to 26 percent of those who attend once or a few times a month and 14 percent of those who attend seldom or never. Most interestingly, nearly four in ten current temple recommend holders (38 percent) say they have consumed at least one of the substances forbidden by the Word of Wisdom in the last six months. This is especially noteworthy because Mormons are required to report to a church leader that they are faithful keepers of the Word of Wisdom to qualify for a temple recommend. Some people may be less than truthful in the recommend interview, or they are interpreting the Word of Wisdom with a certain amount of flexibility. Another possibility is that some of these individuals have temple recommends that are technically still current—recommends now last for up to two years—but they have begun distancing themselves from full Mormon activity since the time of their last recommend interview.

There are interesting patterns regarding specific substances prohibited by the Word of Wisdom. Our survey data shows that about a third of current Mormons report consuming coffee (35 percent), while a quarter (25 percent) have drunk alcohol or nonherbal tea (25 percent). The findings on alcohol are consistent with the data recorded in the General Social Survey (GSS), in which 27 percent of LDS respondents reported that they have not wholly abstained from alcoholic beverages, as opposed to 71 percent of other Americans.[27] Nearly 17 percent of Mormon respondents in the NMS smoked or chewed tobacco, which is slightly higher than the GSS result of 13 percent among Mormons. About one in ten consumed marijuana. Just 3 percent of Mormons reported ingesting psychedelics, while slightly more have used other illegal drugs such as cocaine or heroin (5 percent).

Interestingly, coffee alternatives such as decaffeinated (14 percent) or Postum (4 percent) have lower rates than regular coffee (35 percent). This is surprising because Postum has long been deemed acceptable by LDS leaders, and the Handbook guidelines have historically said nothing about decaffeinated coffee. This prompted the First Presidency to respond in the late 1960s and early 1970s to letters from local leaders who had inquired about "Sanka," the main brand of decaffeinated coffee at that time. "The use of a beverage from which the deleterious ingredients have been removed would not be considered breaking the Word of Wisdom," the First Presidency instructed a Provo stake president in 1969. "This would include Sanka coffee, and a temple recommend should not be denied to those drinking Sanka coffee."[28] Other letters offered the same advice, sometimes identically worded.

As shown in Figure 8.1, there was a visible generational difference in some areas of Word of Wisdom compliance, with younger Mormons less likely to adhere strictly to all aspects of the religion's dietary rules. The rate of alcohol consumption nearly doubles from the Boomer/Silents (14 percent) to the Millennials (29 percent), and the rate of marijuana

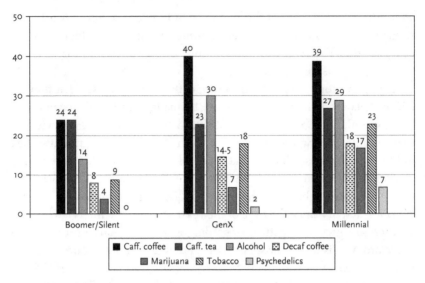

Figure 8.1. Word of Wisdom Noncompliance among Current Mormons, by Generation.

consumption quadruples, from 4 to 17 percent. Coffee and tobacco consumption also increase markedly.

In other questions on the NMS, it became clear that younger Mormons were less likely to regard certain elements of keeping the Word of Wisdom as "essential" to being a good Mormon. For example, only 31 percent of Millennial Mormons say it is essential for a good Mormon not to drink coffee or tea, a twenty-point drop from what the Boomer/Silent generation says. When asked about alcohol, we see more than a thirty-point drop between these generations; just over three-quarters of Boomer/Silent Mormons see eschewing alcohol as an essential part of a Mormon identity, but only 46 percent of Millennials think the same. This suggests that Millennials don't tie Word of Wisdom observance with their Mormon identity as closely as older Mormons do.

This attitude came through in numerous interviews. Most of the Millennials I talked to were keeping the Word of Wisdom, but not without question. Marie, twenty-four, says that some parts of it make total sense to her—"obviously, abstaining from tobacco is a 100 percent good thing"—but others are less clear.[29] "In so many ways, tea is actually good for you and healthy," she explains. She also finds it strange that LDS leaders' interpretation of the Word of Wisdom has changed so much over time. In particular, the founding generations of the church were not teetotalers.[30] "Joseph Smith and Brigham Young drank brandy, they drank beer, they drank wine. And in the Word of Wisdom it says that when you drink wine, it should be wine you made yourself."[31] Still, Marie keeps the

Word of Wisdom as the church interprets it today, and does not seem to mind doing so.

Some wondered why the church has emphasized certain aspects of the Word of Wisdom but ignored others that are also mentioned in the text of the original revelation. Annelise, twenty-five, thinks that "often, as church members, we focus on the five things in the missionary pamphlet: no alcohol, no coffee, no tea, no tobacco, no illegal drugs. But it turns out the Word of Wisdom has a lot more in it than just that."[32] One of those neglected elements is that the scriptural text of the Word of Wisdom stipulates that meat is to be "used sparingly . . . only in times of winter, or of cold, or famine."[33] Yet the near vegetarianism advocated by the scripture is not required for Mormons to get a temple recommend, and in fact one Mormon vegetarian I spoke to has encountered stiff resistance among fellow Mormons who disagree with his choice. Troy, thirty-seven, decided to become a vegetarian when he was just nine years old, but found little support for a plant-based diet in Mormon Utah, where he did not know any other vegetarians.[34] "Sometimes I was basically forced to fast on Scout trips or at other church events because everything had meat in it or was cooked together with meat. I would pretend to eat the potatoes covered in meat grease so as not to cause a scene but I would throw them in the bushes instead." All this, he says, caused him to think seriously about religious authority:

> I felt that my being a vegetarian was inspired by God. So, I had to develop nuance very early in my understanding of God and the church, to separate out what my leaders and teachers were telling me versus what I believed. In the end, that really helped me, to be able to develop that skill when I was young. But as an adolescent, it was difficult to be so different, especially in a culture where difference is not valued.[35]

Troy not only keeps the Word of Wisdom as the church defines it but also has taken his observance a step beyond what the church requires, and feels that God prompted him to do so. Some other interviewees likewise felt that the Word of Wisdom—or at least its modern interpretation—may not go quite far enough. "If we're going to go to coffee and tea and talk about health, then we should talk about sugar too," says Jayne, thirty-seven.[36] "I can totally abuse my body with as much soda and as much cake as I want" and still qualify for a temple recommend, which does not seem right to her.

Those are all statements from people who keep the Word of Wisdom (and even go beyond what it requires), but I also talked to some who consider themselves faithful Mormons but do *not* follow its guidelines. Penny, twenty-five, became sexually active during her sophomore year of college, which changed her relationship with other Mormon expectations as well.[37]

"So at that point I was like, 'It doesn't matter. I've already barred myself from temple worthiness, so there's no reason to cling to the rest of it.'" She began drinking coffee and still does, though she has no plans to leave Mormonism. She questions the way leaders have interpreted the Word of Wisdom:

> I have no idea when they started to interpret the "hot drinks" thing as coffee and tea, but it seems so arbitrary to me. In many respects drinking coffee is healthier than drinking caffeinated soda. I try to eat healthy and live a generally healthy life, which is important for a spiritual and practical perspective. But I don't feel that a sort of one-size-fits-all code makes sense.

K.C., a nineteen-year-old student at a Mormon university, has recently started drinking coffee and says she knows a number of fellow students who do as well—"We don't rat each other out," she assures me. She sees a certain relativism in the church's positions on what is and is not forbidden by the Word of Wisdom. "It's funny, because the church leaders always say that the world will change but God's law will never change. But actually, the church has changed a whole lot. They seem to kind of pick and choose what they want to keep." This last observation—that church leaders have vacillated on which Word of Wisdom standards to uphold and which to discard—is particularly interesting, because the "pick and choose" accusation so often goes the other way, with older Mormons complaining that younger ones only keep the commandments that suit them. When it comes to Word of Wisdom compliance, there is reason to believe that younger Mormons are less rigid in their practice than older ones, less likely to tie its observance to their Mormon identity, and more apt to question the rules even if they do choose to follow them.

POPULAR CULTURE

Another area where young adult Mormons' behavior appears to be deviating from the standards set by church leaders involves engagement with popular culture, which I am defining broadly to include entertainment, fashion, and media. The NMS obtained more information about Mormons' views on popular culture than I can possibly include here, but a few items stood out.

First, it seems that nearly a quarter (23 percent) of Mormon Millennials report having at least one tattoo. This is lower than the percentage of Millennials in the general population that sport a tattoo (38 percent), but of course higher than the rate the LDS Church would presumably like to see, which is zero.[38] In the "For the Strength of Youth" pamphlet, for example, Mormon teens are counseled to "not disfigure" themselves with tattoos and piercings, and former prophet Gordon B. Hinckley—who was president of the church during much of the time that today's Millennials were growing up—made a point of strongly discouraging the practice.[39] In contrast, only 9 percent of the Boomer/Silent cohort reports having at least one tattoo. (One interesting side note is that in that combined group, the rate is driven entirely by the Baby Boomers, since not a single member of the Silent Generation in the NMS had a tattoo.) The growth of tattoos among young Latter-day Saints mirrors a wider trend in American culture, in which the tattoo industry is expected to grow by more than 9 percent annually and surpass $1 billion in sales by 2020.[40] It also demonstrates a widespread cultural easing of previous generations' distaste for tattoos, as a majority of Americans today report feeling comfortable with the idea of police officers, restaurant workers, athletes, or teachers who have tattoos.[41] Young adults today are more likely to see their tattoos as vehicles for individual storytelling—an embodied personal history of loves, losses, and inspiration—than as a form of open rebellion.

Second, some younger Mormons appear to have fewer qualms about watching R-rated movies or television with a "mature" rating. About four in ten Millennials have seen an R-rated film or watched a mature television program in the last six months, as seen in Table 8.6, and almost as many have played graphic video games or listened to songs with explicit lyrics. In the table, those are grouped in an umbrella category of "popular culture deemed unacceptable by LDS leaders," since the Brethren have at various times cautioned church members, especially youth, against participating in any media "that is vulgar, immoral, violent, or pornographic in any way."[42]

It is clear that the consumption of more graphic content is higher among younger Mormons than it is among their parents and grandparents. From this snapshot, we cannot tell whether Millennial Mormons will become more conservative in their viewing habits as they grow older or will continue to watch R-rated content at a higher rate than other generations. Given the fact that GenXers' consumption is the highest of any generation for mature television and nearly equal to Millennials' for R-rated movies, we should be careful about assuming that Millennials will content themselves with a diet of Disney as they age; GenXers did not.

Finally, there is considerable generational spread on the question of pornography (both "soft" and explicit).[43] Overall, the rates for viewing pornography among all Mormons in the NMS increases from about one in twenty in the older generations to just under one in five among Millennials. Since the LDS Church has often and unambiguously cautioned men about pornography but has said less about it to women (except insofar as they might suffer when husbands and fathers used porn), it is also instructive to break

Table 8.6. MORMONS AND POPULAR CULTURE CONSUMPTION IN THE LAST SIX MONTHS, BY GENERATION

	Boomer/Silent	GenX	Millennial
Popular culture deemed acceptable by LDS leaders			
Animated movies	53%	65%	60.5%
PG-13 movies	63%	61%	64%
LDS General Conference	66%	51%	44%
LDS Church videos	51%	52%	47%
Live sporting event on television or online	48%	55%	53%
Popular culture deemed unacceptable by LDS leaders			
Video games with graphic or violent content	6%	26%	35%
Music with sexually explicit or profane song lyrics	6%	25%	37%
R-rated movies	28%	40%	42%
Television with a mature rating	37%	43.5%	40%
"Soft" pornography	7%	14%	19%
Explicit pornography	5%	11%	18.5%

this out by gender to see whether Mormon women are, in fact, viewing pornography themselves.[44] The answer is that some do, though not at the same rate as men, and that younger women report doing so most frequently. Among men, the rate more than doubles from the Boomer/Silents (10 percent) to the Millennials (22 percent). Among women, the generational spread is even more pronounced. Only a tiny number of Boomer/Silent women have viewed explicit porn recently (1.5 percent), while 15 percent of Millennial women have, which is a tenfold increase from the oldest Mormon women to the youngest. Although 15 percent is a small minority, it's not radically smaller than the number for Millennial men (22 percent), which means that Mormon leaders' discourse about pornography as a temptation only for men seems misguided.

Mormon leaders will likely be concerned to see that the rates of viewing explicit pornography have nearly quadrupled from the oldest adult Mormons to the youngest, even though it is still a minority of Latter-day Saints. Let me offer a word of caution about interpreting this last result. It has become a popular narrative in the LDS Church today that pornography is a widespread and pernicious problem, but the numbers in this survey are not dramatic: only 12 percent of Mormons (all generations and both genders combined) say they have viewed any explicit pornography at any time in the last six months. Among Mormon women overall, the figure is 7.5 percent; among men it is 16 percent. Even though pornography exposure among Mormon Millennials is significantly higher than it is for their grandparents, this is still low compared to their non-Mormon peers.[45] Overall, only a minority of Mormons are viewing pornography even in small doses.

It is possible that the numbers are low because Mormons would be reluctant to admit on a survey that they have engaged in behavior that the church regards as immoral and dangerous; however, the fact that this was an anonymous internet survey rather than a telephone survey with a live caller means we were more likely to get a candid and honest response.[46] On the other hand, it was surprising how often people volunteered in interviews that they had experienced problems with pornography. One man said he had been battling with pornography and masturbation since he was nine years old; another began looking at porn online during his freshman year of high school. "It became a thing that was scary and hidden," he told me. "I didn't talk to anybody about it." In some cases, the individuals confessed to their bishops and worked through a repentance process, sometimes repeatedly; in others, they simply hid it from the world, fearful of consequences and the public shame that might occur if, for example, their bishop told them they had to refrain from taking the sacrament for a specified period.[47]

The NMS findings about pornography are in keeping with Millennials' and GenXers' less stringent avoidance of adult content such as R-rated movies, explicit song lyrics and video games, or television with a mature rating. Still, a majority of young Mormons avoid these forms of entertainment.

TITHING

Tithing is an important spiritual practice in Mormonism and is required for anyone seeking a temple recommend. Mormons believe that tithing is a commandment of God that has been in place since the Old Testament, and that they will receive spiritual blessings if they faithfully observe the practice. While the church teaches that a full tithe is 10 percent of income, it has no official stance on the question of whether individuals should tithe based on their gross income (before taxes) or net income (after taxes).[48] Anecdotally, however, there are many stories about individual Sunday School teachers, youth leaders, and ward members who have extolled the superiority of tithing from gross income, so we set out to learn more about actual tithing practices.

Respondents were asked which of the following options best described their charitable donations to the LDS Church: regularly giving 10 percent of their before-tax income, regularly giving 10 percent of their after-tax income, giving less of their after-tax income, rarely giving money, or never giving at all. If we combine the first two categories together, more than two-thirds of Mormons declared themselves to be full tithe-payers (68 percent), which is an astonishing rate but in keeping with other research that has shown Mormons to have the highest rate of giving of any religious group in America.[49]

When we deconstruct this figure a bit more (Table 8.7), we find a striking generational difference. Among Boomers and Silents, only 12.5 percent say they tithe from net income; with GenX that trend nearly doubles to 25 percent; among Millennials it climbs still further to 29 percent. So although Millennials are more likely than any other generation to report that they are full tithe-payers, only 40 percent tithe from their gross income—a double-digit drop from the gross tithe-payers in the oldest generations—while an additional 29 percent pay tithing after taxes.

If there ever was a cultural bias toward paying tithing on gross income, that bias has been diluted among Millennials. Tithing as a practice is alive and well among them; it's only their definition of tithable income that appears to be different. As with some other practices and beliefs, we see some of the usual patterns about which kinds of people are more likely to tithe on gross income: 55 percent of Mormons in Utah do so, for example, versus 41 percent outside of Utah. Education matters too: 56 percent of Mormons with a postgraduate degree pay tithing from gross income, versus 42 percent of those without a college degree. The political difference is even more pronounced, as Republicans are significantly more likely to tithe from gross income than Democrats (54.5 vs. 31 percent).[50] There is no difference whatsoever by gender, however.

Table 8.7. TITHING FROM GROSS OR NET INCOME TO THE LDS CHURCH, BY GENERATION

	Boomer/Silent	GenX	Millennial
Regularly give 10% of gross income	56%	40%	40%
Regularly give 10% of net income	12.5%	25%	29%
Regularly or occasionally give less than 10% of net income	7%	13%	16%
Rarely give	13%	12%	9%
Never give	11%	9%	6%

In interviews, many Millennials were supportive, even enthusiastic, about tithing, though men seemed to enjoy talking about it more than women did. As Ammon, twenty-five, says, "The Lord gave us everything we've got, so what is 10 percent?"[51] He concedes that 10 percent of gross income "does hurt a little" since he is working about sixty hours a week and has a new baby, but "I will always pay my tithing and I think it will work out." In fact, at his wife's suggestion, his family contributes an additional 5 percent of their income in fast offerings for the poor. In Mormon practice, members of the church fast for two meals once a month, typically on the first Sunday of the month, and donate the money they would have spent on food to the church's fast offering fund for needy members. Fast offerings are in addition to tithing, but are often nominal amounts by comparison. Ammon's family's contribution is far above and beyond what is expected, and he says he's honored to do it. "Why say no to extra blessings, right?" he asks. "I have a newborn baby and I want him to stay healthy. I want to have a great career. So part of it is selfish, sure, but I want the blessings." When pressed to explain whether he thinks the Lord will bless him with health and career success if he pays tithing, however, he demurs: "Hmmm. I'm sure blessings come in from paying a faithful tithe, but I don't necessarily know what those blessings will be. . . . I don't necessarily think that because I pay my tithing, the Lord is going to give me a great, high-paying job. I don't think that tithing opens the door to making more money, otherwise the Mormons would be the richest group of people in the world!"

Several people expressed concern that the church does not release any reports or financial statements about what is done with the tithing money it collects. (The last time it did so was in 1959.[52]) Steve, thirty-one, pays tithing but says, "The Church needs to give full transparency to where every dollar of tithing money goes. Until they're willing to do that they'll alienate people."[53] He doesn't necessarily think anything nefarious is being done with the money; he knows, for example, that tithing helps to keep tuition low at BYU, and to erect and maintain chapels and temples. But "as a guy that works in finance or accounting, I'm concerned about the lack of disclosure. I don't think that the Church is hiding anything, but what could disclosure hurt?"

One who has suspended tithing for the time being is Rion, thirty-five, whom we met earlier as someone who rarely attends church but still considers himself an active member. He doesn't like how tithing is required for entrance to the temple, and also thinks that it should count if he contributes money to any charitable organization that is doing good works, not just to the LDS Church. That way, "if you disagree with the decisions" of some LDS leaders, "you can still have the option" of going to the temple. "At some point, if the church begins moving in a direction I can support,

I will pay tithing again," he affirms. "Right now I feel like other community organizations and causes are doing better at that."

We've seen that in terms of religious behavior, Mormon Millennials are stalwart in many areas and less committed in others. Their focus on prayer and the scriptures may reveal a hunger for depth. Millennials, through their religious practices, seem to be hunting for a spirituality that is deep, authentic, and demanding. They exhibit high rates of scriptural devotion, prayer, and relational grassroots interactions with other church members; we've seen elsewhere that they also have strong belief and a particular emphasis on missionary service. However, they have far less of a focus on religious behaviors they may see as superficial or less important, like avoiding tattoos, coffee, or mature entertainment. There is a sharp divide between their theoretical and actual church attendance. They are committed tithe-payers, but appear to accept "net" tithe paying more readily than older Mormons. What is particularly interesting is that their understanding of what it means to be "active" in the church may well be changing from the ways that older Mormons have traditionally understood that term; Millennials are not tying their identities as "active" Mormons as strictly to practices like attending church meetings or keeping the Word of Wisdom. What religious behavior will look like for this generation of Latter-day Saints as they grow older is of course unclear, but it's unlikely to be exactly the same as the generation that preceded them. As the next chapters will show, their political values and views about authority are also distinctly different.

CHAPTER 9

Social and Political Views among Current and Former Mormons

Natalie, a forty-year-old mother of four, knew she had what she refers to as "liberal political leanings" compared to her fellow Latter-day Saints, but she was a rule-following Mormon in just about every way: she had served a mission in Russia, graduated from BYU, and held regular scripture study and Family Home Evening with her husband and kids.[1] She was active in the church, and stayed active even after she began to experience what she calls a faith crisis. Natalie started to feel uncomfortable in the temple endowment, where she realized that women were not given equal access to God without male mediation. And she noticed other ways the church did not seem to value women, including their professional contributions. She had decided to be a stay-at-home mom instead of pursuing a master's degree, and now she regretted it—"absolutely, I felt it as a loss"—despite the deep love she feels for her kids. But it was politics that ultimately pushed her away from the church.

It was the fall of 2016, and Natalie, like many Americans, was closely following the presidential election between Donald Trump and Hillary Clinton. "The 2016 election was very hard for me," she says. "I viewed it as an attack on Hillary Clinton as a woman, less than as a politician." Then, in October 2016, a recorded interview surfaced in which Donald Trump boasted of trying to commit adultery with a married woman and of sexually assaulting women who refused his advances.[2] Natalie was appalled. She was even more devastated when she logged on to social media and saw how many fellow Mormons were rallying around the GOP candidate anyway:

> I went on my Facebook feed and watched active member after active member, male and
> female, defend his vile actions. I literally could not put on my garments after that. This

church literally does not value the equality of women. They're willing to sweep all this under the rug so that they can get him elected so they can ram their conservative agenda through regardless of the cost.

Suddenly, that night and at that moment, I could no longer separate all of the things I had put on a shelf about the temple and women. I saw the far-reaching effects of the second-class nature of women in the temple and how that had infected our Mormon culture to the point where they could ignore Trump's comments and actions.

Natalie was deeply offended by what she perceived as her fellow church members' lack of ethics, excusing Trump's behavior because he was the candidate of their preferred political party. Natalie had not been an unquestioning Mormon, and had sometimes experienced doubts about church history and belief. But ultimately it was politics that pushed her over the edge, not theology. Natalie continues to raise her kids as Mormons and still attends church, but she no longer wears garments and has started drinking coffee.

Since World War II, Mormons have been recognized for their conservative moral values, staunch patriotism, and commitment to the nuclear family. Those core values are still very much present among older Latter-day Saints, though we see changes among Millennials who remain active in the church; the NMS finds that Millennial Mormons are, once again, more conservative than their non-Mormon Millennial peers but more progressive than their Mormon elders.[3] Meanwhile, among former Mormons, we see not a dilution of the conservative political agenda, but an outright rejection of many parts of it.

MORMON PARTY AFFILIATION AND VOTING PATTERNS

Many previous studies of Mormons have found a strong relationship between membership in the LDS Church and political conservatism. Mormons' marriage to the Republican Party has been going strong for seventy years, sealed by the rise of Ezra Taft Benson as President Eisenhower's secretary of agriculture in the 1950s.[4] Republican political affiliation has been the prevailing norm among almost all LDS representatives in Congress and the clear majority of voters in Mormon-dominated districts. While the church maintains a policy of not endorsing candidates, and therefore officially stays out of politics, it has made exceptions for issues it has deemed threats to morality, like same-sex marriage and the Equal Rights Amendment. For the most part, the church's positions on social issues such as abortion and homosexuality have stood largely in line with the GOP's positions.[5] Many Mormons have naturally assumed that the church stands behind the Republican Party, even if the institution remains officially neutral. Research shows that Mormons tend to follow political instructions from the church when its leaders appear unified in their opinions.[6]

But Robin, a convert (see chapter 1) whose born-in-the-covenant Mormon husband has a mother who "is a diehard Fox News listener," sees generational change on politics.[7] "I feel like this generation of Mormons is tackling much more challenging issues and is less insular," she says. Younger Mormons don't take her mother-in-law's approach for granted, assuming that Fox News presents the only side worth listening to; they are "more diverse in their views." While she knows a number of people who have left Mormonism because they weren't Republican and felt they didn't fit in, Robin thinks it's possible to be a "big tent" Mormon, which is how she defines herself. "I think that you can be Mormon with a lot of different perspectives," she concludes.

Robin's impression is correct. Statistically, Millennials are more likely to lean or vote Democratic than older generations of Latter-day Saints, though they are not nearly as Democratic as their non-Mormon peers in the general population (Table 9.1).[8] Mormon Millennials are actually almost as likely to lean or vote Democratic (41 percent) as Republican (46 percent), whereas in GenX the GOP carries the day by a nearly two-to-one margin (59 to 29 percent) and the Boomer/Silent cohort trends even more decisively Republican (68 to 25 percent).[9] Meanwhile, the percentage of Mormons who consider themselves "pure Independents" is small but higher than it is among the oldest generations; 13 percent of Millennials now describe themselves this way.[10]

As has been shown in previous studies of Mormons, men are a bit more likely to lean Republican than women, at 60 percent and 55 percent, respectively.[11] This gender differential is also a trend in the wider US population, though of course the percentages of people of both genders who favor the GOP are significantly higher among current Latter-day Saints than in the

Table 9.1. CURRENT MORMONS' POLITICAL PARTY AFFILIATION, BY GENERATION

	Boomer/Silent	GenX	Millennial
Vote or lean Republican	68%	59%	46%
Vote or lean Democrat	25%	29%	41%
Vote or lean Independent	8%	12%	13%

United States as a whole, especially among women. In 2016, 51 percent of American men favored the Republican Party, compared to just 38 percent of women.[12]

The NMS shows that Mormons' Republican preferences were at work in the 2012 election. Whereas three-quarters of Boomer/Silent Mormons supported Republican Mitt Romney in 2012, only half of Millennials said the same.[13] In 2016, GOP candidate Donald Trump was considerably less popular with Mormons than previous Republican contenders had been, despite Natalie's personal experience of seeing many members of the church defend him. According to the Cooperative Congressional Election Study, 52 percent of Mormons nationally voted for Trump—significantly less than the 82 percent who voted for Mitt Romney in 2012 and the 72 percent who supported John McCain in 2008.[14] The NMS, which was fielded in September and October of 2016, suggests that things could have gone even more badly for Trump among Mormons. Trump was the expected candidate of choice for just 39 percent of Boomer/Silents, 37 percent of GenXers, and 31 percent of Millennials, who were the only generation to favor Democratic candidate Hillary Clinton by even the slimmest of margins (32.5 percent). In the overall sample of Mormons, only 36 percent said Trump was their desired candidate.[15] Many Mormons who might have preferred another candidate did end up voting for Trump. Paul, forty-four, a proud Republican who has not voted for a Democrat in any presidential election since 1992, "felt like he [Trump] was the lesser of two evils." While Paul harbored reservations about Trump's lack of political experience, his anger toward Hillary Clinton was stronger. As a Haitian American immigrant, Paul may seem an unlikely Trump supporter, but his GOP loyalties are unwavering. "I said on social media that I was going to vote for Trump and I was proud about that, and I took a lot of bashing," he says.

Whether Mormons' relative lack of enthusiasm for the GOP in 2016 was an outlier or is indicative of a new trend is a live question. In one sense, Mitt Romney's 82 percent among Mormons was historically unusual, because through most of the 1990s Mormon GOP preference hovered between 60 and 70 percent, and often closer to 60 percent.[16] Perhaps what we are seeing now is simply a reversion to a historic norm in which GOP affiliation holds sway among a majority of Mormons, but not the overwhelming majority that pertained in recent elections. However, it's also possible that Mormons are becoming less enchanted with the Republican Party, and that the GOP's popularity among Mormons is waning. Only time and future research can tell.

Apart from the Trump-Clinton battle, the big story of the 2016 polling was the splintering of the Mormon vote toward multiple Independent candidates, including LDS conservative Evan McMullin. McMullin was twice as popular with the oldest Mormon adults as he was with the religion's youngest, garnering 16 percent support in the Boomer/Silent group and 8 percent among Millennials. Using political scientist Benjamin Knoll's further analysis of the data, we can learn more about which kinds of Mormons tended to support Evan McMullin and which put their trust in Donald Trump.[17] In a word, the most religiously orthodox Mormon Republicans tended to support McMullin, not Trump. McMullin Republicans were more likely to view religion as a positive force in society, for example. They were also twice as likely as Trump voters to think that racial diversity is a positive trend in America and that immigrants strengthen American society. Trump's followers listed terrorism as the most significant concern facing America, while for McMullin supporters it was moral or religious decline, closely followed by "changing views on the traditional family." What this shows us is that even among Mormon Republicans, there are differing interpretations of political conservatism. Such political variation has been present within Mormon conservatism for a long time, but it may have reached a defining moment in the controversial and divisive 2016 election.[18]

The most popular third-party candidate among younger Mormons was Libertarian candidate Gary Johnson, who garnered 16 percent support among Mormon Millennials but only 8 percent among Boomer/Silents. An even more dramatic generational difference existed for Green Party candidate Jill Stein, though the numbers are small: she was a nonpresence among the oldest Mormons surveyed, barely cracking 1 percent, but she received 6 percent among LDS Millennials. It should be noted that support expressed for Independent candidates in the weeks leading up to an election is not necessarily equivalent to an actual vote; many voters swing to a mainstream party candidate in the final days. Still, these early preferences among Mormon adults are interesting. In the United States, there is a trend away from political party affiliation among younger voters. Among Mormons this is slightly less pronounced than it is among Millennials in the wider population, but the apparent drift away from traditional parties is still present.[19]

On the other hand, the data also shows a simultaneous countertrend. Among those who do ally themselves with one of the two major political parties, Millennials are actually more likely than older Mormons to consider themselves "strong" members of those parties. Among current Mormons who say they are Republican, for example, nearly three-quarters of Millennials report being "strong" Republicans, versus just under two-thirds of Boomer/Silents who characterize themselves this way (72 vs. 62 percent). Among Mormon Democrats, Millennials' commitment is even greater—78 percent say they are "strong" Democrats versus 64 percent of

Boomer/Silents. This is an interesting finding that should give us pause when drawing hasty conclusions that Millennials are tuning out of politics or removing themselves from all traditional institutions. Here, they actually show signs of being *more* committed to a traditional institution than older Mormons. They also inhabit less common ground, meaning that with three-quarters of Mormon Millennials allying themselves in a forceful fashion with one of the two major parties, dialogue and compromise may be less possible.[20]

MORMON PATRIOTISM AND MILITARY SERVICE

Political affiliation is not the only area in which there is a generational difference between the oldest Mormon adults and the youngest; we also see change in how each generation views the United States. The NMS asked respondents whether they agreed with the statement "I believe the United States of America is the greatest country in the world." Since this particular point of view reflects more than basic patriotism ("I love my country"), we will refer to it as "American exceptionalism." Current Mormons express a high degree of exceptionalism overall, but there is a deep generational divide on the subject, with older Mormons far more likely than younger ones to agree that America is "the greatest country in the world." In interviews and other conversations, Millennials expressed a general sense of appreciation for the United States but also a greater willingness to criticize it. One Millennial, when asked whether America is the greatest nation, honestly wanted to know, "Greatest at what?" It's a fair question considering that in various studies, the United States has ranked first in private wealth and wealth inequality, eighteenth for quality of life, twenty-seventh for life expectancy, thirty-seventh for health care, and fifty-fifth for infant mortality.[21] The assumption that the United States is the greatest nation of all may not be the default position of Millennials who have grown up in an era of globalization—especially when many Millennial Mormons have served missions that have exposed them to other cultures.

Both current and former Mormons show much the same results on the decline of American exceptionalism, with the oldest respondents being the most enthusiastic and the youngest the least (Figure 9.1). The downward course among both current and former Mormons is similar to the one Pew has registered in the general population, though the rate of exceptionalism is higher among Mormons overall.[22] (The Silent Generation is included in Figure 9.1 as its own entity so that the NMS data can be compared on an equivalent basis to the generational data from Pew on this same question, but as always we should remember that the small number of NMS

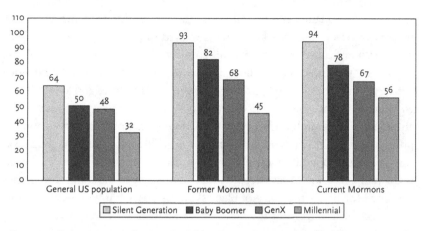

Figure 9.1. Percent Agreeing that America Is "the Greatest Country in the World."

respondents from the Silent Generation calls for prudence in interpreting those specific results.) Between the Silents and the Millennials we see nearly a forty-point drop in American exceptionalism in the current Mormon population; in the former Mormon group it is even more pronounced (93 to 45 percent).[23]

Another major difference that Pew has observed in the general population is that older Americans, especially men, have a much higher chance of having served in the military than Millennials do. This difference reflects a major change in US military policy that occurred in 1973, when the mandatory draft was ended.[24] This trend away from military service holds true for Mormons as well, though Mormons have higher rates of service than non-Mormons. Only 6 percent of LDS Millennials have served in the armed forces, and the rate climbs as the generations rise in age: 10 percent for GenX and 20 percent for the combined Boomer/Silent generation. That is including both genders. If we focus just on men, the rates of military service are 10 percent for Millennials, 19 percent for Generation X, and a remarkable 40 percent for Boomer/Silents. Note that in the general population, just 3 percent of Millennial men have served in the military. This means that while Mormon Millennial men may significantly lag their Mormon elders in military participation, their rate of service is still significantly higher than that of their non-Mormon male peers.[25]

CONCERNS ABOUT ISSUES FACING AMERICA

"Going on my mission was what made me want to be a social worker," says Ryan, a thirty-two-year-old who served a mission in the Pacific Northwest.[26]

"I was woefully inadequate as a nineteen-year-old to address mental illness or poverty or homelessness. I knew that I wanted to help people beyond 'Join my church and all your problems will go away.'" He's now a professional social worker who specializes in homeless outreach, and he credits the mission with teaching him how to approach strangers on the street and start talking with them. But the mission is also where he began experiencing serious doubts about the LDS Church, and some of those doubts stemmed from the church's positions on social issues. He considered himself a Democrat, which he says was unusual among his fellow missionaries, and he questioned some aspects of the religion. "I was always deeply troubled by some of the stuff I read in the Book of Mormon—the curse of black skin, the obsession with war and violence, and the idea that war and violence were always justifiable," Ryan says. "I was on my mission during the Iraq War and would hear people try to justify the violence using Book of Mormon references." When he learned that the church's priesthood/temple ban had been in place until 1978, he came to the uncomfortable realization that his parents had stayed faithful members all that time and did not seem to question the church's racial policies. After marrying a Mormon who was a feminist, Ryan began discovering his own "latent feminist views," and ultimately left the church when he was around thirty.

Ryan's experiences point to some of the differences between Mormon Millennials and their parents and grandparents. In particular, his concern with poverty and homelessness stands out, since Mormons of his generation consider poverty *the* top issue facing the nation today; for older Mormons it did not appear in the top five. All respondents were presented with a list of fifteen current issues and asked to choose the three they saw as the most important. As Table 9.2 shows in presenting each generation's top ten choices, Boomer/Silent Mormons zeroed in on moral or religious decline, with more than four in ten choosing that as one of their top three issues (41 percent). They also expressed concern about "changing views of the traditional family" (26 percent). Both of those items fell further down the list for Mormon Millennials: moral or religious decline was third at 27 percent, and the traditional family barely squeaked into the top ten, at 15 percent. Nearly a third of Boomer/Silents (31 percent) also cited health care as a top concern, probably because they are more likely to face illness than younger people. In contrast, LDS Millennials were more concerned about poverty, racism, and the economy than older Mormons. Issues that did not rank in the top ten for any generation of current Mormons included the environment, high taxes, police brutality, and—most surprisingly—abortion. Abortion took the next-to-last spot for GenXers and Boomer/Silents, and was last for Millennials, though percentage-wise slightly more Millennials said abortion was a top issue for them. In every generation, women and political conservatives were a bit more likely to cite it as a major concern.[27]

Table 9.2. CURRENT MORMONS' VIEWS ON TOP ISSUES FACING AMERICA,
BY GENERATION

	Boomer/Silent	GenX	Millennial
1	Moral or religious decline, 41%	Moral or religious decline, 34%	Poverty/hunger/ homelessness, 30%
2	Health care, 31%	Terrorism, 30%	Terrorism, 27%
3	[Tie] Ineffective government/ political system, 30%	Crime/violence, 29%	Moral or religious decline, 27%
4	[Tie] Terrorism, 30%	Ineffective government/ political system, 27%	Crime/violence, 26%
5	Changing views on the traditional family, 26%	Economic growth/jobs, 25%	Ineffective government/ political system, 24%
6	Poverty/hunger/ homelessness, 21%	Poverty/hunger/ homelessness, 23%	Economic growth/jobs, 23.5%
7	Crime/violence, 21%	Changing views on the traditional family, 22%	Health care, 22%
8	Immigration/undocumented aliens, 19%	Health care, 21%	Racism, 20%
9	Economic growth/jobs, 18%	Racism, 17%	Economic inequality between rich and poor, 18%
10	Economic inequality between rich and poor, 15%	Immigration/undocumented aliens, 16%	Changing views on the traditional family, 15%
11	High taxes, 11%	Economic inequality between rich and poor, 15.5%	High taxes, 14%
12	Racism, 10.5%	High taxes, 12.5%	[Tie] Immigration/ undocumented Aliens, 13%
13	The environment, 9%	The environment, 9%	[Tie] Police brutality, 13%
14	Abortion, 7%	Abortion, 7%	The environment, 12%
15	Police brutality, 6%	Police brutality, 6%	Abortion, 11%

Among former Mormons, several things were different (Table 9.3). Most
striking is that "changing views on the traditional family" did not bother any
generation of people who had left the church, ranking twelfth for Boomer/
Silents, fourteenth for GenXers, and last for Millennials. Likewise, "moral
or religious decline" ranked lower for former Mormons of every generation
than it did for current Mormons. Former Mormons feel other concerns are
more pressing—such as poverty, especially among younger respondents,
and terrorism, which also ranked highly among current Mormons. Health
care again emerges as a source of disquiet for older respondents. Former
Mormons are more worried about the environment and climate change
than current Mormons are, but fewer than one in five former Mormons list

Table 9.3. FORMER MORMONS' VIEWS ON TOP ISSUES FACING AMERICA, BY GENERATION

	Boomer/Silent	GenX	Millennial
1	Terrorism, 40.5%	Terrorism, 37%	Poverty/hunger/homelessness, 33%
2	Ineffective government/political system, 37%	Poverty/hunger/homelessness, 32%	Crime/violence, 32%
3	Health care, 35%	Health care, 29%	Economic inequality between rich and poor, 29%
4	Immigration/undocumented aliens, 31%	Crime/violence, 27%	[Tie] Terrorism, 25%
5	Crime/violence, 26%	Economic inequality between rich and poor, 27%	[Tie] Ineffective government/political system, 25%
6	Economic growth/jobs, 23%	[Tie] Economic growth/jobs, 26%	Health care, 24%
7	Poverty/hunger/homelessness, 22%	[Tie] Ineffective government/political system, 26%	Racism, 24%*
8	Moral or religious decline, 21.5%	Environment/climate change, 17%	Environment/climate change, 18%
9	Economic inequality between rich and poor, 18%	Racism, 15%	[Tie] Economic growth/jobs, 17%
10	Environment/climate change, 17%	Moral or religious decline, 15%	[Tie] Moral or religious decline, 17%
11	Racism, 10%	Police brutality, 13%	Police brutality, 14%
12	Changing views on the traditional family, 5%	Immigration/undocumented aliens, 13%	Immigration/undocumented aliens, 12%
13	High taxes, 4%	High taxes, 11%	High taxes, 11%
14	Police brutality, 3%	Changing views on the traditional family, 8%	Abortion, 10%
15	Abortion, 2%	Abortion, 1.5%	Changing views on the traditional family, 9%

* Health care and racism appear to be tied due to rounding, but health care slightly edged out racism by two-tenths of a percent.

the environment as one of their top anxieties, so it's not an overwhelming difference.

Overall, the most remarkable difference relates to how few former Mormons are concerned with changes to the traditional family, which is an ongoing preoccupation of LDS leaders and features in multiple talks at each General Conference. Conflicting ideas of morality also featured in other responses, where we can see clear differences between current and former

Mormons—and also between older and younger generations of current Mormons.

CHANGING MORAL AND SOCIAL VIEWS

The NMS repeated some questions from Pew about respondents' moral views and added several of our own. Respondents were given three options to describe how they felt about twenty different moral issues, categorizing each one as either morally wrong, morally acceptable, or "not a moral issue." In general, Mormon Millennials tend to disapprove of many of the same things their elders do. On the five measures tracked in Figure 9.2, more than 50 percent of Millennials said the actions were morally wrong, but these were still lower levels than their elders. Among the Boomer/Silent group, for example, very strong majorities said it was morally wrong to have an abortion, an extramarital affair, or a sex reassignment surgery ("sex change"). Among Millennials, censure was still high, but it dropped by double-digit percentages on every one of the five measures—from 95 to 79 percent disapproving of extramarital affairs, for example, or from 83 to 65 percent who considered abortion to be morally wrong. Often these differences tended to crystallize around sexual issues.

It is probably best to describe Millennials as *less disapproving* of these actions than their elders. They're more apt to say that something is not a moral issue. In other cases, though, Mormon Millennials are simply more positive and accepting of the behavior in question. When it comes to having a baby outside of marriage, for example, the church is clearly opposed, to the point that the LDS Handbook recommends that any expectant mother who is unmarried should plan to give her baby up for adoption.[28] Along

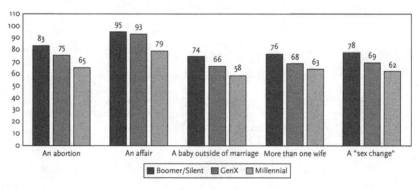

Figure 9.2. Mormons Who Believe It Is Morally Wrong to Have an Abortion, an Affair, or a Baby outside of Marriage.

these lines, almost three-quarters of Boomer/Silent Mormons say that it's morally wrong, and only 10 percent see it as morally acceptable, with the remaining 17 percent classifying it as "not a moral issue." Among Millennials, 58 percent disapprove and 25 percent say it's morally acceptable. This means that two and a half times as many Millennials as Boomer/Silent Mormons approve of having a baby outside of marriage. Approval is still a minority position, but it's higher than it is among older Mormons, perhaps reflecting how much more common out-of-wedlock birth is in this generation. The youngest Millennials have reached adulthood in a time when 42 percent of live births in the United States are to unmarried women. In the 1960s, when some of the older respondents in the NMS were young adults, this was true of only 5 percent of live births. As one researcher put it, "today's kids are eight times more likely to have come into this world without married parents than were Boomers."[29]

Yet on other questions (Figure 9.3), Mormon Millennials proved the least accepting of any generation. Nearly half think it is morally wrong to wear fur, perform stem cell research, or enact the death penalty. Particularly interesting is that four in ten Mormon Millennials say it is morally wrong to get a divorce. Not coincidentally, Millennials are also the generation most likely to have grown up with parents who divorced before they were eighteen. (Twenty-seven percent of Mormon Millennials had this experience, compared to 16 percent of Boomer/Silent Mormons and 17 percent of GenXers.) On some of these issues, LDS Millennials more closely resemble other Millennials than they do older Mormons: on the death penalty, for example, a previous study showed that 46 percent of Millennials nationally oppose it, which is strikingly similar to the NMS's finding that 46 percent of Mormon Millennials think it is morally wrong.[30]

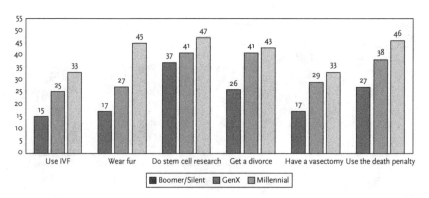

Figure 9.3. Mormons Who Believe It Is Morally Wrong to Use IVF, Wear Fur, or Do Stem Cell Research.

One interesting element of the data on sexual ethics is the strong divide that exists between Utah Mormons and non-Utah Mormons on the question of whether in vitro fertilization (IVF) is morally wrong. Such reproductive technology sometimes makes it possible for an infertile couple to conceive a child by extracting a woman's eggs and fertilizing them in a laboratory setting, then implanting one or more of the resulting fertilized embryos back into the woman's uterus in hopes of a successful pregnancy. In Mormonism, there is no official restriction on IVF other than a policy that states that if IVF is employed, only the sperm from the prospective father and an egg from the prospective mother are to be used; the church strongly discourages egg or sperm donation from others.[31] The kinds of moral challenges that are raised by some Catholics regarding IVF are rarely discussed in Mormon circles, such as what should happen to unused fertilized embryos or the ethics of implantation when there is already such a high risk that those fertilized embryos will fail to transfer successfully.[32]

Overall, Utah Mormons were noticeably more positive about IVF than non-Utah Mormons. Only 9 percent of Utah Mormons think that IVF is wrong, with the remainder divided between those who believe it is morally acceptable (42 percent) or not a moral question (49 percent). In contrast, non-Utah Mormons were split roughly into thirds for those who believe it is morally wrong (31 percent), morally acceptable (36 percent), or not a moral issue (33 percent). It is unclear why three times as many non-Utah Mormons feel IVF is inappropriate compared to those who live in Utah, especially when there is no official censure of the practice other than the specific caveat mentioned earlier. Several Mormon Millennials and GenXers I interviewed had taken advantage of assisted reproductive technology, and none of them raised ethical qualms about it. Most, in fact, were thrilled at the chance science had provided them to fulfill their religion's expectation of "multiply and replenish." Interestingly, a few were single Mormons who had either frozen their eggs or were thinking about it. Jennifer, thirty-four, had recently done this after overcoming her own reservations, mostly because "I never thought I would be that person, that I would be a statistic." But the thought kept coming back. "After many prayers, the answer I got from Heavenly Father was, 'Do everything you can do on your end to prepare, and leave the rest up to me.'. . . What that meant to me was that we live in a time with advanced technology, so I was going to take this opportunity to freeze my eggs as insurance to be able to have a family one day, even if the timing's not right now." Some of her peers, she says, got married at age twenty and never had to face these questions.

Jennifer's comment points to another interesting finding about IVF: it was Millennials who disapproved of IVF the most, and Boomer/Silents the least. A third of Millennials think IVF is morally wrong (33 percent) versus half that many Boomer/Silents (15 percent). Perhaps this is a life cycle effect at work, since most Millennials in our survey are still well within the years when they may assume they'll be able to bear children without medical assistance, and their views may change if they experience infertility in themselves or others. A third of LDS Millennials also say it is immoral to have a vasectomy, and only 17 percent of the Boomer/Silent cohort agrees. In my personal conversations with Millennials it became clear that a few did not know what a vasectomy was, so it's possible that this data is skewed by ignorance: people may be more likely to disapprove of something they don't understand. On the other hand, vasectomy is expressly discouraged by the LDS Church Handbook of Instructions, so perhaps Mormon Millennials do understand and are simply articulating a more orthodox, by-the-book position that is in accordance with what their religion teaches. If so, that would be surprising given this generation's apparent flexibility about other policies of the LDS Church.

HOMOSEXUALITY

We saw in chapter 7 that Millennials are more accepting of the idea of homosexuality than the oldest Mormons are, and are warming to the legality of same-sex marriage. So it's not surprising that in this battery of questions about morality, LDS Millennials are also more accepting of the specific idea of homosexual sex. For example, only half of Millennial Mormons (50 percent) say that homosexual sex is wrong if the individuals involved are married, while nearly three-quarters of the Boomer/Silent respondents believe it's wrong (73 percent). And Millennial Mormons aren't wholly convinced that *un*married homosexual sex is wrong either—only 60 percent think so, versus 84 percent of Boomer/Silents. In both questions we see a drop even within the Millennial generation itself, in which younger Millennials (ages eighteen to twenty-six) are several points less likely to view homosexual sex as morally wrong. And former Mormons of all ages are considerably less likely to frown upon homosexual sex than current Mormons are. Only four in ten former Mormons say sex between unmarried homosexuals is morally wrong, which is more than a thirty-point drop from the disapproval rate of current Mormons.

Given these deep divisions, it's not surprising that one interviewee after another brought up LGBT issues as particularly significant in their decision about whether to leave Mormonism. One Millennial who is trying to stay in the church despite her misgivings about LGBT equality is Blaire, thirty-three.[33] Once a Primary president in her local ward, she now has no calling, and several years ago her temple recommend became a casualty of her outspokenness on women's ordination and LGBT rights. What she said was "nothing aggressive or defiant," she notes, but the bishop called her into his office to discuss the possibility of a disciplinary council. She found his response "shocking and frustrating," especially after all the time and energy she had poured into serving the ward. After a couple of meetings the bishop told Blaire she could either stop speaking about controversial issues or have a disciplinary council about her temple recommend. Since she hadn't been to the temple in a while and didn't want to participate in what she calls "the authority power plays of local leadership," she surrendered her temple recommend. "The bishop may control my standing in the LDS Church, but not my standing with God or Mormonism," she says.

Now she is at a crossroads. When the church's new LGBT policy was leaked in November 2015, she and her husband were planning to baptize their eight-year-old son, the oldest of their three children. At the time of our interview the following summer, they still had not done so. "The only reason we were exempt from that policy was because I married a man, when I am equally attracted to women," explains Blaire, who is bisexual but has been quiet about that fact at church. "I really do want to baptize him, but I don't know how I can be true to my Mormon community and to my queer community. It's extremely conflicting. I'm very devoted to Mormonism, but I also can't deny my queer side. It's frustrating."

Despite her anger and sadness about the LGBT policy, Blaire has no desire to leave the fold. A ninth-generation Mormon, she has ancestors who numbered among Joseph Smith's inner circle and were some of the earliest members of the faith. "If there is Mormon DNA, I have it," she explains simply. Although she willingly yielded her temple recommend, she promises she would fight to retain her church membership. "If someone wants to take away my temple recommend, let them have it, but they're going to have to kick me out because I'm not planning to leave the Church."

People leaving the church over LGBT issues seems to be a relatively recent development; as we will see in chapter 11, it is the third-most-cited reason for Millennials to leave, but did not even rank in the top ten reasons for leaving for former Mormons of the Boomer/Silent generation. Char, age forty-two, is old enough to have seen friends leave the LDS Church because of its involvement in Proposition 8 in California in 2008.[34] Politics, she says, proved very divisive—and ultimately fatal to her friends' engagement with the church. "What I find is that for many of them [who have left], they still believe" in the church's basic doctrines, "but if the thing they are struggling with is political, they no longer feel comfortable in Mormon society. I know people who are essentially believers, but there is that one thing."

What is happening here? Why is politics the "one thing" that is strong enough to push some Millennials out of Mormonism, whether it's Natalie's disgust at active members' support for a misogynist presidential candidate or Char's friends leaving the church over LGBT issues despite still believing the religion's core doctrines? We are seeing here the fruit of the politicization of religion in America. Conservative Christianity's single-minded focus on certain social and political issues has created a situation in which anyone who holds contrary opinions no longer feels comfortable within the faith. It used to be a truism in American politics that when people's political positions collided with those of their religious tradition, they would likely privilege belonging to the tradition. That cannot be taken for granted any longer, especially among younger Americans. There is a strong correlation among them between progressive views on sexuality and disaffiliation from organized religion.[35] Researchers have long noted that people's religious views could influence their political behavior; now they are finding that the relationship points the other way too, as political views can drive *religious* behavior.[36] In particular, those who feel their churches are hostile toward their own political values are more likely to leave them. This research has focused on the visibility of the religious Right as a catalyst for people leaving organized religion, as the conservative political agenda has "led liberals and young people who already had weak attachment to organized religion to drop that identification."[37] But it translates well to Mormonism, whose leaders have been as politically vocal on issues such as same-sex marriage as the principal players of the Christian Right. In doing so, LDS leaders have created an uncomfortable situation for Mormons who disagree, a discomfort that is heightened when apostles appear to anathematize such disagreement. Elder Dallin H. Oaks, for example, stated in 2017 that "converted Latter-day Saints" are ones who believe the church's teachings on traditional marriage, suggesting that Mormons who approve of same-sex marriage have not truly understood their own religion. And in 2016, then-Elder Russell M. Nelson implied that church members who did not accept the 2015 LGBT policy as divine revelation were acting under the influence of Satan.[38] Such remarks indicate that leaders may see Mormons with differing social views as unconverted at best or demonic at worst.

What's particularly interesting is how thoroughly young adults who leave organized religion over this issue have assimilated their churches' overall lesson that these sexual issues are paramount; they are essential; they are not to be ignored. Churches have forced people to choose, so that young adults who disagree with their religions' LGBT stance can either compromise their personal values or obey their consciences and leave the faith. Churches have sent the message that homosexuality is a make-or-break issue, and many young people are choosing to break with their churches. We'll see in the next chapter that this is a bit more complicated for Mormons, who tend to have a high regard for institutional authority, but it is increasingly true that even Mormons, when faced with the crisis of siding with their beloved religious institution on political matters or following their own values, will make the heartrending decision to obey their consciences.

FORMER MORMONS

We've seen in this chapter that views on homosexuality differ greatly between current and former Mormons. As shown in Table 9.4, though, this divide is true of most sexual issues we measured, in which current Mormons are more likely to disapprove of various behaviors than former Mormons are. Homosexuality is an obvious one, in that current Mormons are more than twice as likely to disapprove of homosexual sex. But former Mormons did not register strong disapproval for any of these other behaviors either, except for polygamy and extramarital affairs, in which their disapproval was equivalent to or even a little stronger than current Mormons'.

Former Mormons appear to disagree sharply with the LDS Church's position on most sexual issues. They are about evenly divided on whether it's morally acceptable to have a baby outside of marriage, for example, with a third disapproving, a third approving, and another third saying it's not a moral issue. Another way of looking at this data is that two-thirds of former Mormons either approve of having a baby outside of marriage or don't agree with the church's opinion that doing so is automatically

Table 9.4. CURRENT AND FORMER MORMONS' VIEWS ON SEXUAL ISSUES, COMPARED

Percent Who See This as "Morally Wrong"	Former Mormons (All)	Current Mormons (All)
Sex between unmarried heterosexual adults	32%	68%
Sex between unmarried homosexual adults	40%	72%
Sex between married homosexual adults	33.5%	63%
Having a baby outside of marriage	34%	65%
Sex reassignment surgery ("sex change")	44%	69%
Stem cell research obtained from human embryos	29%	42%
Surgical sterilization/vasectomy	15%	27%
Surrogate motherhood	12%	26%
In vitro fertilization (IVF)	16%	25%
Polygamy (having more than one wife)	68%	69%
Having an extramarital affair	90%	88%
Having an abortion	52%	74%

immoral. Also, only four in ten think that a sex reassignment surgery—which is discussed in the LDS Handbook as grounds for losing a temple recommend—is wrong, compared to nearly seven in ten current Mormons. Barely half of former Mormons think abortion is morally wrong, compared to nearly three-quarters of current Mormons. On all these matters former Mormons deviate strikingly from the moral views expressed by the institutional church: the Handbook makes clear, for example, that having an abortion is grounds for excommunication unless the pregnancy resulted from rape or incest, the pregnancy is a danger to the mother, or the fetus has severe defects that would not allow it to survive past birth.[39]

On two other issues, the church *does* have a position that is either unknown to many members or ignored by them. The Handbook "strongly discourages surgical sterilization as an elective form of birth control."[40] This includes vasectomy, but as we can see from the data, most Latter-day Saints do not have a problem with the practice. Neither do the vast majority of former Mormons, with only 15 percent viewing permanent sterilization as morally wrong. It also includes surrogate motherhood, in which an egg is fertilized by means of assisted reproductive technology but then not implanted in the uterus of the intended mother, whose body may not be capable of carrying a pregnancy to term. Another woman carries the pregnancy and gives birth to the baby, who is then raised by the biological parents. The Handbook expressly discourages surrogacy, yet in Mormonism's decidedly pronatalist culture it occurs among otherwise wholly orthodox Mormon families, including most famously Mitt Romney's oldest son Tagg and his wife.[41]

On many social issues, current and former Mormons differ markedly, and that difference is also apparent in political party preference (Figure 9.4). Not surprisingly, former Mormons are significantly less likely to be Republican. In fact, there is a nineteen-point difference between the current Mormons who identify with the GOP (57 percent) and the former Mormons who do (38 percent). There is a corresponding rise in affiliation with the Democratic Party (+14 percent) and in Independent voting (+5 percent). Generationally, fewer than one in three former Mormon Millennials identify with the GOP, while more than half (55.5 percent) vote or lean Democratic. This is more than twenty points higher than the 35 percent of Boomer/Silent former Mormons who do.

In some ways, though, former Mormons are similar to current ones in their political views and involvement. In both groups, just over half say they enjoy following the news, with former Mormons enjoying it a bit more (60 percent) than current ones (53 percent). In both groups, more

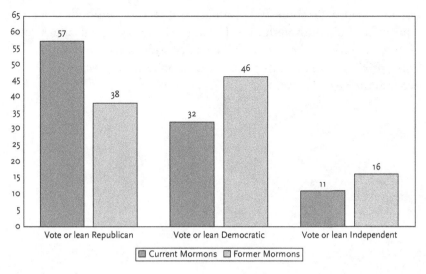

Figure 9.4. Current and Former Mormons' Political Party Affiliation.

than half feel that government "is almost always wasteful and inefficient" (57 percent of former Mormons and 56 percent of current ones). Like current Mormons, those who have left the LDS Church are not persuaded that a larger government necessarily equals a better one. Barely a quarter of former Mormons (28 percent) "prefer a bigger government that provides more services rather than a smaller government that provides fewer services," which is only eight points higher than among current Mormons (20 percent). Among both current and former Mormons, then, small government is decidedly more popular.

We have seen that there are deep political divisions in two separate areas: between current and former Mormons, most obviously, but also more subtly between different generations of those who are still active in the LDS Church. Elaine, thirty-five, reflected on this generational change at the end of our interview. "I think my generation of Mormons is more liberal-minded than my parents' generation, both politically and ethically," she said. "My generation—not everyone—is more open to things like gay marriage, and less politically conservative. As far as women's rights and gay marriage and women working outside the home, my generation is a little more open to that."[42] The problem with Millennials' greater liberalism on these social issues is that the church has often staked its claim in the opposite direction, such as with repeated public opposition to same-sex marriage or the Equal Rights Amendment for women. Modern Mormonism has carved out an identity that capitalizes on conservative family values, so what happens when those values begin to be a liability for some of its youngest adherents? This boils down to a question of religious authority: If young Mormons' social values come into conflict with those of their religious leaders, whose opinions will they privilege—their own or the institution's? This question forms the core of the next chapter.

CHAPTER 10

The Realignment of Mormon Religious Authority

When you're a Mormon kid, going to high school in a non-Mormon area can be difficult. You're in the minority everywhere except at church. You often have to explain, or even defend, your religion to people who don't understand it. (Several of the people I interviewed told me about standing up to teachers who made anti-Mormon remarks, for example.) It is challenging under the best of circumstances. But it wasn't the best of circumstances in 2008 in California, when Mikey, now twenty-five, was attending high school. Rather, it was the height of the controversy over Proposition 8.[1]

And this was terribly confusing for Mikey, because he was not exactly sure how he felt about Prop 8. He was sure how his church and his parents *wanted* him to feel—his parents, in fact, put a pro–Prop 8 bumper sticker on his car without asking his permission. In response, some students wrote "bigot" on his car. Mikey was aware that some of his friends were probably gay, so he "didn't bring it up on purpose," preferring to avoid discussion. He was relieved that when the measure passed and there was so much anti-Mormon backlash, all of his friends who had opposed the measure remained friends with him. He was glad he didn't "have a target on [his] back anymore," but he knew the issue of same-sex marriage was not truly resolved, either in national politics or in his own mind.

In our interview, Mikey never directly stated that he felt the church was wrong about Prop 8, but it was also clear he was not a knee-jerk supporter. He had to be persuaded to adopt the church's position. During the Prop 8 controversy, he attended a broadcast in which LDS leaders were encouraging church members to donate money to the measure and to give their time to phone banks and door-to-door canvassing. Although Mikey says, "On the question of gay marriage, I wasn't able to form an opinion about it," he listened to everything the leaders said and prayed about it. During the broadcast he had a spiritual impression that he should support the initiative, not because it was how he felt himself, but because beloved church leaders were asking him to follow their counsel:

> I think the biggest takeaway for me was that I don't know everything in the big scheme of life, and that even if leaders were wrong about Prop 8, I could feel safe as a member by supporting the prophet. It's a feeling; I can't describe it. It wasn't anything specific, except feeling that I can be at peace. I don't need to be obnoxious about what I believe, but I can support the prophet.

In the end, Mikey backed the church's actions because bowing to prophetic authority was part of how he demonstrated his loyalty to, and love for, his religion. He says he would probably follow the same course now. "I think I would still have a really hard time," he admits. "I would do the same things—pray and fast and go to the temple. And eventually I probably would support it, but quietly. I wouldn't post things on Facebook telling other people they're wrong." Heeding prophetic authority, he says, is a vital part of what it means to be Mormon. "I feel like it's very important to follow the prophet even if you don't know the answer," he explains. He adds that as an academic, it's not like he is anti-intellectual; he thinks "there's plenty of room for discussion or disagreement" in the church. But he places a high value on listening to the prophet, even if he is inclined at first to disagree:

> I need to, at the very least, have spiritual insight on what the prophet has to say. A lot of times it's that I disagree but I follow. . . . We are just a bunch of men and women who don't know the full picture and are trying to do the best with the information we are given . . . and then we update our belief system when there is new information. Line upon line.

Mikey's thoughtful ruminations about ecclesiastical authority get to the heart of this chapter. Millennial Mormons have grown up in a religious tradition that places a premium on obeying the leaders of the church, and they have inherited modern Mormonism's expanded view of the role of the prophet. However, they're also embedded within a generation that takes a dim view of many traditional institutions, including religious ones, and has tended to qualify claims to exclusive truth. How are young adult Mormons reconciling these tensions within themselves? In what ways do they regard authority differently than older Mormons do?

Mormons stand apart from many other faiths because they believe their leaders are the only men authorized by Jesus Christ himself to exercise all the authority of the holy priesthood. Given this belief—that Mormonism's uniqueness stretches from its ecclesiastical authority in the form of prophets and apostles—it's not surprising that the religion strongly emphasizes obeying the teachings of those leaders.

Mormonism currently holds two different ideals in tension. At one extreme is the rulebook of following the prophet, encoded by the late church president Ezra Taft Benson as "fourteen fundamentals." These included the ideas that the teachings of a living prophet always supersede those of a former one, that the living prophet "is more vital . . . than the standard works" of scripture, and that the Lord would never permit the prophet to lead the people of the church astray.[2] Benson advised church members that if they ever experienced a conflict between "earthly knowledge" and the prophet's teachings, they should "stand with the prophet." Even the notion that Mormons would call the president of their church "the prophet" is a mid-twentieth-century innovation; the practice can be dated to 1955, during the presidency of the exceptionally popular David O. McKay. Before 1955 the term "prophet" was used in LDS periodicals to refer to founding leaders Joseph Smith and Brigham Young, or else to prophets from scripture.[3] Recently, obedience and following the prophet have become regular topics in LDS curriculum. In 2016, for example, they were reinforced in the revised seminary Doctrinal Mastery program for high school students. For the church as a whole, words such as "authority" and "obedience" have increased in frequency in General Conference usage in the last two decades.[4]

On the other hand, there has also been a countervailing trend in which some LDS leaders have reiterated that the prophet is not infallible and general authorities can make mistakes, as when Elder Dieter Uchtdorf acknowledged in 2013 that "there may have been things said or done that were not in harmony with our values, principles, or doctrine."[5] These are difficult approaches to hold in balance, and the fact that Uchtdorf did not specify which mistakes may have been made and by which leaders is an indication of just how taboo it is to criticize or publicly disagree with an LDS prophet or apostle. It is remarkably rare for the church to disavow statements or actions from its leaders, even long-dead ones.[6] Even doctrines that were taught in the distant past and have not been emphasized in decades are almost never publicly renounced. Instead, they quietly slip out of leaders' teachings and disappear from church publications.

Mormonism, then, places a premium on the church's institutional authority, to the point of regarding its prophet as the only person in the world who is fully authorized to speak for God. This belief is potentially a hard sell with a generation of young Americans that has little trust in institutional authority. Generational researchers have noted that both GenXers and Millennials seem averse to large institutions—the stereotype being that GenXers are suspicious of them, and Millennials are not suspicious so much as disengaged or apathetic.[7] There is some truth to those stereotypes. Pew has tracked Millennials' disaffection from various institutions, including religious ones, and noted steep declines in even a few short years. In 2010, for example, 73 percent of Millennials said they believed churches and religious organizations had a positive effect on where the country was going, but when the question was asked again just five years later, only 55 percent still felt that way.[8] The NMS showed Mormon Millennials to be more positive about religious institutions than their non-Mormon Millennial peers, but not as enthusiastic as their Mormon elders. It invited respondents to agree or disagree with the statement "I think that religious organizations are a great force for good." In general, Mormons were quite positive about this statement, with 71 percent agreeing. Predictably, however, older Mormons were far more sanguine about it than younger ones: eight out of ten members of the Boomer/Silent cohort agreed (with the Silents garnering more than 90 percent consensus), compared to just six in ten Millennials (Figure 10.1).

There are other indications in the survey that Millennials are less vigorous in their embrace of institutional authority. For example, Millennials

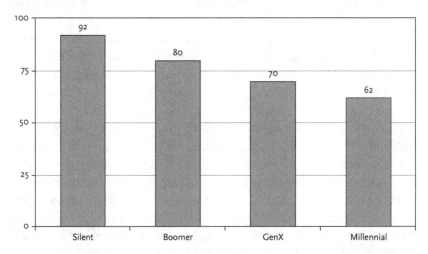

Figure 10.1. Mormons Who Think "Religious Organizations Are a Great Force For Good," by Generation.

Table 10.1. MORMONS WHO ARE TROUBLED BY "THE CHURCH'S EMPHASIS ON CONFORMITY AND OBEDIENCE," BY GENERATION

	Boomer/Silent	GenX	Millennial
Very troubling	12%	19%	26%
A little troubling	19%	32%	30%
Not at all troubling	69%	49%	44%

are less likely to name "having a prophet on the earth today" as a favorite aspect of being Mormon. This ranked seventh of nine possible choices for Millennials, with 22 percent choosing it as one of their top three features. For Boomer/Silents it was fourth, chosen by 34 percent of people. Millennials were also slightly less likely than older Mormons to say that obeying leaders was essential to being a good Mormon: 70 percent of Boomer/Silents agree, compared to 59 percent of Millennials.

We see even larger differences on the question of whether Mormons are troubled by the church's culture of obedience (Table 10.1). Nearly seven in ten Boomer/Silent Mormons said they were "not at all troubled" by "the Church's emphasis on obedience and conformity." In contrast, only 44 percent of Millennials were not at all troubled, a twenty-five-point drop from the Boomer/Silents.

These various data points signal something important: Millennial Mormons hold institutional authority more lightly than their elders. It's not a massive or dramatic change, but it is noticeable. That's not to say that Millennials differ in every way on questions of institutional authority. For instance, the NMS asked respondents to select which characteristics made general authorities "more effective leaders" in their eyes, and offered two pairs of traits to choose from: strength and confidence or authenticity and vulnerability. Six in ten Mormons said they prefer LDS leaders to project strength and confidence, while four in ten chose authenticity and vulnerability. This did not vary by more than a couple of points from one generation to another, so age was not a factor.[9] Yet Mormon Millennials do have a more distant relationship to the LDS Church as an institution, which we can measure in several ways, including how they make moral decisions.

COMPETING SOURCES OF AUTHORITY

The NMS asked Mormon respondents to rank a dozen sources of authority on a scale of one to five, based on which sources they consult most when making moral decisions.[10] Given how essential the counsel of LDS general authorities is considered for Mormon life, I was expecting to see church leaders at the top of the list for Mormons in general, with some possible dilution of their importance in the lives of younger respondents. What the NMS showed instead is that this kind of prophetic counsel ranked fifth overall on the list of twelve items, after respondents' own conscience, promptings of the Spirit, family advice, and the scriptures. Looking at Table 10.2, we can see that on average, church members were significantly more likely to privilege their own conscience and spiritual impressions than they were the authority of high-ranking church leaders. Mormons do not perceive themselves to be following the prophet at the expense of their own spiritual authority or the opinions of those closest to them. Prophetic counsel is one of several sources they consult when making moral decisions, but it is hardly the only one. In fact, half of the respondents didn't have LDS general authorities in their top five. As we might expect, highly orthodox Mormons were the most likely to do so, and doubters the least, based on their answers to the survey's theological questions.[11]

This does break down generationally in some expected ways. Older Mormons are more inclined than younger ones to say that LDS general authorities are a major authority in their decision making: nearly six in ten Boomer/Silent Mormons listed this in their top choices, while only four in ten Millennials did. That a majority of LDS Millennials would not include Mormonism's institutional leadership as a major source of moral authority in their personal decision making might seem to be a clear indication that they are following their generation's rejection of institutional authority in

Table 10.2. MORMONS' TOP SOURCES
OF AUTHORITY

		Average
1	Own conscience	2.43
2	Promptings from Spirit	2.3
3	Family members	2.0
4	Scriptures	1.71
5	LDS general authorities	1.58
6	LDS local authorities	1.35
7	Friends/coworkers	0.83
8	Philosophy and reason	0.73
9	Societal norms/values	0.44
10	Professional counselor/therapist	0.38
11	Media	0.27
12	Celebrities (Brené Brown/Colbert)	0.19

favor of their own moral conscience and personal experience. Except that they're not—not exactly. Mormon Millennials may be paying less attention to LDS general authorities, but they are not replacing that source with a reliance on their own ability to make moral choices. The NMS shows, instead, that Millennial Mormons are much *less* likely than Boomer/ Silent Mormons and GenXers to regard their own conscience or spiritual promptings as authoritative (Figure 10.2).

So if Millennials are not turning to their own experiences to fill the void left by prophetic counsel, where are they turning? It's not celebrities, despite the criticism this generation has taken from elders who might accuse them of being too easily persuaded by the opinions of the famous. And it's not human reason, despite the fact that Mormon Millennials are, for example, more likely than older Mormons to believe in evolution.[12] Rather, it seems to be the influence of the people they love—family members especially, but also friends and local bishops. (The authority of local church leaders in

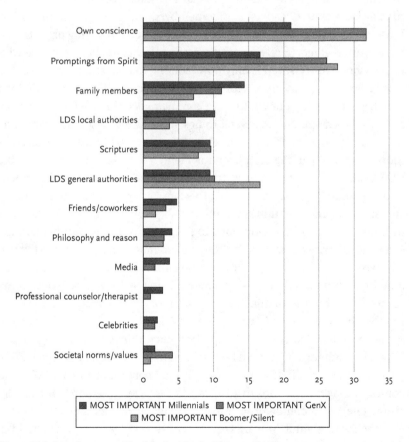

Figure 10.2. Most Important Moral Authorities for Mormons, by Generation.

the lives of this generation is something we'll explore later in the chapter.) Mormon Millennials report they are listening to and allowing themselves to be swayed by the people closest to them, which should come as good news to their parents and other family members. The darker side of this is that some generational researchers have labeled this generation as perpetually immature for just this reason: a need for prolonged coddling compared to previous generations when they entered adulthood.[13] The whole concept of "delayed adulthood" has been largely dismissed throughout this book because some of its classic markers—such as putting off jobs and living at home with parents—are largely absent among Mormon Millennials compared with other Millennials.[14] However, their uncertainty about trusting in their own experience or relationship with God may signal that in other ways, Mormon Millennials are not immune to the need to find authority outside of themselves.

Perhaps the ability to regard one's own spiritual experiences and interpretations as authoritative is something people grow into with age. Millennials are likely to credit personal relationships with trusted adults such as local church leaders, family members, and professional therapists. I would suggest that as some people age, they drift from relying primarily on those trusted elders to relying on themselves.[15] That has been the case with Jayne, who at thirty-seven is only now "coming to understand that I am the best person to make decisions for me. And in saying that, I know that I don't even believe that right now! But I am coming to believe it."[16] Her hesitation, she says, is wrapped up in several things about being raised Mormon. She feels that as a woman, she has never been encouraged to trust her own authority, especially in the temple endowment. She's also concerned that the LDS Church's claim to exclusive truth and priesthood authority "automatically sets one person up to feel that they are better than the other person," and such judgment is unhealthy. Above all, though, she senses that as a Mormon she has been conditioned to put her trust in the prophet and the external authority of the church. "Relying too much on a prophet to tell you what you can and cannot do creates problems. . . . I never actually relied on how I felt about anything. I always referred to what other people told me I should feel about something, to their authority, and that created problems in other areas of my life." Jayne claims she "didn't own" the decisions she made and tended to blame other people when things went wrong. "I was always second-guessing myself because I thought someone else knew more about me than me. That's a message that I got somehow, and a lot of it did come from my religious life, that I always had to get permission to make a decision. I never felt confident spiritually to make strong decisions for myself."

Other young adult Mormons have had the opposite experience. Lisa, thirty-two, grew up in a Mormon family that privileged spiritual experiences of God and often shared their dreams and impressions with each other at home: "I felt the Spirit when this happened" or "I had this revelation." The miraculous was as normal in their home as the weather. Her dad would read to her from the journals of their pioneer ancestors, who seemed to regularly have extraordinary encounters with God. Then Lisa went on a mission to Canada and ran headlong into the church's culture of obedience, which had never been her primary experience of Mormonism even though she grew up in a small Utah town that was more than 90 percent LDS. The mission was an eye-opener for Lisa, and not in a good way. "My own spiritual experiences had always been my own authority, and on my mission I was told that the Church's authority was more important," she says. "Somewhere I decided that this was the voice I should listen to." Lisa stopped journaling, and her personal prayer life suffered as she emphasized keeping the mission rules but neglected the devotional habits that had long been her spiritual lifeline. About halfway through the mission she realized she was "very disconnected with myself and with God." In the decade since her mission, she has remained somewhat active in the LDS Church but never with the conviction and peace she used to have. She would like to reclaim her sense of spiritual authority and the deep, automatic connection she once felt with God, but the LDS Church "has become so institutional, which is not at all the way I experienced Mormonism in my childhood," and it no longer feels like home.

FOLLOWING THE PROPHET

Both Jayne and Lisa are struggling with the church's authority in their lives, even though their stories are so different: Jayne is trying to conjure a sense of spiritual authority she has never truly felt, while Lisa hopes to reclaim one. At critical times in their journeys, both women received the message that their own ideas and relationships to divinity were less important than obeying the mandates of the institutional church. They're not alone in feeling ambivalent about LDS leaders' power in their everyday lives; we can see from the data that Millennials struggle with how to balance their own authority with that of the church.

The NMS had other ways of assessing how Mormons regard the church's institutional authority in their lives. The first is fairly straightforward: determining how often Mormons watch General Conference. What's interesting about this question is that it set a very low bar for participation: respondents could answer "yes" to it even if they had watched as little as one Conference talk in the last six months. (The question did not encompass those who *read* copies of the talks, just those who watched them in some way.)

Overall, it was surprising that many otherwise orthodox Mormons seem to be skipping General Conference, particularly when so many options now exist for streaming sessions online after Conference is over. There was also a clear generational divide in General Conference viewing habits, with the event exerting the most pull on the oldest Mormons and the least on the youngest. As we can see from Figure 10.3, fewer than half of Millennial Mormons had seen any of Conference in the last six months, compared to more than three-quarters of the Silent Generation.[17]

Perhaps the church's curricular focus on General Conference talks in other contexts has driven viewing rates down, especially for younger people; there may be less impetus to watch Conference if the next week's sacrament meeting talks will focus on it, it will be dissected over the next year in Relief Society and priesthood meetings, and it is always available online. There is also, in the United States at least, a paradigm shift in the location of General Conference viewing with so many people now watching it at home, versus the late twentieth-century model of getting dressed up and going to the church to watch it via satellite with other members. This domestication is desirable for its convenience, but social science research has found that people tend to showcase their best selves when other people can see them.[18] There's no longer a social cost attached to *not* watching General Conference; in fact, other members of the community probably won't even know if people don't.[19]

But why are young adults in particular more likely to tune out of General Conference? One possibility is that they don't see themselves represented. When members of the Silent Generation watch, they are guaranteed to see

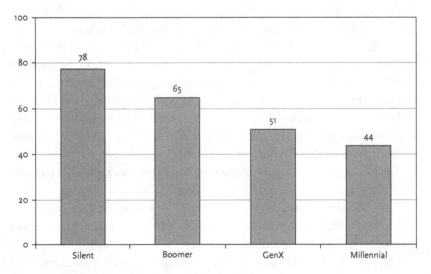

Figure 10.3. Viewing General Conference, by Generation.

and hear men from their own generation, since several of the members of the First Presidency and Quorum of the Twelve are members of the Silent or Greatest Generation.[20] Baby Boomers too can find kindred spirits of their own age in the other members of the Quorum and a majority of the Seventies and auxiliary leaders, who also speak. This is not the case for GenXers and Millennials, who will be hard pressed to find any leaders from their generations. The cultural touchstones that general authorities refer to are often events that occurred before those younger generations were even born. And of course, the entire paradigm of sitting passively for a weekend of ten hours of lectures and sermons may not be appealing to a generation that has not been trained to enjoy that scenario in any other areas of life.

The question about General Conference is not the only way to gauge Millennials' enthusiasm for, or distance from, the church's leadership. We also asked which kinds of topics church members want to hear about from top LDS leaders. Respondents were instructed to check as many topics as applied from a list of sixteen items. Some of them were spiritual (prayer, kindness, Sabbath behavior), while others were pragmatic (career and educational goals, parenting standards, financial preparedness), and others cultural or external (tattoos, clothing). What I was expecting to see from this exercise was that Mormon Millennials might welcome leaders' advice about religious topics but be lukewarm or even hostile toward advice about superficial issues like whether men can have beards or women can wear skirts above the knee. I also anticipated that Boomer/Silent Mormons would welcome guidance from prophets and other church leaders on just about any topic. However, the data showed a lower-than-expected desire for guidance on the part of all Mormons, not just Millennials (Table 10.3). The highest-rated topics in the entire current Mormon sample were prayer and kindness, at 61 percent and 56 percent, respectively; these were in fact the only areas that achieved a majority consensus among all Mormons. The least popular topics were all related to physical appearance. The fact that most topics generated such a low average response from members is surprising. Even more surprising is that the average is not that much higher among the survey's most orthodox members. Usually in the data, we see a more statistically significant divergence between the most and least active Mormons.

When we break this down by generation, we see that Millennials are somewhat less keen about receiving guidance from LDS general authorities than older Mormons are, and that this is not limited to topics related to physical appearance—in fact, Millennials seem a tiny bit *more* receptive than older Mormons to hearing about such matters, though fewer than one in five consider such guidance useful (Table 10.4). Other topics that sparked Millennials' interest compared to older Mormons included career

Table 10.3. DESIRED GUIDANCE FROM LDS
CHURCH LEADERS

It is useful when LDS Church leaders give me clear
guidance about (CHECK ALL THAT APPLY):

Prayer	61%
Kindness	56%
Financial preparedness	46%
Sabbath Day behavior	44%
Sexual purity	40%
Tithing	40%
Parenting	37%
Educational goals	34%
Media standards	29%
Career goals	28%
Social media use	27.5%
Tattoos/piercings	21.5%
Skirt length	18%
Shoulder coverage	15%
White shirts	13%
Facial hair	12%

Table 10.4. DESIRED GUIDANCE FROM LDS CHURCH LEADERS,
BY GENERATION

	Boomer/Silent	GenX	Millennial
Prayer	72%	59%	54%
Kindness	65%	56%	48.5%
Financial preparedness	55%	43%	40.5%
Sabbath Day behavior	57%	42%	34.5%
Sexual purity	48%	37%	37%
Tithing	54%	40%	29%
Parenting	45%	37%	30%
Educational goals	33%	32%	36%
Media standards	37%	25%	25%
Career goals	20%	32%	30.5%
Social media usage	33%	25%	25%
Tattoos/piercings	25%	19%	21%
Skirt length	19%	16%	18%
Shoulder coverage	14%	13%	17%
White shirts	11%	13%	15%
Facial hair	9%	10%	16%
Average	37%	31%	30%

and educational goals, which makes sense given that many are just beginning their adult lives and are making important decisions about jobs and education. On average, though, Millennials showed less zeal for leaders' guidance, with a topical average of 30 percent compared to the Boomer/Silents' 37 percent. And whereas the Boomer/Silent generation had five topics that attained majority status, for Millennials only prayer cracked that barrier—and only barely, with 54 percent.

On a third measure of how Mormons regard institutional authority, Millennials scored the lowest of any generation. Mormon respondents were presented with two statements and asked which came closer to their view: "Good Latter-day Saints should obey the counsel of priesthood leaders even if they don't necessarily know or understand why," or "Good Latter-day Saints should first seek their own personal revelation on a matter and act accordingly, even if it is in conflict with the counsel of priesthood leaders." This was adapted from a question on a prior survey but changed to add the "even if it is in conflict with the counsel of priesthood leaders" statement at the end.[21] We wanted to force the issue of what would happen if Mormons' own feelings ever came into conflict with those of church leaders. A slim majority of Mormons selected the first option: 56 percent would choose obedience to church leaders, and the remaining 44 percent would act on their personal revelation. Many of the usual trends are evident in this data: women, political conservatives, people in Utah, and those with a college degree are more likely to obey church leaders, while other groups (men, liberals, non-Utah Mormons, and those with a high school education) lean toward personal revelation.

Generational differences were also evident, as seen in Figure 10.4. Two-thirds of Boomer/Silent Mormons said they would obey priesthood leaders even if they didn't know why (65 percent), but barely half of Millennials would (51 percent). This is still a majority, which shows that the Mormon reverence for ecclesiastical authority runs deep, even among Millennials. Many are like Mikey, who supported Proposition 8 despite his reservations. Still, it's clear that any sense of default obedience is diminishing.

CALLINGS

In addition to the previous questions, the NMS also explored the area of "callings"—the assigned jobs that Mormons have in their local wards and branches. Most church members have a calling, especially outside of well-established Utah wards (in fact, in some fledgling areas of the church, members might have two or more callings). Callings are assigned by bishops, branch presidents, and stake presidents after consulting with the

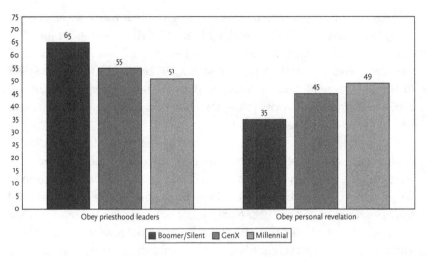

Figure 10.4. Current Mormons Who Would Obey Priesthood Leaders Versus Personal Revelation, by Generation.

individual church member, and then are affirmed by the congregation. In Mormonism, there has long been an institutional bias against ever saying "no" to a calling from a church leader. This was elevated to the status of an apostolic utterance in 1996 when Elder Boyd K. Packer instructed members that "we do not aspire to calls in the Church, nor do we ask to be released. We are called to positions in the Church by inspiration."[22] It would be unwise to refuse, he indicated, because callings come from the Lord.

To better understand how Mormons regard callings from local church leaders, the NMS asked respondents when, if ever, it is permissible to refuse such service, offering seven hypothetical scenarios that included saying no because of family responsibilities or because a person already felt overwhelmed. Most Mormons appear to have taken Packer's idea to heart: each possible reason for refusing only garnered minority support, and a third of Mormons said that it's never appropriate under any circumstances. But among those who did consider it sometimes appropriate to say no, there were some generational differences.

Millennials are more likely than older Mormons to believe it's sometimes proper to refuse (Figure 10.5). In the Boomer/Silent group, nearly half (47 percent) say that it is "never appropriate" to say no to a calling except in "very exceptional circumstances." But barely a quarter (27 percent) of Millennial Mormons agree, with GenXers falling in the middle with 36 percent. This means that among Millennial Latter-day Saints, nearly three-quarters feel it is sometimes acceptable to turn down a calling from the bishop.

Most of the Millennials I talked to were happy with their callings and not overly concerned with how or why those callings were issued. Several mentioned that their callings had helped them to grow in various ways, whether that was by teaching them how to work with different kinds of people or more effective ways to lead a class. Steve, thirty-one, describes his high school self as "wildly inactive" religiously and admits that he used to sleep through seminary. But in his senior year, the seminary teacher sat him down and gave him a job to do.[23] "I at that point did not believe at all in the church," Steve admits. "He asked me to be the president of the seminary and I told him I didn't believe and was doubting God. But he put me in charge of the seminary, which is for whatever reason a huge deal in Utah." Steve served successfully as the student president, and at the end of the year, the teacher challenged him to go on a mission, which he eventually did. In this case, having a rigorous calling proved to be a catalyst for greater activity in the church. But Steve says he's also not afraid to turn down a calling, and has done so in the past when he understood the calling would take more time than he was able to give it. His current bishop, who was apparently accustomed to people saying yes even if they had major time constraints, initially thought Steve was joking when he said no to an offered calling. The bishop soon realized Steve wasn't kidding; in fact, Steve insists it was because he *was* taking the invitation seriously that he believed someone else would be a better fit. Eventually he and the bishop settled on a calling that required less time, and Steve is happy with that. In balancing the authority of the institution with his own desires, he found a way to serve the church while also protecting his free time.

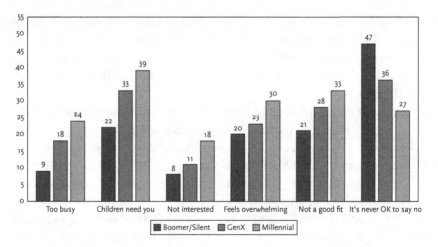

Figure 10.5. Mormon Attitudes toward Refusing a Calling, by Generation.

The NMS does not have data on whether callings help individuals stay active in the LDS Church, though as discussed in chapter 4, some other research would suggest that among single members at least, having a calling does help to increase involvement. But the fact that the NMS data shows marked positivity toward callings should be considered a hopeful sign by anyone who is interested in better engaging LDS Millennials. On questions measuring the church's authority at the institutional level—namely, how church members respond to the highest leaders and to pronouncements coming out of Salt Lake City—Millennials are lukewarm. In this question on local callings, however, most do appear to obey the church's authority. While three-quarters said that it was theoretically permissible to refuse a calling, on each of the specific hypothetical scenarios provided, only a minority actually would refuse. Callings at the local level appear to be an area where Millennials have generally warm feelings, even if they're less by the book than their elders.

RELATIONAL AUTHORITY AND THE IMPORTANCE OF BISHOPS

The data on callings hints that Millennials might regard local authority figures more favorably than they do institution-wide ones, which is a trope that emerges from the survey in other ways as well. For example, the NMS asked respondents how often they seek counsel from their local bishop or branch president when making major decisions or experiencing significant problems. I was wondering whether Boomer/Silent Mormons, with their higher regard overall for authority figures, would be more likely to consult their local leaders in such situations. This was not at all the case (Table 10.5). Fewer than one in ten Boomer/Silent Mormons consult their bishop "very often," compared to nearly a quarter of Millennials. Looked at from the other side, more than half of Boomer/Silent Mormons rarely or never seek counsel from the bishop, a situation that applies to fewer than a third of Millennials.

In part, this may be due to Millennials' relational sensibility, and to their upbringing: some generational researchers argue that Baby Boomers, possibly reacting against an authoritarian strain many experienced in their own childhoods, raised their Millennial children to regard adults more as friends than as authority figures.[24] This tendency to view adults as caring mentors in a nonadversarial partnership may apply to Mormon Millennials' strong ties with local church leaders. In part, of course, their apparent eagerness to receive counsel from the bishop is also due to where they are in the life cycle—many are seeking endorsements for missionary service, acceptance at a church-owned university, or entrance to the temple for their own or

Table 10.5. MORMONS WHO SEEK COUNSEL FROM THE LOCAL BISHOP, BY GENERATION

	Boomer/Silent	GenX	Millennial
Very often	7%	13.5%	23%
Sometimes	37%	40%	47%
Rarely or never	56%	46.5%	30%

friends' weddings. All of those milestones require an ecclesiastical endorsement from at least one local leader. From the data we aren't in a position to say definitively why Millennials are more likely to meet with local leaders, but the question did specifically mention "when making major decisions or experiencing significant problems." That would suggest an element of personal trust, not just a situation in which a young adult would need a bishop to sign off on a letter of recommendation.

Over and over again in interviews—even with people who had left Mormonism—Millennials had positive things to say about the local bishops and stake presidents they had known throughout their lives. One told me about a bishop who, out of his own pocket, supplemented the Young Women's activities so their budget would equal the boys', and encouraged all the girls in the ward to go on missions. I heard of Young Single Adult (YSA) ward bishops who regularly opened their homes to students and other Millennials, welcoming them for meals and fellowship, and of young adults who confessed difficult truths about themselves to bishops and received compassion in return. Jon, twenty-nine, a gay man in California, told me that the first person he ever came out to was his bishop.[25] He was, Jon remembers, "humble and unassuming," and did not rush to issue advice or behavioral mandates. Instead, the bishop listened carefully before asking for a few days to pray and fast. "A week later, he had fasted and gone to the temple, and the main message he had for me was that I would have all of the resources I needed to have a happy and successful life," Jon says.

There were a few negative stories, like one woman whose bishop had told her to *not* serve a mission but to jump at a chance to get married, which she had determined from personal revelation was not the right decision for her at that time. (She followed her own revelation.) But overall, the thrust of the stories about bishops was overwhelmingly friendly. Some Millennials were cognizant of the tremendous amount of time bishops spend on church work, with no remuneration. Several mentioned that they had won "bishop roulette"—a phrase we've already heard from at least two interviewees—indicating that they felt lucky, in the hierarchical system that is Mormon leadership, to have been assigned bishops who loved and understood them. In fact, the phrase and the sentiment came up often enough that it was rarer to find interviewees who *didn't* feel they had at some point won the bishop lottery.

HYPERPERSONALIZED AUTHORITY: THE PATRIARCHAL BLESSING

This chapter was supposed to end here: in the divide between institutional and relational authority, Millennials demonstrate a clear preference for the latter. However, one issue kept coming up again and again in oral history interviews: patriarchal blessings. At the core of understanding how Millennials feel about their patriarchal blessings lurks this larger question of institutional versus relational authority. Patriarchal blessings inhabit a fascinating middle space, in that they occur through the authority of the institutional church but exist to bolster an individual's own spiritual authority.

In Mormonism, a patriarchal blessing is a once-in-a-lifetime experience that often, but not always, occurs during adolescence. As a typical example we'll consider the story of Chrissy, who was sixteen when she went with her parents to receive her blessing at the stake patriarch's house.[26] A stake patriarch is a man ordained specifically to do this one thing: lay his hands on church members' heads and communicate to them what the Lord would have them know about their divine lineage, their spiritual gifts, their future life, and their family. The practice of patriarchal blessings is one of the last remaining holdovers of Mormonism's more charismatic early beginnings.[27] For Chrissy, the experience was deeply meaningful. "I felt really peaceful and I felt the Spirit a lot as he was talking, and as he had his hands on my head. I felt like his words were inspired." Although Chrissy did not imagine that the blessing should be treated like a fortune cookie predicting the contours of her future life, it did have some specific content that she felt was unique to her. "There's one spot that talked about particular leadership skills that I had and specific things I could offer because of those. And lines about my relationship with God and how I stood out previously, before we came to earth," she says. "That has always meant a lot to me." After the blessing, her parents hugged Chrissy and told her she was a special young lady, and they felt blessed to have her in their family. Chrissy remembers the event with great fondness and appreciation, but more important, she still consults her patriarchal blessing as spiritually authoritative: "Even now, I feel a particular closeness to God when I read it."

In Mormonism, the specific content of patriarchal blessings is considered sacred, and there is a reticence to share it with others who are not close family members. Yet in interviews, many Millennials seemed eager to talk about their blessings and their interpretations of them. In fact, when I first began interviewing Millennials, there was no question on my interview template about patriarchal blessings, but I added two questions midway through the interview process because so many people had broached the topic on their own.[28] I began raising the open-ended question, "Tell me about your patriarchal blessing," and then, if applicable, inquired whether people had found the counsel in their blessings useful as they made decisions and choices in their adult lives.

For many, the answer was yes. Jack, twenty-six, whose story opens this book, memorized his blessing and recited it silently to himself every day on his mission, over and over again while jumping rope.[29] Since then, he and his wife have consulted it regularly when making decisions relevant to their family. Ammon, twenty-five, also revisits his patriarchal blessing when he is at a crossroads:

> Like, right now I am looking for a new career. This job isn't what I want to do in the future. So my wife looks at my blessing, which says I will have a good career and . . . that I will make a lot of money and have a lucrative career in business, but not to worry about that. It says to focus on my kids, as my top priority. So that's nice to hear, but I'd like to know what that career is and when that day will come.[30]

For some people, patriarchal blessings are not just a roadmap to the future but a powerful memory of a spiritual experience in the past. Lillian, a thirty-eight-year-old woman who received her blessing when she was seventeen, says it was one of the most meaningful religious moments of her life, and that she sobbed most of the way through it.[31] "I felt like God really did know me. I felt that in a way that I had never felt before," she says. That does not mean, however, that aspects of the blessing don't confuse her now. A good deal of it concerned the husband she would one day have, and how her influence would help him reach his full potential. She did marry but is now divorced, so that part of the blessing is cloudy to her: "I have no idea where to put that right now." Other interviewees also mentioned the confusion they feel if certain aspects of their patriarchal blessings, especially related to marriage and family, don't "come true." For example, Kristi, forty-seven, who struggled with infertility for years, fully expected that having children would be no problem at all because it was an assumed fact in her patriarchal blessing.[32] She remains childless.

The power of patriarchal blessings for young adult Mormons lies in their individualized counsel. There appears to be wide variation in just how specific patriarchal blessings can be from one person to another. Some recipients are disappointed to get blessings that feel fairly generic, declaring an individual's lineage in the tribe of Ephraim (which is quite common), mentioning basic future elements like having a family and serving faithfully in the church, and expressing that the Lord is pleased with this person, his child. Other blessings are fiercely unique. Natalie, now forty, was told in the blessing she got as a teenager that she would serve a mission in a former Eastern bloc country; this was in the mid-1990s, several years after the fall of the Berlin Wall.[33] She later received a call to serve a mission in Russia.[34] More important, the "incredibly long, very detailed" blessing she received made a lasting impact in the way she viewed herself:

> Those were important words to a young woman who felt so small, so insecure, like I didn't have talents or abilities to do great things. And my patriarchal blessing speaks of an incredible woman, a woman of faith and fortitude and ambition. It says I have the ability to do incredible things, to persuade and influence my family and the world around me. When I read my patriarchal blessing I think that if I truly live up to this, I will die happy. That is a worthy picture of a person I would love to be.

Natalie has had her own struggles with the church, as we saw at the start of chapter 9. She still attends, but she no longer wears her garments, and she has started drinking coffee. She holds to the beauty of her patriarchal blessing, though, and finds particular comfort in its words even now, after her faith transition. "One of the things that my patriarchal blessing says ... is that I will never be capable of doing anything that would bring shame on my family or the church. It also encourages me in my life to always seek counsel from my parents, as well as church leaders. To take their counsel because they will always have my best interest at heart."

For Natalie, and many other people I talked to, the patriarchal blessing is taken as a word from God, directed to the individual person, as a kind of North Star to follow. It can provide consolation in disappointment and guidance in decision making, but its authority comes from the fact that Mormons regard it as a divine projection of what constitutes a meaningful life. The fact that such blessings are received and pronounced only through the authority of the priesthood of the LDS Church actually helps to underscore the value of the church's authority in the eyes of Miranda, thirty-five. "My patriarchal blessing is probably the reason I'm still a Mormon today, in that it was a very powerful experience that I felt was just for me," she says. "It was the moment I felt that God knew me and was aware of me, and that for whatever reason, this church was a vehicle through which that could be accessed. I'm probably a Mormon because of that. I believe in God because of it."

These startling statements—that Miranda remains a Mormon because of her patriarchal blessing, and that it has even sustained her belief in

God—speak to the complex interplay between patriarchal blessings, institutional authority, and personal connection to the divine. For Miranda, the institutional authority of the LDS Church feels more true because the church was the "vehicle" through which she felt personally known by God. On the one hand, patriarchal blessings are a church-sanctioned experience every step of the way: you have to have a bishop's interview before getting one, the blessing is pronounced by a stake leader who holds that particular office of the Melchizedek priesthood, and it is forever after tied to your church membership number and available to you only by requesting a copy through the church. The process could hardly be described as anything but institutional. On the other hand, there is a strong element of the unpredictable and the individual—things that have become pretty thin on the ground in the post-Correlation LDS experience. Millennials seem to be affected by the way a patriarchal blessing empowers their *own* spiritual authority but does so through the auspices of the institutional church. The fact that Mormons are discouraged from discussing their blessings openly with one another has a perhaps unintended side effect in that individuals are free to interpret and reinterpret those blessings any way they wish, probing the words at various stages of life and arriving at new understandings they come up with themselves. No one in authority ever sits a Mormon down and declares, "This is what your patriarchal blessing means." Because the blessings are so private, church members claim authority for their own evolving perceptions. This places the tradition of patriarchal blessings at a unique crossroads in Mormonism today: they have enough of an institutional overlay to provide structure, but the lived experience of them is so localized—indeed, sometimes hyperpersonalized—that they hold a claim on a rising generation that appears to prefer a more grassroots and intimate experience of Mormonism.

CHAPTER 11

Exodus

Millennial Former Mormons

Every Sunday, James, a thirty-three-year-old graduate student, attends sacrament meeting with his wife and young children.[1] The couple met when they were in the same BYU student ward, and they married in an LDS temple when she was only twenty and he, a returned missionary, was twenty-four. Both were raised Mormon, and his father-in-law has held high callings as a mission president and temple president. James was by all accounts heading in a similar direction of strong Mormon faith and lifelong service to the church. He was not only a believer but also an apologist for the religion, taking advantage of BYU's massive library to research his many questions about Mormonism so he would be better equipped to argue with skeptics.

Yet there were fault lines, certain aspects of his religion that James couldn't quite reconcile. "I first began to have a lot of questions about social concerns—racism within the Book of Mormon and the history of the church, and an official narrative about Official Declaration 2 that did not quite work with the facts," he says.[2] Then not long after he got married, the LDS Church began vocally advocating for Proposition 8 in California, which made James "very uncomfortable." His father had come out as gay not long before, first to James and then to other members of their family. "So where a couple years earlier I probably wouldn't have blinked at the church's position, and would have unquestioningly defended the [traditional] family, my dad's coming out as gay changed my perspective."

For a time, James was able to hold his concerns at bay, partly by throwing himself into church service. He spent several years in a branch presidency in a small and struggling congregation in the Midwest. "For that period, I was just trying to help the branch survive, so I stopped thinking about all the questions I'd had," he says. It was when he moved to Utah to take a position at BYU, ironically, that he was "forced to confront a widening array of questions about church history, practice, and theology." He was working at BYU when the church adopted its 2015 LGBT exclusion policy, which hit him hard and "was the beginning of the end for my affiliation with the church." He was vocal about his disagreement on social media, which put him in an awkward position because he was employed at a church-owned university. His contract was due to expire at the end of the school year anyway, so rather than face institutional reprisal, James was allowed to finish out his contract and then quietly disappear.

In our interview nearly two years later, James was still learning how to negotiate his new life, characterizing his faith transition as a "slow burn" rather than an overnight change. He no longer considers himself Mormon, but he still attends church with his family out of respect for his wife's faith. He'll stay for sacrament meeting, but not for priesthood or Sunday School; he drinks alcohol and coffee sometimes, but never at home; he no longer pays tithing. He recently stopped wearing his garments, a change he has found liberating. "I felt like I was finally being honest with myself in my outward practices," he explains.

Telling his family and friends has been difficult. His orthodox in-laws "are fairly bewildered about what to do," though his own parents, who are now divorced, have been supportive. He has been telling his siblings one by one. "The best way to put it is that they are grieving the loss. They are going through the stages of grief, including anger and sadness." He wants to maintain close relationships with his family without kindling any hope that he will change his mind. He is not coming back to Mormonism, but neither is he planning to have his name formally removed from the church's records. "I view my Mormonness as a sort of ethnicity or heritage. So I don't think I would remove my name of my own accord. My ancestors were pioneers and early converts."

For that matter, James is a pioneer of sorts himself: one of the first in his family to leave Mormonism. And if there's a lesson that cradle Mormons learn from their history, it's that pioneers never have it easy. Deconversion, James says, has been "a very emotional and difficult process." But he's not alone in blazing this particular pioneer trail. As shown in this book's introduction, as many as half of Millennials who were raised Mormon may be leaving the faith, which is a significant change from previous generations, when the retention rate was closer to three-quarters. The picture of former Mormons that emerges from our survey is complex; leaving a religion is often the result of multiple areas of conflict, not just one. Yet there are common threads that weave the stories of people like James together.

DEMOGRAPHIC CHARACTERISTICS OF FORMER MORMONS

In some ways, it's not that surprising to see someone like James leave the church, because he shares a few broad demographic characteristics with former Mormons. In case it needs to be said again, however, correlation is not causation; a person's having one or more of these does not *cause* a person to leave Mormonism.

The first such factor is that James is a man, and as I've noted elsewhere, there's a large body of research suggesting that in this country, men are generally less religious than women. They are also more likely to disaffiliate from organized religion. In the American population, more than a quarter of men have no religious affiliation (27 percent), while this is true of less than a fifth of women (19 percent).[3] Among current Mormons, women slightly outnumber men, so it makes sense that men would logically outnumber women among former Mormons. And that does indeed seem to be true. In Pew's 2014 Religious Landscape Study, 55 percent of former Mormons were male and 45 percent female. A regression analysis of the NMS data shows that men are slightly more likely to leave Mormonism than women, after controlling for other factors.[4]

Something else James shares with other former Mormons is that his parents were divorced. Overall, 37 percent of former Mormons' parents divorced before they turned eighteen, with the highest numbers coming among Millennials. By contrast, only 20 percent of currently identified Mormons had divorced parents.[5] This connection between having divorced parents and not having a religious affiliation is also present in other studies, including research by PRRI on the Nones: in that study, 35 percent of respondents who had divorced parents were religiously unaffiliated, versus 23 percent whose parents were still married.[6] Divorce might make it more difficult to give children a religious upbringing. One parent might be more zealous than the other about taking children to church when it's his or her weekend for custody, for example, or one or both parents might remarry someone of another religion.

James is also in step with other former Mormons politically. They are noticeably less likely to be Republican, as we saw in chapter 9. Only 38 percent of former Mormons identify as or lean Republican, compared to 57 percent of current Mormons. Higher percentages of former Mormons, instead, identify as or lean Democratic or as political Independents. So James, as an

Independent who often votes for Democrats, fits right in with the political inclinations of many former Mormons.

In other areas, James is *not* typical. One of these is education. Generally speaking, less educated people are more likely to leave Mormonism, but James is pursuing his second master's degree.[7] Generally, a person with the highest level of education (postgraduate) is less likely to leave Mormonism than someone who has not finished college.[8] Other major differences are that James is heterosexual and married. Nonheterosexual respondents were more likely to leave Mormonism than "straight" people, and married individuals are noticeably more likely to stay than those who have never married.[9] Recall the statistics from chapter 4: more than two-thirds of the sample's current Mormons are married (65 percent), but fewer than half of former Mormons are (46 percent). Moreover, James was a little older than the norm: he left Mormonism in his early thirties, whereas two-thirds of former Mormons in the NMS left Mormonism before that age, with the median age being nineteen. This is also true more widely of people who leave their religious traditions: most do so in their late teens or early twenties.[10] Somewhat to my surprise, other factors that we might think would be significant—like racial identification (though there is greater racial diversity in the former Mormon sample) or living outside of Utah—do not seem to matter much in whether people leave the faith.[11]

James's case should remind us that every individual story is unique. There is no single "type" of person who disaffiliates from the LDS Church, though a constellation of characteristics and situations may illuminate larger themes. *In general*, leaving Mormonism is often correlated with being male, politically liberal, less educated, never married, from a divorced family, and/or LGBT. In all my conversations I did not find a single former Mormon who personified all of those categories simultaneously, though many, like James, embodied two or more. These various factors are considered "additive," which means that the more of these traits people have, the greater the likelihood becomes that they will be former and not current Mormons.

FORMER MORMONS' RELIGIOUS BELIEFS

Former Mormons are, not surprisingly, less likely to express belief in God and in core Mormon teachings than current Mormons are. But what is surprising is that a substantial number still hold these beliefs—especially in the youngest generation. This may reflect the fact that many young former Mormons have left the church more recently than former Mormons of older generations, and retain more of the religion's core tenets.

Recall that in the current Mormon sample, three-quarters of Mormons said they believed in God and had no doubts about it (see chapter 1). Among former Mormons, that number has been cut nearly in half, to 42 percent (Figure 11.1). Women are a little more likely than men to be in this category: 45 percent of women believe without any doubts, versus 39 percent of men.[12]

Very few former Mormons do not believe in God at all. Only 6 percent fall into this category, with another 8 percent choosing the agnostic option of "I don't know whether there is a personal God and I don't believe there is any way to find out." This means that in our sample of former Mormons, 86 percent say they believe in God, though they may have doubts at times or feel God is more like a "higher power" than a personal deity. It is therefore not accurate to characterize former Mormons as having rejected all religious belief. For most, the reality is far more nuanced and complicated.

One interesting difference between current and former Mormons is that generationally, Millennials are actually *more* likely to be strong theists than former Mormons who are older. Remember that among current Mormons, Millennials were more likely than older Mormons to say they believed in God despite having some doubts. Among former Mormons, this pattern is reversed. There's a ten-point difference between Millennials who believe

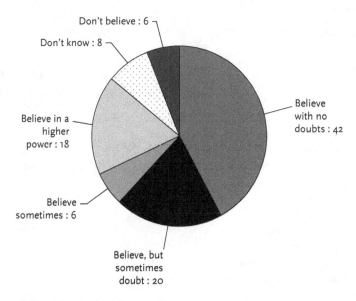

Figure 11.1. Former Mormons' Belief in God.

in God without any doubts (47 percent) and Boomer/Silents who do (37 percent). This is a difference that we will see in some other areas of belief as well. For people who are concerned about Millennials leaving the LDS Church, the silver lining is that many still have some common ground with their friends and family members who remain in the church. The flip side, however, is that merely believing in God may not be enough to hold these young adults in the fold when they disagree on social issues or feel they do not fit in to the culture.

In other questions about Christian belief, a majority of former Mormons reported that they believed in Jesus Christ, in life after death, and that God had a plan for their lives (Table 11.1). In fact, of these questions on basic Christian doctrines, the only question that did not reach 50 percent support concerned the biblical Adam and Eve.[13] Many former Mormons, then, retain belief in or even certainty about core Christian doctrines about salvation and heaven. Sometimes, these beliefs are not held as literally as they would be by churchgoing Mormons. Rob, thirty-eight, was impressed by a friend who used to be a Mormon but then was able to hold on to his belief in Christ after leaving the LDS Church.[14] Rob studied his friend's example and realized he didn't have to throw out the proverbial baby with the bathwater. "I can be a Christian by following His teachings. You don't necessarily have to believe that he was the Son of God, or physically resurrected. He's resurrected in what we do, every day."

Table 11.1. FORMER MORMONS' BELIEFS ABOUT TRADITIONAL CHRISTIAN TEACHINGS

	Those Who Are "Confident and Know This Is True"	Those Who "Believe and Have Faith That This Is Probably True"
Jesus Christ was literally resurrected and rose from the dead.	38%	15.5%
Jesus Christ is the Savior of the world and died to reconcile humanity to God.	38%	20%
God is real.	47%	15.5%
There is life after death.	40%	22%
God has a plan for my life and I will be happier if I follow that plan.	32%	21%
God created Adam and Eve sometime in the last 10,000 years and humans did not evolve from other life forms.	23%	15%

Former Mormons' belief in specifically Mormon teachings is significantly less robust than their belief in God. Overall, just one in five believe most or all of the church's teachings (20 percent), meaning that four out of five do not. Again, Millennials were a little more likely to choose the most believing option ("I believe wholeheartedly in all of the teachings of the LDS Church"), but at only 9 percent, it's still a very small minority who feel this way. (By comparison, 3 percent of GenXers and 2 percent of Boomer/ Silent respondents are complete believers in Mormon teachings.) Roughly half of each generation says that most or all of the church's teachings are difficult or impossible for them to believe. With regard to specific LDS doctrines, only about a fifth of respondents either knew or believed that Joseph Smith was a prophet or the LDS Church was the only true faith leading to exaltation (Table 11.2).

Millennials were, again, more likely to believe in specific LDS doctrines. More than two in five still believe God is a being of flesh and bone, compared to only one in five Boomer/Silent respondents.[15] A third of former LDS Millennials believe Joseph Smith was a prophet of God, while only about 12 percent of the oldest former Mormons think this is true. More than a quarter of former Mormon Millennials feel the LDS Church is the "only true faith leading to exaltation," while just 4 percent of Boomer/Silents

Table 11.2. FORMER MORMONS' BELIEFS ABOUT SPECIFIC MORMON TEACHINGS

	Those Who Are "Confident and Know This Is True"	Those Who "Believe and Have Faith That This Is Probably True"
God is an exalted person of flesh and bone.	16%	17%
Joseph Smith was a prophet of God.	8%	15%
The Book of Mormon is a literal, historical account of God's dealings with people who lived in the ancient Americas.	7%	13.5%
The LDS Church is the only true faith leading to exaltation.	6%	10%
LDS temple ordinances are ultimately the only way for families to be eternal.	6%	10%
God's priesthood authority is reserved only for men, not for women.	8%	13.5%

agree; more than a quarter think that LDS sealing ordinances are the only way for families to be eternal, compared with 6 percent of former Mormons over age fifty-two.

We also asked former Mormons how they felt about these same theological and doctrinal questions when they were in high school. What emerges most clearly when we compare these beliefs side by side is that a majority of former Mormons, especially older ones, already had significant cracks in their testimony during adolescence. For example, 42 percent believed as teenagers that the leaders of the LDS Church were God's prophets on the earth today, meaning that nearly six in ten did not; six in ten also did not believe that God's priesthood authority was reserved only for men or that the Book of Mormon was factual history. What all this suggests is that many, though not all, former Mormons were already doubters as adolescents. It's helpful to remember that this retrospective question is asking respondents to reach back years or even decades into the past, and sometimes in hindsight, we all have a tendency to remember things differently based on our circumstances and beliefs *now*. Thus, it's possible that former Mormons remember themselves as being more critical in high school than they actually were. On the other hand, the median age for defection was nineteen in the NMS, so it's reasonable that many of today's former Mormons were doubters even back then.

Charles is one of those.[16] "Since maybe age twelve or thirteen, I had been someone who asked harder questions than most," he says. One of the earliest seeds of doubt he remembers was asking how ancient fossils could exist if the earth were only a few thousand years old. His father responded that God had taken bits and pieces from other planets and enmeshed them in this world "so there would be a mixture of things that were older." (While hardly a mainstream explanation among Mormons, this theory had its proponents.[17]) Even at that age, Charles found such a circuitous explanation hard to swallow. He also questioned the church's teaching at that time that gay people had "chosen" to embrace a deviant lifestyle ("There's just no way that gays are choosing to be gay just out of a desire for sin, when being gay comes with all sorts of psychic and social pain," he protested). Yet he continued to be active in the church and served a mission. In fact, shortly before he left for his mission he was walking with a friend in a Utah cemetery and it struck them both how improbable the whole Mormon story must seem to other people. "We were looking at all the gravestones and both of us said, 'It's just implausible that we happened to be born into the only true church on the planet in history.' Numbers-wise, it's too far-fetched. What kind of God would only give the real, one truth to a tiny sliver of humanity?"

Charles completed a successful mission in Spain despite his doubts, and in fact broke his mission's record for baptizing the most new converts.

Though struggling with depression, he staved off his most serious questions until he returned home. Then, late at night after his homework was finished, he would stay awake reading on the internet about his many questions about the Book of Mormon and the veracity of Joseph Smith's claims to be a prophet. He was particularly devastated when he learned about Joseph's mendacious behavior toward women and other details about early Mormon polygamy. Charles lost his belief entirely, but unlike most people profiled in this chapter, he still considers himself Mormon and holds a calling. From all outward appearances, he is a fully orthodox Mormon, even to his own parents, who don't know the extent of his nonconformity. "I think they suspect that I'm maybe less of a believer—I freaking moved to Cambridge, after all!—but I got married in the temple, I am going to church, I blessed my babies. So as far as they know, I am keeping up with the things they care about," he says. He is attracted to the beauty of Catholic or Episcopal worship, but stays with the LDS Church because he finds value in how well Mormons create community. "I'll put up with ugly chapels and ugly art if it means that I can be part of a community where there are so many meaningful opportunities to serve and to love."

POST-MORMON RELIGIOUS LIFE

Charles's churchgoing behavior is unusual among those who have lost faith in Mormonism. Many former Mormons have a spiritual life, but it typically takes place outside of the LDS Church. Only four former Mormons in a hundred have watched any of General Conference in the last six months, for example. On the other hand, 56 percent pray at least once a week, with little variation from one generation to another. Fifty-one percent feel God's presence at least weekly; 54 percent experience a deep sense of peace and well-being; four in ten feel guided by God in their lives (42 percent). Other behaviors and experiences are less common. Only about a quarter (26 percent) say they read the scriptures at least once a week, and just one in ten have had personal faith strengthened by reading religious books.

One of the survey's most significant findings is about happiness. When asked to make a binary choice about which better described their feelings after leaving Mormonism, "freedom, possibility, and relief" or "loss, anger, or grief," 93 percent of former Mormons chose "freedom, possibility, and relief." This finding is at odds with a standing narrative in the LDS Church that to exit the fold is to leave warmth and happiness behind.[18] Despite any difficulties that their decision to leave may have caused them, the vast majority of former Mormons—more than nine out of ten—do not seem to be looking back with regret.[19]

That's not to say that such peace and happiness are achieved overnight. Rob, the thirty-eight-year-old who says it's possible to hold on to a belief in Christ even after leaving Mormonism, was initially blindsided by the loss he felt when his family left the church—first his wife, while he was still serving on his stake's high council, and then eventually him as well. During that period of questioning and doubting, Rob went on a business trip and had a profound experience while standing in line at the security checkpoint and looking around at all the other people waiting. "There was suddenly just this feeling of 'I am just like everybody else here. I am no more special than this person or that person. And I don't know who I am anymore.'" He went on:

> My whole identity had been so associated with the church. Every decision that I made was based on what was best for my family, and what my church leaders say, and what the scriptures teach. Before, I had this thing that very few people had. I was special, right? And even though I tried to be humble about it, I always felt like, "I have this thing that you need, and I should share it with you so you can discover true happiness and find salvation." And now I didn't have that anymore.

He spiraled downward for a time, questioning everything about his identity and beliefs. Over time, however, the same realization of his own nonspecialness "actually became empowering: *I am* like everyone else, and that's a good thing. We all have so much to give. I shouldn't have been on that pedestal to begin with." Rob now says he finds beauty in approaching new people by focusing on what he might learn from them, not what he might teach.

Rob and his family have tried attending Unitarian Universalist services, but he says that although people were welcoming and that church is in line with his family's social views—"on the same battlefront," as he puts it—it has not become a regular habit. Their kids like not having to go to church on Sunday mornings, and the Unitarian Universalist church didn't offer the kind of instant community he was used to having in Mormon wards. Rob also occasionally drops in on a Catholic mass, but has made no commitments there either. In this, Rob and his family are typical of most former Mormons. Just under half (44 percent) have not become involved with another religious tradition since leaving Mormonism; these are represented in Figure 11.2 under the categories atheist, agnostic, and nothing in particular. Another fifth consider themselves "just Christian" but do not specify a particular church, which likely means they have retained Christian beliefs but are not regular attenders.[20] The remaining third (33 percent) now identify as something else, mostly remaining within the Christian orbit.[21]

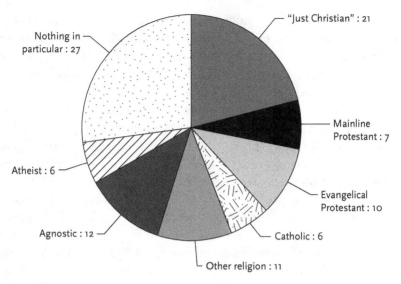

Figure 11.2. Current Religious Affiliation of Former Mormons.

Men were a little more likely than women to choose a new faith; 34 percent of former Mormon men say they are now members of other religions, and just over 31 percent of women, with Christian faiths leading in both cases. But men were also more likely than women to describe themselves as atheist, agnostic, or "nothing in particular," by a margin of about five points. Women, conversely, were more likely than men to select "just Christian" (26 percent for women, 18 percent for men).

Racially, former Mormons of color were more likely than white former Mormons either to have joined another Christian denomination or to declare themselves "just Christian"; 59 percent of nonwhites did this, compared to 41.5 percent of whites. By the same token, former Mormons of color were only half as likely to consider themselves atheists or agnostics: 10 percent, compared to 20 percent for white former Mormons.

Former Mormons' religious life is something we do have a bit of longitudinal data about. Two Utah-based studies in the early 1980s—when the church was growing numerically at a rate of 5 or 6 percent per year—show that even during that period of rapid growth, the rate of Mormons dropping out or switching to another religion actually exceeded the rate of people converting to the LDS Church in Utah. At that time, nearly six in ten Utah residents who had left Mormonism switched to other denominations, particularly Catholicism, Methodism, Lutheranism, Presbyterianism, and Baptist churches.[22] In the 2016 NMS data, as we've seen, the trajectory goes in the opposite direction: two-thirds of former Mormons have *not* reaffiliated. This change reflects the tenor of the times; in contrast to the

1980s, when those earlier studies were completed, the early twenty-first century has been an age of widespread religious disaffiliation. It is more socially acceptable than ever before to not be associated with any kind of organized religion; most people no longer need it as a social support that will advance their careers, provide opportunities for their children, or give them standing in the community. All of those things were true as recently as the mid-twentieth century. Today, in general, if people are going to be involved in organized religion, it is presumably less for social reasons than religious ones—though the persistence of Mormonism as a majority religion in Utah has meant that Mormon culture has held on to some of those advantages far longer than other pockets of America have. For example, Sarah, thirty-eight, grew up in a small Utah town and attended a public school that was more than 90 percent LDS.[23] She still lives in that community with her husband and their six children, but over the years her faith has been challenged and reshaped by various questions about women's roles and LGBT issues. She has remained active in the church despite her doubts, and continues to hold a temple recommend, though she was tempted not to renew it after the 2015 policy change about children of same-sex marriage being barred from baptism. She has a gay family member and says it "felt very disingenuous" to her to hold a temple recommend when she disagreed so strongly with the policy. In the end, though, she decided to renew it because in her small community, she and her family could have "been blacklisted" without it. For some Mormons and former Mormons in Utah, the social standing associated with church activity remains important.

Sarah is holding on to her faith and her heritage, choosing to remain active despite some misgivings. For others, occupying that middle ground has proven impossible and they leave. In interviews with those former members, I often asked them about their post-Mormon religious choices. Very few had taken the step of formally removing their names from church records, so they are still counted as members on the official rolls even though they do not attend and no longer consider themselves Mormon. In LDS polity, officially removing names is a surprisingly complicated process that requires sending a letter to the membership records department at church headquarters in Salt Lake City. It can take months.[24] Yet in most cases, it is not bureaucratic hoops that people cite as barriers to making their disaffection official. Jamie, thirty-three, says her reluctance "started as that I didn't want to hurt my family, and it also started out as kind of a sense that I would be making it a bigger deal than it needs to be if I remove my name." She is thinking about it but sees no rush.[25] Another former Mormon who has not removed his name from the church's official records is James, whose story opened this chapter. He still sees Mormonism as a core part of his identity and a link to his ancestry, a piece of himself he is unwilling to relinquish. It is interesting that despite this generation's lukewarm attitude toward institutions, Mormon identity is still so enmeshed with the institution of the LDS Church that some interviewees feel they might lose the identity if they forfeited official membership.

If removing a name from the rolls feels like a major step, one that most former Mormons are unwilling to take, then switching to another religion feels even more drastic. Jamie brought this idea to the fore. "When you come from that kind of authoritarian structure, it will foster a sense that you never want to be part of that kind of system again," she explains. She understands why many former Mormons are not very trusting of organized religion in general, having been burned in various ways in the past. She is content to satisfy her curiosity by reading about other religions, but has no desire to join any of them.

WHY THEY LEFT

As I've suggested, people's reasons for leaving Mormonism are generally varied and complex, but with the help of survey data we can tease out larger themes that transcend individual stories.[26] The NMS presented former Mormons with two lists of possible reasons for their disaffection and asked them to select up to three from each list that were the most relevant for them personally.[27] Overall, personal and social reasons outweighed any specific doctrinal or historical concerns. Combining the items from both lists, the top answer was "I could no longer reconcile my personal values and priorities with those of the Church," closely followed by "I stopped believing there was one true church" (Table 11.3). These findings are consistent with the 2016 PRRI study of Nones, for whom the top reason for disengaging from their religion was that they stopped believing its teachings.[28]

That's not to say that individual historical issues weren't important, but rather that in the context of a person's whole journey out the door, several issues work in combination, making them more likely to choose an overall loss-of-testimony option like "I stopped believing" rather than isolated historical or doctrinal issues like seer stones (6.5 percent) or the lack of DNA evidence to verify the Book of Mormon's traditional geography (3 percent). The only specific historical or doctrinal issue to rank among the top ten was concern about the historicity of the Book of Mormon and the Book of Abraham.

Consider the case of Michael, a twenty-six-year-old student at a church-owned university.[29] When I asked him the usual getting-to-know-you questions at the start of our interview—including whether he considered himself LDS now—he responded slowly, "That is a complicated question.

Table 11.3. REASONS FOR LEAVING MORMONISM

Ranking	Reason for Leaving	
1	"I could no longer reconcile my personal values and priorities with those of the Church."	38%
2	"I stopped believing there was one true church."	36.5%
3	"I did not trust the Church leadership to tell the truth surrounding controversial or historical issues."	31%
4	"I felt judged or misunderstood."	30%
5	"I drifted away from Mormonism."	26%
6	"I engaged in behaviors that the Church views as sinful."	25%
7	"The Church's positions on LGBT issues."	23%
8	"The Church's emphasis on conformity and obedience."	21%
[Tie for 8th]	"Lack of historical evidence for the Book of Mormon and/or Book of Abraham."	21%
10	"The role of women in the Church."	18%
11	"I was hurt by a negative experience at church."	17%
12	"Joseph Smith's polyandry (sealing himself to women who were already married)."	16%
13	"Excommunications of feminists and intellectuals."	16%*
14	"Joseph Smith's polygamy (sealing himself to more than one woman)."	16%
15	"I disagreed with the top-down, hierarchical structure of the Church."	15%
16	"Multiple and somewhat conflicting accounts of the First Vision."	12%
[Tie for 16th]	"I did not have meaningful friendships and social relationships at church."	12%
18	"The Church's teachings on deification (becoming like God)."	11%
[Tie for 18th]	"I was troubled by my experience with the temple."	11%
20	"Denial of priesthood and temple endowment to members of African descent before 1978."	10%
21	"Lack of financial transparency with tithing, donations, and spending."	10%
22	"I preferred to do other activities on Sunday."	10%
23	"The Church's strong culture of political conservatism."	9%
24	"I moved to a new area and stopped attending church meetings."	7%
[Tie for 24th]	"I was bored."	7%
26	"Too many difficult events [were] going on in my life outside of church."	7%
27	"Seer stones."	6.5%
28	"I had an unsuccessful mission experience."	4%
29	"DNA evidence that Native Americans do not have Middle Eastern ancestry."	3%
30	"My spouse left the church."	1%

* Because of rounding up or down to the nearest integer, some items may appear to be ties (in this case, 16 percent). However, only the items specifically marked as ties were exactly the same down to a tenth of a point.

I'm going to say yes." He considered himself a four on the one-to-ten scale where a ten indicated he was certain he would remain a Mormon for the rest of his life. Even though he was enrolled at a church school, he was leaning toward leaving Mormonism after graduation. As a gay man, he was deeply hurt by the 2015 LGBT exclusion policy, which catalyzed a "spiritual free-fall and explosion where suddenly, everything that I felt was certain was no longer certain for me." He had been mostly living in the closet, but shortly after he heard about the policy, he sought out a gay-straight alliance group in his community and came out to his mom. Other questions came to the surface about his faith. When I asked him what teachings in particular he was struggling with, he rattled off quite a list: he had problems with the temple, the idea that prophets and apostles are inspired by God, LGBT issues, and the church's treatment of women. "Basically, everything is falling apart, Jana!"

If Michael's story reflects the complexities of people's reasons for leaving—again, it's almost never just about one thing—he also voices some particular concerns of his Millennial generation. Table 11.4 shows each generation's top ten reasons for leaving side by side, and there were

Table 11.4. FORMER MORMONS' TOP TEN REASONS FOR LEAVING, BY GENERATION

	Boomer/Silent	GenX	Millennial
1	Couldn't reconcile personal values	Stopped believing there was one true church	Felt judged or misunderstood
2	Stopped believing there was one true church	Couldn't reconcile personal values	[Tie for 1st] Did not trust the church leadership
3	Did not trust the church leadership	Felt judged or misunderstood	LGBT issues
4	Book of Mormon/Book of Abraham	Sinful behaviors	Couldn't reconcile personal values
5	[Tie for 4th] Drifted away	Did not trust the church leadership	Drifted away
6	Emphasis on conformity	LGBT issues	Stopped believing there was one true church
7	Felt judged or misunderstood	[Tie for 6th] Drifted away	Book of Mormon/Book of Abraham
8	Sinful behaviors	Role of women in the church	[Tie for 8th] Sinful behaviors
9	Joseph Smith's polygamy	Joseph Smith's polyandry	Emphasis on conformity
10	Deification	Emphasis on conformity	Role of women in the church

interesting and significant differences. (I've abbreviated the terminology in Table 11.4; for the complete original wording, refer back to Table 11.3.) Social issues appear much more pressing to younger former Mormons. LGBT issues, for example, did not even crack the top ten for former Mormons over age fifty-two. This is not something that Baby Boomers and members of the Silent Generation appear terribly concerned about—or at least they were not concerned about it at the time they left the LDS Church. But for Millennials it was the third most important reason for leaving, and among GenXers it was sixth. Women's roles, as well, do not appear to be a primary source of anxiety for many Boomer/Silent former Mormons, while for GenXers that issue was eighth and for Millennials it was tenth. Not only age but also gender matters significantly in whether the role of women was disturbing enough to be a factor in disaffiliation. Among all former Mormon women, the role of women was the third-most-cited reason for leaving. Among former Mormon men, however, women's roles ranked twenty-fourth out of thirty possible reasons for leaving. Very few men—about 8 percent—cited women's issues as one of their top motives for leaving the church.

Generationally, then, we can see that social issues like the church's treatment of women and the LGBT community appear to be galvanizing disaffection among younger former Mormons. Another major concern for them was feeling judged or misunderstood, which tied for first place among Millennials and ranked third among GenXers. This was a theme I heard many times in interviews, especially from women. One shared the humiliation of getting ready to speak in sacrament meeting and having an elderly lady cover her legs with a coat in front of the whole congregation, because the speaker's skirt was deemed too short. Another told of a Primary president who booted two autistic boys out of Primary one day because they weren't sitting quietly; she also told them that they would not be worthy to hold the priesthood when they turned twelve. I heard so many painful stories. Obviously, these were balanced by other stories of love and acceptance, but those who had experienced the sting of judgment did not forget. It was also interesting how many Millennials, in describing their own religious beliefs and values, used phrases like "I don't want to judge them, but . . ." or "We all struggle with different things, so let's not judge each other." This is a generation that does not want to be judged harshly themselves, and seems careful about not judging others in turn.

As those women's stories might suggest, there is a gender divide on the question of judgment. Women in the NMS were almost twice as likely as men to say they left Mormonism because they felt judged or misunderstood, and among all women judgment ranked as the top reason for leaving the church.[30] In the overall sample of all generations, two in five women cited judgment as a factor that precipitated their departure, while only one in five men did. By the same token, in answer to a question about what, if anything, might have helped them to remain in the church, women were more likely than men to say they could have stayed if the church had been less judgmental and more inclusive (Figures 11.3 and 11.4). This was women's number one response to the question of what would have helped them to stay, while for men it did not factor into the top five.

A final thought on the question of why Mormons might disaffiliate: there is a prevailing narrative within certain segments of the LDS Church that when people leave, they do so because they "got offended." For example, a Gospel Doctrine lesson about apostasy in the Kirtland era of the early

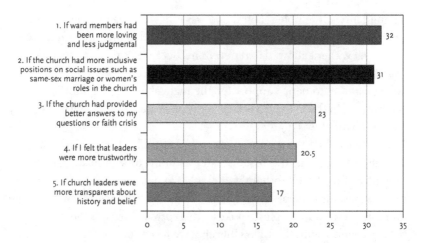

Figure 11.3. Former Mormon Women on What Would Have Helped Them to Stay.

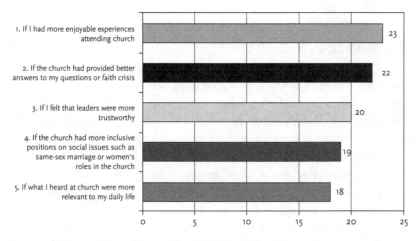

Figure 11.4. Former Mormon Men on What Would Have Helped Them to Stay.

1830s places blame squarely on the shoulders of those who left, suggesting they did so for trivial reasons and were susceptible to Satan's deceptive wiles.[31] In a 2006 General Conference talk, Elder David A. Bednar gave several modern examples, including a member who was insulted by a comment made in Sunday School and had not darkened the door of a church since, and another person who disagreed with some advice from the bishop and refused to attend until that bishop was released.[32]

According to the NMS, Elder Bednar is correct that many people leave because they became offended, but often the reasons are far more serious than he seemed to indicate. Among the write-in reasons that former Mormons provided when given an additional opportunity to explain their defection, some spoke of serious breaches of trust with the LDS Church. One woman wrote, "When I was divorcing my husband because of abuse and infidelity, his temple recommend was renewed, even though I knew he was drinking and sleeping with prostitutes (and beating me and my children . . .). I was not allowed to renew mine, because I might fall again before I was married." Another respondent cited a "lack of assistance for domestic violence and automatic support for the male abuser." Still another wrote, "As a woman in the military I was treated coldly and shunned by most of my peers as if what I was doing was wrong."

Individuals like these would certainly fall under the general category of taking offense, but the first two stories point to significant failures on the part of the church to help vulnerable women who needed it, and the third suggests a general lack of warmth and acceptance when someone didn't fit the mold. People I spoke with expressed frustration that legitimate grievances with the LDS Church were too often hastily dismissed by orthodox members who shut down or took over the discussion, refusing to listen as they tried to describe the reasons for their loss of faith.

WILL THEY COME BACK?

In chapter 8 we met Thomas, who grew up in an ultra-conservative Mormon family but then rejected that legacy by turning to drugs and alcohol as a teenager.[33] After barely graduating from high school, Thomas resisted his parents' attempts to have him serve a mission, instead working in different places in the United States and abroad, including Spain and China. There was, he says, a "deep restlessness" in him. "I know the word 'trauma' gets thrown around a lot now, but I felt like I was working through such deep trauma from my family life that I had to disappear." He discovered that he could support himself anywhere he went, which was a marvelous realization. "I was not at the mercy of the Mormon world I'd left behind. So that was really empowering." He also delved deeply into Buddhist mindfulness and meditation, finding a peace he had not known before.

Eventually, however, Thomas returned home, because he instinctively knew that Salt Lake City was the only place he could fully heal the wounds he had experienced growing up. He slowly reconnected with his family members and now regularly attends the clan's Sunday dinners. No one is more surprised than Thomas that he also began reasserting his Mormon identity, gradually returning to church as an active member. He does so on his own terms, however, practicing a more "subtle Mormonism" that honors the uniqueness of each person's journey. "I see countless people in my generation who are spiritually orphaned, so to speak. People who don't feel like they can bring their complexity or their authenticity to the religious experience." He dreams of a Mormonism that is less tribal, less judgmental, less either/or than the faith of his parents' generation. He wants people to be able to come to church and bring their whole selves.

It hasn't always been smooth sailing. Mormons didn't effusively welcome this prodigal son home—"No one killed a fatted calf for me," as Thomas puts it. Instead, he has sometimes been greeted with suspicion because his views are so different, so influenced by Buddhism. People in the ward don't quite know what to do with him:

> Leaders will come into my class on Sundays and it sometimes feels like they're there to watch what I'm going to say more than to participate in the lesson. It feels like because I'm not Mormon in the way we expect Mormons to be on the Wasatch Front, I'm suspect. Kind of guilty until proven innocent. For every one person who celebrates the diversity I bring to conversation, it feels like there are ten more who are suspicious of me.

Thomas's re-entry to Mormonism has been bumpy enough that he worries about other former members who may wish to return but may not have the thick skin he has developed, as well as his natural stubbornness when he sets his mind to something. Those fellow exiles, he says, may not "tolerate the scrutiny and the treatment they'll likely face," because it is so painful to experience the distrust of people within one's religious community. Leaving Mormonism, he says, "feels a little bit like a one-way door."

Perhaps this is one reason it seems that relatively few people come back, or at least come back for good. We don't have exact statistics on this, but the fact that more than nine in ten former Mormon respondents say they feel primarily "freedom, possibility, and relief" rather than grief about their choice suggests the lay of the land. The NMS also asked them how long it took to make their decision to leave the LDS Church: A few weeks? A few months? Years? The answers ranged widely, but seven in ten respondents said their faith transition took at least six months. In other words, leaving was not a decision most reached lightly. We can imagine that they would be similarly unlikely to rush into a lasting return.

Moreover, we have enough information about the broad strokes of America's changing religiosity to say that Mormonism would need to be extraordinary in its ability to resist its environment in order for a majority of leavers to return. Few young adults who leave other religions appear to be returning, judging from the fact that almost with every passing year, the percentage of Nones increases and the percentage of young adults who are affiliated with traditional religion continues to shrink. When Pew asked Nones in 2012 whether they were looking for a religion that would be right for them, nearly nine in ten said no, results that were largely duplicated when PRRI asked a similar question in 2016.[34] Some researchers point hopefully to the historical example of the Boomer generation, which saw two-thirds of its members leave organized religion for a time during their teens and twenties.[35] Some came back, especially when they had children themselves and discovered that they wanted to raise those children within the scaffolding of organized religion. But as Wade Clark Roof points out, it's important to remember that more Boomers did *not* return to their religions of origin than did: 33 percent never left, 25 percent left but eventually returned, and 42 percent left but never came back.[36] What's more, the religious landscape has changed since the 1970s and 1980s, when some Boomers returned with their children; disaffiliation has become normalized, and it is more socially acceptable for individuals to leave organized religion for good. As well, many Millennials are having fewer children and having them later in life, so if having children has traditionally been the main catalyst prompting people to return to religious activity, that is not good news for organized religion.

Because Mormonism is such a high-sacrifice religion, leaving its orbit can be shattering. Everything changes when a formerly orthodox Mormon leaves, from diet and clothing to decisions about how much money to donate to charity and which charities to choose. Then there are relational matters, like how to communicate with family members when you no longer have the LDS Church as your shared frame of reference—or whether those relationships will survive at all. For several people I spoke to, family relationships became fraught with anguish. One of Rob's orthodox sisters told him it would have been better if he had died—not that she wished that on him, but she would have been more prepared for that, since Mormonism teaches that families are eternal so long as everyone is sealed together in the temple and everyone keeps their covenants. She was not prepared for Rob to *not* keep those covenants. Another sister wrote him out of her will because she no longer wanted Rob and his wife to be the legal guardians of her children if she were to die prematurely. Gradually, Rob's relationships with his siblings have begun to mend and his sisters have expressed their love for him, even though they are baffled by his choices.

With the passage of months and years, former Mormons seem less and less interested in rejoining the fold. Some expressed to me that they look back on all the time they once invested in Mormonism—including, in some cases, a two-year mission—and are amazed by the free time they have now by comparison. Ryan, thirty-two, says he and his wife have developed a new Sunday ritual where they read the *New York Times* together and make breakfast, consciously enjoying their time as a couple.[37] "When we were in the church we didn't see each other as much. Now, Sunday mornings are our mornings." There were some aspects of Mormonism that he missed, however. "I miss having that community. Knowing that no matter what, I could call some people and get help with something. I miss knowing that a group of people were invested in my life, and I like that I didn't get to choose them." Still, he likes his new life far more.

Another major reason many people are reluctant to return is that the issues that steered them out of Mormonism in the first place have not budged much. Gay Mormons are still essentially second-class citizens in the church, allowed to be members but not to be in same-sex partnerships without facing excommunication. Women are still excluded from most leadership positions, despite small recent concessions, such as including one female representative in a few previously all-male councils at the highest level of church governance. Testimony questions still abound, though many people welcomed the church's recent efforts toward historical transparency and theological nuance in the Gospel Topics essays.

So the short answer is that most young adults who leave Mormonism are unlikely to come back. Some will, certainly. And perhaps they will be like Thomas, returning on their own terms with innovative ideas of how to make Mormonism more inclusive and welcoming. It remains to be seen whether, as Luke's Gospel says, the church will be waiting on the road, watching for these prodigals from a long way off, filled with compassion and warmth. So far, that has not been the experience of most former Mormons.

Conclusion

A Mormonism for the Twenty-first Century

In the 1950s, sociologist Thomas O'Dea published an insightful book called *The Mormons*, in which he argued, among other things, that higher education would introduce such a strain of theological relativism to the LDS Church that it would decrease faithfulness among the religion's brightest and best. In fact, the opposite happened; as we saw in chapters 1 and 11, it is often the best-educated individuals who have the strongest ties to Mormon orthodoxy.[1] A blind spot of O'Dea's book was that he read the present situation through a narrow lens and then projected that current assessment into the future.[2] Then in the 1980s, Rodney Stark famously predicted that Mormonism would be the "next world faith," with as many as a quarter of a billion adherents by 2080.[3] Stark chronicled Mormonism's astonishing growth in its first century and a half, then predicted that because of Mormons' vigorous missionary activity, high fertility, and seeming tendency to be an attractive alternative in nations beset by secularization, it would continue to grow at a rate of between 30 and 50 percent every decade. Mormonism's postwar explosion showed no sign of slowing in the early 1980s; in the year that Stark published his article, membership grew by more than 5 percent. In fact, Mormonism obliged him for a decade—so much so that Stark gamely published a follow-up article called "So Far So Good"—but has slowed noticeably since, especially in the last few years.[4] Stark's work was a critical contribution in getting scholars and others to take Mormonism seriously as an emerging religion, but his membership projections now seem impossible.

I bring up these two examples to point out that the literature about Mormonism and social science is so littered with failed theories that anyone should be humbled by the prospect of adding one more tombstone to that graveyard. If there's a lesson to be learned from O'Dea's unrealized anxieties on the one hand and Stark's unbridled optimism on the other, it's that present conditions are no guarantee of future results.

But if I were to offer a prognostication, it would be that in the next few years at least, the polarization I am seeing within Mormonism will continue, in which those who remain in the LDS Church will be ardent believers but those who don't fit in, which includes many young adults, will pull up stakes and leave. What should worry LDS leaders is not simply that the church will lose ground numerically—though for any institution of course that is a valid concern—but that it will become an echo chamber of its own making, a dogged remnant whose followers retreat to their own safe subculture. How the church chooses to finesse the social shifts we saw in Part Two of this book—specifically, those regarding marriage, gender, racial diversity, and LGBT issues—will signal which trajectory it is going to follow. Will it become an entrenched, embattled subculture, or will it accommodate its message to retain cultural relevancy? As of this writing, both avenues seem plausible, as evidenced by two actions that occurred in rapid succession in 2017. In August of that year, the LDS Church publicly supported the LoveLoud festival in Utah, building bridges with the LGBT community and proclaiming its commitment to "foster a community of inclusion" in society. A few weeks later, however, the church added its name to an amicus brief in support of a Colorado baker who refused to bake a wedding cake for a same-sex couple.[5]

That odd give and take over LGBT issues encapsulates the acute tensions the church is experiencing. How much should it adapt to American society, which is changing rapidly in its views on marriage, sexuality, and the family—particularly when the church's conservative stance on those issues was recently considered an asset rather than a liability in the United States, and continues to be an asset in some areas of the world where Mormonism is still growing? If there is a brilliant sociological theory that explains where Mormonism is now and how it might navigate these new challenges, it is not found in O'Dea's pessimism about Mormon secularization or Stark's buoyant assurances that all will be well; it's in Armand Mauss's 1994 book *The Angel and the Beehive*. Mauss argued that Mormons always exist in a state of tension between a desire to accommodate their host culture and a simultaneous need to stand apart as a peculiar people.[6] The "angel," according to Mauss, is the other-worldly spirit of Mormonism, the charismatic strain that embraces exclusive truth claims and distinctive theology. The "beehive" is the industry of Mormon culture in its quest to assimilate into

American society. This ever-present pendulum between assimilation and retrenchment has ensured that Mormonism has successfully maintained a distinctive edge even while making theological changes that might have been unthinkable to previous generations: it eliminated polygamy in 1890, theocracy in the early twentieth century, and a racially determined priesthood/temple ban in 1978. At one time, those would have been considered unimaginable concessions—particularly polygamy, which is enshrined in LDS scriptures, not just policy or precedent. And yet the church changed. When those doctrines and policies were seen as standing in the way of its mission as LDS leaders understood it, those leaders jettisoned aspects of Mormonism that were impeding the religion's progress.

The question ahead for the LDS Church as it moves further into the twenty-first century is how far it is willing to accommodate new social norms if the risk of not doing so is that, in the United States at least, a substantial percentage of its young people may exit the doors. Is that loss a cost the church will deem unacceptable, changing its course to stem the tide? Or will those exiles be considered necessary collateral damage as the institution clings to its postwar brand identity as a religion devoted to a particular configuration of the nuclear family? While I said I would not be proffering a grand theory about Mormonism's future, I will end by pointing to the historically informed wisdom of Mauss's thesis: the LDS Church has accommodated change before, and it can do so again. The issue is whether it will choose to.

THE 2016 NEXT MORMONS SURVEY

BY BENJAMIN KNOLL WITH JANA RIESS

DATA SOURCES AND FUNDING

The 2016 Next Mormons Survey (NMS) is an online public opinion survey designed and fielded by Jana Riess and Benjamin Knoll in 2016. We contracted with the firm Qualtrics, an online data collection company based out of Seattle, Washington, and Provo, Utah, to gather responses for this survey. Funding for this contract came from a Kickstarter campaign fielded by Jana Riess from July 15 through July 29, 2016. In all, the campaign raised $19,665 from 245 individual donors (an average of about $80 per donor), which was supplemented by more than $6,000 in additional donations after the Kickstarter campaign had ended. The Kickstarter campaign was advertised on a variety of online Mormon social media sites, as well as through personal contacts. All donors are listed in the acknowledgments of this book.

We chose Qualtrics and its online data collection method for several reasons. First, it is difficult to reliably measure public opinion among small subsets of a population using traditional random-digit-dialing telephone survey methods. This is because when analysts want to measure public opinion of a particular group, it is necessary to obtain a randomized sample so that everyone in the population has an equal chance of participating in the survey. That way we can be confident that the results of the survey are generalizable to the wider population within a particular margin of error. Mormons constitute less than 2 percent of the American population, making it extremely costly to gather a sufficiently large sample from such a small group using traditional telephone-based survey methods. Second, the NMS is lengthy, with more than 130 separate survey questions in all (though not all questions applied to every respondent). It is much, much faster to complete the survey online versus over the telephone. Third, on-line data collection firms often reward their respondents for completing surveys and thus require that all questions are answered. Incentives for taking surveys can include points to earn store gift cards or even small cash payments. This results in fully completed surveys that do not suffer from the same "missing data" problem as many other telephone- or internet-based voluntary surveys.[1]

These various issues make online survey firms such as Qualtrics a viable option for studying small populations that are difficult to capture in tradi-tional telephone-based surveys. These firms use a "panel matching" tech-nique to acquire sufficient responses. Surveyors can specify a variety of demographic or response quotas to increase the representativeness of the survey respondents to the population of interest. Research has shown that online samples from reputable firms such as Qualtrics produce samples that are comparable in representativeness to randomized telephone surveys.[2] Online panel-matching surveys are becoming increasingly common in high-quality, peer-reviewed scholarship, including research on Mormon public opinion.[3]

The NMS was in the field from September 8 to November 1, 2016, though the majority of responses were collected during September. In all, 1,156 self-identified Mormons were included in the final sample, as well as 540 former Mormons, for a total of 1,696 completed surveys. The current Mormon sample has a standard survey margin of error of 2.9 percent and the former Mormon sample one of 4.2 percent, based on the sample sizes and the estimated size of those populations in the United States. For sim-plicity, we consider the margins of error to be ±3 percent and ±4 percent, respectively. The survey design and question wording received approval from Centre College's Institutional Review Board (IRB) on September 1, 2016 (Centre College IRB Assurance #FWA00017871; IRB approval code 140-Knoll-NMS-F16).

HOW WE DEFINE MORMONS AND FORMER MORMONS

The LDS Church defines its members and former members by their status on official membership registration rolls, regardless of their level of activity and social or emotional attachment to the faith. In contrast, public opinion researchers of social topics such as religion must rely on survey respondents to describe their own demographic characteristics and are not usually able to independently verify the accuracy of these self-reported responses. In our case, we allowed respondents to self-select into the survey based on the nature of their identification with Mormonism. This means that "current

Mormons" and "former Mormons" in our survey are those who *say* they are Mormons (or once were) regardless of their current status on the LDS Church's membership rolls.[4] Using self-identification as a basis of survey categorization is a standard procedure for social science public opinion research data. To find these self-identified Mormons, all potential survey respondents received this initial screening question:

Do you currently identify, or have you ever identified, as a member of the Church of Jesus Christ of Latter-day Saints (Mormon)? Please read these options carefully before selecting.

1. *I currently identify as LDS and was LDS <u>for at least one year before turning 18</u>. This could include:*
   o   *Being born and raised in the LDS Church.*
   o   *Converting to the LDS Church before age 17.*
2. *I currently identify as LDS but joined the LDS Church only <u>after turning 17</u>.*
3. *I identified as LDS at one point in my life <u>for **at least one year** starting before age 18</u> but **no longer do**. This could include:*
   o   *Being born in an LDS family but no longer identifying as LDS.*
   o   *Converting to the LDS Church as a child/adolescent and being involved for at least a year but no longer identifying as LDS.*
4. *I identified as LDS at one point in my life <u>for less than one year starting before age 18</u> but **no longer do**. This could include:*
   o   *Being born in an LDS family but my family stopped involvement/identification with the LDS Church while I was still a baby.*
   o   *Converting to the LDS Church as a child/adolescent and staying involved for a few weeks or months but ceasing involvement with the LDS Church within a year.*
5. *I currently identify as a member of the Community of Christ or Fundamentalist Church of Jesus Christ of Latter-day Saints.*
6. *None of the above.*

The vast majority of the 23,080 potential respondents queried by Qualtrics selected "none of the above" and were thus excluded from the final survey sample. Those who indicated identification with the Community of Christ or Fundamentalist Church of Jesus Christ of Latter-Day Saints (FLDS) were likewise excluded. While adherents of those faiths certainly qualify as members of the wider Mormon tradition, we were specifically interested in members of the Latter-day Saint branch for the purposes of this project. We also excluded from the survey those who said that they identified as LDS for less than a year as children or adolescents but no longer do so, as the sample of interest was specifically those who identified as LDS long enough for it to have a substantive impact on their religious and social lives. Otherwise, those who selected the first or second options were defined as "current Mormons" in our survey and those who selected the third option as "former Mormons." It is important to note that "former Mormons" for our purpose are those who were raised LDS or converted as children/adolescents (but not adults) and later stopped identifying. This is because one of the key objectives of this book is to analyze long-term trends of youth who grow up in the LDS culture/tradition, as well as retention patterns.

We requested that Qualtrics provide us a finished sample of which 50 percent of responses would come from current Mormons and the other 50 percent from former Mormons so that we could treat each group as separate and then combine when needed. We also specifically requested that one-quarter of current Mormons be converts (i.e., selecting the second option in the original screening question) so that we could be sure to analyze how convert Mormons compare to native (or "cradle") Mormons in future research. We selected one-quarter as the quota for convert Mormons because that is close to the proportion of Mormons who identify as converts in the 2014 Pew Religious Landscape Study (specifically, 31 percent). In all, it proved impossible for Qualtrics to find enough respondents to fill the quotas for convert Mormons and former Mormons (given that they are very small population subsamples) and so the data collection ended with a final distribution of 943 native Mormon (55.6 percent of total), 213 convert Mormons (12.6 percent of total), and 540 former Mormons (31.8 percent of total) with fully completed surveys.

OTHER SURVEY PARAMETERS

A primary objective of the NMS is to compare religious behaviors and attitudes across generational lines. To this end, we requested that Qualtrics be sure to sample for respondents across four major generational patterns: 35 percent Millennials (born 1980 to 1998), 25 percent GenXers (born 1965 to 1979), 25 percent Baby Boomers (born 1945 to 1964), and 15 percent Silent Generation (born 1928 to 1944). These age quotas were established to ensure that we would obtain a representative sample of each generation given that internet surveys tend to bias toward younger respondents. Our quotas were based on the age distributions as given in the 2007 Pew Religious Landscape Study (RLS).[5] According to the 2014 RLS, the age distribution for current and former Mormons is 35 percent Millennials, 30 percent GenXers, 25 percent Baby Boomers, and 10 percent Silent Generation. Thus, our age quotas were designed to mirror the wider LDS population as much as possible. After data collection commenced, however, we were informed that there were not enough Baby Boomers and Silent Generation respondents to fill our quotas, especially for those in the Silent Generation. At the end of the data collection, the sample had finished at 42 percent Millennials, 30 percent GenXers, and 28 percent for the Baby Boomers and Silents combined together. We use these three principal age cohorts throughout the book.

We originally did not include any quotas by way of gender on the assumption that men and women would respond to the survey roughly in proportion to their distribution in the wider population of interest. It became apparent as data commencement began, however, that more women were responding to the survey than men. We thus quickly implemented a quota of 46.5 percent male and 52.5 percent female, with 1 percent left "open" to provide for potential self-identification of transgender or gender nonconforming respondents. Again, this breakdown was based on results from the Pew Religious Landscape Study. Despite this more stringent quota, the survey ended with a final sample of current/former Mormons that was 36.4 percent male, 63.3 percent female, and 0.4 percent "other." This necessitated a weighting of the sample, as described later, to achieve representativeness for gender so that men's opinions would be weighted according to men's actual percentage of the LDS population.

A final original quota regarded geography. We requested that 30 percent of the sample of current and former Mormons report currently living in Utah and 70 percent outside of Utah, again based on the geographical distribution revealed in the 2007 Pew Religious Landscape Study. We wanted to ensure to the extent possible that our results did not describe Utah Mormons only. After data collection commenced, it became apparent that the non-Utah sample was disproportionally drawing from states with major urban centers (California, New York, Florida, Illinois, Pennsylvania, etc.). We thus quickly implemented a more stringent geographic quota: 30 percent Utah, 20 percent Mountain states (Arizona, Colorado, Idaho, Montana, Nevada, New Mexico, Wyoming), 15 percent Pacific states (Alaska, Hawaii, California, Washington, Oregon), 15 percent South Atlantic (Delaware, Washington, DC, Florida, Georgia, Maryland, North Carolina, South Carolina, Virginia, West Virginia), 10 percent Midwest (Illinois, Indiana, Michigan, Ohio, Wisconsin, Iowa, Kansas, Minnesota, Missouri, Nebraska, North Dakota, Oklahoma, South Dakota), 5 percent South Central (Arkansas, Louisiana, Texas, Alabama, Kentucky, Mississippi, Tennessee), and 5 percent Northeast (Connecticut, Maine, Massachusetts, New Hampshire, Rhode Island, Vermont, New Jersey, New York, Pennsylvania), these proportions being based on results from the 2007 Pew Religious Landscape Study that were available online. Given the extremely small population subgroups, we eventually were forced to combine some categories to complete data collection. In all, 27 percent of our final sample of current/former Mormons reported currently living in

Utah, 15 percent in the Mountain states, 12 percent in the Midwest, 6 percent in the Northeast, 18 percent in the Pacific states, 16 percent in the South Atlantic states, and 6 percent in the South Central states, still very close to our goal distribution based on Pew data.

ASSESSING THE SURVEY'S REPRESENTATIVENESS

After data collection was complete for all 1,696 respondents, we compared our survey results with those of other reputable and nationally representative public opinion surveys based on random-digit-dialing methods to assess the degree of representativeness that we achieved with the NMS. Specifically, we compared our results with those of the 2014 Pew Religious Landscape Study (which had been released just after the NMS's data collection process) on several demographic and socioeconomic indicators such as gender, income, education, age, and race/ethnicity.[6]

Table NMS_0.1 shows us that for the current Mormon sample, our internet-based NMS survey achieved a level of demographic and socioeconomic representativeness very close to that of the random-digit-dialing telephone-based RLS with a few moderate exceptions. Specifically, the NMS oversampled women compared to men by about 7 percent. It undersampled those with a high school education by about 10 percent and oversampled those with a college degree by the same amount. Millennials were oversampled compared to Baby Boomers and Silent Generation members. In terms of income, race/ethnicity, and geographical residence, however, the two surveys were virtually identical and certainly within the margin of sampling error.

Table NMS_0.1 also shows us that for our former Mormon sample, the NMS did an even better job of approximating demographic and socioeconomic distributions in the wider population (as indicated by the 2014 RLS). The only two categories where the NMS differed appreciably was that it substantially oversampled women compared to men and those with a college degree compared to those with a high school education.

It is important to note that these sampling differences are extremely common in public opinion survey research. When this happens, researchers can create "poststratification sample weights," which minimize potential biases in the survey results due to disproportionate sampling of one group over another. In other words, we can statistically correct for these sample biases to a large extent by artificially inflating the weight of the responses from groups that were undersampled in the survey while artificially contracting the weight of the responses from the groups that were oversampled, in direct proportion to the degree to which they were over- or undersampled in the survey. Assuming that there are correlations with

Table NMS_0.1. DEMOGRAPHIC VARIABLES OF THE NMS BEFORE WEIGHTING

	Current Mormons – 2014 RLS (Weighted) MoE ±4%	Current Mormons – 2016 NMS (Unweighted) MoE ±3%	Difference	Former Mormons – 2014 RLS (Weighted) MoE ±7%	Former Mormons – 2016 NMS (Unweighted) MoE ±4%	Difference
Male	46%	39%	-7%	55%	32%	-23%
Female	54%	61%	7%	45%	67%	22%
Less than college degree	67%	55%	-12%	79%	64%	-15%
College	21%	31%	10%	14%	25%	11%
Postgraduate	12%	14%	2%	8%	11%	3%
Income < $50K	47%	47%	0%	51%	54%	3%
Income $50K–$100K	33%	37%	4%	35%	32%	-3%
Income > $100K	20%	45%	-3%	14%	14%	0%
Millennial	31%	44%	13%	40%	38%	-2%
GenXer	31%	27%	-4%	32%	37%	5%
Boomer/Silent	38%	29%	-9%	28%	25%	-3%
White	85%	86%	1%	81%	84%	3%
Black	1%	4%	3%	3%	5%	2%
Hispanic	8%	5%	-3%	5%	6%	1%
Other race/ethnicity	6%	5%	-1%	12%	6%	-6%
Utah	28%	29%	1%	21%	24%	3%
Non-Utah	72%	71%	-1%	79%	76%	-3%

Categories may not add up to 100 percent due to rounding. The 2014 Pew Religious Landscape Survey samples of comparison include 664 self-identified Mormons and 215 self-identified former Mormons.

the particular survey question and a demographic or socioeconomic factor like age, education, gender, and so forth, this procedure increases our confidence that our survey findings are representative of the wider population of interest.

For the purposes of this research project, we created two separate sample weights, one for current Mormons and one for former Mormons, to correct for these survey biases. The sample weight for current Mormons accounts for gender, education, and age, while the sample weight for former Mormons accounts for gender and education. We used the weighted 2014 Pew Religious Landscape Study as our basis of comparison when constructing our sample weights. Unless otherwise noted, these sample weights were applied for all analyses reported throughout this book. We again emphasize that this is a regular best practice among public opinion survey researchers and has consistently been shown to increase the accuracy and representativeness of survey results. It is a methodology routinely employed by virtually every reputable survey firm including Pew, Gallup, Economist/YouGov, and the *Washington Post*.[7]

With these data weights applied, our survey results become even more representative of both current and former Mormons on almost every demographic category, as shown in Table NMS_0.2. They are often nearly identical to those of the 2014 Pew Religious Landscape Study (or within the margin of error). We note as well that the majority of our weighted survey results for key religious and political attitudes/behaviors also approximate those found for current and former Mormons in the 2014 Pew Religious Landscape Study. We thus argue that the results we report in this book are representative of the wider Mormon and former Mormon populations in the United States within the standard margins of error (±3 percent and ±4 percent, respectively) for public opinion survey research.

SURVEY QUESTION WORDING

In designing a survey with over 130 questions (and more than 600 separate variables), we consulted a variety of sources and questionnaires from other religious and social surveys conducted by reputable research firms, including those who have specifically surveyed Mormons. In particular, many survey questions came from standard batteries of survey questions on religion and social behavior used by the Pew Religious Landscape Study, the General Social Survey, the American National Elections Survey, the 2012 Pew Mormons in America Survey, the Pew Political Typology surveys, the 2012 Peculiar People Survey, the 2011 Understanding Mormon Disbelief Survey, and the 2015 Mormon Gender Issues Survey.[8] Many other questions we wrote ourselves according to the goals of our research project, striving in

Table NMS_0.2. DEMOGRAPHIC VARIABLES OF THE NMS AFTER WEIGHTING

	Current Mormons – 2014 RLS (Weighted) MoE ±4%	Current Mormons – 2016 NMS (Weighted) MoE ±3%	Difference	Former Mormons – 2014 RLS (Weighted) MoE ±7%	Former Mormons – 2016 NMS (Weighted) MoE ±4%	Difference
Male	46%	47%	1%	55%	54%	-1%
Female	54%	53%	-1%	45%	44%	-1%
Less than college degree	67%	65%	-2%	79%	79%	0%
College	21%	22%	1%	14%	13%	-1%
Postgraduate	12%	12%	0%	8%	8%	0%
Income < $50K	47%	48%	1%	51%	55%	4%
Income $50K–$100K	33%	36%	3%	35%	31%	-4%
Income > $100K	20%	16%	-4%	14%	14%	0%
Millennial	31%	35%	4%	40%	33%	-7%
GenXer	31%	35%	4%	32%	37%	5%
Boomer/Silent	38%	30%	-8%	28%	30%	2%
White	85%	87%	2%	81%	83%	2%
Black	1%	4%	3%	3%	6%	3%
Hispanic	8%	4%	-4%	5%	5%	0%
Other race/ethnicity	6%	4%	-2%	12%	6%	-6%
Utah	28%	28%	0%	21%	22%	1%
Non-Utah	72%	72%	0%	79%	76%	-3%

each case to follow best practices for public opinion survey question design.[9] After the original survey was drafted, we sought input from other scholars and experts of religion, public opinion, and Mormonism, who are listed in the acknowledgments. Throughout the book the survey question wordings are provided in the text and are footnoted if otherwise. The entire final survey is also available at thenextmormons.org as a downloadable PDF.

QUALITATIVE ORAL HISTORY INTERVIEWS

To flesh out and enhance the survey data, I (Jana Riess) conducted sixty-three oral history interviews with young adult Mormons and former Mormons, as well as additional background interviews with experts in areas I was researching. The vast majority of the oral history interviewees were Millennials, with a few GenXers in the mix. None of the interviewees was part of the NMS. Most of these interviews were conducted over the phone, with a smaller number done in person, covering an interview template that included seven sections on demographic characteristics, childhood, adolescence, mission experiences (if applicable), religious beliefs and behaviors, temple experiences (if applicable), and the families that interviewees have created or hope to create as adults. This template evolved from 2012, when I first began conducting interviews less formally for a book that was then conceived as being about Mormon childhood and spiritual formation, and 2017, when I was writing this book about young adults and conducting the last of the interviews. The interviews were a separate, but no less important, part of the research.

Almost all of the interviewees were raised in the LDS Church, though a few had converted to Mormonism in their adolescence or young adulthood. Whereas every pain was taken to ensure a nationally representative sample of survey respondents for the quantitative data, these oral history interviews are *not* representative of Mormons or former Mormons as a whole. I would not say this was a socioeconomically diverse sample; most interviewees were middle class. A higher proportion of interviewees had completed a college education than we know from nationally representative surveys is true of Mormons generally. Whereas nationally, over a quarter of adult Mormons have only a high school education, in the interview pool, this circumstance applied to very few—and only because they were barely out of high school. For these interviews I have also intentionally oversampled some subgroups within the Mormon and former Mormon populations, such as African Americans and LGBT persons, so that no one person's experiences would represent an entire minority group. At the close of the interview process I had 768 pages of single-spaced interview transcripts, which means it was not possible to fully tell everyone's stories, but I have endeavored to give many young Mormons' voices a fair hearing.

I found people to interview in various ways. Most interview subjects were not people I knew personally, but young people from whom I had one degree of separation. Many referrals came from friends or acquaintances who knew I was looking to discuss a broad range of Millennials' experiences with the LDS Church and put me in contact with their relatives, students, neighbors, and ward members. Some of those Millennials then introduced me to other people their age they knew to have had interesting experiences they were willing to talk about. Sometimes, interview subjects simply showed up—either randomly or providentially, depending on your perspective. One was a cheerful young man in Salt Lake City who worked for the rental car company I frequented on repeated trips to Utah, and whose very obviously Mormon first name led to a conversation about his religious background. Several others were people I met at conferences of various kinds, or when I had a speaking engagement and mentioned I was looking for people who could speak to particular questions.

Five of the seven sections of the interview template were given to every interviewee, while the sections on mission and temple were only presented to those who affirmed they had served a mission or been through the temple to receive their endowments. The interview template changed slightly as the process evolved, especially as I encountered my own missteps. For example, early on I added a question about sexual orientation to the opening demographic section because of a dope-slap moment that occurred in an interview. A young woman who was married to a man and had young children revealed in passing near the end of our conversation that she considered herself bisexual, and I realized to my great embarrassment that I could not make assumptions about people's sexual orientation merely based on their external circumstances. After that I made sure to inquire about people's sexual orientation at the start of every interview when I asked about age, education, race, occupation, and other demographic characteristics.

Other sections of the interview template changed over time as well. The section on childhood was shortened because it became clear as I began to write that there was no place in the book where we could delve into childhood experiences in much depth. I also added several questions to other sections of the formal template, especially to the section on religious beliefs and behaviors, because individual people kept volunteering information and bringing up certain topics that were not in the original script, such as their patriarchal blessings and how they felt about tithing. These questionnaire additions resulted in some interesting interview excerpts that were included in the final book.

A few weeks after the conversations, participants were provided the opportunity to go through the edited transcript of their interview and return it to me with changes or additions. More than half of those who responded elected to make revisions or expand on things they had told me. If they did not choose to make any changes, I used the version I had sent to them. The majority of interviewees quoted in the book are identified by their actual first names, though a few with common first names were asked to choose a different one to avoid confusion, and others elected to use an invented name to protect their identity. Several mentioned not wanting to hurt their parents' feelings if they had left the church or had expressed views that would make their family members uncomfortable. In every case I honored the interviewees' wishes about how they would like to be identified, and if some information was designated as being off the record, I kept it out of the book.

Throughout, it was an honor and a pleasure to speak in such depth to young adult Mormons about their families, sacred experiences, and, occasionally, their tragedies. One of the people I interviewed subsequently passed away of cancer, which grieves me. I hope I have conveyed a small sense of her vibrancy and spiritual intelligence in life. In the majority of the interviews I conducted, I was struck by the thoughtfulness of young Mormons and former Mormons, and by the community ethos that pervaded their eagerness to share their stories. Such conversations made me wary of the Millennial bashing that has become a beloved sport for some older people, and the apparent desire some have to characterize this generation as overly self-involved. That more people volunteered to be interviewed than I could possibly talk to was not a case of Millennials' much-criticized desire for fame or wanting to see their names in a book, nor was it merely an instance of their predilection for public confessionalism (though many interviewees *were* remarkably candid, at least in the eyes of this buttoned-up GenXer).[10] Instead, many told me their willingness to help was motivated by a desire to know more about this research: Were things really changing in the LDS Church? Was their generation as different from their parents' as they observed it to be? And, often, were they alone in feeling uncertain of whether their generation has a place in Mormonism?

These are young adults who clearly care about their faith community, even if they are no longer practicing members of it. So in the interviews we sometimes went off script to discuss particular areas of the survey results, which I would ask if they found predictable or surprising. More than once, Millennials' own framing of research findings I had not anticipated pointed me toward explanations I hadn't thought to consider, such as some interviewees' interpretations of the Word of Wisdom (is iced coffee really coffee if it isn't a "hot drink," some wondered?). Overall, then, what began as a facet of the project that was intended primarily to "flesh out the data" and "give a face to the name" of various trends we were seeing in the quantitative research became much more than that, and actually helped to influence the ways I was interpreting the survey results.

ACKNOWLEDGMENTS AND DONORS

It's customary in the acknowledgments of any book or major project to thank a number of people without whom, the author insists, the project could not have happened. Well, I've written a fair number of books, and I have never meant this more than I do right now: without the people listed here, this project could not have happened. At all. It's a major and costly undertaking to do a nationally representative survey of a minority population, and these are the people who made it possible.

A number of social scientists, marketing researchers, and historians helped in crafting the survey and interpreting the results. Chief among these is Benjamin Knoll, who has been a leader in this project from the beginning. Ben's help has been invaluable in many ways, his insights profound and his patience for multivariate regression analyses inexhaustible. Two graduate students, Alexis Straka and Jelena Vicic, ran additional regressions and performed other research tasks. I'm also grateful to social scientists David Campbell, Ryan Cragun, Armand Mauss, Rick Phillips, Gary Shepherd, and Gordon Shepherd; Pew Research Center associate Anna Schiller; and the team at Qualtrics for helping us to field the study (especially Nathan Richard and Royce Hackett). Greg Prince provided valuable introductions to a network of people working on related research questions, while Judy Dushku and Sharon Harris were instrumental in finding young adults to interview. Many individuals offered feedback on one or more of the eighteen drafts of the survey, including Angela Black, Matthew Bowman, Joanna Brooks, Tona Hangen, Sharon Harris, Tania and John Lyon, Armand Mauss, Allison Pond, Bob Rees, Travis Stratford, Toria Trendler, Bill and David Turnbull, and Sara Vraneš. Thanks also to Ashley Mae Hoiland, Ardis Parshall, Dan Wotherspoon, and Thomas Hatton for helping me to understand Kickstarter and publicize the Kickstarter campaign via blogs and podcasts. And finally, thank you to my friends at Paraclete Press, who designed the layout for my initial top-line report about the data—especially Paul Tingley, Sister Martina, and Brother Christopher.

Two foundations provided especially key funding and support, organizations that are notable for being both old and new. The Dialogue Foundation offered a generous grant to this project as one that would advance Mormon scholarship and understanding in ways that are in keeping with Dialogue's mission over its first half century. It's an honor to have my work recognized as worthy of Dialogue's venerable tradition of Mormon scholarship. The other foundation began just as my project was getting underway, so the two initiatives have been growing up together. The Faith Matters Foundation, created by Bill, Susan, David, and Kristin Turnbull, seeks to provide deeper engagement with Mormonism and the world. I am proud to serve on its board of advisers. For more information, visit https://www.faithmatters.org/about/.

I've worked in and around the publishing industry for a long time and have long admired the religion and history books from Oxford University Press, so it is a dream come true for me to be part of that tradition of excellence. I am particularly grateful to Theo Calderara for being excited about this project when I first floated the idea for it years ago; he deserves a gold medal for his patience and his mad skills with a red pen. I also thank my literary agent, Gail Ross of the Ross Yoon Agency, for facilitating this collaboration.

Parts of this book were written at the Mercantile Library in Cincinnati, a very special "third place" that has for nearly two hundred years supported the work of writers and readers in our city. I am grateful to the librarians there for their welcome and the important work they do. Since I was also writing *The Prayer Wheel* at the same time I was working on this project, I want to thank my coauthors, Patton Dodd and David Van Biema, for their flexibility as I juggled multiple deadlines, as well as my colleagues at Religion News Service for their patience and their interest in both projects.

I had an amazing team of early readers who provided feedback on one or more chapter drafts. For this I thank Kim Matheson Berkey, Matthew Bowman, Joanna Brooks, David Campbell, Erik Freeman, Bobbie Givens Goettler, Ryan Gottfredson, Craig Harline, Sharon Harris, J. B. Haws, Shon Hopkin, Paula Ison, Robin Jensen, Andrew Lewis, John Lyon, Tania Lyon, Patrick Mason, Armand Mauss, Mitch Mayne, Adam Miller, John Morehead, Jacob Rennaker, Gordon Shepherd, Joseph Spencer, Jonathan Stapley, Alexis Straka, Chelsea Sue, Charlotte Hansen Terry, Jeffrey James Turner, John Turner, Jelena Vicic, and Jenny Webb. Benjamin Knoll commented on *every* chapter, double-checked my analyses, and performed additional analyses to strengthen my arguments. The Mormon-Evangelical Dialogue Group, started by Rich Mouw and Bob Millett, has been a rich source of conversation and feedback, as has the Mormon History Association preconference workshop, where I presented two of these chapters, and the Mormon Social

Science Association. I am also grateful to the professors I had in seminary and graduate school who taught me about American religious history, including Randall Balmer, Richard Bushman, Claudia Bushman, Edwin Gaustad, James Moorhead, Albert Raboteau, Leigh Schmidt, and Judith Weisenfeld; all of them have encouraged me throughout my career, and several of them cheered on this particular project.

My family has supported me through many long hours of researching and writing this book. I'm grateful to my in-laws for letting me come to their old Kentucky home for an intensive writing retreat (and bring my dog). My daughter picked up some slack through the last months of my writing by running errands and doing the grocery shopping, while my husband, Phil, took care of—well, everything. He is my rock. After more than a quarter century of marriage, he is still the person I want to spend the most time with. And now that this book is finished, I will actually be able to.

Contributions to this project came primarily through Kickstarter in donations large and small, from families and individuals who wanted more information about how Mormonism is faring in a changing world. Their names are listed below, according to the information provided by Kickstarter. I hope I have not forgotten anyone. I am beyond grateful.

Jana Riess

May 2018

Name in the acknowledgments, a signed copy of the book, a PDF of the executive summary of the research, and an author appearance in your city: Jonathan Arnell, Katy Bettner, David Campbell, Taylor Dix, Eric Canfield, Dialogue Foundation, Faith Matters Foundation, Jeannie Hamblin, Richard and Karen Ji, Armand Mauss, Kim McCall, Richard and Sheila Ostler, Steve Otteson, Chris and Toria Trendler.

Name in the acknowledgments, a signed copy of the book, and a PDF of the executive summary of the research: Rich Baker, Philip Barlow, Elise Erikson Barrett, Gail Berkey, Ray and Roberta Black, Scott Blackwelder, Jen Blair, Matthew Bowman, David Broadbent, David Brower, Paul and Sharon Brown, Ronda Callister, Angie Carter, Karen Carter, T. L. Choate, Bryce Cook, Doe Daughtrey, Ben Dolman, "Duck," Walt Eddy, Jonathan Ellis, Steve Evans, Peter Faleschini, Ryan Farr, Matthew Ferrell, Jennifer Finlayson-Fife, Russell M. Frandsen, Adriane Gill, Holly Griffin, Douglas Harmon, Robert Hatch, Ben Heaton, Len Hoffman, Mike Holmstrom, Tim Irwin, Linda Hoffman Kimball, Collette Larsen, Rachelle Lopp, Tania and John Lyon, Heather Marx, Jean-Francois Mayer, Colleen McDannell, Kate McKay, Quin Monson, Nate Munson, David Conley Nelson, Brandon Palmer, Charles Randall Paul, Cinco Paul, Courtney Peck, Simon Phipps, Kristin G. Pingree, Bill Reel, Robert A. Rees, Jonathan Reid, Robert

Riley-Mercado, Chelsea Robarge, Hannah Schell, Debra D. Smith, George Andrew Spriggs, Tamra Thacker, Rob Van Dam, Chris Wei, Ann and Bob Wicks, Casey Willard, Charla Willian, Charlotte Johnson Willian, Dan Wotherspoon.

Name in the acknowledgments and a signed copy of the book: Lauren Ard, Michael Arnell, Kevin Barney, Jeanine Bean, Dean R. Bender, Gary Bergera, Marilyn Bushman-Carlton, Dan Carter, Wendy Chapman, Leighton Connor, Leslie Dalton, Margaret E. Dansie, Michael Reed Davison, Nathan Day, Douglas Dickson, Mike Duffy, Wendy Christian Dunn, Sheila Duran, Julia Durrant, Lori Bolland Embree, Brady Emmett, Brad Farmer, Richard Finlinson, Lindsay Hardin Freeman, Andy Frost, Bob Fryling, Emily Geddes, Cathy Lynn Grossman, P. J. Hafen, Josephine E. Hansen, Sharon J. Harris, Mette Harrison, Sarah Hodson, Andrew Hudson, Kelly Hughes, Sandra Clark Jergensen, Mary Johnson, Melissa Leilani Larson, Megan Linton, Allison Mack, Michael J. Mannino, Lynsie Mortensen, Max Mueller, Barbara Falconer Newhall, Kerry Norman, Jon Ogden, Paul Otterstrom, Taylee Robinson Pardi, Ardis E. Parshall, JaneAnne Peterson, Margaret Britsch Peterson, Curtis Roberts, Scott Roby, Gordon Shepherd, Chelsea Shields, Brooke Shirts, Nancy Sidhu, Lori Laurent Smith, Megan Moore Smith, Fara Sneddon, Richard Stanger, Chris Taber, Larissa Taylor, Three Coin Productions, Morris A. Thurston, Sara Vraneš, Jordan M. Waite, Carol Watson, Jennifer Webb, Valerie Weeks, Sharman Wilson, Anna Woofenden, Christian Wright, Anne Wunderli.

Name in the acknowledgments: Bob Ahlender, Phyllis Barber, Robert A. Barney, Nancy Beck, Christopher Bigelow, Marie Blanchard, Stephanie Bliese, Richard Bushman, Alethea Teh Busken, Dustin Cammack, Brad Carmack, Derek Christensen, Derrick Clements, Lisa Ann Cockrel, John Draper, James Egan, Eric Elnes, Matt Evans, Keri Ford, Carey Foushee, Jedd Fowers, Sheryl Fullerton, Travis Hall, Soren Harward, Andrew Heiss, Hannah Herman, Aimee Hickman, Chad Hinkson, Kathy Hollett, Amie Houser, Nathan Hoyt, Corwin Hudson, Mariah Jackson-Christensen, Rob and Emily Jensen, Matthew Kern, Katie Langston, Jeremy Larsen, Tiago Sá Maia, Matt Martin, Brad Mortensen, John Lewis Needham, Twila Newey, Steven Peck, Christopher Phillips, Ge Pop, Lee Poulsen, Kimberly Pratt, Robert Rees, Bruce Reyes-Chow, Richard Roitlinger, Marion Fust Sæternes, Jessica Sagers, David Scoville, Aaron Taylor, Devin D. Thorpe, Brent Tubbs, David Wood, Margaret Blair Young.

NOTES

INTRODUCTION

1. Jack, twenty-six, telephone interview, October 12, 2017.
2. Emily, thirty-four, telephone interview, September 12, 2017.
3. As explained in chapter 8, caffeinated soda was never expressly forbidden by the LDS Church, but many Latter-day Saints made a point of avoiding it. Memoirist Joanna Brooks, for example, notes that in her orthodox LDS childhood, she was the "root beer among the Cokes," the only child at birthday parties who couldn't partake in what everyone else was drinking. In recent years that unwritten code against caffeinated soft drinks has been changing, with an LDS spokesman declaring in 2012 that the church did not "prohibit the use of caffeine." Associated Press, "LDS Church Clarifies Stance on Caffeine," September 2, 2012, http://www.heraldextra.com/news/state-and-regional/lds-church-clarifies-stance-on-caffeine/article_e4e357d0-ba5d-5a6c-8e78-dd1e791a34b2.html. See also Joanna Brooks, *The Book of Mormon Girl: A Memoir of an American Faith* (New York: Free Press, 2012), 13.
4. In Mormon congregations for unmarried adults (singles wards), a thirtieth birthday is also a time of transition, since at age thirty-one, Mormons who are still single are taken out of singles wards and moved to either a "midsingles" ward for ages thirty-one to forty-five or to a multigenerational ward that has members of all ages. For more on single Mormons, see chapter 4.
5. Elaine Jarvik, "LDS Teens Tops in Living Faith," *Deseret News,* March 15, 2005, https://www.deseretnews.com/article/600118667/LDS-teens-tops-in-living-faith.html; Christian Smith with Melinda Lundquist Denton, *Soul Searching: The Religious and Spiritual Lives of American Teenagers* (New York: Oxford University Press, 2005), 35, 37, 46.
6. Kenda Creasey Dean, *Almost Christian: What the Faith of Our Teenagers Is Telling the American Church* (New York: Oxford University Press, 2010), 51.
7. This notion of a "traditional" family is a contested one, as there has been a surprising amount of diversity in how the family has been configured throughout history. In modern LDS usage, however, the word refers to something particular: a family in which the father presides, the mother is primarily responsible for nurturing children, and marriage is between a man and a woman.
8. Pew's 2014 Religious Landscape Study had a sample size of 35,071 respondents, including 661 Mormons. Of these, 200 were Millennials, resulting in a margin of error of about 7 percent. The 62 percent retention rate Pew found for Mormon Millennials, then, could be as low as 55 percent or as high as 69 percent.

9. Darren E. Sherkat, *Changing Faith: The Dynamics and Consequences of Americans' Shifting Religious Identities* (New York: NYU Press, 2014), 62. I am grateful to Professor Sherkat for updating his table to include General Social Survey (GSS) data through 2016.

10. The margins of error for the first four cohorts in the GSS are between 7 and 9 percent, but that jumps to plus or minus 14 percent for Cohort 5, the Millennials. So while we can't speak definitively of the exact retention number for this cohort (which could range in this study from a low of 32 percent to a high of 60 percent), we can say with 95 percent confidence that the *rate* of retention has decreased from the oldest respondents to the youngest.

11. Robert P. Jones, Daniel Cox, Betsy Cooper, and Rachel Lienesch, "Exodus: Why Americans Are Leaving Religion—and Why They're Unlikely to Come Back," report of the Public Religion Research Institute, September 22, 2016, http://www.prri. org/research/prri-rns-poll-nones-atheist-leaving-religion/. The GSS longitudinal data puts the unaffiliated rate slightly lower: 30 percent for those born after 1981. Still, that is a sixfold increase over the 5 percent of "Nones" in the generation born before 1943.

12. See Sherkat, *Changing Faith*, 63. As David E. Campbell and Robert D. Putnam report, Catholic retention would actually be far lower than this were it not for a healthy influx of Latinx immigrants whose presence has significantly bolstered the ranks, especially among young adults. See Putnam and Campbell, *American Grace: How Religion Divides and Unites Us* (New York: Simon and Schuster, 2012), 146, 285–286, and 296–300. There is in general a greater tendency toward disaffiliation among Anglo-Americans than among many other racial or ethnic groups.

13. Carol Pipes, "ACP: Churches up in 2016; Baptisms, Membership Decline," *Baptist Press*, June 8, 2017, http://www.bpnews.net/49005/acp--churches-up-in-2016-baptisms-membership-decline; Bob Allen, "Southern Baptists Have Lost a Million Members in 10 Years," *Baptist News Global*, June 9, 2017, https://baptistnews.com/article/southern-baptists-lost-million-members-10-years/#.Wjkb-0tG1E9.

14. In the United States, LDS membership growth has slowed in the twenty-first century from a combination of decreased fertility and fewer conversions. See Matthew Martinich, "United States," *Cumorah.com: International Resources for Latter-day Saints*, http://www.cumorah.com/index.php?target=countries&cnt_res=2&wid=231&wid_state=&cmdfind=Search.

15. "Membership by Country Statistics Released for 2016," LDS Church Growth blog, April 4, 2017, http://ldschurchgrowth.blogspot.com/2017/04/membership-by-country-statistics.html. Mormonism's growth rate in the United States had slowed to .93 percent in 2016, but the worldwide average was somewhat better: 1.59 percent. The area of the world that experienced the most rapid growth was West Africa.

16. Matthew Martinich, "Top Ten Most Encouraging and Top Ten Most Discouraging LDS Growth and Missionary Developments in 2017," December 30, 2017, http://cumorah.com/index.php?target=view_case_studies&story_id=481&cat_id=8.

17. "In Which They Fret Over the Young Single Adults," YouTube video, 50:03, from a meeting of LDS leaders taped November 12, 2008, posted by MormonLeaks, October 2, 2016, https://www.youtube.com/watch?v=FBH045ooaY0.

18. There were two small differences. The NMS extended the Millennial generation to 1998 instead of 1997 so that we could include those who, at age eighteen, had just entered adulthood at the time of our survey. We also ended GenX in 1979 instead of 1980. See "The Generations Defined," Pew Research Center, May 8, 2015, http://www.pewresearch.org/fact-tank/2015/05/11/millennials-surpass-gen-xers-as-the-largest-generation-in-u-s-labor-force/ft_15-05-11_millennialsdefined/.

19. Tim B. Heaton and Cardell K. Jacobson, "The Social Composition of Mormonism," in Terryl L. Givens and Philip L. Barlow, *The Oxford Handbook of Mormonism* (New York: Oxford University Press, 2015), 309–333, esp. 314, 316–317.

CHAPTER 1

1. Daniel, twenty-eight, telephone interview, September 2, 2016.
2. Gordon and Gary Shepherd, *A Kingdom Transformed: Early Mormonism and the Modern LDS Church*, 2nd ed. (Salt Lake City: University of Utah Press, 2016), 73. Since that time, family has been in the top three themes in every decade. Ibid., 205.
3. Christian N. K. Anderson, "Do We Have to Believe That?: Canon and Extra-Canonical Sources of LDS Belief," *Dialogue: A Journal of Mormon Thought* 50, no. 1 (Spring 2017): 79–135; esp. 124–125.
4. Shepherd and Shepherd, *A Kingdom Transformed*, 73 and 205.
5. The choices included Mormonism's emphasis on the Savior, Jesus Christ; the knowledge that families can be together forever; the comfort of having a prophet on the earth today; the opportunities the church provides to serve other people; the freedom from addiction that comes with keeping the Word of Wisdom; the strong community at church; the peace faith provides in hard times; the focus on children and youth; and temple worship. These nine options were randomized from one respondent to another, which was generally the case for all questions with many possible choices.
6. It is common in survey research to encounter a social desirability bias on certain types of questions. People may hesitate to admit to surveyors that they have an attitude or engage in a behavior that society, friends, or family might frown upon. This may be the case here, given that there is a strong norm in Mormon culture against expressing doubt or disbelief. Levels of doubt may thus be *underestimated* in our sample. At the same time, this survey was conducted online where respondents were answering in private and were assured on multiple occasions that their responses were 100 percent anonymous. This suggests that respondents may well have been more candid with their answers than they might have been in a live telephone survey. Research has shown that online surveys tend to produce more accurate answers on questions that are socially sensitive or that would be embarrassing to the respondent. Frauke Kreuter, Stanley Presser, and Roger Tourangeau, "Social Desirability Bias in CATI, IVR, and Web Surveys: The Effects of Mode and Question Sensitivity," *Public Opinion Quarterly* 72, no. 5 (December 2008): 847–865; Scott Keeter, "Methods Can Matter: Where Web Surveys Produce Different Results Than Phone Interviews," *Pew Research Center*, May 14, 2015, http://www.pewresearch.org/fact-tank/2015/05/14/where-web-surveys-produce-different-results-than-phone-interviews/.
7. I am grateful to Ryan Cragun of the University of Tampa for suggesting that we structure the question in this way.
8. "Age Distribution among Adults Who Believe in God with Absolute Certainty by Generational Group," 2014 Religious Landscape Study, Pew Research Center, n.d., http://www.pewforum.org/religious-landscape-study/compare/age-distribution/by/generational-cohort/among/belief-in-god/believe-in-god-absolutely-certain/.
9. I am grateful to Benjamin Knoll for pointing out this possibility.
10. In one case—the priesthood/temple ban—Millennials are rather surprisingly even more likely to uphold a conservative view than GenXers, at 37 percent and 30 percent, respectively.
11. Jean Twenge, *Generation Me: Why Today's Young Americans Are More Confident, Assertive, Entitled—and More Miserable Than Ever Before*, rev. ed. (New York: Atria, 2014), 6.
12. Millennials' distrust in institutions is not monolithic, according to Pew data. While their views of organized religion are less trustful than older generations', in other

areas—notably, their views about labor unions, banks, businesses, and universities—they report higher levels of trust than Silent and Boomer respondents. Hannah Fingerhut, "Millennials' Views of News Media, Religious Organizations Grow More Negative," Pew Research Center, January 4, 2016, http://www.pewresearch.org/fact-tank/2016/01/04/millennials-views-of-news-media-religious-organizations-grow-more-negative/.

13. Christian Smith with Melinda Lundquist Denton, *Soul Searching: The Religious and Spiritual Lives of American Teenagers* (New York: Oxford University Press, 2005), 40–43. The NMS did not ask about beliefs in angels, miracles, or heaven.
14. Smith and Denton, *Soul Searching*, 119–121.
15. Robin, thirty-eight, telephone interview, September 30, 2017.
16. Brittany, thirty, telephone interview, November 12, 2016.
17. Annabel, twenty-nine, in-person interview, Provo, Utah, September 23 2017.
18. Twenge, *Generation Me*, 139.
19. "Kingdoms of Glory," *True to the Faith* (Salt Lake City: Church of Jesus Christ of Latter-day Saints, 2004), https://www.lds.org/manual/true-to-the-faith/kingdoms-of-glory?lang=eng.
20. Rachel, thirty-two, telephone interview, October 26, 2016.
21. "What Is Sticky Faith?," Fuller Youth Institute, n.d., https://fulleryouthinstitute.org/stickyfaith.
22. See Vern L. Bengtson, *Families and Faith: How Religion Is Passed Down across Generations* (New York: Oxford University Press, 2013), 65–67, 119–124, 187–188; Naomi Schafer Riley, *'Til Faith Do Us Part: How Interfaith Marriage Is Transforming America* (New York: Oxford University Press, 2013), 24–26, 190–194.
23. In studies of Mormonism, the primary example of this assumption that higher education would result in widespread religious disaffection is found in sociologist Thomas O'Dea's foundational 1957 book *The Mormons*. For helpful critiques of that book half a century later, see Howard M. Bahr, "Finding Oneself among the Saints: Thomas F. O'Dea, Mormon Intellectuals, and the Future of Mormon Orthodoxy," *Journal for the Scientific Study of Religion* 47, no. 3 (September 2008): 463–484, and Cardell K. Jacobson, John P. Hoffmann, and Tim B. Heaton, *Revisiting Thomas F. O'Dea's The Mormons: Contemporary Perspectives* (Salt Lake City: University of Utah Press, 2008), esp. chapters 2 and 14.
24. As Damon Mayrl and Jeremy E. Uecker summarize, "Contrary to longstanding scholarly wisdom, attending college appears to have no liberalizing effect on most dimensions of religious belief. In fact, on some measures, college students appear to liberalize *less* than those who never attended college." "Higher Education and Liberalization among Young Adults," *Social Forces* 90, no. 1 (September 2011): 181–208.
25. This includes all kinds of college education, both secular and religious. It would be interesting in a future study to include separate categories for respondents who attended LDS universities.
26. Some high school students also take seminary by correspondence course, especially if they live in an area where there are too few students to make up a class or they are involved in sports in the early morning.
27. Nicole, twenty-six, telephone interview, October 20, 2016.
28. Rebecca de Schweinetz, "Holding on to the 'Chosen Generation': The Mormon Battle for Youth in the 1960s and Early 1970s," in *Out of Obscurity: Mormonism since 1945*, ed. Patrick Q. Mason and John G. Turner (New York: Oxford University Press, 2016), 278–301.
29. Marie Cornwall, "The Influence of Three Agents of Religious Socialization: Family, Church, and Peers," in *The Religion and Family Connection: Social Science Perspectives*, ed.

Darwin L. Thomas (Provo, UT: Religious Studies Center, Brigham Young University, 1988), 207–231.

30. Seminary did not, however, make a difference among those who were less active church attenders in their youth.

31. This finding is supported by some studies but not others. Armand Mauss, in a local study comparing Mormons in Salt Lake City and San Francisco in the late 1960s, found that regardless of their levels of education, the San Francisco Mormons were "consistently lower" in orthodoxy than the Utah Mormons, "usually by a third or more." Armand Mauss, *The Angel and the Beehive: The Mormon Struggle with Assimilation* (Urbana: University of Illinois Press, 1994), 68–73. In contrast, David E. Campbell, John C. Green, and J. Quin Monson found few appreciable differences between Utah Mormons and non-Utah Mormons except in the strength of their LDS kinship and friendship networks—Utah Mormons, not surprisingly, had more Mormon friends and family members than Mormons elsewhere in the United States. *Seeking the Promised Land: Mormons and American Politics* (New York: Cambridge University Press, 2014), 67–68.

32. This finding has also been true in previous studies of Mormon converts. On converts' religiosity being lower than lifelong Mormons', see Campbell, Green, and Monson, *Seeking the Promised Land*, 69, and Bruce A. Chadwick, Brent L. Top, and Richard J. McClendon, *Shield of Faith: The Power of Religion in the Lives of LDS Youth and Young Adults* (Provo, UT: BYU Religious Studies Center, 2010), 27. Another study found very little difference in either direction: see Stan L. Albrecht and Howard M. Bahr, "Patterns of Religious Disaffiliation: A Study of Lifelong Mormons, Mormon Converts, and Former Mormons," *Journal for the Scientific Study of Religion* 22, no. 4 (December 1983): 366–379, esp. 373–374.

33. Rick Phillips, "Saints in Zion, Saints in Babylon: Religious Pluralism and the Transformation of Mormon Culture" (dissertation, Rutgers University, 2001), 8; Matt Canham, "Salt Lake County Is Becoming Less Mormon—Utah County Is Headed in the Other Direction," *Salt Lake Tribune*, July 16, 2017, http://archive.sltrib.com/article.php?id=5403049&itype=CMSID; Public Religion Research Institute, *America's Changing Religious Identity: Findings from the 2016 American Values Atlas*, 12.

34. Colby, twenty, telephone interview, January 27, 2017.

35. In Mormonism, a patriarchal blessing is a once-in-a-lifetime pronouncement by a "stake patriarch" who is ordained specifically for this purpose. The blessing typically proclaims a person's lineage among the twelve tribes of Israel and offers guidance from God about future directions in life. Church members become eligible to receive their patriarchal blessings when they are in early adolescence, though some wait until adulthood to do so. For more about interviewees' specific experiences with patriarchal blessings, see chapter 10.

36. Brooke, thirty-six, telephone interview, October 20, 2017.

37. Catherine, thirty-seven, telephone interview, October 9, 2017.

38. Parts of this section are adapted from Benjamin Knoll and Jana Riess, "Infected with Doubt: An Empirical Overview of Belief and Nonbelief in Contemporary American Mormonism," *Dialogue: A Journal of Mormon Thought* 50, no. 3 (Fall 2017): 1–38, with the permission of *Dialogue*. Ben was the primary author of several paragraphs in this section of the chapter.

39. This includes respondents who selected any of the bottom three responses, saying that some, most, or all of the teachings of the LDS Church were hard for them to believe.

40. Seminary attendance makes a difference. Those who attended seminary all four years are ten points less likely to identify as doubters than those who did not attend (15 vs. 5 percent).

41. Henry B. Eyring, "Bind Up Their Wounds," October 2013 General Conference, https://www.lds.org/general-conference/2013/10/bind-up-their-wounds?lang=eng.

CHAPTER 2

1. Lee, thirty-eight, telephone interview, June 1, 2016.
2. In October 2012, the LDS Church lowered the missionary age from nineteen to eighteen for men and from twenty-one to nineteen for women.
3. In Mormonism, an "investigator" is someone who is learning more about the church and likely meeting with the missionaries about the possibility of joining.
4. The possible responses to this question were "randomized," meaning that the order presented was randomly generated for each respondent.
5. In 2017, the LDS Church announced that it would discontinue its Scouting programs for older teens, dramatically changing a relationship that had existed between the two organizations for over a century. Tad Walch, "Mormons Drop Scout Programs for Older Teens," *Deseret News*, May 11, 2017, http://www.deseretnews.com/article/865679711/Mormons-drop-Scout-programs-for-older-teens.html. The following year, the church announced it would withdraw entirely from the Boy Scouts at the end of 2019, and said that it planned instead to create its own program for Mormon youth around the world. Laurie Goodstein and Christine Hauser, "Mormon Church Ends Century-Long Partnership with Boy Scouts of America," *New York Times*, May 9, 2018, https://www.nytimes.com/2018/05/09/us/boy-scouts-mormon-church.html.
6. Sarah, thirty-eight, in-person interview, Salt Lake City, Utah, October 1, 2016.
7. Missionaries who come from areas of the world where $400 would be a hardship pay a reduced monthly amount. Eric Hawkins, spokesman for The Church of Jesus Christ of Latter-day Saints, email correspondence with the author, August 25, 2017.
8. Lynn Arave, "Top 10: Most/Least Expensive LDS Missions," *Standard-Examiner*, December 29, 2014, http://www.standard.net/Faith/2014/12/28/Most-least-expensive-LDS-Church-missions.
9. According to the church's guidelines, "Parents who send extra money so missionaries can eat fast food rather than cook their own food not only detract from one of the great learning experiences of the mission, but also encourage missionaries to break mission rules." See the "Becoming a Supportive Missionary Mom or Dad" section of Robert K. Wagstaff, "Preparing Emotionally for Missionary Service," March 2011, https://www.lds.org/ensign/2011/03/preparing-emotionally-for-missionary-service.p28-p36?lang=eng.
10. At LDSBookstore.com, piggy banks are available for both boys (blue) and girls (pink), the main difference being that the boys' bank has slots for tithing, mission, and spending, while the girls' bank offers slots for tithing, "savings," and spending. See https://ldsbookstore.com/girl-tithing-bank and https://ldsbookstore.com/boytithing-bank.
11. Taylor, thirty-seven, telephone interview, October 11, 2017.
12. There may be some variation in these times if, for example, the missionaries live in an area where it is unsafe to be out teaching after dark; see R. Scott Lloyd, "Changes to Missionaries' Daily Schedule Allows More Time to Teach Gospel," *LDS Church News*, February 6, 2017, https://www.lds.org/church/news/changes-to-missionaries-daily-schedule-allows-more-time-to-teach-gospel?lang=eng.
13. As of this writing, there are fifteen MTCs, but two—the centers in Chile and Spain—will be discontinued in January 2019. "Two Missionary Training Centers to Close," Mormon Newsroom, March 29, 2018, https://www.mormonnewsroom.org/article/two-missionary-training-centers-closing.
14. Armand Mauss, *Shifting Borders and a Tattered Passport: Intellectual Journeys of a Mormon Academic* (Salt Lake City: University of Utah Press, 2012), 10.

15. James Dennie LoRusso, "'The Puritan Ethic on High': LDS Media and the Mormon Embrace of Free Enterprise in the Twentieth Century," in *Out of Obscurity: Mormonism since 1945*, ed. Patrick Q. Mason and John G. Turner (New York: Oxford University Press, 2016), 119. One casualty of the restructured missionary program was the discontinuation of missions for young married couples, who had never been many in number. For Eugene England's experiences serving a mission in Samoa as a twenty-year-old newlywed with his wife Charlotte, see "Mission to Paradise," *BYU Studies* 38, no. 1 (1999): 170–185.

16. According to Gregory Prince's biography of President David O. McKay, Henry D. Moyle, one of McKay's counselors in the First Presidency who chaired the Missionary Committee, had a strong preference for calling younger mission presidents. "I want younger men out there, vigorous, that know how to motivate people and get this missionary work going." Quoted in Prince and Wm. Robert Wright, *David O. McKay and the Rise of Modern Mormonism* (Salt Lake City: University of Utah Press, 2005), 233.

17. Gary Shepherd and Gordon Shepherd, *Mormon Passage: A Missionary Chronicle* (Urbana: University of Illinois Press, 1998), 10.

18. This General Conference talk was directed at an entirely male audience in a priesthood session; there have not been similar General Conference talks directed at women and girls in which a mission is presented as an obligation rather than merely an option.

19. M. Russell Ballard, "The Greatest Generation of Missionaries," October 2002 General Conference, https://www.lds.org/general-conference/2002/10/the-greatest-generation-of-missionaries?lang=eng/.

20. See Benjamin Hyrum White, "The History of *Preach My Gospel*," in *Go Ye into All the World: The Growth and Development of Mormon Missionary Work*, ed. Reid L. Neilson and Fred W. Woods (Provo, UT: BYU Religious Studies Center, 2012), 151–188, esp. 162–165.

21. "President Nelson Signs Mission Calls as Presiding Apostle," Mormon Newsroom, January 9, 2018, https://www.mormonnewsroom.org/article/president-nelson-signs-calls-new-missionaries.

22. See Armand Mauss, *The Angel and the Beehive: The Mormon Struggle with Assimilation* (Urbana: University of Illinois Press, 1994), 90 and 131–132, and Bruce A. Chadwick, Brent L. Top, and Richard J. McClendon, *Shield of Faith: The Power of Religion in the Lives of LDS Youth and Young Adults* (Provo, UT: BYU Religious Studies Center, 2010), 15. Interestingly, the generation of young men that would have been of missionary age when Mauss was writing in the early 1990s were largely GenXers, one-third of whom were believed to serve. In our data we see a far higher percentage of GenX men who served: 53 percent, or slightly more than half. In understanding this double-digit discrepancy we have to remember that this part of the NMS is canvassing only those who are *still self-identifying members of the church*, rather than everyone who served a mission from that generation.

23. According to the church's public affairs department, approximately 15 percent of young missionaries were women prior to the 2012 age change. Now it is closer to 30 percent. Hawkins, email correspondence, August 25, 2017.

24. Courtney L. Rabada and Kristine L. Haglund, "The Great Lever: Women and Changing Mission Culture in Contemporary Mormonism," in *Voices for Equality: Ordain Women and Resurgent Mormon Feminism*, ed. Gordon Shepherd, Lavina Fielding Anderson, and Gary Shepherd (Salt Lake City: Greg Kofford Books, 2015), 259–275.

25. Rob, thirty-eight, in-person interview, Cincinnati, Ohio, May 5, 2017.

26. Gloria, thirty-one, in-person interview, Salt Lake City, Utah, October 3, 2016.

27. Nicole, twenty-six, telephone interview, October 20, 2016.

28. Jamie, thirty-three, telephone interview, July 13, 2016.

29. Lisa, thirty-two, in-person interview, New York City, February 4, 2012.
30. It is surprising that Millennial RMs are the most likely of any generation to say their missions were "very valuable" in helping to gain converts for the LDS Church (53 percent), since the average number of baptisms per missionary noticeably decreased during the time they served their missions. The number of baptisms per missionary has fallen from about eight in 1989 to about three and a half in 2014. See David G. Stewart Jr., "Growth, Retention, and Internationalization," in *Revisiting Thomas F. O'Dea's* The Mormons: *Contemporary Perspectives,* ed. Cardell K. Jacobson, John P. Hoffmann, and Tim B. Heaton (Salt Lake City: University of Utah Press, 2008), 330.
31. Research on short-term missions in adolescence has shown them to have a surprisingly robust effect on personal religiosity and feelings of closeness to God. Jenny Trinitapoli and Stephen Vaisey, "The Transformative Role of Religious Experience: The Case of Short-Term Missions," *Social Forces* 88, no. 1 (September 2009): 121–146, esp. 125 and 135. Specific follow-up research on several thousand LDS missionaries confirms that most RMs remain deeply committed to Mormonism, with high rates of church attendance and temple marriage. See Chadwick, Top, and McClendon, *Shield of Faith,* 265–294.
32. Craig Harline, *Way Below the Angels: The Pretty Clearly Troubled but Not Even Close to Tragic Confessions of a Real Live Mormon Missionary* (Grand Rapids, MI: Eerdmans, 2014), 257–258.
33. Note that those who returned home early are still counted in a generation's cumulative total of RMs. Among the Millennials, for example, 38 percent served for their designated tenure and an additional 17 percent served a mission but came home early, creating the 55 percent figure cited earlier. In this survey, missionary service "counts" whether it was for one month or twenty-four.
34. Levi S. Peterson, "Resolving Problems for Missionaries Who Return Early," *Sunstone* 127 (May 2003): 42.
35. Russell Arben Fox, "Are More Missionaries Returning Early?," By Common Consent, July 22, 2014, https://bycommonconsent.com/2014/07/22/are-more-missionaries-returning-early/.
36. Tad Walch, "Many Mormon Missionaries Who Return Early Feel Some Failure," *Deseret News,* December 6, 2013, http://www.deseretnews.com/article/865591983/LDS-missionaries-developing-strategies-to-cope-with-stress.html. While this is the best data we have on the subject, it should be noted that it was obtained from a convenience sample (also called a "snowball sample"), in which respondents are invited through social media networks, and can also invite other respondents they know who fit the study's criteria. This gives researchers the ability to target tiny populations—in this case, LDS missionaries who returned early from their missions—but it has some disadvantages that don't pertain to a nationally representative sample, such as the reinforcement of the socioeconomic, religious, and/or educational biases that may exist in a person's social networks.
37. I am grateful to Benjamin Knoll for running this and many other analyses of the data.
38. Zachary, twenty-one, telephone interview, September 8, 2016.
39. FLDS stands for the Fundamentalist Church of Jesus Christ of Latter-Day Saints, one of several polygamous sects that traces its history back to a schism that occurred when the LDS Church, then led by Wilford W. Woodruff, disavowed polygamy in 1890. The FLDS Church's leader, Warren Jeffs, is serving a sentence of life imprisonment for child abuse.

CHAPTER 3

1. Chrissy, thirty-three, telephone interview, September 18, 2017.
2. Chelsea, twenty-five, telephone interview, August 10, 2017.

3. Brittany, thirty, telephone interview, November 12, 2016.
4. Colby, twenty, telephone interview, January 27, 2017.
5. Karianne, twenty-five, telephone interview, October 17, 2016.
6. In LDS temples, sacred names rotate on a daily basis, so that on a given day all men will be given the same sacred name at any temple in the world, and all women will. This practice may be an emotional letdown, but it serves a pragmatic purpose because people who forget their sacred name can rediscover it by having the church search for it based on the date they received their temple ordinances.
7. Eleven percent of former Mormons say their experience was very positive, 48 percent somewhat positive, 25 percent somewhat negative, and 17 percent very negative. (As elsewhere in the book, not all percentages add up to 100 because of rounding to the nearest whole number.)
8. James E. Faulconer, "The Mormon Temple and Mormon Ritual," in *The Oxford Handbook of Mormonism*, ed. Terryl L. Givens and Philip L. Barlow (New York: Oxford University Press, 2015), 199.
9. Conventional wisdom has dictated that the closer people get to death, the more religious they become. Recent social science research, however, calls that theory into question. Data from the Longitudinal Study of Generations from 1971 to 2016 suggests that "gerotranscendance"—the theory that people become more altruistic and religiously observant when they are in close proximity to death—is misguided. People in the study not only became slightly less religious the closer they got to death but also said they valued religion less highly, which was surprising. Merril Silverstein and Vern Bengtson, "Changes in Religiosity with Aging and the Approaching End of Life" (paper presented at the annual convention of the Society for the Scientific Study of Religion, Washington, DC, October 13–15, 2017).
10. Troy, thirty-seven, telephone interview, September 9, 2016.
11. Jason, thirty-one, telephone interview, September 13, 2016.
12. Miranda, thirty-five, telephone interview, September 19, 2017.
13. Another young Mormon couple's very different choice to have a "Gentile" wedding instead of one in the temple is recounted in Katherine Taylor Allred, "I, Katherine, Having Been Born of Goodly Parents . . .," in *Baring Witness: 36 Mormon Women Talk Candidly about Love, Sex, and Marriage*, ed. Holly Welker (Urbana: University of Illinois Press, 2016), 100–103.
14. The language that would have been used in Miranda's temple endowment did not include the word "obey." It was removed in 1990 in an attempt to update the ceremony so that, in the words of a church spokesperson, it would be "more in keeping with the sensitivities we have as a society." Peter Steinfels, "Mormons Drop Rites Opposed by Women," *New York Times*, May 3, 1990, http://www.nytimes.com/1990/05/03/us/mormons-drop-rites-opposed-by-women.html. However, the fact that this interviewee and others *perceived* a requirement to obey their husbands shows that the 1990 change did little to correct the underlying problem of women's relationship with God being mediated through male authority.
15. Roe, thirty-two, telephone interview, June 9 and June 16, 2017.
16. Some Latter-day Saints leaders have proffered the language that the temple is "sacred, not secret." David O. McKay, "The Purpose of Temples," *Ensign* (January 1972): 38. But the temple is *both* sacred and secret. When individuals are told to conceal certain information from others, that is the definition of a secret, even if such concealment has a holy purpose. As Kathleen Flake's research has shown, the temple was always intended to be such, from the endowment's beginnings in 1842 when Joseph Smith apparently gave instructions that the ceremony was "not to be riten" down. For its first several decades, the temple endowment existed as a purely oral ritual that was maintained only in the

memory of its participants; in 1877, it was committed to paper, but with the clear understanding that the written version, like the ritual itself, was not for outsiders. Kathleen Flake, " 'Not to Be Riten': The Mormon Temple Rite as Oral Canon," *Journal of Ritual Studies* 9, no. 2 (Summer 1995): 1, 5.

17. Linda King Newell, "A Gift Given, a Gift Taken Away: Washing, Anointing, and Blessing the Sick among Mormon Women," *Sunstone* 6 (September/October 1981): 16–25; Laurel Thatcher Ulrich, *"A House Full of Females": Plural Marriage and Women's Rights in Early Mormonism, 1835–1870* (New York: Vintage Books, 2017), 193, 369; Jonathan A. Stapley and Kristine Wright, "Female Ritual Healing in Mormonism," *Journal of Mormon History* 37 (Winter 2011): 1–85.

18. Sarah, thirty-eight, in-person interview in Salt Lake City, Utah, October 1, 2016.

19. Devery S. Anderson, *The Development of LDS Temple Worship, 1846–2000: A Documentary History* (Salt Lake City: Signature Books, 2010), Kindle location 8963.

20. Elaine, thirty-five, telephone interview, September 29, 2017.

21. Taylor, thirty-seven, telephone interview, October 11, 2017.

22. Jamie, thirty-three, telephone interview, July 13, 2016.

23. Daniel, twenty-eight, telephone interview, September 2, 2016.

24. Janelle, thirty-six, telephone interview, June 23, 2016.

25. "Sacred Temple Clothing," LDS Media Library, n.d., https://www.lds.org/media-library/video/2014-01-1460-sacred-temple-clothing?lang=eng.

26. Mikey, twenty-five, in-person interview, St. Louis, Missouri, June 3, 2017.

27. Jacob, thirty-five, telephone interview, July 20 and July 28, 2016.

28. See "Church Updates Temple Garment Video," Mormon Newsroom, October 22, 2014, http://www.mormonnewsroom.org/article/church-updates-temple-garment-video.

29. As historian Matthew Bowman writes, "Intended to be reminiscent of the skins in which God clothed Adam and Eve after the expulsion from the Garden of Eden in the third chapter of Genesis, the garment, Mormons are told, is a constant reminder of their dependence on God and the covenants they make in the temple to obey him." Bowman, *The Mormon People: The Making of an American Faith* (New York: Random House, 2012), 77. See also Colleen McDannell, *Material Christianity: Religion and Popular Culture in America* (New Haven, CT: Yale University Press, 1995), 211–214.

30. The only explicit instructions about how to wear garments are found in the Church Handbook of Instructions: "Endowed members should wear the temple garment both day and night. They should not remove it, either entirely or partially, to work in the yard or for other activities that can reasonably be done with the garment worn properly beneath the clothing. Nor should they remove it to lounge around the home in swimwear or immodest clothing. When they must remove the garment, such as for swimming, they should put it back on as soon as possible." Section 21.1.42 of *Handbook 2: Administering the Church*, https://www.lds.org/handbook/handbook-2-administering-the-church/selected-church-policies?lang=eng#21.1.42.

31. On the other hand, Millennials are less likely to approve of shedding garments to have sex, which was a very surprising finding. A significant portion of those Millennials who say it is not appropriate to remove the garment during sex have never been married, and may therefore be sexually inexperienced. In the sample as a whole, an individual is almost twice as likely to disapprove of removing garments during sex if he or she has never been married.

32. Emily, thirty-four, telephone interview, September 12, 2017.

33. Garments' arm and leg length have undergone significant changes. In 1906, LDS Church President Joseph F. Smith chastised members who rolled up their union-suit-like garments to accommodate changing fashions. In 1918, he followed that up with a statement that the prescribed length—to the ankles and to the wrists—was part of

the "approved pattern" that was "revealed from heaven." Members were not authorized to alter it in any way. But Smith's successor, Heber J. Grant, allowed the garment to be shortened to the elbows and just below the knees in 1923, and further changes in the twentieth century shortened it even more. The church began allowing for a two-piece version in 1979, which is the standard today. McDannell, *Material Christianity*, 214–215, and Anderson, *The Development of LDS Temple Worship, 1846–2000*, Kindle locations 578, 9832, and 10307.

34. "Church Offers New Stretch Cotton Garments for Women," January 24, 2018, https://www.lds.org/church/news/church-offers-new-stretch-cotton-garments-for-women?lang=eng. The article states that the garment changes were tested on more than a thousand women and implemented with their concerns and preferences in mind. A men's version of the stretch cotton garment was expected to follow.

35. Catherine, thirty-seven, telephone interview, October 9, 2017.

36. See McDannell, *Material Christianity*, 208.

CHAPTER 4

1. Naomi, thirty-eight, telephone interview, August 8, 2017.

2. Claire Cain Miller, "The Divorce Surge Is Over, but the Myth Lives On," *New York Times*, December 2, 2014, https://www.nytimes.com/2014/12/02/upshot/the-divorce-surge-is-over-but-the-myth-lives-on.html?mcubz=1.

3. Pew Research Center, "The Decline in Marriage among the Young," March 5, 2014, http://www.pewsocialtrends.org/2014/03/07/millennials-in-adulthood/sdt-next-america-03-07-2014-0-02/.

4. Ibid. See also Paul Taylor, *The Next America: Boomers, Millennials, and the Looming Generational Showdown* (New York: Public Affairs, 2015), 143.

5. "Historical Marital Status Tables, Table MS2: Estimated Median Age at Marriage by Sex: 1890 to the Present," United States Census Bureau, updated November 2016, https://www.census.gov/data/tables/time-series/demo/families/marital.html.

6. Ibid.

7. Kay Hymowitz, Jason S. Carroll, W. Bradford Wilcox, and Kelleen Kaye, "Knot Yet: The Benefits and Costs of Delayed Marriage in America," n.d., http://twentysomethingmarriage.org/summary/.

8. Gordon B. Dahl, "Early Teen Marriage and Future Poverty," *Demography* 47, no. 3 (August 2010): 689–718, cites research that women who marry while still in their teens are two-thirds more likely to divorce within the first fifteen years than women who were older. They are also considerably less likely to obtain a college education. For an analysis of factors correlating with early marriage (but not outcomes of it), see Jeremy E. Uecker and Charles E. Stokes, "Early Marriage in the United States," *Journal of Marriage and the Family* 70, no. 4 (November 2008): 835–846.

9. Taylor, *The Next America*, 145.

10. This figure includes not only those who are married to their first spouse but also those who have remarried after divorce or bereavement. According to Public Religion Research Institute (PRRI) data, Orthodox Jews have the highest rate of marriage among all religious groups (74 percent), while Mormons are second (68 percent) and Hindus are third (66 percent). Mormons have the highest rate when considering only Christian groups. Robert P. Jones and Daniel Cox, "America's Changing Religious Identity: Findings from the 2016 American Values Atlas," PRRI, 33.

11. Naomi Schafer Riley, *Got Religion? How Churches, Mosques, and Synagogues Can Bring Young People Back* (New York: Oxford University Press, 2014), 92.

12. In the NMS, 5 percent of all Mormons were cohabiting, and 10 percent of Mormon Millennials ages eighteen to thirty-six were doing so. In the general population, 7 percent

of US adults were cohabiting in 2016, and 14 percent of US Millennials ages twenty-five to thirty-four were doing so. Although the age ranges for both studies are slightly different, both show a doubling between the popularity of cohabiting in the general population and its prevalence among Millennials. Renee Stepler, "Number of U.S. Adults Cohabiting with a Partner Continues to Rise, Especially Among Those 50 and Older," Pew Research Center, April 6, 2017, http://www.pewresearch.org/fact-tank/2017/04/06/number-of-u-s-adults-cohabiting-with-a-partner-continues-to-rise-especially-among-those-50-and-older/.

13. Lydia Saad, "Fewer Young People Say I Do—to Any Relationship," Gallup, June 8, 2015, http://www.gallup.com/poll/183515/fewer-young-people-say-relationship.aspx. In Gallup's research on US adults, 68 percent of all men ages eighteen to twenty-nine had never married, compared to 60 percent of women.

14. In Utah, 69 percent of never-married women reported attending church at least weekly, compared to just 31 percent of never-married men. I thank Benjamin Knoll for performing this analysis. We should keep in mind that the margin of error is high when we focus only on never-married Mormons in Utah. However, this NMS finding may confirm previous research indicating that a gender imbalance in Utah was the result of higher disaffiliation among men than women there. See Rick Phillips and Ryan T. Cragun, "Mormons in the United States 1990–2008: Socio-demographic Trends and Regional Differences: A Report Based on the American Religious Identification Survey 2008" (Hartford, CT: Institute for the Study of Secularism in Society & Culture, n.d.), 4–5, https://commons.trincoll.edu/aris/publications/2008-2/mormons-in-the-united-states-1990-2008-socio-demographic-trends-and-regional-differences/.

15. Mala, thirty-six, telephone interview, March 29, 2017.

16. Jessica, twenty-seven, telephone interview, June 22, 2016.

17. Among former Mormons, egalitarian marriage is more popular than the traditional, gender-specific model. In fact, the numbers seem to be an almost exact reversal of current Mormons' views: 60 percent of former Mormons say the egalitarian model is ideal, while just four in ten opt for the traditional one. Here again we see generational movement, with two-thirds of Millennial former Mormons preferring the egalitarian marriage.

18. Troy, thirty-seven, telephone interview, September 9, 2016.

19. In Mormonism it is a commonly repeated aphorism that a single man over the age of twenty-five is a menace to society, but the attribution to Brigham Young does not bear up under scrutiny. According to Young's biographer John G. Turner, it is not present in his collected discourses, and he never apparently used the word "menace" as a noun. Moreover, the phrase "menace to society" did not become common until after Young's death in 1877; according to the Oxford English Dictionary, its earliest usage in the *New York Times* occurred in 1884, the *Chicago Tribune* in 1890, and the *Wall Street Journal* in 1893. John Turner, email correspondence with author, November 9, 2017, and Ken Greenwald, "Menace to Society," WordWizard, May 26, 2005, http://wordwizard.com/phpbb3/viewtopic.php?f=7&t=17987.

20. Brandon, forty-one, telephone interview, July 12, 2017.

21. LDS Church growth researcher Matthew Martinich, email to author, February 3, 2018.

22. Bishop interview, in person, Provo, Utah, August 2, 2017.

23. Heaton, Bahr, and Jacobson, *A Statistical Profile of Mormons*, 49.

24. "In Which They Fret Over the Young Single Adults," YouTube video, 50:03, from a meeting of LDS leaders taped November 12, 2008, posted by MormonLeaks, October 2, 2016, https://www.youtube.com/watch?v=FBH04SooaY0. According to data presented in the meeting, in 2008 the rate of activity in North America was around 30 percent for YSAs, and 20 percent internationally. In the video, the presenter tells LDS leaders,

"What's interesting about that to us is that . . . young adults . . . of the same age who get married are twice as active as singles. So there's something about being single."

25. Median age at first marriage, however, is strikingly similar for both groups: twenty-two for current Mormons, and twenty-three for former Mormons. Three-quarters of former Mormons who marry do so by the time they turn twenty-seven.

26. According to Pew, for example, 60 percent of married Americans say they pray daily, versus 43 percent of those who have never married. "Frequency of Prayer by Marital Status," 2014 Religious Landscape Study, http://www.pewforum.org/religious-landscape-study/compare/frequency-of-prayer/by/marital-status/.

27. In this tabulation, the data of the small number who are cohabiting is included with the "never married" respondents so that a three-point data scale is created: those who are married, remarried, or widowed are in one group; those who are divorced or separated are in a second group; and those who are either never married or are cohabiting are in a third group.

28. Drawing from the National Study of Youth and Religion, Mark Regnerus found that Mormon teenagers had the highest support for abstinence before marriage; 77 percent of LDS youth believed in waiting until marriage to have sex. Their abstinence is not just aspirational, either, which may be the case with evangelical youth who were found to strongly support abstinence in theory but had less robust follow-through in practice. Mormon abstinence was the highest of any religious group surveyed, at 72.5 percent, and the few Mormon teens who had engaged in intercourse were considerably less likely to have repeated the experience than other teens. Mark Regnerus, *Forbidden Fruit: Sex and Religion in the Lives of American Teenagers* (New York: Oxford University Press, 2007), 87, 132–133, 205.

29. Bruce A. Chadwick, Brent L. Top, and Richard J. McClendon, *Shield of Faith: The Power of Religion in the Lives of LDS Youth and Young Adults* (Provo, UT: BYU Religious Studies Center, 2010), 213, 200–201.

30. Not all of these are represented in the table; the others included holding hands, hugging, kissing, and masturbation with partner present.

31. Regnerus finds conflicting evidence on whether virginity loss might be a causative factor in an individual's decision to leave religion; overall, he suspects it is not. See Regnerus, *Forbidden Fruit*, 125–126. However, he notes elsewhere that Mormons can be quite different from other religious groups, such as in the low numbers of Mormon teens who repeat sexual activity once they have lost their virginity. So it is certainly possible that Mormons are different in another way as well—that for some people, loss of virginity is such a cultural and religious taboo that they see no way back to full fellowship.

32. Sharon J. Harris, "Shifting Boundaries and Redefining Adulthood: LDS Singles and Their Wards," Neal A. Maxwell Institute 2014 Summer Seminar, 1, copy in author's possession; Peggy Fletcher Stack, "Loss of Members Spurred LDS Singles Ward Changes," *Salt Lake Tribune*, April 29, 2011, http://archive.sltrib.com/article.php?id=51700209&itype=CM SID.

33. In its 2014 Religious Landscape Study, Pew found that "more than three-quarters of U.S. Hindus (91%), Mormons (82%) and Muslims (79%) who are married or living with a partner are with someone of the same religion. This is somewhat less common among Jews (65%), mainline Protestants (59%) and religiously unaffiliated people (56%)." Caryle Murphy, "Interfaith Marriage Is Becoming More Common in U.S., Particularly among the Recently Wed," Pew Research Center, June 2, 2015, http://www.pewresearch.org/fact-tank/2015/06/02/interfaith-marriage/.

34. Vern Bengtson, Norella M. Putney, and Susan Harris, *Families and Faith: How Religion Is Passed Down across Generations* (New York: Oxford University Press, 2013), 123–128. "In our sample, more than two-thirds of the same-faith marriages produced children

who followed their parents' religious tradition, whereas less than one in four mixed marriages resulted in a child who followed either the mother's or the father's religious tradition" (127).

35. Jason, thirty-one, telephone interview, September 13, 2016.

36. Emily, thirty-four, telephone interview, September 12, 2017.

37. Clayton Christensen, "The Need to Be Needed," Plenary address at the symposium "Of One Body: The State of Mormon Singledom" in New York City, May 16, 2015, video at https://www.youtube.com/watch?v=gDOHPx5K4fk.

38. Nicole Hardy, *Confessions of a Latter-day Virgin: A Memoir* (New York: Hyperion, 2013), 111.

39. Janelle, thirty-six, telephone interview, June 23, 2016.

40. Tinesha, twenty-three, telephone interview, July 8 and August 14, 2017.

41. Chelsea, twenty-five, telephone interview, August 10, 2017.

42. Char, forty-two, in-person interview, Cincinnati, Ohio, February 29, 2012.

CHAPTER 5

1. Elysse, twenty-six, telephone interview, September 20, 2016.

2. Robert D. Putnam and David E. Campbell, *American Grace: How Religion Divides and Unites Us* (New York: Simon and Schuster, 2012), 24–26; Pew Research Center, "The Gender Gap in Religion around the World," March 22, 2016, http://www.pewforum.org/2016/03/22/the-gender-gap-in-religion-around-the-world/. Researchers James T. Duke and Barry L. Johnson have contributed a nuanced analysis of Mormon women's religiosity in different stages of life, finding that while women were more religious overall than men, their religiosity was also more variable: public devotion, for example, is high when women are single, while private devotional habits such as prayer increase when they are raising teenagers. Duke and Johnson, "The Religiosity of Mormon Women through the Life Cycle," in *Latter-day Saint Social Life: Social Research on the LDS Church and Its Members* (Provo, UT: Religious Studies Center, Brigham Young University, 1998), 315–344. John P. Hoffmann and John P. Bartkowski have shown that among conservative evangelical Christians, women are more likely to adopt an inerrant view of the Bible than men are, which the authors see as a "compensatory mechanism"; because women are blocked from most positions of authority, they "offset their exclusion" by strategically doubling down on biblical literalism. In mainline denominations, where women have greater access to positions of leadership, gender differences are not as pronounced in their religious views. Hoffmann and Bartkowski, "Gender, Religious Tradition, and Biblical Literalism," *Social Forces* 86, no. 3 (March 2008): 1245–1272. It's a valid question, therefore, how much the gender differences we see in Mormons' theological views might be lessened if Mormon women had greater access to positions of leadership.

3. Not present in this analysis is one of two questions on evolution: "Evolution is the best explanation for how God brought about the emergence and development of life on earth." This was removed from the averages because it is the only one of the fifteen testimony questions for which a "yes" response would involve opposing what some (but not all) LDS leaders have historically taught about evolution. A "yes" response is therefore not necessarily a marker of religious orthodoxy.

4. Men surpassed women in a few areas, including the claim to have stored more than a year's supply of food in case of emergencies and in counseling with the bishop about personal issues or decisions. While there may be a cultural stereotype of women running to the bishop's office with their problems, in the data it is men, not women, who more often seek such consolation (62 vs. 51 percent). Of course, this may also reflect the reality that because men are more likely to have meetings with the bishop in the normal course of

fulfilling their priesthood callings, men have natural access and proximity without having to make a formal appointment.

5. See, for example, Quentin L. Cook, "LDS Women Are Incredible!," April 2011 General Conference, https://www.lds.org/general-conference/2011/04/lds-women-are-incredible?lang=eng; D. Todd Christofferson, "The Moral Force of Women," October 2013 General Conference, https://www.lds.org/general-conference/2013/10/the-moral-force-of-women?lang=eng; and Gordon B. Hinckley, "To the Women of the Church," October 2003 General Conference, https://www.lds.org/general-conference/2003/10/to-the-women-of-the-church?lang=eng.

6. Ammon, twenty-five, telephone interview, November 4, 2017.

7. The three levels of the Aaronic priesthood are deacon (for twelve- and thirteen-year-old boys), teacher (ages fourteen and fifteen), and priest (ages sixteen and seventeen). Paul VanDenBerghe, "Your Aaronic Priesthood Duties," *New Era* (June 2012), https://www.lds.org/new-era/2012/06/your-aaronic-priesthood-duties?lang=eng.

8. Quoted in ibid.

9. Miranda, thirty-five, telephone interview, September 19, 2017.

10. See, for example, Spencer W. Kimball, "The Role of Righteous Women," LDS Women's Fireside, September 15, 1979, https://www.lds.org/general-conference/1979/10/the-role-of-righteous-women?lang=eng.

11. The greatest spike in emphasis on traditional duties occurred in the 1970s, when three-quarters of church magazines' articles mentioning women limited their acceptable roles to that of wife and mother. Laura Vance, "Evolution of Ideals for Women in Mormon Periodicals, 1897–1999," *Sociology of Religion* 63 (Spring 2002): 91–112. Carrie Miles also points out that a 1942 First Presidency statement that instructed mothers to stay home with their children may have been the first time that motherhood was referred to as a "divine" calling, a trope that became standard in the decades to come. Miles, "LDS Family Ideals versus the Equality of Women: Navigating the Changes since 1957," in *Revisiting Thomas F. O'Dea's* The Mormons: *Contemporary Perspectives,* ed. Cardell K. Jacobson, John P. Hoffmann, and Tim B. Heaton (Salt Lake City: University of Utah Press, 2008), 101–134.

12. Neil J. Young, " 'The ERA Is a Moral Issue': The Mormon Church, LDS Women, and the Defeat of the Equal Rights Amendment," *American Quarterly* 59, no. 3 (September 2007): 623–644; Sonia Johnson, "My Revolution," excerpted in *Mormon Feminism: Essential Writings,* ed. Joanna Brooks, Rachel Hunt Steenblik, and Hannah Wheelwright (New York: Oxford University Press, 2016), 66–68. Although two-thirds of Mormons in Utah had approved of the ERA before the LDS Church took an official stance against it in 1975, those numbers plummeted once the church published an un-favorable *Deseret News* editorial. Subsequent LDS anti-ERA activism included stacking local and state women's conventions with Relief Society sisters who had been trained by the church to vote against every measure proposed—ironically, in the case of Utah's 1977 state convention, even opposing a measure to stop pornography. See Young, " 'The ERA Is a Moral Issue,' " 626, 634–635.

13. Peggy Fletcher Stack, "April Mormon Conference Will Make History: Women Will Pray," *Salt Lake Tribune,* March 22, 2013, http://archive.sltrib.com/article.php?id=56026380&itype=CMSID; Tad Walch, "In a Significant Move, Women to Join Key, Leading LDS Church Councils," *Deseret News,* August 18, 2015, https://www.deseretnews.com/article/865634860/In-a-significant-move-women-to-join-key-leading-LDS-Church-councils.html; Tad Walch, "Pants for Women, Parental Leave for All LDS Employees," *Deseret News,* June 28, 2017, https://www.deseretnews.com/article/865683828/Pants-for-women-parental-leave-for-all-LDS-Church-employees.html.

14. Camille West, "Ministering to Replace Home and Visiting Teaching," *LDS Church News,* April 1, 2018, https://www.lds.org/church/news/ministering-to-replace-home-and-visiting-teaching?lang=eng.

15. Marianne Holman Prescott, "Changes to Young Women Camp Invite Youth Leadership Opportunities," *LDS Church News,* March 14, 2018, https://www.lds.org/church/news/changes-to-young-women-camp-invites-youth-leadership-opportunities?lang=eng.

16. The practice began to be more limited in the early twentieth century and was officially discouraged in 1946, when Joseph Fielding Smith wrote that barring special circumstances, women should cease the practice of anointing other sisters and "send for the Elders of the Church to come and administer to the sick and afflicted." Linda King Newell, "A Gift Given, a Gift Taken Away: Washing, Anointing, and Blessing the Sick among Mormon Women," *Sunstone* 6 (September–October 1981): 16–25.

17. "Mother in Heaven," Gospel Topics, October 2015, https://www.lds.org/topics/mother-in-heaven?lang=eng.

18. Penny, twenty-four, telephone interview, July 14, 2017.

19. See Lori G. Beaman, "Molly Mormons, Mormon Feminists and Moderates: Religious Diversity and the Latter-day Saints Church," *Sociology of Religion* 62, no. 1 (Spring 2001): 65–86, esp. 75.

20. Pew Research Center, "Mormons in America: Certain in Their Beliefs, Uncertain of Their Place in Society," January 12, 2012, http://www.pewforum.org/2012/01/12/mormons-in-america-executive-summary/; Putnam and Campbell, *American Grace,* 244; Ryan T. Cragun, Stephen M. Merino, Michael Nielsen, Brent D. Beal, Matthew Stearmer, and Bradley Jones, "Predictors of Opposition to and Support for the Ordination of Women: Insights from the LDS Church," *Mental Health, Religion & Culture* 19, no. 2 (2016): 124–137.

21. This finding about generational difference is consistent with prior research about the importance of "cohort replacement" in shifting attitudes about women's roles. Cohort replacement—the simple fact of younger people aging into the survey pool and older respondents dying off—was responsible for 55 percent of the movement toward more liberal gender policies in the General Social Survey from 1985 to 1998. Clem Brooks and Catherine Bolzendahl, "The Transformation of US Gender Role Attitudes: Cohort Replacement, Social-Structural Change, and Ideological Learning," *Social Science Research* 33 (2004): 106–133, esp. 110 and 124.

22. David E. Campbell, John C. Green, and J. Quin Monson, *Seeking the Promised Land: Mormons and American Politics* (New York: Cambridge University Press, 2014), 112–113.

23. This finding was replicated almost exactly when we asked the same question in a different context elsewhere in the survey, with near-identical generational differences.

24. Benjamin Knoll and Cammie Jo Bolin, *She Preached the Word: Gender and Leadership in Modern America* (New York: Oxford University Press, 2018), chapter 8 (religious identity and efficacy) and chapter 6 (education and employment).

25. Annabel, twenty-nine, in-person interview, Provo, Utah, September 23, 2017.

26. Gary Gates of UCLA's Williams Institute estimated the transgender population at three-tenths of a percent, research that has been widely quoted, including by Pew in its 2013 study of LGBT Americans. However, he says that was "an educated guess based on two state-level surveys." See Pew Research Center, "A Survey of LGBT Americans," June 13, 2013, http://www.pewsocialtrends.org/2013/06/13/a-survey-of-lgbt-americans/; Katy Steinmetz, "How Many Americans Are Gay?: Inside Efforts to Finally Identify the Size of the Nation's LGBT Population," *Time,* May 18, 2016, http://time.com/lgbt-stats/. A more recent estimate by the Williams Institute places the percentage higher, at 0.6 percent, and that study was nationwide, not extrapolating from two

states. See "1.4 Million Adults Identify as Transgender in America, Study Says," NPR, June 30, 2016, http://www.npr.org/sections/thetwo-way/2016/06/30/484253324/1-4-million-adults-identify-as-transgender-in-america-study-says.

27. "A person who is considering an elective transsexual operation may not be baptized or confirmed. Baptism and confirmation of a person who has already undergone an elective transsexual operation require the approval of the First Presidency." *Church Handbook of Instruction, 1: Stake Presidents and Bishops*, 16.4.16.

28. Grayson, in-person interview in Provo, Utah, September 23, 2017; telephone interview October 2, 2017.

29. In 2015, man buns were outlawed at BYU-Idaho, but not at BYU-Provo or BYU-Hawaii. Lexi Harrison, "BYU-Provo Talks about BYU-Idaho's Man-Bun Ban," *BYU Universe*, September 24, 2015, http://universe.byu.edu/2015/09/24/byu-provo-talks-about-byu-idahos-man-bun-ban/.

30. Darren Sherkat, *Changing Faith: The Dynamics and Consequences of Americans' Shifting Religious Identities* (New York: NYU Press, 2014), 124.

31. Armand L. Mauss, *The Angel and the Beehive: The Mormon Struggle with Assimilation* (Urbana: University of Illinois Press, 1994), 133.

32. Doctrine and Covenants 93:36.

33. Because LDS leaders have framed higher education as a way for women to better prepare for motherhood, the way is clear for even the most orthodox Mormon women to pursue a college degree. See John Mihelich and Debbie Storrs, "Higher Education and the Negotiated Process of Hegemony: Embedded Resistance among Mormon Women," *Gender and Society* 17, no. 3 (June 2003): 404–422, esp. 406–408 and 413–417.

34. According to Pew, "In 1994, 63% of recent female high school graduates and 61% of male recent high school graduates were enrolled in college in the fall following graduation. By 2012, the share of young women enrolled in college immediately after high school had increased to 71%, but it remained unchanged for young men at 61%." Mark Hugo Lopez and Ana Gonzalez-Barrera, "Women's College Enrollment Gains Leave Men Behind," Pew Research Center, March 6, 2014, http://www.pewresearch.org/fact-tank/2014/03/06/womens-college-enrollment-gains-leave-men-behind/.

35. Millennials are left out of this comparison because many have not yet completed their educations.

36. Tim B. Heaton and Cardell K. Jacobson provide a different perspective on the educational levels of Mormon women by drawing on the GSS. Like we see in the NMS, the GSS shows Utah Mormon women's educational attainment to be lower than Mormon women's elsewhere. One difference, however, is that the GSS showed the educational gap between Mormon men and women to be widening, not narrowing as the NMS seems to show among the younger generations. Heaton and Jacobson, "The Social Composition of Mormonism," in *The Oxford Handbook of Mormonism*, ed. Terryl L. Givens and Philip L. Barlow (New York: Oxford University Press, 2015), 309–333, esp. 312–313.

37. For a popular summary of this research, see Emma Green, "Why Educated Christians Are Sticking with Church," *Atlantic*, April 26, 2017, https://www.theatlantic.com/politics/archive/2017/04/education-church-attendance/524346/. See also Philip Schwadel, "The Effects of Education on Americans' Religious Practices, Beliefs, and Affiliations," *Review of Religious Research* 53, no. 2 (November 2011), 161–182; and Damon Maryl and Jeremy E. Uecker, "Higher Education and Religious Liberalization among Young Adults," *Social Forces* 90, no. 1 (2011): 181–208.

38. "Changes in Women's Labor Force Statistics in the 20th Century," United States Department of Labor, Bureau of Labor Statistics, February 16, 2000, https://www.bls.gov/opub/ted/2000/feb/wk3/art03.htm.

39. Ezra Taft Benson, "The Honored Place of Woman," October 1981, https://www.lds.org/general-conference/1981/10/the-honored-place-of-woman?lang=eng.

40. In 1994, Carrie Miles and Laurence R. Iannaccone posited that LDS membership growth "has tended to accelerate as the church has accommodated change," particularly regarding women's roles, and that data suggests that "younger and less experienced members' favorable reaction to accommodation outweighs the older and more committed members' opposite reaction." Miles and Iannaccone, "Dealing with Social Change: The Mormon Church's Response to Change in Women's Roles," in *Contemporary Mormonism: Social Science Perspectives,* ed. Marie Cornwall, Tim B. Heaton, and Lawrence A. Young (Urbana: University of Illinois Press, 1994), 265–286.

CHAPTER 6

1. Chelsea, twenty-five, telephone interview, August 10, 2017.

2. As defined by Merriam-Webster, a microaggression is "a comment or action that subtly and often unconsciously or unintentionally expresses a prejudiced attitude toward a member of a marginalized group (such as a racial minority)." https://www.merriam-webster.com/dictionary/microaggression.

3. Chelsea asked me to note that she only learned about this years later, after the two had become good friends.

4. Bruce Drake, "6 New Findings about Millennials," Pew Research Center, March 7, 2014, http://www.pewresearch.org/fact-tank/2014/03/07/6-new-findings-about-millennials/. As one researcher put it, this Millennial generation has not had "to *learn* multiculturalism but instead has embraced it as a core value and norm." Elisabeth A. Nesbit Sbanotto and Craig L. Blomberg, *Effective Generational Ministry: Biblical and Practical Insights for Transforming Church Communities* (Grand Rapids, MI: Baker Academic, 2016), 170–171.

5. Robert D. Putnam and David E. Campbell, *American Grace: How Religion Divides and Unites Us* (New York: Simon and Schuster, 2012), 260.

6. Rebecca, thirty-seven, telephone interview, June 17, 2017.

7. Lillian, thirty-eight, in-person interview, Cincinnati, Ohio, April 6, 2012.

8. Spencer W. Kimball, "Marriage and Divorce," in *Eternal Marriage Student Manual* (Salt Lake City: Church Educational System, 2003) 168–174, esp. 169.

9. Alex, twenty-three, telephone interview, November 2, 2016.

10. Char, forty-two, in-person interview, Cincinnati, Ohio, February 29, 2012.

11. Char's adopted family came to include twenty-three children over the course of four decades.

12. Tinesha, twenty-three, telephone interview, July 8 and August 14, 2017.

13. Mormonism is not unique in this, however, and in fact shows more racial diversity than the Episcopal Church (90 percent white), the United Methodist Church (94 percent), and the Evangelical Lutheran Church in America (96 percent). Michael Lipka, "The Most and Least Racially Diverse U.S. Religious Groups," Pew Research Center, July 27, 2015, http://www.pewresearch.org/fact-tank/2015/07/27/the-most-and-least-racially-diverse-u-s-religious-groups/.

14. Putnam and Campbell, *American Grace,* 25, 28–29.

15. Research on black Mormons in the 1980s found exceptionally high overall levels of religious beliefs and commitments, but also that "the intensity of conviction" was lower "for more distinctive Mormon claims" about Joseph Smith and the Book of Mormon. Jessie Embry, *Black Saints in a White Church: Contemporary African American Mormons* (Salt Lake City: Signature Books, 1994), 99.

16. "Race and Ethnicity in Utah: 2016," Kem C. Gardner Policy Institute at the University of Utah, July 2017, http://gardner.utah.edu/wp-content/uploads/RaceandEthnicity_FactSheet20170825.pdf.

17. Robert P. Jones, *The End of White Christian America* (New York: Simon and Schuster, 2016), 127. The 2017 American Values Atlas of the Public Religion Research Institute (PRRI) found for the first time that same-sex marriage had achieved majority support among African Americans, with 52 percent saying they favored it being legal. In 2013, just 41 percent had supported it. Alex Vandermaas-Peeler, Daniel Cox, Molly Fisch-Friedman, Rob Griffin, and Robert P. Jones, "Emerging Consensus on LGBT Issues: Findings from the 2017 American Values Atlas," May 1, 2018, https://www.prri. org/research/emerging-consensus-on-lgbt-issues-findings-from-the-2017-american-values-atlas/.

18. Embry, *Black Saints in a White Church*, 88–89.

19. Camille L. Ryan and Kurt Bauman, "Educational Attainment in the United States: 2015," US Census Bureau, March 2016, https://www.census.gov/content/dam/Census/library/publications/2016/demo/p20-578.pdf.

20. The secondary literature on Mormonism and race in the nineteenth century is now substantial, but it began with Lester E. Bush Jr., "Mormonism's Negro Doctrine: An Historical Overview," *Dialogue: A Journal of Mormon Thought* 8 (Spring 1973): 229–270. Bush's article traced the ban to Brigham Young rather than Joseph Smith and was read carefully by Spencer W. Kimball, the president of the church, according to Kimball's son. Five years after the article was published, President Kimball announced the revelation extending the priesthood to all worthy men. See also Newell G. Bringhurst, *Saints, Slaves, and Blacks: The Changing Place of Black People within Mormonism*, 2nd ed. (Salt Lake City: Greg Kofford Books, 2017); W. Paul Reeve, *Religion of a Different Color: Race and the Mormon Struggle for Whiteness* (New York: Oxford University Press, 2015); and Armand L. Mauss, *All Abraham's Children: Changing Mormon Conceptions of Race and Lineage* (Urbana: University of Illinois Press, 2003).

21. Brigham Young, "Speech in Joint Session of the Legislature," February 5, 1852, reprinted in Matthew L. Harris and Newell G. Bringhurst, *The Mormon Church and Blacks: A Documentary History* (Urbana: University of Illinois Press, 2015), 37–40. The idea of the "curse of Cain" stems from the Genesis 4 story of Cain murdering his brother Abel and subsequently being marked by God in some unspecified physical way. In the nineteenth century, many Americans interpreted that physical mark as being black skin, and then conflated it with the curse of a later Genesis character, Ham, who had been consigned to a lifetime of servitude. See David M. Goldenberg, *The Curse of Ham: Race and Slavery in Early Judaism, Christianity, and Islam* (Princeton, NJ: Princeton University Press, 2003), esp. 141–144 and 178–179.

22. Letter from Joseph Smith to Oliver Cowdery, April 1836, reprinted in Harris and Bringhurst, *The Mormon Church and Blacks*, 22–25.

23. 3 Nephi 2:14–16.

24. Max Perry Mueller, *Race and the Making of the Mormon People* (Chapel Hill: University of North Carolina Press, 2016), 40–44, 95, 143.

25. Brian Walton, "A University's Dilemma: BYU and Blacks," *Dialogue: A Journal of Mormon Thought* 6 (Spring 1971): 31–36.

26. Even if one adopts a purely instrumental view of the lifting of the ban—that is, that it occurred in response to worldly circumstances—it is unlikely that the civil rights movement was the provocation. As Armand Mauss points out, by 1978 the negative media attention about Mormonism's racial ban had eased. However, the church's missionary outreach was rapidly expanding in areas of the world that were racially mixed, such as Brazil. The policy reversal was therefore catalyzed by "an *internal* imperative to increase church membership worldwide, rather than as a capitulation to *external* pressure from the American civil rights movement." Armand Mauss, "The Peril and Promise of Social Prognosis: O'Dea and the Race Issue," in *Revisiting Thomas F. O'Dea's The*

Mormons: *Contemporary Perspectives,* ed. Cardell K. Jacobson, John P. Hoffmann, and Tim B. Heaton (Salt Lake City: University of Utah Press, 2008), 160–183, esp. 171; and Mauss, "The Fading of the Pharaoh's Curse: The Decline and Fall of the Priesthood Ban against Blacks in the Mormon Church," *Dialogue: A Journal of Mormon Thought* 14 (Fall 1981): 10–45, esp. 29–31.

27. Doctrine and Covenants 130:22; Kent M. Van De Graaf, "Physical Body," in *Encyclopedia of Mormonism* (1992), http://eom.byu.edu/index.php/Physical_Body.

28. See, for example, Del Parson, *God the Father and Jesus Christ,* LDS Media Library, https://www.lds.org/media-library/images/god-christ-art-lds-37728?lang=eng; and uncredited, "Joseph Smith's First Vision," https://www.lds.org/media-library/video/2010-06-03-chapter-2-joseph-smiths-first-vision-1820?lang=eng&_r=1.

29. See Edward J. Blum and Paul Harvey, *The Color of Christ: The Son of God and the Saga of Race in America* (Chapel Hill: University of North Carolina Press, 2012).

30. Jason Horowitz, "The Genesis of a Church's Stand on Race," *Washington Post,* February 12, 2012, https://www.washingtonpost.com/politics/the-genesis-of-a-churchs-stand-on-race/2012/02/22/gIQAQZXyfR_story.html?utm_term=.60fdcfef2427.

31. "Race and the Church: All Are Alike unto God," Mormon Newsroom, February 29, 2012, https://www.mormonnewsroom.org/article/race-church.

32. "Race and the Priesthood," Gospel Topics Essay, December 2013, https://www.lds.org/topics/race-and-the-priesthood?lang=eng.

33. John T. Jost, Mahzarin R. Banajli, and Brian A. Nosek, "A Decade of System Justification Theory: Accumulated Evidence of Conscious and Unconscious Bolstering of the Status Quo," *Political Psychology* 25, no. 6 (2004): 881–919.

34. This view that Joseph Smith is absolved of responsibility for racism in Mormon history is popular but only partly accurate, according to historian Max Perry Mueller. See Mueller, *Race and the Making of the Mormon People,* esp. chapter 4.

35. Janan Graham-Russell, "Choosing to Stay in the Mormon Church despite Its Racist Legacy," *The Atlantic,* August 28, 2016, https://www.theatlantic.com/politics/archive/2016/08/black-and-mormon/497660/.

36. Pew Research Center, "Race, Immigration, and Discrimination," October 5, 2017, http://www.people-press.org/2017/10/05/4-race-immigration-and-discrimination/.

37. According to Pew, 59 percent of blacks in the United States say that racial discrimination is the main reason many black people can't get ahead in the country today, while only 35 percent of whites do. Pew Research Center, "Race, Immigration, and Discrimination," http://www.people-press.org/2017/10/05/4-race-immigration-and-discrimination/. In the NMS, every nonwhite racial group was more likely than white Mormons were to see racial discrimination as a root cause if African Americans do not succeed; Latinx Mormons, for example, were split about half and half on the question.

38. The fact that Millennial Mormons are less likely than other Americans their age to point to systemic racism is related to the greater racial diversity in the United States than within Mormonism.

39. Pew Research Center, "Beyond Distrust: How Americans View Their Government," November 23, 2015, http://www.people-press.org/2015/11/23/9-views-of-the-nation-how-its-changing-and-confidence-in-the-future/.

40. Armand Mauss, *The Angel and the Beehive: The Mormon Struggle with Assimilation* (Urbana: University of Illinois Press, 1994), 52–54.

41. Cardell K. Jacobson, "African American Latter-day Saints: A Sociological Perspective," in *Black and Mormon,* ed. Newell G. Bringhurst and Darron T. Smith (Urbana: University of Illinois Press, 2004), 118–121.

42. Tatishe M. Nteta and Jill S. Greenlee, "A Change Is Gonna Come: Generational Membership and White Racial Attitudes in the 21st Century," *Political Psychology* 34, no. 6 (December 2013): 877–897.

43. Tad Walch, "LDS Church Releases Statement on Religious Freedom as Donald Trump's Muslim Controversy Swirls," *Deseret News,* December 8, 2015, https://www.deseretnews.com/article/865643265/LDS-Church-releases-statement-on-religious-freedom-as-Donald-Trumps-Muslim-controversy-swirls.html. See also Bob Mims and David Noyce, "New LDS First Presidency Takes Its First Public Stance, Calls on Congress to Make Room for 'Dreamers,'" *Salt Lake Tribune,* January 26, 2018, https://www.sltrib.com/news/politics/2018/01/26/mormon-church-calls-on-federal-politicians-to-provide-hope-and-opportunities-for-former-daca-recipients/.

44. Latinx Mormons exhibited high support for immigration, at 80 percent. Asian American Mormons were even more favorable, at 86 percent. (However, there were only 28 Asian Americans in the NMS, so this finding should be interpreted with caution.)

45. Pew Research Center, "Race, Immigration, and Discrimination," http://www.people-press.org/2017/10/05/4-race-immigration-and-discrimination/.

46. This positive view of immigration was also apparent in the 2012 Peculiar People survey. David E. Campbell, John C. Green, and J. Quin Monson, *Seeking the Promised Land: Mormons and American Politics* (New York: Cambridge University Press, 2014), 122–125.

47. Campbell, Green, and Monson found that "Mormons who learned a new language as a missionary are significantly more likely to say that immigrants strengthen the United States than LDS Church members who have not served a mission at all." Ibid., 126.

48. In 2015, according to Pew, "immigrants from South and East Asia combined accounted for 27% of all immigrants, a share equal to that of Mexico. Other regions make up smaller shares: Europe/Canada (14%), the Caribbean (10%), Central America (8%), South America (7%), the Middle East (4%) and sub-Saharan Africa (4%)." Gustavo López and Kristen Bialik, "Key Findings about U.S. Immigrants," Pew Research Center, May 3, 2017, http://www.pewresearch.org/fact-tank/2017/05/03/key-findings-about-u-s-immigrants/.

49. "Worldwide Statistics," https://www.mormonnewsroom.org/facts-and-statistics.

50. Christina Caron, "Mormon Church Selects Two Senior Leaders, and Neither Is a White American," *New York Times,* April 2, 2018, https://www.nytimes.com/2018/04/02/us/mormon-church-minority-leaders.html.

51. Jana Riess, "Changes for Mormons: 12 Takeaways from LDS General Conference," Religion News Service, April 2, 2018, https://religionnews.com/2018/04/02/changes-for-mormons-12-takeaways-from-lds-general-conference/.

52. David Rock and Heidi Grant, "Why Diverse Teams Are Smarter," *Harvard Business Review,* November 4, 2016, https://hbr.org/2016/11/why-diverse-teams-are-smarter.

53. See Charlan Nemeth, *In Defense of Troublemakers: The Power of Dissent in Life and Business* (New York: Basic Books, 2018).

54. Mikey, twenty-five, in-person interview, St. Louis, Missouri, June 3, 2017.

55. On the other hand, there are many critiques of the ways the LDS Church expects local wards in other countries to replicate the way things are done in the United States, with little apparent acknowledgment that those customs represent white American culture. See Gina Colvin, Elise Boxer, Laurie Maffly-Kipp, Melissa Inouye, and Janan Graham-Russell, "Roundtable Discussion: Challenging Mormon Race Scholarship," *Journal of Mormon History* 41, no. 3 (July 2015): 258–282.

56. Paul L. Anderson, "Sacred Architecture and the Widow's Mite: Aesthetics, Economics, and Cultural Adaptation in LDS Temples, 1967–2017," in *The Kimball Challenge at*

Fifty: Mormon Arts Center Essays, ed. Glen L. Nelson (New York: Mormon Arts Center, 2017), 14–23, esp. 21–22.

57. "Primary voice" is difficult to define, but I think I know what Lillian means: a sweet, even saccharine, intonation and a slow delivery, as though the woman in question is speaking to kindergartners even when she is addressing adults.

58. Roe, thirty-two, telephone interview, June 9 and 16, 2017.

CHAPTER 7

1. Ellis, twenty-four, telephone interview, July 26, 2016. A portion of Ellis's personal story is also recounted in his essay for the *New York Times* Modern Love column. Ellis Jeter, "White Shirt, Black Name Tag, Big Secret," *New York Times,* May 12, 2017, https://www.nytimes.com/2017/05/12/style/modern-love-white-shirt-black-nametag-big-secret.html.

2. Jana Riess, "Mormons 50% More Likely to Accept Homosexuality Than in 2007, Says New Pew Study," Religion News Service, November 3, 2015, http://religionnews.com/2015/11/03/mormons-50-more-likely-to-accept-homosexuality-than-in-2007-says-new-pew-study/. Meanwhile, the general population's acceptance rose from 50 to 63 percent. Note that here as with many other Pew questions, the Pew version allowed for a "don't know" option that was not available in the NMS.

3. Neil J. Young, "Mormons and Same-Sex Marriage," Patrick Q. Mason and John G. Turner, eds., *Out of Obscurity: Mormonism since 1945* (New York: Oxford University Press, 2016), 147.

4. Spencer W. Kimball, *The Miracle of Forgiveness* (Salt Lake City: Bookcraft, 1969), chapter 6, full text available at https://archive.org/stream/MiracleOfForgiveness/MoF_djvu.txt.

5. Throughout the book, Kimball's depiction of homosexuality is entirely male centered, as seen in his anxiety that male masturbation served as a kind of gateway drug to homosexual behavior. Even the chapter's chosen epigraph from Romans 1:26–27 suggests that in Kimball's mind, part of the sin of homosexuality was that it made men into women. One exception to the early invisibility of lesbians to LDS leaders occurred in 1952, when J. Reuben Clark, second counselor in the LDS First Presidency, mentioned to Relief Society sisters that the "tragic" sin of homosexuality was "found in both sexes." See Seth Anderson, "Timeline of Mormon Thinking about Homosexuality," Rational Faiths, November 3, 2013, http://rationalfaiths.com/timeline-of-mormon-thinking-about-homosexuality/.

6. D. Michael Quinn, *Same-Sex Dynamics among Nineteenth-Century Americans: A Mormon Example* (Urbana: University of Illinois Press, 2001), 382.

7. "Homosexual Behavior and Same-Gender Attraction," *Handbook of Instruction 2: Administering the Church,* 21.4.6, https://www.lds.org/handbook/handbook-2-administering-the-church/selected-church-policies/21.4.12?lang=eng&_r=1#214.

8. Braley Dodson, "LGBT BYU Students Want Honor Code Clarification," *Provo Daily Herald,* November 18, 2016, http://www.heraldextra.com/news/local/education/college/byu/LGBT-byu-students-want-honor-code-clarification/article_5da9be08-d0f1-5558-b16d-a13a1027a1f1.html.

9. The outstanding memoir *Good-bye, I Love You* chronicles Carol Lynn Pearson's marriage in the late 1960s to a man who later confessed to her that he was gay. Many themes in that book are paradigmatic of the church's approach to homosexuality in the 1960s and 1970s, particularly the heartbreaking lengths LGBT Mormons went to in order to change themselves. Gerald, Carol Lynn's husband, entered into the marriage still fighting his homosexuality. "I tried to beat it to death, to strangle it, to smother it," he told her. "And it has not died. . . . If my homosexuality is wrong, then *I* am wrong, the fact of my *being* is wrong. Because that's what *I am!*" Pearson, *Good-bye, I Love You: The True*

Story of a Wife, Her Homosexual Husband—and a Love Honored for Time and All Eternity (New York: Random House, 1986), 92.

10. According to Quinn, what was then called "aversion therapy" began at BYU shortly after a 1959 meeting of the Church Board of Education. Young men who had been referred by their bishops, counselors, or mission presidents were entered into a study in which they were shown erotic photos of both nude women and men. The punishment for getting an erection at the sight of a naked man was eight seconds of 1,600 volts into the subject's arm. See Quinn, *Same-Sex Dynamics among Nineteenth-Century Americans*, 379; and Pearson, *Good-bye, I Love You*, 98–99.

11. Alex Cooper was fifteen when her Mormon parents signed over her custody to a couple promising to cure her. As part of her "treatment" she was forced to wear a backpack full of rocks each day, to represent the burden she was carrying in "choosing to be gay." If her behavior on a day was acceptable, she might have a rock removed. Some days, she would be forced to stand for hours at the wall in isolation, wearing the backpack, while the family and their guests (including Mormon missionaries) had dinner and talked to one another. They alternated between ignoring Alex entirely or taunting her for being a "dyke." Alex Cooper with Joanna Brooks, *Saving Alex: When I Was Fifteen I Told My Mormon Parents I Was Gay, and That's When My Nightmare Began* (San Francisco: HarperOne, 2016), 87–90, 104–109.

12. In 2014, Evergreen ceased operation and merged its membership with North Star, which is also LDS but does not sanction conversion or "reparative" therapy. Peggy Fletcher Stack, "Longtime Support Group for Gay Mormons Shuts Down," *Salt Lake Tribune*, January 14, 2014, http://archive.sltrib.com/story.php?ref=/sltrib/news/57344806-78/north-star-evergreen-gay.html.csp.

13. "The Surgeon General's Call to Action to Promote Sexual Health and Responsible Sexual Behavior," Centers for Disease Control and Prevention, July 9, 2001, https://www.ncbi.nlm.nih.gov/books/NBK44225/.

14. "Frequently Asked Questions," n.d., https://mormonandgay.lds.org/articles/frequently-asked-questions?lang=eng.

15. Michael J. Klarman, *From the Closet to the Altar: Courts, Backlash, and the Struggle for Same-Sex Marriage* (New York: Oxford University Press, 2013), 65, 67.

16. Ibid., 85–86.

17. This statement is available on the church's official public relations website. "California and Same-Sex Marriage," June 30, 2008, http://www.mormonnewsroom.org/article/california-and-same-sex-marriage.

18. Joanna Brooks, "On the 'Underground': What the 'Yes on 8' Campaign Reveals about the Future of Mormons in American Political Life," in *Mormonism and American Politics*, ed. Randall Balmer and Jana Riess (New York: Columbia University Press, 2016), 198. Klarman provides a slightly lower estimate of $15 million to $20 million being contributed by Mormons. Klarman, *From the Closet to the Altar*, 122.

19. Jessica Garrison and Joanna Lin, "Prop 8 Protesters Target Mormon Temple in Westwood," *Los Angeles Times*, November 7, 2008, http://www.latimes.com/local/la-me-protest7-2008nov07-story.html.

20. Colin Moynihan, "At Mormon Temple, a Protest over Prop 8," *New York Times* City Room, November 13, 2008, https://cityroom.blogs.nytimes.com/2008/11/13/at-mormon-temple-thousands-protest-prop-8/.

21. Kimball, *The Miracle of Forgiveness*, https://archive.org/stream/MiracleOfForgiveness/MoF_djvu.txt.

22. Peggy Fletcher Stack, "Packer Talk Jibes with LDS Stance after Tweak," *Salt Lake Tribune*, October 25, 2010, http://archive.sltrib.com/story.php?ref=/sltrib/home/50440474-76/packer-church-question-speech.html.csp.

23. The question "Which bests describes your current sexual orientation?" was followed by four options: "heterosexual/straight, homosexual/gay/lesbian, bisexual, or other (specify)." A question about gender identity was treated separately, giving individuals the opportunity to identify themselves as male, female, or transgender/other.

24. "In US, More Adults Identifying as LGBT," Gallup, January 11, 2017, http://www.gallup.com/poll/201731/LGBT-identification-rises.aspx.

25. Brian W. Ward, James M. Dahlhamer, Adena M. Galinsky, and Sarah S. Joestl, "Sexual Orientation and Health among U.S. Adults: National Health Interview Survey, 2013," *National Health Statistics Reports* 77 (July 15, 2014), Center for Disease Control and Prevention, National Center for Health Statistics, 3. Although the CDC has done its National Health Interview Survey for many years, respondents were not asked about sexual orientation until 2013. The survey was conducted with a sample of 34,557 US adults over the age of eighteen. These CDC statistics about the occurrence of self-reported homosexual identity in the United States are considerably lower than the 5 to 10 percent estimate that has been sometimes reported, and certainly than the 10 percent estimate that Albert Kinsey put forward in 1948 in *Sexual Behavior of the Human Male*. Kinsey was reporting on his observations of sexual *behavior*, not self-reported sexual *identity*, which is how individuals define themselves. Incidence of homosexual behavior is higher; for example, 4.1 percent of respondents in the General Social Survey report having had sex with someone of the same sex in the last five-year period. See Darren Sherkat, *Changing Faith: The Dynamics and Consequences of Americans' Shifting Religious Identities* (New York: NYU Press, 2014), 119. The CDC reports that over their life history (rather than just in the last five years), 17 percent of women and 6 percent of men had sexual contact with someone of their own sex. David Deschamps and Bennett Singer, *LGBT Stats: Lesbian, Gay, Bisexual, Transgender, and Queer People by the Numbers* (New York: New Press, 2017), 61.

26. "In US, More Adults Identifying as LGBT," Gallup. The organization postulates that Millennials may also be more likely to identify as LGBT because Millennials "are more comfortable than their older counterparts with the idea of sharing what some might consider private information on surveys."

27. Robert P. Jones, Daniel Cox, and Juhem Navarro-Rivera, "A Shifting Landscape: A Decade of Change in American Attitudes about Same-Sex Marriage and LGBT Issues," Public Religion Research Institute, February 26, 2014, 39–40.

28. The heterosexual population was measured as 96.6 percent of US respondents in 2013. Ward et al., "Sexual Orientation and Health among U.S. Adults," 3.

29. Ibid., 4–5.

30. GLAAD, "Accelerating Acceptance 2017: A Harris Poll Survey of Americans' Acceptance of LGBT People," 3–4.

31. In the GLAAD study, 65 percent of Millennials said they personally know someone who is gay or lesbian, compared to 78 percent of Baby Boomers. "Accelerating Acceptance 2017," 4. In the NMS, 60.5 percent of current Mormon Millennials said they personally know "at least one person who is gay, lesbian, or transgender," compared to 77 percent of the combined Boomer/Silent generation.

32. Alex, twenty-three, telephone interview, November 2, 2016.

33. There is some evidence that conservative religious beliefs may be associated with a higher incidence of suicidal thoughts and attempts in teens who are gay, bisexual, or questioning their sexuality. Whereas religion has functioned as a protective factor against suicide for heterosexual youth, it seems to have the opposite effect on nonheterosexuals, whose odds of suicidal thoughts and attempts increased significantly when they attached great importance to religion in their lives. Religious youth who were questioning their sexuality were almost three times as likely to have attempted suicide as those

who were sexually questioning but nonreligious, one 2011 study showed. Carol Kuruvilla, "Chilling Study Sums Up Link between Religion and Suicide for Queer Youth," *Huffington Post,* April 18, 2018, https://www.huffingtonpost.com/entry/queer-youth-religion-suicide-study_us_5ad4f7b3e4b077c89ceb9774?ncid=engmodush pmg00000003.

34. For a helpful overview of the history of the terminology used to describe sexuality and gender, see the "Brief History of Changing Terminology" prologue to Lillian Faderman, *The Gay Revolution: The Story of the Struggle* (New York: Simon and Schuster, 2015), xix–xx.

35. Falencia, twenty-seven, telephone interview, June 15, 2017.

36. Lauren, thirty-one, telephone interview, November 10, 2016.

37. Mormon bishops are required to be married. They usually serve for a period of several years, but this term may vary. It is a volunteer position.

38. The sample size when we group all nonheterosexual Mormons and former Mormons together is 125.

39. Troy, thirty-seven, telephone interview, September 9, 2016. The policy was later clarified as applying only to children who are living with parents who are in a same-sex marriage.

40. This is of course quite conservative compared to the general population. Pew research has demonstrated that among all Millennials in America, 73 percent favor same-sex marriage—more than twice the support as seen among all Millennial Mormons (33 percent). So despite the growing support for same-sex marriage among younger Mormons, it is not comparable to Millennials' support in the nation. See Paul Taylor and the Pew Research Center, *The Next America: Boomers, Millennials, and the Looming Generational Showdown* (New York: Public Affairs, 2015), 155.

41. Daniel Cox, Rachel Lienesch, and Robert P. Jones, "Who Sees Discrimination? Attitudes on Sexual Orientation, Gender Identity, Race, and Immigration Status: Findings from PRRI's American Values Atlas," Public Religion Research Institute, June 21, 2017, https://www.prri.org/research/americans-views-discrimination-immigrants-blacks-LGBT-sex-marriage-immigration-reform/.

42. In 2017, a follow-up study from PRRI saw Mormons move several more points toward support (40 percent) and away from opposition (53 percent), which continued the overall trajectory, albeit more slowly than in the year before. Alex Vandermaas-Peeler, Daniel Cox, Molly Fisch-Friedman, Rob Griffin, and Robert P. Jones, "Emerging Consensus on LGBT Issues: Findings from the 2017 American Values Atlas," May 1, 2018, https://www.prri.org/research/emerging-consensus-on-lgbt-issues-findings-from-the-2017-american-values-atlas/.

43. Robert P. Jones, *The End of White Christian America* (New York: Simon and Schuster, 2016), 237.

CHAPTER 8

1. Elaine, thirty-five, telephone interview, September 29, 2017.

2. Rachel, thirty-two, telephone interview, October 25, 2016.

3. Brittany, thirty, telephone interview, November 12, 2016. Taylor, thirty-seven, telephone interview, October 11, 2017.

4. Lauren, thirty-one, telephone interview, November 10, 2016.

5. Thirty-nine percent of younger US Millennials report praying every day, according to Pew, while 46 percent of older Millennials do. "Frequency of Prayer among Younger Millennials," Pew 2014 Religious Landscape Study, http://www.pewforum.org/religious-landscape-study/frequency-of-prayer/among/generational-cohort/younger-millennial/.

6. One difference in the wording of this Pew question when we asked it in the NMS was to change "Bible" to "scriptures" so that Mormons might also include their additional sacred texts, such as the Book of Mormon and the Doctrine and Covenants.

7. Seventy-one percent of LDS Millennials in the NMS sample read their scriptures at least once a week, compared with 67 percent for the oldest Mormons and 68 percent of GenXers.

8. The number of Boomer/Silent generation members in our survey favoring a literal interpretation is consistent with earlier research that showed that 35 percent of Mormons thought the Bible should be taken word for word. See Tim B. Heaton and Cardell K. Jacobson, "The Social Composition of Mormonism," in *The Oxford Handbook of Mormonism,* ed. Terryl L. Givens and Philip L. Barlow (New York: Oxford University Press, 2015), 317.

9. "Interpreting Scripture by Generational Group," Pew 2014 Religious Landscape Study, http://www.pewforum.org/religious-landscape-study/interpreting-scripture/. About four in ten members of the Silent Generation say Scripture is the word of God and should be taken literally, compared to only two in ten Millennials. Lydia Saad, "Record Few Americans Believe Bible Is Literal Word of God," Gallup News, May 15, 2017, http://news.gallup.com/poll/210704/record-few-americans-believe-bible-literal-word-god.aspx.

10. I am grateful to John Lyon and Patrick Mason for suggesting this possible reason for growing scriptural literalism.

11. See, for example, "Jonah and the Second Chance," *Ensign* (September 2002), https://www.lds.org/ensign/2002/09/jonah-and-the-second-chance?lang=eng. For a deeper and nonliteral LDS engagement with Job, see Michael Austin, *Re-Reading Job: Understanding the World's Greatest Poem* (Salt Lake City: Greg Kofford Books, 2014), esp. 11–19, 110–117.

12. Elysse, twenty-six, telephone interview, September 20, 2016.

13. Grayson, twenty-three, in-person interview in Provo, Utah, September 23, 2017; telephone interview, October 2, 2017.

14. Jessica Martinez, "Study: Millennials Stay in Churches Focused on Being Relational," *Christian Post,* September 20, 2013, https://www.christianpost.com/news/study-millennials-stay-in-churches-focused-on-being-relational-104962/.

15. Karl Vaters, "Ministering to Millennials by Leveraging the Relational Power of Healthy Churches," Pivot blog of *Christianity Today,* October 12, 2016, http://www.christianitytoday.com/karl-vaters/2016/october/ministering-millennials-relational-power-healthy-churches.html?paging=off.

16. Robert Wuthnow, *Inventing American Religion: Polls, Surveys, and the Tenuous Quest for a Nation's Faith* (New York: Oxford University Press, 2015), 48.

17. David Kinnaman, *You Lost Me: Why Young Christians Are Leaving Church . . . and Rethinking Faith* (Grand Rapids, MI: Baker Books, 2011), 161.

18. As a reminder, the NMS and other surveys are only considering the experiences of people who claim the identity "Mormon," which naturally lends itself to include mostly active, believing individuals. The fact that three-quarters of NMS respondents say they attend church weekly does not mean that all people on the LDS rolls do. In the United States, well below half of the people on the rolls attend regularly, and it is even lower abroad. "LDS Church Growth, Member Activity, and Convert Retention: Review and Analysis," cumorah.com, n.d., http://www.cumorah.com/index.php?target=church_growth_articles&story_id=13.

19. The wording of this first question is important: "Aside from weddings and funerals, how often do you attend the regular religious services in your congregation (not including weekday activities), regardless of whether you currently attend LDS services or those of

another religious tradition?" The question was designed to rule out weeknight activities (Institute, church-related book clubs, impromptu basketball games in the church gym) and focus on "religious services," but it did not stipulate that those services had to take place at an LDS church. So it is possible that at least some of the discrepancy could be due to Mormon Millennials attending other religions' services.

20. The desirability bias is particularly relevant when respondents are speaking to a live interviewer over the telephone, which was not the case with the NMS. Stanley Presser and Linda Stinson, "Data Collection Mode and Social Desirability Bias in Self-Reported Religious Attendance," *American Sociological Review* 63 (February 1998): 137–145.

21. Heaton et al. reported in 2004 that GSS data showed LDS attendance at 61 percent—which would seem to be on par with the Mormons in our study (57 percent), except that the GSS asked respondents to report on their activities within the last *week* and the NMS within the last *month*. See Tim B. Heaton, Stephen J. Bahr, and Cardell K. Jacobson, *A Statistical Profile of Mormons: Health, Wealth, and Social Life* (Lewiston, NY: Edward Mellen Press, 2004), 59.

22. Thomas, thirty-six, in-person interview, Salt Lake City, Utah, October 3, 2016.

23. Rion, thirty-five, in-person interview, Salt Lake City, Utah, September 29, 2016.

24. Among former Mormons, three-quarters (76 percent) had consumed coffee in the last six months, while two-thirds had drunk alcohol (62 percent) and about one in five had tried marijuana (18 percent). Those coffee and alcohol percentages are a bit lower than the national average, though it's difficult to compare exactly because the NMS question asked about consumption in the last six months, and other surveys measure at different intervals ranging from daily to "have you ever."

25. Several paragraphs of this section have been adapted from John E. Ferguson III, Benjamin R. Knoll, and Jana Riess, "The Word of Wisdom in Contemporary American Mormonism: Perceptions and Practice," *Dialogue: A Journal of Mormon Thought* 51, no. 1 (Spring 2018): 39–78. I am grateful to *Dialogue* for permission to reuse this material.

26. We did not include the consumption of caffeinated soda/energy drinks in this part of the analysis given that it has generally been accepted as not violating the Word of Wisdom in recent years by Mormon leaders, as described in Bob Mims, "Holy Brigham Young (University)! Caffeinated Sodas Allowed on Mormon Church School's Campus," *Salt Lake Tribune*, September 21, 2017, http://www.sltrib.com/news/2017/09/21/reversing-decades-old-policy-byu-sells-caffeinated-drinks-on-campus/, and Peggy Fletcher Stack, "OK, Mormons, Drink Up—Coke and Pepsi Are OK," *Salt Lake Tribune*, September 5, 2012, http://archive.sltrib.com/article.php?id=54797595&itype=CMSID.

27. See Heaton, Bahr, and Jacobson, *A Statistical Profile of Mormons*, 144. Other dramatic differences between Mormons and the rest of the US population in alcohol and drug use are reported by Bruce A. Chadwick, Brent L. Top, and Richard J. McClendon, *Shield of Faith: The Power of Religion in the Lives of LDS Youth and Young Adults* (Salt Lake City and Provo, UT: Deseret Book and BYU Religious Studies Center, 2010), 100–103.

28. LDS First Presidency, "Letter to President A. Harold Goodman of the BYU Fifth Stake," February 12, 1969. PDF available at Jana Riess, "Hello! Most Mormons Actually Do Drink Caffeinated Soda," Religion News Service, September 25, 2017, http://religionnews.com/2017/09/25/hello-most-mormons-actually-do-drink-caffeinated-soda/. A nearly identical letter about decaffeinated coffee was sent to Curt Bench of Salt Lake City on October 17, 1966, from Claire Middlemiss, secretary to LDS President David O. McKay. Middlemiss states that President McKay had directed her to provide Bench with the same answer that the church had sent others who inquired about decaf: "that the drinking of Sanka coffee is not regarded as a violation of the Word of Wisdom." The letter to Bench goes further in saying that "Sanka, being 97 percent caffein

[*sic*] free, is not considered harmful, and there is no objection to anyone's using it as a warm drink." Copy in Curt Bench's possession.

29. Marie, twenty-four, in-person interview, St. Louis, Missouri, June 2, 2017; followed by telephone interview, June 13, 2017.

30. Laurel Thatcher Ulrich, *A House Full of Females: Plural Marriage and Women's Rights in Early Mormonism, 1835–1870* (New York: Alfred A. Knopf, 2017), 165.

31. The verse Marie is referring to instructs Mormons about taking the sacrament (communion) and reads, "And, behold, this should be wine, yea, pure wine of the grape of the vine, of your own make" (Doctrine and Covenants 89:6).

32. Annelise, twenty-five, telephone interview, September 15, 2017.

33. Doctrine and Covenants 89:12–13.

34. Troy, thirty-seven, telephone interview, September 9, 2016.

35. Later, Troy was called to serve a mission in Italy, and one of his main worries was that as a missionary he would be expected to eat whatever food was presented to him. However, it turned out that one of the main areas where he worked was a branch of the church where "half the members were vegetarians." He "took it as a sign that God was okay with me being vegetarian and didn't condemn me for it as many people had tried to tell me."

36. Jayne, thirty-seven, telephone interview, September 26, 2017.

37. Penny, twenty-five, telephone interview, July 14, 2017.

38. Paul Taylor and the Pew Research Center, *The Next America: Boomers, Millennials, and the Looming Generational Showdown* (New York: Public Affairs, 2015), 58. In a separate 2015 study, the Harris Poll found that overall, 29 percent of American adults had at least one tattoo, and nearly half (47 percent) of Millennials did. The study noted that the majority of people who have a tattoo do not stop at one, but have two or more. http://www.theharrispoll.com/health-and-life/Tattoo_Takeover.html.

39. Hinckley cautioned, "Now comes the craze of tattooing one's body. I cannot understand why any young man—or young woman, for that matter—would wish to undergo the painful process of disfiguring the skin with various multicolored representations of people, animals, and various symbols. . . . Fathers, caution your sons against having their bodies tattooed. They may resist your talk now, but the time will come when they will thank you. A tattoo is graffiti on the temple of the body." Hinckley, "Great Shall Be the Peace of Thy Children," October 2000 General Conference, https://www.lds.org/general-conference/2000/10/great-shall-be-the-peace-of-thy-children?lang=eng&_r=1.

40. Gavan Blau, "Business You Can Count On: 7 Growing Industries for Accountants," Media Center, June 9, 2015, https://media.ibisworld.com/2015/06/09/business-you-can-count-on-7-emerging-industries-for-accountants/.

41. "Tattoo Takeover: Three in Ten Americans Have Tattoos, and Most Don't Stop at Just One," Harris Poll, February 10, 2016, https://www.prnewswire.com/news-releases/tattoo-takeover-three-in-ten-americans-have-tattoos-and-most-dont-stop-at-just-one-300217862.html.

42. "For the Strength of Youth" pamphlet, https://www.lds.org/youth/for-the-strength-of-youth/entertainment-and-media?lang=eng.

43. After much debate about the wording of the survey, we removed specific examples from the questions about soft and explicit pornography and simply allowed respondents to define those for themselves.

44. Warnings about pornography use have often come in the all-male priesthood session of General Conference. See, for example, Gordon B. Hinckley, "A Tragic Evil among Us," October 2004, https://www.lds.org/ensign/2004/11/a-tragic-evil-among-us?lang=eng&_r=1; Dallin H. Oaks, "Pornography," April 2005, https://www.lds.org/ensign/2005/05/pornography?lang=eng&_r=1#footnote1; and H. David Burton,

"Honoring the Priesthood," April 2000, https://www.lds.org/general-conference/2000/04/honoring-the-priesthood?lang=eng.

45. For example, while 18.5 percent of Millennial Mormons in our study reported viewing explicit pornography at some point in the last six months, in a different study of eighteen- to twenty-three-year-old non-Mormons at two universities, the overall finding was that 47 percent had done so. Moreover, that study is ten years old; it is possible those numbers would be even higher today. Timothy Buzzell, Drew Foss, and Zack Middleton, "Explaining Use of Online Pornography: A Test of Self-Control Theory and Opportunities for Deviance," *Journal of Criminal Justice and Popular Culture* 13, no. 2 (January 2006): 96–116, http://www.albany.edu/scj/jcjpc/vol13is2/Buzzell.pdf.

46. Keeter, "Methods Can Matter," Pew Research Center, http://www.pewresearch.org/fact-tank/2015/05/14/where-web-surveys-produce-different-results-than-phone-interviews/.

47. In Mormonism, the content of what is confessed to a bishop is confidential. However, ward sacrament meetings are public, so if a young person attends church but does not take the sacrament for a period of some weeks, his or her parents (and others) are likely to notice.

48. The LDS First Presidency stated in 1970 that "no one is justified in making any other statement" about the gross-net question. "What Is Tithing?," in *Tithing and Fast Offerings* (Salt Lake City: LDS Church, 2007), https://www.lds.org/manual/tithing-and-fast-offerings/what-is-tithing?lang=eng.

49. Mormons rank first among all religious groups in the percentage of their income that is tithed (5.2 percent). In fact, the next-most-generous group gave away considerably less—3.5 percent among certain groups of Protestants. See Christian Smith, Michael O. Emerson, and Patricia Snell, *Passing the Plate: Why American Christians Don't Give Away More Money* (New York: Oxford University Press, 2008), 34–35, 83–84.

50. Republicans are also more likely to tithe. Combining those who tithe from gross and net income together, three-quarters of LDS Republicans are full tithe-payers (77 percent) compared to 56 percent of Democrats and 54 percent of Independents.

51. Ammon, twenty-five, telephone interview, November 4, 2017.

52. Samuel D. Brunson, "The Past, Present, and Future of LDS Financial Transparency," *Dialogue: A Journal of Mormon Thought* 48, no. 1 (Spring 2015): 1–44. In 1959, according to historian D. Michael Quinn, the LDS Church engaged in deficit spending for the first time in twenty-one years. Overspending during these years "erased the massive reserve fund" the church had accumulated since the 1930s and resulted in second counselor N. Eldon Tanner curtailing planned building projects. Because of Tanner's retrenchment on spending, coupled with shrewd investments, he is credited with "methodically rescuing the church from the brink" of financial disaster. Quinn, *The Mormon Hierarchy: Wealth and Corporate Power* (Salt Lake City: Signature Books, 2017), 120–123.

53. Steve, thirty-one, in-person interview, Cincinnati, Ohio, May 27, 2014.

CHAPTER 9

1. Natalie, forty, telephone interview, September 25, 2017.

2. "Transcript: Donald Trump's Taped Comments about Women," *New York Times*, October 8, 2016, https://www.nytimes.com/2016/10/08/us/donald-trump-tape-transcript.html.

3. Whether Mormon Millennials will veer to the right as they age is unclear; there may be an age effect associated with political views, since conventional wisdom dictates that people tend to become at least slightly more conservative as they grow older. However, recent studies have called this into question. See Leslie A. Morgan and Suzanne

R. Kunkel, *Aging, Society, and the Life Course* (New York: Springer Publishing Company, 2007), 312.

4. Jan Shipps, "Ezra Taft Benson and the Conservative Turn of 'Those Amazing Mormons,'" in *Mormonism and American Politics,* ed. Randall Balmer and Jana Riess (New York: Columbia University Press, 2015), 73–84. With the exception of 1964, Utah has voted Republican in every presidential election since 1952.

5. The exception to this is immigration, on which the LDS Church has taken positions that challenge the GOP's recent platform; see chapter 6.

6. According to political scientists David E. Campbell and J. Quin Monson, Mormons have not always "fallen in line" when LDS leaders have instructed them how to vote. For example, in 1933, LDS Church President Heber J. Grant made "frequent appeals" for voters to uphold Prohibition, but Utah repealed it anyway. Campbell and Monson argue that for the church to successfully mobilize members to vote a certain way, it has to "publicize an official position on the issue" and demonstrate consensus among leaders. Consensus was not achieved in 1933, despite Prohibition being supported by the highest-ranking leader of the church. Campbell and Monson, "Following the Leader?: Mormon Voting on Ballot Propositions," *Journal for the Scientific Study of Religion* 42, no. 4 (2003): 605–619.

7. Robin, thirty-eight, telephone interview, September 30, 2017.

8. In the general population, 57 percent of Millennials either identify or lean toward the Democratic Party, while 36 percent favor the Republicans. Pew Research Center, "Party Affiliation among Voters: 1992–2016," September 13, 2016, http://www.people-press.org/2016/09/13/2-party-affiliation-among-voters-1992-2016/.

9. The overall percentage of Republicans in our current Mormon sample—57 percent—is lower than the percentage the GOP garnered in Pew's 2011 survey of Mormons, which was closer to three-quarters. The timing of both surveys is significant. Pew's was fielded in a season when not one but two Mormons were vying for the Republican presidential nomination; there was little reason for conservative-leaning Mormons to be at cross-purposes with the GOP. Our survey, however, was fielded in September and October of 2016, as Mormons were faced with the prospect of voting for one of the most controversial candidates the Republican Party had ever fielded. This makes it less surprising that we see lower numbers of Mormons claiming affiliation with the GOP. For more on the rise of Republican affiliation within Mormonism, see Patrick Q. Mason, "Ezra Taft Benson and Modern (Book of) Mormon Conservatism," in *Out of Obscurity: Mormonism since 1945,* ed. Patrick Q. Mason and John G. Turner (New York: Oxford University Press, 2016), 63, and David E. Campbell, Christopher F. Karpowitz, and J. Quin Monson, "A Politically Peculiar People: How Mormons Moved into and Then out of the Political Mainstream," in *Mormonism and American Politics,* ed. Balmer and Riess, 133–154.

10. This trend toward young adults voting or leaning Independent is also seen in Pew data; from 2008 to 2016, Millennial voters shifted in that direction by eight percentage points. Pew Research Center, "Party Affiliation among Voters," http://www.people-press.org/2016/09/13/2-party-affiliation-among-voters-1992-2016/.

11. See David E. Campbell, John C. Green, and J. Quin Monson, *Seeking the Promised Land: Mormons and American Politics,* Cambridge Studies in Social Theory, Religion and Politics series (New York: Cambridge University Press, 2014), 89.

12. Pew Research Center, "Party Affiliation among Voters: 1992–2016," September 13, 2016, http://www.people-press.org/2016/09/13/2-party-affiliation-among-voters-1992-2016/. In 2017, the GOP had lost a bit of market share among both men and women: men's Republican allegiance declined from 51 to 48 percent, while women's fell to 37 percent from 38. Pew Research Center, "Wide Gender Gap, Growing Educational

Divide in Voters' Party Identification," March 20, 2018, http://www.people-press.org/2018/03/20/wide-gender-gap-growing-educational-divide-in-voters-party-identification/.

13. This question was worded to include "support" for a candidate in 2012, even if some of the youngest respondents were not old enough at that time to cast a ballot. Also, it's worth noting that the percentage of Mormons of any generation who voted for Mitt Romney is likely higher than this hindsight perspective might show as recounted four years later. Political scientists have noted that some voters tend later to side with the person who eventually won, even if those voters actually cast a ballot for the other candidate at the time (or did not vote at all).

14. The Cooperative Congressional Election Study results are quoted in Sarah Pulliam Bailey, "Romney Is Running for Senate. Even If He Wins, the Mormon Church Has Already Lost Powerful Status in D.C.," *Washington Post,* February 16, 2018, https://www.washingtonpost.com/news/acts-of-faith/wp/2018/02/16/romney-is-running-for-senate-even-if-he-wins-the-mormon-church-has-been-losing-powerful-status-in-dc/?noredirect=on&utm_term=.11c28576d002. These numbers are slightly different than the exit polls immediately afterward, which indicated that Trump had won 61 percent of the Mormons' votes nationally and 45 percent in Utah. Gregory A. Smith and Jessica Martínez, "How the Faithful Voted: 2016 Preliminary Analysis," November 9, 2016, http://www.pewresearch.org/fact-tank/2016/11/09/how-the-faithful-voted-a-preliminary-2016-analysis/; Robert Gehrke, "While Mormons Nationally Stuck with Trump, in Utah He Lagged," *Salt Lake Tribune,* November 18, 2016, http://archive.sltrib.com/article.php?id=4573783&itype=CMSID.

15. Mormons appeared to rally around Trump, however, not only at the polls but also during the first year of his presidency. According to Gallup, Trump garnered a 61 percent approval rating from Mormons in January of 2018, a year after he first took office. Frank Porter, "Trump Approval Highest among Mormons, Lowest among Muslims," Gallup News, January 12, 2018, http://news.gallup.com/poll/225380/trump-approval-highest-among-mormons-lowest-among-muslims.aspx.

16. For Mormons' political preferences every four years from 1992 to 2016, see Pew Research Center, "The Parties on the Eve of the 2016 Election: Two Coalitions, Moving Further Apart," September 13, 2016, 29.

17. Benjamin Knoll, "Mormons, Trump, and McMullin: A 2016 Postmortem by the Numbers," Religion News Service, July 17, 2017, http://religionnews.com/2017/07/17/mormons-trump-and-mcmullin-a-2016-postmortem-by-the-numbers/.

18. Jeffrey C. Fox, "A Typology of LDS Sociopolitical Worldviews," *Journal for the Scientific Study of Religion* 42, no. 2 (June 2003): 279–289. Fox concludes that "there is more ideological variation among active Mormons than conventional wisdom has suggested," particularly where economic issues are concerned, and says that "past research has overestimated political constraint among Mormons because Utah-based samples are unrepresentative of all Mormons" (286).

19. Samantha Smith, "5 Facts about America's Political Independents," July 5, 2016, http://www.pewresearch.org/fact-tank/2016/07/05/5-facts-about-americas-political-independents/.

20. Sociologist Robert Wuthnow has chronicled an apparent entrenchment of religious Americans on both sides politically and the disappearance of moderate voices. For example, from the 1960s to the 1980s, Republican presidential candidates "enjoyed an advantage of about 1.2 among frequent church goers," but this advantage increased between 2.6 and 3.9 after the 1980s. Robert Wuthnow, *After the Baby Boomers: How Twenty- and Thirty-Somethings Are Shaping the Future of American Religion* (Princeton, NJ: Princeton University Press, 2007), 169.

21. Erik Sherman, "America Is the Richest—and Most Unequal—Country," *Forbes*, September 30, 2015, http://fortune.com/2015/09/30/america-wealth-inequality/; "Rankings," *U.S. News and World Report*, https://www.usnews.com/news/best-countries/united-states#ranking-details; Organisation for Economic Cooperation and Development, "OECD Better Life Index: Health," n.d., http://www.oecdbetterlifeindex.org/topics/health/; World Health Organization, "World Health Organization Assesses the World's Health Systems," June 21, 2000, http://www.who.int/whr/2000/media_centre/press_release/en/; Central Intelligence Agency, "The World Factbook: Infant Mortality," n.d., https://www.cia.gov/library/publications/the-world-factbook/rankorder/2091rank.html.

22. Young adults' public opinion on American exceptionalism appears to be changing rapidly. When Pew asked a version of this question in 2011, 27 percent of all Americans in the eighteen-to-twenty-nine age group said America was the greatest country in the world, and 38 percent of those ages thirty to forty-nine said so. When Pew repeated the question just three years later, both of those cohorts' responses had declined by twelve points (to 15 and 26 percent, respectively). See Alec Tyson, "Most Americans Think the U.S. Is Great, but Fewer Think It's the Greatest," Pew Research Center, July 2, 2014, http://www.pewresearch.org/fact-tank/2014/07/02/most-americans-think-the-u-s-is-great-but-fewer-say-its-the-greatest/.

23. For more on eroding patriotism in the younger generations, see Robert Wuthnow, *The Restructuring of American Religion* (Princeton, NJ: Princeton University Press, 1988), 273–274.

24. Although men are required to register with the Selective Service upon turning eighteen, they have not been involuntarily conscripted from its rolls for over forty years.

25. Paul Taylor, *The Next America: Boomers, Millennials, and the Looming Generational Showdown* (New York: Public Affairs, 2015), 62.

26. Ryan, thirty-two, in-person interview, Cincinnati, Ohio, February 7, 2017.

27. I am grateful to Jelena Vicic for her detailed analysis of the question on respondents' top three issues, including which groups of respondents were most and least likely to consider abortion one of their main concerns.

28. According to the Handbook, "unmarried parents are generally unable to provide the stability and the nurturing environment that a married mother and father can provide. Unmarried parents should give prayerful consideration to the best interests of the child and the blessings that can come to an infant who is sealed to a mother and father." Bishops and expectant single parents are then directed to the church's resources for adoption services. *Handbook 2: Administering the Church*, 21.4.12, https://www.lds.org/handbook/handbook-2-administering-the-church/selected-church-policies/21.4.6?lang=eng&_r=1#214.

29. David Kinnaman, *You Lost Me: Why Young Christians Are Leaving Church ... and Rethinking Faith* (Grand Rapids, MI: Baker Books, 2011), 46.

30. "Attitude toward the Death Penalty for Convicted Murderers in the U.S. in 2011 by Generation," Statista, https://www.statista.com/statistics/207065/attitude-towards-death-penalty-for-convicted-murderers-in-the-us-by-generation/.

31. *Handbook 2: Administering the Church*, 21.4.7 and 21.4.13, https://www.lds.org/handbook/handbook-2-administering-the-church/selected-church-policies/21.4.6?lang=eng&_r=1#214.

32. Depending on the age of the mother, successful IVF rates from nondonor eggs might range from 46.5 percent of women under age thirty-five giving birth to less than 2 percent success for women over age forty-four. In the latter case, then, 98 percent of fertilized embryos do not result in a live birth. Centers for Disease Control and Prevention, *2015 Assisted Reproductive Technology Summary Report*, October 2017, 5, https://www.cdc.gov/art/pdf/2015-report/ART-2015-National-Summary-Report.pdf.

33. Blaire, thirty-three, telephone interview, July 28, 2016.

34. Char, forty-two, in-person interview, Cincinnati, Ohio, February 29, 2012.

35. Political scientist David Campbell argues that the religious Right itself is partly to blame for the rise of secularization in the United States, which can be understood as a backlash against the close ties Christian conservatives have formed with the GOP. Tad Walch, "At BYU, Speaker Says Religious Right's Ties to Republican Party Spurred Secularization," *Deseret News*, November 8, 2017, https://www.deseretnews.com/article/865692420/At-BYU-speaker-says-religious-rights-ties-to-Republican-party-spurred-secularization.html. See also Putnam and Campbell, *American Grace: How Religion Divides and Unites Us* (New York: Simon and Schuster, 2012), 130.

36. Paul A. Djupe, Jacob R. Neiheisel, and Anand E. Sokhey, "Reconsidering the Role of Politics in Leaving Religion: The Importance of Affiliation," *American Journal of Political Science* 62, no. 1 (January 2018): 161–175. The authors found that disaffiliation was most prevalent among Christians who already had a tenuous connection with their churches, "and hence fewer benefits to outweigh the costs" of being politically different than others in the pews.

37. Michael Hout and Claude S. Fischer, "Explaining Why More Americans Have No Religious Preference: Political Backlash and Generational Succession, 1987–2012," *Sociological Science* 1 (October 2014): 423–447. The quotation is on page 423.

38. "Converted Latter-day Saints believe that the family proclamation . . . is the Lord's reemphasis of the gospel truths we need to sustain us through current challenges to the family," Elder Oaks said in 2017. "Two examples are same-sex marriage and cohabitation without marriage." Dallin H. Oaks, "The Plan and the Proclamation," October 2017 General Conference, https://www.lds.org/general-conference/2017/10/the-plan-and-the-proclamation?lang=eng. Russell M. Nelson, "Becoming True Millennials," Worldwide Devotional for Young Adults, January 10, 2016, https://www.lds.org/broadcasts/article/worldwide-devotionals/2016/01/becoming-true-millennials?lang=eng.

39. *Handbook 2: Administering the Church*, 21.4.1, https://www.lds.org/handbook/handbook-2-administering-the-church/selected-church-policies/21.4.6?lang=eng&_r=1#214.

40. *Handbook 2: Administering the Church*, 21.4.15.

41. Joanne Kenen, "Mitt's Son Has Twins via Surrogate," Politico, May 4, 2012, https://www.politico.com/story/2012/05/romneys-son-has-twin-boys-through-surrogate-075939.

42. Elaine, thirty-five, telephone interview, September 29, 2017.

CHAPTER 10

1. Mikey, twenty-five, in-person interview, St. Louis, Missouri, June 3, 2017.

2. Ezra Taft Benson, "Fourteen Fundamentals of Following the Prophet," devotional address at Brigham Young University, February 26, 1980, https://www.lds.org/liahona/1981/06/fourteen-fundamentals-in-following-the-prophet?lang=eng. Benson was not yet the president of the church himself when he gave this address.

3. From the newspaper's beginnings until 1955, for example, no headline of the *Church News* ever used "prophet" to connote the current LDS president. By the 1960s, however, such references to McKay as "our prophet" and "the prophet" were becoming routine. D. Michael Quinn, *The Mormon Hierarchy: Extensions of Power* (Salt Lake City: Signature Books, 1997), Kindle location 16376. McKay's immediate successor, Harold B. Lee, expressed concern with the "almost worshipful attitude" Mormons had begun expressing toward the president of the church and sought to stop it; during his administration only one headline referred to him as "prophet." However, his tenure of less than a year was "too brief

to reverse the accelerating adoration by the rank-and-file" (Kindle location 16441).

4. Christian N. K. Anderson, "Do We Have to Believe That?: Canon and Extra-Canonical Sources of LDS Belief," *Dialogue: A Journal of Mormon Thought* 50, no. 1 (Spring 2017): 79–135; esp. 120, 125.

5. Dieter Uchtdorf, "Come, Join with Us," October 2013 General Conference, https://www.lds.org/general-conference/2013/10/come-join-with-us?lang=eng.

6. However, a notable example of exactly this occurred in the Gospel Topics essay on race, released in 2013. As explored in chapter 6, the church's essay strongly suggests that Brigham Young, the second LDS president, was wrong in his statements about African Americans.

7. Jean Twenge asserts that the rising generation "doesn't just question authority—they disregard it entirely." Twenge, *Generation Me: Why Today's Young Americans Are More Confident, Assertive, Entitled—and More Miserable Than Ever Before* (New York: Atria Books, 2014), 36.

8. Hannah Fingerhut, "Millennials' Views of News Media, Religious Organizations Grow More Negative," Pew Research Center, January 4, 2016, http://www.pewresearch.org/fact-tank/2016/01/04/millennials-views-of-news-media-religious-organizations-grow-more-negative/.

9. According to a regression analysis by Benjamin Knoll, respondents who want "authenticity and vulnerability" are those with more education, those who were born and raised LDS, those who express less belief in Mormon teachings, those who don't currently have temple recommends, and those who live in Utah. Of these, education levels and levels of belief orthodoxy are the largest predictors.

10. Respondents were presented all options shown in Table 10.2 and asked to rank their top five sources of authority. The "average" shown in Table 10.2 shows the numerical mean of rankings on this option for all Mormon respondents, computing the options they didn't rank as "0." An average of "5" would mean that all Mormons ranked that option as their top source of individual authority.

11. Benjamin Knoll and Jana Riess, " 'Infected with Doubt'?: An Empirical Overview of Belief and Non-Belief in Contemporary American Mormonism," *Dialogue: A Journal of Mormon Thought* 50, no. 3 (Fall 2017): 1–38, esp. 21–23. Fifty-seven percent of believers ranked LDS general authorities in their top five sources of authority in making moral decisions, but only 16 percent of doubters did so.

12. The NMS asked two questions about Mormons' views on evolution. On the first ("Evolution is the best explanation for how God brought about the emergence and development of life on Earth"), just under 50 percent of Mormons know or believe it is true, and just over 50 percent either doubt it or reject it outright. Millennials are more likely to agree than older Mormons (58 to 38 percent). On the second ("God created Adam and Eve sometime in the last 10,000 years and humans did not evolve from other life forms"), 74 percent of Mormons know or believe that it is true, and just over a quarter (26 percent) do not. This suggests an interesting dichotomy in which about half of Mormons think that evolution occurred but about three-quarters see human evolution as standing apart from it; most current Mormons hold to a literal view of Adam and Eve, even if they accept the concept of an old earth and the theory of evolution for non-human life. For more on this, see Benjamin Knoll, "A Detailed Look at Mormon Beliefs on Evolution and Human Origins," Huffington Post, December 21, 2017, https://www.huffingtonpost.com/entry/a-detailed-look-at-mormon-beliefs-on-evolution-and_us_5a3aff30e4b0d86c803c6ec0.

13. See Twenge, *Generation Me*, 114–117; Christian Smith and Patricia Snell, *Souls in Transition: The Religious and Spiritual Lives of Emerging Adults in America*

(New York: Oxford University Press, 2009), 279–281 and 290–292; and Paul Taylor, *The Next America: Boomers, Millennials, and the Looming Generational Showdown* (New York: Public Affairs, 2015), 47–59.

14. It has been widely reported that Millennials as a whole are the first generation since the nineteenth century to be more likely to still be living at home with their parents than in their own households or with peers, giving rise to the nickname the "Boomerang" generation. According to Pew, 32 percent of Americans ages eighteen to thirty-four were living in their parents' homes in 2016; in our survey, only 23 percent of Mormon Millennials (eighteen to thirty-six at the time of the survey, so very slightly older than that particular Pew sample) were still at home with mom and/or dad. That represents a nine-point drop in Mormon young adults currently living at home compared to their peers in the general US population. Richard Fry, "For First Time in Modern Era, Living with Parents Edges Out Other Living Arrangements for 18-34-Year-Olds," Pew Research Center, May 24, 2016, http://www.pewsocialtrends.org/2016/05/24/for-first-time-in-modern-era-living-with-parents-edges-out-other-living-arrangements-for-18-to-34-year-olds/. It should be noted, however, that 2016 research showed a lower percentage of Millennials still at home—just 15 percent. "It's Becoming More Common for Young Adults to Live at Home—and for Longer Stretches," Pew Research Center, May 5, 2017, http://www.pewresearch.org/fact-tank/2017/05/05/its-becoming-more-common-for-young-adults-to-live-at-home-and-for-longer-stretches/.

15. Smith and Snell, *Souls in Transition*, 150–151.

16. Jayne, thirty-seven, telephone interview, September 26, 2017.

17. After performing a multivariate regression analysis to isolate individual factors, there's still a clear age difference in General Conference viewing habits. Statistically significant variables included age, gender, geographic location, race, educational levels, and activity level. General Conference viewers are more likely to be white, female, older, Republican, college-educated, and living in Utah. See Benjamin Knoll, "Who's Not Watching General Conference," Religion News Service, November 7, 2017, http://religionnews.com/2017/11/07/whos-not-watching-mormon-general-conference/.

18. Roy F. Baumeister, "A Self-Presentational View of Social Phenomena," *Psychological Bulletin* 91, no. 1 (1982): 3–26. Charitable donations, for example, tend to be "dramatically greater" when there is an audience than when they are entirely private (5, 7).

19. Rick Phillips has demonstrated that among Mormons, for example, church attendance and male priesthood ordination are markedly higher in Utah than in other areas of the United States where Mormonism is a tiny minority. "Mormons are more active in areas where they *predominate*." Phillips, "Religious Market Share and Mormon Church Activity," *Sociology of Religion* 59, no. 2 (1998): 117–130.

20. By comparison, in 2014, just 11 percent of Mormons in America were of the Silent Generation, and 1 percent of the Greatest Generation. "Generational Cohort among Mormons," Pew Research Center, http://www.pewforum.org/religious-landscape-study/religious-tradition/mormon/.

21. The original response options were "A good Latter-day Saint should obey the counsel of priesthood leaders without necessarily knowing why" and "A good Latter-day Saint should first seek his or her own personal revelation as the motivation to obey." See R. T. Cragun, Stephen M. Merino, Michael Nielsen, Brent D. Beal, Matthew Stearmer, and Bradley Jones, "Predictors of Opposition to and Support for the Ordination of Women: Insights from the LDS Church," *Mental Health, Religion & Culture* 19, no. 2 (2016): 124–137.

22. Boyd K. Packer, "The Unwritten Order of Things," BYU Devotional Address, October 15, 1996, http://emp.byui.edu/huffr/The%20Unwritten%20Order%20of%20Things%20--%20Boyd%20K.%20Packer.htm. This idea was also expressed in 1951 by

Second Counselor J. Reuben Clark, who noted that "in the service of the Lord . . . one takes the place to which one is duly called, which place one neither seeks nor declines." "Not Where You Serve, But How," *Conference Report*, April 1951, 153–154, http://scriptures.byu.edu/gettalk.php?ID=522. I am grateful to Matthew Bowman for the reference.

23. Steve, thirty-one, in-person interview, Cincinnati, Ohio, May 27, 2014.
24. Sbanotto and Blomberg, *Effective Generational Ministry*, 192.
25. Jon, twenty-nine, telephone interview, October 10, 2016.
26. Chrissy, thirty-three, telephone interview, September 18, 2017.
27. On patriarchal blessings in early Mormonism, see, for example, John Turner, *Brigham Young: Pioneer Prophet* (Cambridge, MA: Harvard University Press, 2012), 48, 88, and 115, and Jonathan Stapley, *The Power of Godliness: Mormon Liturgy and Cosmology* (New York: Oxford University Press, 2018), chapter 3.
28. For more on how patriarchal blessings became part of the interview template, see the appendix at the end of the book.
29. Jack, twenty-six, telephone interview, October 12, 2017.
30. Ammon, twenty-five, telephone interview, November 4, 2017.
31. Lillian, thirty-eight, in-person interview, Cincinnati, Ohio, April 6, 2012.
32. Kristi, forty-seven, telephone interview, October 27, 2016.
33. Natalie, forty, telephone interview, September 25, 2017.
34. Natalie notes, however, that in the town where she lived, Russian was taught in the local high school, and she and many of her Mormon friends studied it. It is possible the stake patriarch was aware of this history.

CHAPTER 11

1. James, thirty-three, telephone interview, October 16, 2017.
2. Official Declaration 2 is the statement issued by the LDS Church in 1978 that extended the priesthood to all worthy adult males, regardless of race. For the full text, see https://www.lds.org/scriptures/dc-testament/od/2.
3. Pew Forum, "The Gender Gap in Religion around the World," http://www.pewforum.org/2016/03/22/the-gender-gap-in-religion-around-the-world/.
4. I am grateful to Alexis Straka for performing the data analyses on Pew's findings about former Mormons, and for the multivariate regression analyses that populate this chapter. Here, the controlled variables are gender, education, age, sexual orientation, residence in Utah, political party identification, and income.
5. The generational trajectory is the same in both samples, with younger respondents more likely to have had divorced parents. For example, in the current Mormon sample, only 16 percent of the combined Boomer/Silent generation grew up with divorced parents, but among the younger Millennials (ages eighteen to twenty-six), the rate is nearly double, at 31 percent.
6. Betsy Cooper, Daniel Cox, Rachel Lienesch, and Robert P. Jones, "Exodus: Why Americans Are Leaving Religion—and Why They're Unlikely to Come Back," Public Religion Research Institute, September 22, 2016, 7–8, https://www.prri.org/research/prri-rns-poll-nones-atheist-leaving-religion/.
7. The NMS findings challenge the educational pattern observed by some sociologists of religion, in which education correlates with decreased religiosity. See Zuckerman, *Faith No More*, 105, 115–116, for a defense of the idea that education and disaffiliation often go together. That thesis has already been questioned in other contexts, including by Ray M. Merrill, Joseph L. Lyon, and William J. Jenson, "Lack of a Secularizing Influence of Education on Religious Activity and Parity among Mormons," *Journal for the Scientific Study of Religion* 42, no. 1 (March 2003): 113–124; Putnam and Campbell, *American Grace*,

28, 276–277; and Jeremy E. Uecker, Mark Regnerus, and Margaret L. Vaaler, "Losing My Religion: The Social Sources of Religious Decline in Early Adulthood," *Social Forces* 85, no. 4 (June 2007): 1667–1692, esp. 1668–1670 and 1676–1678. Uecker et al. found that respondents who did not go to college showed decreased religious attendance, gave less weight to the importance of religion, and were less likely to have a religious affiliation.

8. This is true for the sample as a whole, but the results were somewhat different when we consider women by themselves; see the education section of chapter 5.

9. The link between marriage and increased religious affiliation is also noted by Uecker et al., "Losing My Religion," 1671, 1684.

10. Zuckerman, *Faith No More*, 6; Zuckerman, Luke W. Galen, and Frank L. Pasquale, *The Nonreligious: Understanding Secular People and Societies* (New York: Oxford University Press, 2016), 93–94; and PRRI, "Exodus," 6.

11. The lack of a geographical connection was a little surprising, because throughout the data we saw that non-Utah Mormons were less orthodox in their beliefs and in their practice of Mormonism. In other words, living outside of Utah is correlated with a less strict interpretation of the faith, but after controlling for other factors like politics and education, it does not seem any more connected with actually leaving the church.

12. In the former Mormon sample, eight respondents chose the other/transgender option. (There were no trans respondents at all in the current Mormon sample.) Because the margin of error for a sample size of eight is far too high to draw conclusions, this chapter will only present the findings of self-identified women and men.

13. Despite this, former Mormons may be *less* open than current Mormons to the theory of evolution. Asked whether "evolution is the best explanation for how God brought about the emergence and development of life on earth," 44 percent of former Mormons knew or believed that was true, compared to almost 50 percent of current Mormons. Of course, one complication is that the question inquired specifically about theistic evolution, or the idea that God directed the evolutionary process. It is possible that some former Mormon respondents were objecting not to the overall theory of evolution but to the particular circumstance of God's involvement. More research is needed on this question before conclusions can be drawn.

14. Rob, thirty-eight, in-person interview, Cincinnati, Ohio, May 5, 2017.

15. As earlier, here I am combining the number who chose "I am confident and know this to be true" and "I believe and have faith that this is probably true."

16. Charles, thirty-three, telephone interview, September 28, 2017.

17. See FAIR Mormon, "How Do Dinosaurs Fit into God's Plan?" for an apologetic overview of several ways Mormons have attempted to resolve the seeming contradiction of ancient fossils and a young creation. The theory that fossils "are actually from the destroyed remains of other planets" is not, according to FAIR, "a popularly held notion today" even if it was taught earlier by some LDS leaders. N.a., n.d., https://www.fairmormon.org/answers/Mormonism_and_science/Dinosaurs.

18. See, e.g., Elder M. Russell Ballard, "To Whom Shall We Go?," LDS General Conference, October 2016, https://www.lds.org/general-conference/2016/10/to-whom-shall-we-go?lang=eng.

19. In Elizabeth Drescher's research on Nones in America, she finds that many who had left organized religion are happy with their choice, feeling that it has broadened their horizons. "The Nones who talked with me consistently saw themselves as active creators in the story of their own spiritual lives," she writes. "Their narratives were populated with the language of 'discovery,' 'freedom,' 'escape,' 'liberation,' 'maturation,' 'journeying,' 'enlightenment,' and 'self-realization,' or growth in 'awareness,' 'knowledge,' 'self-understanding,' or 'insight.'" Elizabeth Drescher, *Choosing Our Religion: The Spiritual Lives of America's Nones* (New York: Oxford University Press, 2016), 54.

20. This is in line with what Pew found about former Mormons in its 2014 Religious Landscape Study; in that research, of the 36 percent of people who had left Mormonism, 21 percent (just under two-thirds of the total) had not rejoined another tradition and the others were scattered across various religious traditions. http://www.pewforum.org/2015/05/12/chapter-2-religious-switching-and-intermarriage/pr_15-05-12_rls_chapter2-02/.

21. However, in a related question where the NMS asked people whether they were "actively involved as a regular member of another religious tradition," only 23 percent of former Mormons said yes. So some of the people who said they "identify" as being part of another religion seem to be less than regular, active members of it. An additional quarter were "interested in other religions" but had not "committed to any of them" (25 percent), and the remaining half were flat-out "not interested in joining another religion" (52 percent).

22. Stan L. Albrecht and Howard M. Bahr, "Patterns of Religious Disaffiliation: A Study of Lifelong Mormons, Mormon Converts, and Former Mormons," *Journal for the Scientific Study of Religion* 22, no. 4 (December 1983): 366–379, esp. 372–376.

23. Sarah, thirty-eight, in-person interview, Salt Lake City, Utah, October 1, 2016.

24. For example, Karianne, twenty-five, hired an attorney to submit her resignation in the summer of 2016, because she felt she could not continue as an official member in the wake of the 2015 LGBT policy. She was not notified of her name's removal from the church records until shortly before our interview, which occurred by telephone on October 17, 2016.

25. Jamie, thirty-three, telephone interview, July 13, 2016.

26. As well, there are certain narrative complications that a survey simply cannot capture: namely, that people's explanations of difficult faith transitions tend to change over time. What may have felt like the most pressing reasons at the actual time of departure from a religion may not be the aspect of the narrative that is emphasized later. See Seth Payne, "Ex-Mormon Narratives and Pastoral Apologetics," *Dialogue: A Journal of Mormon Thought* 46, no. 4 (Winter 2013): 85–121.

27. The NMS asked respondents to name their top reasons for leaving the church, choosing from thirty randomized options that were loosely broken down into two main categories: (1) doctrinal/institutional reasons (concerns about the Book of Abraham, for example, or the lack of financial transparency about what happens with tithing money) and (2) personal/social reasons (like being excluded, not feeling able to trust the leadership, or losing a testimony of the "one true church"). Each respondent could choose up to three possible reasons from each category, or up to six reasons overall.

28. Cooper, Cox, Lienesch, and Jones, "Exodus," PRRI, September 22, 2016, https://www.prri.org/research/prri-rns-poll-nones-atheist-leaving-religion/, 6. Linda Mercadante cites research that two-thirds of former Catholics and half of former Protestants left those religions because they stopped believing what was taught. Linda Mercadante, *Belief without Borders: Inside the Minds of the Spiritual but Not Religious* (New York: Oxford University Press, 2014), 229.

29. Michael, twenty-six, telephone interview, May 10, 2017.

30. Women's top five reasons, in order, were that they felt judged or misunderstood, could no longer reconcile personal values and priorities with those of the church, found women's roles problematic, stopped believing there was one true church, and did not trust in the church leadership to tell the truth surrounding controversial or historical issues. For men, the top three were that they stopped believing, could not reconcile their values with the church's, and did not trust leaders. Fourth on men's list was "I drifted away from Mormonism," while number five was historical concerns about the Book of Mormon and Book of Abraham.

31. "Be Not Deceived, but Continue in Steadfastness," Lesson 24, *Doctrine and Covenants and Church History: Gospel Doctrine Teacher's Manual*, https://www.lds.org/manual/doctrine-and-covenants-and-church-history-gospel-doctrine-teachers-manual/lesson-24-be-not-deceived-but-continue-in-steadfastness?lang=eng.

32. See David A. Bednar, "And Nothing Shall Offend Them," October 2006, https://www.lds.org/general-conference/2006/10/and-nothing-shall-offend-them?lang=eng.

33. Thomas, thirty-six, in-person interview, Salt Lake City, Utah, October 3, 2016.

34. Drescher, *Choosing Our Religion*, 24–25; PRRI, "Exodus," 15.

35. Rodney Stark, for example, is a vocal critic of the widely accepted thesis that young adults are leaving organized religion. Such data, he insists, "merely shows that when young people leave home, some of them tend to sleep in on Sunday morning rather than go to church. That they haven't defected is obvious from the fact that a bit later in life when they have married, and especially after children arrive, they become more regular attenders. This happens every generation." Rodney Stark, *What Americans Really Believe* (Waco, TX: Baylor University Press, 2008), 11. This may have been true of some Baby Boomers, but so far we have no reason to see it as true of Generation X or Millennials.

36. Wade Clark Roof, *A Generation of Seekers: The Spiritual Journeys of the Baby Boom Generation* (New York: HarperCollins, 1994), 154–155.

37. Ryan, thirty-two, in-person interview, Cincinnati, Ohio, February 7, 2017.

CONCLUSION

1. Cardell K. Jacobson, John P. Hoffmann, and Tim B. Heaton, *Revisiting Thomas F. O'Dea's* The Mormons: *Contemporary Perspectives* (Salt Lake City: University of Utah Press, 2008).

2. Not one of O'Dea's interviewees was female, for example, a blind spot that seems astonishing in retrospect. Howard Bahr, "Finding Oneself among the Saints: Thomas F. O'Dea, Mormon Intellectuals, and the Future of Mormon Orthodoxy," *Journal for the Scientific Study of Religion* 47, no. 3 (September 2008): 463–484, esp. 481 n. 5.

3. Rodney Stark, "The Rise of a New World Faith," in *Latter-day Saint Social Life: Social Research on the LDS Church and Its Members* (Provo, UT: Religious Studies Center, Brigham Young University, 1998), 1–8, https://rsc.byu.edu/archived/latter-day-saint-social-life-social-research-lds-church-and-its-members/1-rise-new-world. The range Stark gave in the original article was anywhere between 63,415,000 and 265,259,000 adherents by 2080.

4. Rodney Stark, "So Far So Good: A Brief Assessment of Mormon Membership Projections," *Review of Religious Research* 38, no. 2 (December 1996): 175–178.

5. Dennis Romboy, "LDS Church, 22 Utah Senators Back Colorado Baker in Supreme Court Case," *Deseret News*, September 12, 2017, https://www.deseretnews.com/article/865688650/LDS-Church-22-Utah-senators-back-Colorado-baker-in-Supreme-Court-case.html.

6. Armand L. Mauss, *The Angel and the Beehive: The Mormon Struggle with Assimilation* (Urbana: University of Illinois Press, 1994).

THE 2016 NEXT MORMONS SURVEY

1. For more detailed information about missing data in survey research, see Therese D. Pigott, "A Review of Methods for Missing Data," *Educational Research and Evaluation* 7, no. 4 (2001): 353–383.

2. Courtney Kennedy, Andrew Mercer, Scott Keeter, Nick Hatley, Kyley McGeeney, and Alejandra Gimenez, "Evaluating Online Nonprobability Surveys," May 2, 2016, http://www.pewresearch.org/2016/05/02/evaluating-online-nonprobability-surveys/ ; Miliaikeala S. J. Heen, Joel D. Lieberman, and Terance D. Miethe, "A Comparison of

Different Online Sampling Approaches for Generating National Samples," UNLV Center for Law and Justice Policy, September 2014, https://www.unlv.edu/sites/default/files/page_files/27/ComparisonDifferentOnlineSampling.pdf.

3. For example, David E. Campbell, Joel C. Green, and Quin Monson gathered a representative sample of Mormon respondents using an online panel-matching approach from YouGov. Campbell, Green, and Monson, *Seeking the Promised Land: Mormons and American Politics* (New York: Cambridge University Press, 2014), 45–46, 63–67, 265–267.

4. To conduct a reliable public opinion survey of those that the LDS Church defines as members, we would need to have access to the contact information for all individuals currently on the LDS membership records from which to draw a random sample. The church, however, does not make such information available to either academic researchers or members of the general public.

5. The 2014 Pew Religious Landscape Survey would have been more ideal, but at the time the NMS was being fielded, certain essential portions had not yet been released for public analysis.

6. Here we compare against the results from 2014 Pew Religious Landscape Survey using the standard poststratification weighting process. Pew created its weights compared to US Census-level data.

7. See http://www.applied-survey-methods.com/weight.html, http://www.aapor.org/Education-Resources/For-Researchers/Poll-Survey-FAQ/Weighting.aspx, and http://www.pewresearch.org/methodology/u-s-survey-research/our-survey-methodology-in-detail/ for more information.

8. http://www.mormonstories.org/understanding-mormon-disbelief-survey-results-and-analysis/.

9. See https://www.amazon.es/Polling-Public-Every-Citizen-Should/dp/1604266066 for a primer.

10. Jean M. Twenge chronicles a rise of generational narcissism in *Generation Me*, especially chapter 2.

INDEX

Figures, notes, and tables are indicated by f, n, and t following the page number.

retention rates of, 5*t*
same-sex marriage and, 143–146, 144*t*
seminary attendance of, 26
sexual diversity and, 137–138, 276n31
sharing faith and, 154, 154*t*
temple, preparation for, 60, 61*t*, 62
temple experiences and, 54–55, 54*t*, 55*f*
temple garments and, 64–66, 65*t*
tithing and, 166, 166*t*
Word of Wisdom adherence,
159–160, 160*f*
Bowman, Matthew, 262n29, 288n22
Brandon (interview), 79–80, 88–89, 264n20
Brigham Young University (BYU)
Honor Code, 141
on LGBT issues, 132, 141, 275n10
on men's hair styles, 269n29
racism of, 117–118
tuition rates, 167
wards for students, 85
youth sexual behavior, study on, 83
Brittany (interview), 22, 51, 59, 150, 256n16,
261n3, 277n3
Brooke (interview), 29–30, 257n36
Brooks, Joanna, 253n3, 267n12, 275n11
Bush, Lester E., Jr., 271n20
Bushman, Claudia, 97
Bushman, Richard, 97
BYU. *See* Brigham Young University

caffeine consumption, 2, 158–162, 160*f*,
253n3, 279n24, 279n26, 279–280n28.
See also Word of Wisdom
Cain (biblical figure), 117, 271n21
California, opposition to same-sex marriage
in, 134, 183, 189–190
callings, 201–204, 203*f*, 287–288n22
Campbell, David E., 98, 111*t*, 257n31,
273n47, 282n6, 292n3
Catherine (interview), 30, 67–68,
257n37, 262n35
Catholicism, 134, 254n12, 281, 290n28
Celestial Room, 51
celibacy, 141. *See also* chastity
Centers for Disease Control and Prevention
(CDC), 136, 137, 276n25
chapel meetinghouses. *See also* singles wards
acceptance of all, 49
attendance, importance of, 3, 4, 7, 46, 156
attendance by generational cohort,
155–157, 155*t*

attendance rates, 77, 81, 88, 264–265n24,
264n14, 287n19
designs of, 127–128
family wards, 86
gender segregation and, 94–97
Primary for children, 35, 129, 151
spiritual inspiration and, 157
student wards, 85
Char (interview), 88, 114, 183, 266n42,
270nn10–11, 285n33
charity, 167. *See also* tithing
Charles (interview), 218–219, 289n16
chastity
endowment ceremonies, worthiness
for, 49
former Mormons and, 84
homosexuality and, 132, 141, 143
Mormon teachings on, 82–83
weddings outside temple and, 57
Chelsea (interview), 50–51, 62, 66,
88–89, 109–110, 121–122, 260n2,
266n41, 270n1
child abuse, 228, 260n39, 275n11
children. *See also* adolescents and teenagers
adoption of, 179, 284n28
exclusion from temple, 49
gender segregation and, 94–95
instilling traits in, 34–35, 258n4
parental influence, religious orthodoxy
and, 24, 26
Primary, participation in, 35, 95
of same-faith marriages, 265–266nn33–34
of same-sex marriage/couples, 2,
142–146, 144*t*
unmarried parents and, 179–180, 179*f*,
185, 284n28
Chrissy (interview), 49–50, 56, 58, 206,
260n1, 288n26
Christensen, Clayton, 86–87
Christian teachings
continuity of belief in, 14–18, 16*f*, 17*t*,
142, 255n6
former Mormons' belief in, 215–216,
215*f*, 216*t*, 289n13
political issues and, 184, 285n35
scripture as literal word of God, 152
churches. *See* chapel meetinghouses; temple
civil rights movement (1960s),
117–118, 271n26
Clark, J. Reuben, 274n5, 288n22
climate change, 177–178

Clinton, Hillary, 169, 172
clothing, 36, 95, 96, 103, 180*f. See also*
   temple garments
coffee. *See* caffeine consumption
cohabitation
   gender and, 77*t*
   rates of, 81
   trends in, 75, 75*t*, 263–264n12
cohort replacement, 268n21
Colby (interview), 29, 51, 60,
   257n33, 261n4
college degrees, 72–73, 104–105, 116,
   201, 236n33
colonialism, 126–128
Community of Christ, 239
confirmation as "normal order of
   things," 13
continuity of belief, 13–32
   doubters who remain, 30–32, 31*t*
   factors associated with, 24–30, 27*f*, 28*t*
   in God and Christian teachings, 14–18,
      16*f*, 17*t*, 120, 142, 255n6
   in Jesus Christ, 120, 142, 216, 216*t*
   in Mormon teachings, 18–21, 19*t*, 152
   relationship with God and, 21–24
conversions
   of deceased persons, 49, 53
   decrease in, 254n14, 260n30
   investigators and, 258n3
   of Mormons to Mormonism, 14
   political issues and, 184, 285n38
   relationship with God and, 22
   religious orthodoxy and, 28, 257n32
conversion therapy for homosexuals,
   129–130, 133, 275nn10–12
Cooper, Alex, 133, 275n11
Cooperative Congressional Election
   Study, 172
Court of Honor, 35
Cragun, Ryan, 111*t*, 255n7, 264n14,
   268n20, 287n21
creation, 218, 286n12, 289n17
cultural changes, 4, 179–182
cultural differences among international LDS
   Churches, 127, 273n55
current events and national issues,
   175–179, 177*t*
"Curse of Cain," 117, 271n21

DACA (Deferred Action for Childhood
   Arrivals), 125

Daniel (interview), 13–14, 32, 62,
   255n1, 262n23
dating
   challenges in, 79, 140–141
   former Mormons and, 72
   interracial, 110, 112–113, 114
   singles wards and, 80–81
Dean, Kenda Creasey, 3–4
death and deceased people
   baptisms of, 49, 53
   beliefs about, 23
   endowment and ordination of,
      53–54, 54*t*
   sealing ceremonies for (*see* sealing)
death penalty, 180, 180*f*
Deferred Action for Childhood Arrivals
   (DACA), 125
delayed adulthood, 196
desirability bias, 155–156, 255n6, 279n20
dietary restrictions
   alcohol consumption and, 150, 157–160,
      160*f*, 279n24, 280n31
   caffeine consumption and, 158–162, 160*f*,
      253n3, 279n24, 279n26, 279–280n28
   Millennials and, 4
   rates of adherence to, 157–162, 160*f*
   temple recommend cards and, 49, 56,
      159, 161
   vegetarianism and, 161, 280n35
disaffiliation from Mormonism. *See* former
   Mormons
discrimination, 123–126, 123*t*, 272nn37–38
diversity
   appreciation for, 42, 126, 270n4
   benefits of, 127
   in LDS Church leadership, 126–127
   of Mormonism, 111–114, 111*t*, 272n8
   Mormon views on, 123–126, 123*t*
divorce
   doubting, correlation with, 31
   former Mormons and, 81, 213,
      214, 288n5
   gender and, 77*t*
   morality and, 180, 180*f*
   rates of, 72–73, 75*t*
   risk factors for, 74
   temple recommend cards and, 228
domestic abuse, 228
doubt
   causes of, 2, 13–14, 22
   education and, 24, 30, 31

faith, strengthening, 14, 122
  folk beliefs and, 218
  NMS results on, 15–16, 16f, 17t,
    255n6
  remaining Mormon and, 30–32, 31t
Drescher, Elizabeth, 289n19
drug use, 157–160, 160f, 279n24. *See also*
    Word of Wisdom
Duke, James T., 266n2

Eagle Scouts, 35, 258n5
early return from missionary work, 44–48,
    260n33, 260n36
education
  doubt and, 24, 30, 31
  fertility rates and, 104–105
  former Mormons and, 106, 214,
    288–289n7
  gender and, 104–106, 269n33, 269n36
  leaders, preferred traits in, 192, 286n9
  marriage and divorce rates, 72–73, 73t, 74,
    76, 263n8
  for missionary work, 37, 39
  on obedience and following prophet, 191
  post graduate, 106
  race and, 116–117
  role in religious orthodoxy, 24–25, 30, 31,
    106, 233, 256nn23–26
  seminary attendance, continuity of belief
    and, 25–27, 27f, 257n30
  tithing rates and, 166
  youth programs, 35, 95, 96, 258n5
Elaine (interview), 61, 149–150, 187,
    262n20, 277n1, 285n42
electric shock therapy, 133, 275n10
Ellis (interview), 129–130, 273n1
Elysse (interview), 91–92, 152,
    266n1, 278n12
Emily (interview), 2–3, 4, 66–68, 86, 253n2,
    262n32, 266n36
employment, gender and, 107–108, 107t,
    115–116
endowment ceremonies, 50–51, 53, 57–59,
    60f, 61t, 110, 122
environmental issues, 177–178
Equal Rights Amendment (ERA),
    96, 267n12
ethnicity. *See* race and ethnicity
Eve (biblical figure), 58
Evergreen (conversion therapy organization),
    133, 275n12

evolution, 195, 266n3, 286n12, 289n13
excommunication, 96, 132, 142, 186
extended families, role in religious
    orthodoxy, 31–32, 31t
extramarital affairs, 179, 179f
Eyring, Henry B., 32

FAIR Mormon, 289n17
Faith Matters Survey, 111t
Falencia (interview), 140, 277n35
families. *See also* parental influence
  birth rates and, 6, 39, 103–105,
    104t, 254n14
  extended, role in religious orthodoxy,
    31–32, 31t
  of former Mormons, 230–231
  LDS Church emphasis on, 9, 15, 55, 72,
    76, 89, 176–178, 255n2
  non-Mormon families compared, 34
  sealing, 23, 114, 218
  trends in size and composition, 34,
    103–104, 104t
  values of, 92, 96, 195–196
"The Family: A Proclamation to the World"
    (First Presidency statement), 100–101,
    135, 285n38
family-to-family relationships, 153
family wards, 86
fasting, 167
feminism, 96–97, 142, 176
fertility rates, 6, 39, 103–105, 104t, 254n14
First Presidency
  on caffeinated beverages, 159,
    279–280n28
  "The Family: A Proclamation to the
    World," 100–101
  on homosexuality and gender, 274n5
  members as prophets, 24, 115
  mission program and, 38, 259n16
  on motherhood, 267n11
  racial composition of, 126
  on same-sex marriage, 134
  Silent Generation members, 199
  on tithing, 281n48
  on transsexual operations, 269n27
Flake, Kathleen, 261–262n16
FLDS (Fundamentalist Church of Jesus
    Christ of Latter-Day Saints), 47,
    239, 260n39
folk beliefs, 112, 117, 118–119, 218
food storage, 266n4

women's subordination to men and, 58, 95, 97

Gender and Religious Representation survey, 100

gender dysphoria, 101–102

general authorities, 127, 133, 191, 193–195, 199

General Conference
family, emphasis on, 15, 178, 255n2
former Mormons and participation rate, 219
gender and, 82, 92, 96
on homosexuality and pornography, 135
married Mormons and participation rates in, 82
on missionary work, 38–39, 259n18
Mormons' viewing frequency, 197–199, 198f, 287n17
on obedience and authority, 191
on pornography, 280n44
race and leadership, 128
on reasons for leaving Mormonism, 228

general population. *See also specific surveys*
on American exceptionalism, 174, 175f
education and gender, 106
family size and, 34
homosexuality, societal acceptance of, 129–133, 131f, 182, 274n2
marriage trends, 72–74, 73t, 75, 263n8
political values and, 170, 171–172
religious affiliation and gender, 213
religious orthodoxy and practice of, 278n18
on systemic racism, 124, 272n38

General Social Survey (GSS)
on education and gender, 269n36
on gender policies, 268n21
on LDS chapel attendance, 279n21
on LDS Church retention rates, 4–7, 5t
on marriage trends, 75
on Nones, 254n11
on racial segregation, 125
on sexual orientation, 276n25
on tobacco use, 159
wording of questions in, 244

generational transmission of religion, 24

Generation X (GenXers)
age quotas in surveys, 240–241
age range for, 8, 8t
attendance of chapel and sabbath keeping, 155–156, 155t

authority, competing sources of, 195, 195f
belief in God and Christian teachings, 15, 16f, 17t
belief in Mormon teachings, 18–21, 19t, 217–218, 255n10
belief in priesthood/temple ban of black people and, 120t, 121
bishops, counseling with, 204, 205t
callings, refusal of, 202–203, 203f
current national issues and, 176–179, 177t
education and gender, 105
employment and gender, 107, 107t
family size and, 104, 104t
general conference viewing frequency of, 198, 198f
as home teachers and, 153, 153t
institutional authority and obedience, 192–193, 192f, 193t, 201, 202f
leaders from this generation, 199
leaving Mormonism, reasons for, 225t, 226
marriage trends and, 73
missionary work and, 39, 45, 259n22
moral and social views of, 179–182, 179f
patriotism and military service of, 175, 175f
political party affiliation of, 171–172, 171t
popular culture and, 163–165, 164t
prayer and scripture study, 151, 151t
preferred topics addressed by leaders, 199–201, 200t
priesthood and gender, 98–99, 98t
racial discrimination, 123t, 124
relationship with God, 21
retention rates of, 5–6, 5t
returning to religion, 291n35
same-sex marriage and, 143–145, 144t
seminary attendance of, 26
sharing faith and, 154, 154t
temple, preparation for, 60, 61t
temple experiences and, 53–55, 54t, 55f
temple garments and, 64–66, 65t
tithing and, 166, 166t
Word of Wisdom adherence, 159–160, 160f

Generation Z, 7, 146

geographical location. *See also* Utah
continuity of belief and, 28–30, 28t, 214, 257n31, 289n11
survey quotas and, 241

gerotranscendance, 261n9

Jones, Robert P., 146, 254n11, 263n10, 271n17, 276n27, 277n43
judgmentalism, 20, 72, 80, 226–227, 287n16

Karianne (interview), 52–53, 222, 261n5, 290n24
K.C. (interview), 162
Kelly, Kate, 96
Kimball, Spencer W., 118, 271n20
  The Miracle of Forgiveness, 131–133, 135
Kinsey, Albert, *Sexual Behavior of the Human Male*, 276n25
Klarman, Michael J., 134
Knoll, Benjamin, 7, 100, 173, 237, 255n9, 257n38, 260n37, 264n14, 268n24, 286n9
Kristi (interview), 207, 288n32

language training, 37
Latinx Mormons
  on discrimination, 272n37
  on immigration issues, 273n44
  racial composition of Mormonism and, 111*t*
Lauren (interview), 140–142, 151, 277n4, 277n36
LDS Church and Mormonism
  on afterlife, 23
  on caffeinated beverages, 159, 279–280n28
  change, acceptance of, 235, 270n40
  on chapel attendance, 156
  on children outside of marriage, 179, 284n28
  children's role and, 34–35
  conservative political views of, 170
  continuity of belief in, 18–21, 19*t*, 152
  corporatization of teachings, 25
  criticism of, 134
  on dark skin, 117, 176
  defining members and former members, 238–239
  disaffiliation with (*see* former Mormons)
  on education, 105, 269n33
  on embodied God, 118
  on Equal Rights Amendment, 96, 267n12
  excommunication, grounds for, 132, 142
  family, emphasis on, 4, 9, 15, 55, 72, 76, 89, 176, 253n7, 255n2
  favorite teachings of, 15, 28–29, 55, 94*t*, 193, 255n5

on feminism, 96
financial reports of, 167, 281n52
folk beliefs of, 112, 117, 118–119, 218
former Mormons' belief in teachings of, 217–218, 217*t*
on gender issues, 1, 96–97, 100–103, 169–170
General Conference of (*see* General Conference)
as global religion, 126–127, 273n55
growth rates, 6, 254nn14–15, 270n40
Handbook (*see* LDS Handbook of Instruction)
history of, 25, 30, 37–38, 47, 62, 170, 259n16, 261–262n16, 282n6
on immigration issues, 125–126, 282n5
international, cultural differences among, 127, 273n55
leadership in, 86–87, 95–100, 98*t* (*see also* specific leadership roles)
leaving, 211–231 (*see also* former Mormons)
on LGBT issues, 2, 22, 110, 130–133, 131*f*, 142–146, 144*t*, 170, 183–184, 225, 234, 274n5
LoveLoud festival (2017), support for, 234
on marriage, 1, 2, 76–78, 86, 134–135, 253n7
membership records, removing names from, 222, 290n24
on missionary work, 38–39, 45, 258nn9–10
on motherhood, 77–78, 96, 105, 236n33, 267n11
other Americans compared to (*see* general population)
other religions compared to (*see* religions (non-Mormon))
as percentage of American population, 237
political party affiliation and, 170–173
on politics, 282n6, 282n9
on polygamy, 260n39
on popular culture, 162–163, 235, 280n39
on pornography, 163, 280n44
president as prophet, 191, 285–286n3
on priesthood, 288n2
racial diversity in, 111–114, 111*t*, 126–128, 270n13, 272n8
racial prejudice of, 110, 113

National Study of Youth and Religion
(NSYR), 3–4, 20, 83, 265n28
Native American Mormons, 111*t*
Nebraska, opposition to same-sex marriage
in, 134
Nelson, Russell M., 184
New York, protests against LDS Church
in, 134
Next Mormons Survey (NMS), 237–248
on attendance of chapel and
sabbath keeping, 155–157, 155*t*,
278–279nn18–19
on authority, competing sources of, 193–
197, 194*t*, 195*f*, 286n10, 286n12
on belief in God and Christian teachings,
15–18, 16*f*, 17*t*, 215–216, 215*f*,
216*t*, 255n6
on belief in Mormon teachings, 18–21,
19*t*, 217–218, 217*t*, 255n10
on bishops, counseling with, 204, 205*t*
on callings, refusal of, 202–204, 203*f*
creation of, 7
current national issues and, 176–179, 177*t*
data sources and funding for, 237–238
on diversity and immigration,
123–126, 123*t*
on doubting Mormons, 30–32, 31*t*
on education and religious
orthodoxy, 288n7
education levels of respondents, 24
on education of women, 105
on employment and gender,
107–108, 107*t*
on family size, 103–104, 104*t*
on favorite aspects of Mormonism, 15,
28–29, 55, 94*t*, 193, 255n5
on folk beliefs, 119
on former Mormons' religious lives, 219–
223, 221*f*, 290n21
on General Conference, Mormons' viewing
frequency, 197–199, 198*f*, 287n17
generational parameters of, 8, 8*t*, 254n18
on instilling traits in children,
34–35, 258n4
on institutional authority and obedience,
192–193, 192*f*, 193*t*, 201, 202*f*, 287n21
on leaving Mormonism, reasons for, 223–
228, 224*t*, 227*f*, 290nn26–27, 290n30
on LGBTQ issues, 131, 131*f*, 142, 277n38
limitations of, 8–9
on marriage trends, 74–77, 75*t*, 77*t*

on missionary work and Millennials, 39–
48, 40*f*, 260n36
on moral and social views, 179–182, 179*f*
Mormons and former Mormons defined,
238–240
on patriotism and military service,
174–175, 175*f*
on political views, 170, 171–172, 171*t*,
282n9, 283n13
on popular culture, 162–165,
164*t*, 280n43
on prayer and scripture study, 151–152,
151*t*, 278nn6–8
on preferred topics addressed by leaders,
199–201, 200*t*
on priesthood and gender, 98–100, 98*t*
on priesthood/temple ban of black
people, 119–121, 120*t*
qualitative oral history interviews, 246–248
on race and Mormonism, 111*t*, 114–117
racial composition of respondents,
114–115
on relationship with God, 21–24
on religious affiliation and gender,
213, 288n4
on religious orthodoxy and gender,
92–94, 93*t*
on same-sex marriage/couples,
143–146, 144*t*
on seminary attendance, 26–27, 27*f*
on sexual activity, 83–84, 84*f*, 84*t*
on sexual diversity within LDS Church,
135–138, 136*t*
sexual orientation of participants,
135–136, 276n23
on sharing faith with others, 153–155,
153*t*, 278n18
on single Mormons and religious
practices, 81–82
survey parameters, 240–242
survey question wording, 238, 244, 246
survey representativeness, assessment of,
242–244, 243*t*, 245*t*
on temple, preparation for, 60–63, 61*t*
on temple experiences, 50, 53–55, 54*t*,
55*f*, 59, 60*f*
on temple garments, 64–66, 65*t*
on tithing, 165–168, 166*t*
on "Utah effect," 28–30, 28*t*
on Word of Wisdom adherence,
159–160, 160*f*

LDS Church on, 165, 281n48
Mormons compared to other religions
    and, 166, 281n49
NMS on, 165–168, 166t
partisanship and, 166, 281n50
as percentage of income, 4, 165, 281n48
support for political issues and, 134
temple recommend cards and, 165
tobacco use, 159–160, 160f
transcendence, 25, 261n9
transformative religious experiences
    doubt and, 32, 122
    missionary work and, 47–48
    patriarchal blessings, 206–209
    relationship with God and, 21–24
    as seminary challenge, 46
    summer camp attendance and, 149
transgender people
    experiences in LDS Church, 100–103
    in NMS sample, 102, 241
    as percentage of population, 268n26
    sex reassignment surgery and, 102, 179f,
        186, 269n27
Troy (interview), 55–56, 57, 79, 142–143,
    161, 261n10, 264n18, 277n39,
    280nn34–35
Trump, Donald, 125, 169–170, 172–173,
    283nn14–15
Turner, John G., 256n28, 259n15, 264n19,
    274n3, 282n9, 288n27

Uchtdorf, Dieter F., 126, 191
underclothes. See temple garments
Understanding Mormon Disbelief
    Survey, 244
unmarried Mormons. See single Mormons
unmarried parents, 179–180, 185, 284n28
Utah
    2016 presidential election and, 283n14
    church attendance and priesthood
        ordination rates in, 287n19
    education and gender, 106, 269n36
    history of, 282n6
    leadership in LDS Church from, 126, 128
    LoveLoud festival (2017), 234
    racial homogeneity of, 109, 116
    religious orthodoxy in, 28–30,
        214, 289n11
    single adults and church attendance, 77
    survey quotas and, 241
    tithing in, 166

in vitro fertilization, views of Mormons
    on, 181
voting patterns in, 282n4
"Utah effect," 28–30, 28t, 257n31

vasectomy, 180f, 182, 186
vegetarianism, 161, 280n35
video games, 163
virginity, 83, 265n31. See also chastity
visiting teachers, 153, 153t
volunteers. See missionary work; specific
    leadership roles
voting patterns, 170–174, 171t

Williams Institute, 268–269n26
women and girls, 91–108. See also gender;
    motherhood
    clothing of, 36, 95, 96, 103
    domestic abuse and, 228
    education and, 104–106, 269n36
    employment and, 107–108, 107t,
        115–116
    endowment ceremonies and, 50, 57, 59
    feminism and, 96–97, 142, 176
    homosexuality and, 132, 274n5
    initiatory experience and, 59
    leadership positions and, 95–100,
        98t, 266n2
    leaving Mormonism, reasons for, 226–
        227, 227f, 290n30
    marriage and, 71, 76–79, 77t
    missionary work and, 39, 40, 40f, 258n2,
        259n18, 259n23
    priesthood and, 98–100, 98t
    religious orthodoxy of, 92–94, 93t, 215
    religious responsibilities of, 35
    single Mormons, 76–77, 77t, 80
    social changes and, 103–108,
        107t, 270n40
    subordination to men, 58, 95, 100
    survey quotas for, 241
    temple garments and, 66–67
Woodruff, Wilford W., 260n39
wording of survey questions, 238, 244, 246
Word of Wisdom
    addiction and, 150
    endowment ceremonies, worthiness for, 49
    rates of adherence to, 157–162, 160f
    temple recommend cards and, 56,
        159, 161
Wuthnow, Robert, 278n16, 283n20, 284n23